CONTENTS

Chapters

Appendices

PREFACE TO THE SECOND EDITION

May I begin with two paradoxes?

Firstly, copyright happens to be one of those subjects which are particularly difficult to explain clearly. On the one hand 'multum in parvo' or conciseness should be a prime aim when trying to make copyright 'easier'. On the other hand, it can be all too obvious that piling in more and more words of 'clarification' may obscure the meaning more and more on a 'seeing wood among trees' basis as well as exhaust readers' patience. Those unfamiliar with the details of copyright law are liable to lose patience for another reason: namely, they do not at all like being told that they cannot legally do what they want to do, especially if they have already been doing it for some time! Yet, the simplification of legal language and/or its translation into generalisations can be dangerously misleading practices.

Secondly, the continuing CEC work towards harmonisation of copyright law in order to make the EU a 'level playing field' for the market in copyright media, however laudable the aim, has so far had the effect of increasing the detail and complexity of the law.

So a problem which has increased during the preparation of this second edition is 'How on earth can one continue trying to make this subject "easier" when others are so busy making it more difficult?' Surely this cannot be allowed to prevail, or people will so far lose respect for copyright law that they will 'do their own thing' anyway and await any consequences? If accused of infringement, they may then apologise sweetly or – if unconvinced of the viability of an accusation and able to afford time and money for defence – go to court.

Faced with the fascinating task of updating this book, I have tried to help users through the difficult period ahead by emphasising the compensatory or 'what to do if' approach. The Quick Reference section at the front has been revised and expanded, and additional problems appear in the last chapter. New law has been incorporated throughout, often along with some comments of my own.

People naturally approach copyright with different attitudes. Some readers may regard copyright as something of a 'quagmire', hence it is recommended that readers engaged in 'heavy' matters should avoid relying on just one opinion to keep their heads above the mire. Moreover, for the sake of my own head, please note that no indemnity of any kind can be offered in respect of decisions made as a result of studying this book. Other readers may have already discovered interesting and quite remarkable ramifications in copyright, and adopt a more positive attitude to the subject.

Ten years hence there may indeed be a 'level playing field' in the EU (if only the Champs Elysees?), and it may even have achieved a simpler overall structure of copyright law. The danger is that the latter might be achieved mainly by effectively forcing users to get licences for just about every need, and to do just as they are told by the big commercial rights holders. Thus complexities would be largely transferred into the contracts arena, out of sight of the average user, who would pay up more or less as he or she may now with the 'phone bill or online service account. But the interim period may tax user patience in yet another way, for the process of change itself might well build up further complexities for at least the next few years. However, this may not be so bad if users 'keep their cool' – as this goes to press, the collaboration between publisher and user representatives towards solutions has accelerated remarkably, as some of the items in Appendix 4 should demonstrate. It will be essential for authors (as the larger and more important proportion of users!) to monitor the situation and urge such permissions as may prove possible in the new climate.

Those who need to track their way through transitional provisions will have special difficulties. For example, the drafters of SIs now avoid the problem of incorporating new points into an amended CDPA88 Schedule 1. Instead, new 'transitional provisions and savings' are being added at the end of SIs which implement new EU law, apparently for readers to 'mix and match' as they may. It is no longer of any use to recommend readers to keep a copy of the full Act handy, for it is much out of date. Those who require to study full details exactly as passed by Parliament should refer instead to a looseleaf work (or online service at greater cost) which holds an updated version of the Act together with the SIs which supplement it. However, the contents of this book are up to date as at January 1998. In any event, I have tried to reduce the need for such detailed research, especially by information service professionals. I have sought to convey enough understanding for them to keep in line with the law in day to day work, and to make a strong defence of the case for flexibility for users during the next decade. (Otherwise we might be carried into the new millennium kicking and screaming.)

For those who may find unusual stress in copyright observance, my advice is primarily to avoid deliberate offence to rights owners, especially infringement which can be linked to commercial publication. Those rights owners who might wish to make some point or other should be found reasonable and sympathetic in approach, unless dealing with a video pirate or the like. So, users accessing libraries or information services who cannot spare time to absorb why's and wherefore's are recommended simply to follow notices beside photocopying machines and electronic, etc. equipment and/or the access regulations – and, if in a firm, get the managements to become appropriately licensed. There is in any case 'life beyond copyright' as I myself am often told! This seems to be my opportunity to wish all my colleagues, friends – and everyone who enters this interesting and ever-changing area of law – a most happy and successful future.

Otherwise, the aims of this edition are unchanged from those of 1993. Permissions in respect of the contents of Appendix 4 from The Publishers Association, the JISC/PA Working Party on Fair Dealing in an Electronic Environment, EBLIDA and the Ad Hoc Alliance for a Digital Future are greatly appreciated. My thanks are again due to the Aslib editorial team for excellent work, and of course to my wife for her forbearance! Lastly (and perhaps continuing a train of thought), in the hope of soothing a savage reader's breast, Appendix 5 hazards a guess at the possibility of a serene 'copyright Nirvana' for users at some future date, when electronic systems might make life easier – but not necessarily cheaper!

Ray Wall, January 1998

PREFACE TO THE FIRST EDITION

Having wide interests, I turned to librarianship as a key to all subjects, and on the whole it has not let me down in that respect. So how did I come to specialise in Copyright towards the end of a career spanning the public and private sectors? Perhaps it was because Copyright, whenever it cropped up at all, seemed to aim itself at me – I wish sometimes it had missed. This volume is addressed broadly to professionals -- information managers, librarians, teachers, students, authors and other users of copyright materials. Apart from the obvious qualification and career connotations, I believe that a person who does a job as well and carefully as possible, especially in a team context and in accordance with standards of behaviour, is a professional. Copyright is particularly demanding in respect of care with detail, for even the legally permitted actions have ifs and buts. To base actions on an outline would be like giving a chemist an abstract on preparing a compound and expecting him to produce that compound without further data. So why begin this book with outlines and summaries? These are partly as introductions for those who prefer a bird's eye view to start with; and partly for quick reference as reminders.

In short, this book is an attempt to provide what I myself could never find in the literature:

- guidelines by publishers and others, together with the law itself, sufficient for a user to practice
- licensing availability and terms
- a form of 'companion to the Act' – main points of new law (Appendix 2 and Appendix 3), supplementary legislation (Appendix 4) and an index to the Act itself incorporated into the index to this volume – for readers who wish to consult the law directly (not in the second edition)
- a quick reference guide, containing outlines and summaries, linked to the main text for detailed descriptions of permissions and guidelines
- controversial issues which it is hoped that others will take up and pursue
- examples of specific user problems on which advice has been given at various times.

The emphasis on user needs is thus clear enough. To me, a user of copyright media is anyone who has need to interact with the creative work of others, whether to educate, solve particular problems, or produce new creative works. I have tried to bear in mind the needs of both the more experienced and the new users.

At the height of the licensing controversy around 1986, it was possible to break the ice at seminars by comparing the schools licensing scene with an old-style melodrama, before pointing out the rationale or Hobson's choice of collective licensing for schools. For example, the fair maiden Zeeroxana, observed by Pounding Prints (noble scion of a commercial publishing dynasty) to be practically papering her walls with photocopies from her Speed-Kop machine, is threatened with espousal to Lai-Sen Sing. However, Z sees this as a fate worse than death, until all is sorted out amicably over some royal-tea ... and so on. Then came the Act and the need to explain the essentials without satisfactory literature references as back-up in half-hour presentation periods, which made for heavy going. Question-answer sessions after a brief introduction, with maximal audience participation and some humour, preferably with some preparatory reading and advance gathering of participants' problems for discussion, are now recommended for half-day programmes.

For past involvement in Copyright, my thanks are due to colleagues in the various working groups mentioned in Appendix 2, and indeed all those with whom I have worked or talked about this subject, whether representing publisher or user viewpoints. This applies especially to Aslib colleagues, for my work with them dates from the early 1950s in general and from 1977 on Copyright. Aslib has always attempted to stand the middle ground in the quest for balance in Copyright law, and has provided a means of prompt publication as well as a forum for helpful debate.

Thanks are also due to the Library Association for having asked me – and financed me part-time – to act as a focus for the lobbying campaign in the run-up to new law and its immediate aftermath during 1985 to 1989 on behalf of all UK information and library professional bodies. And I shall always remember with gratitude those in Parliament who helped so much, especially in the Lords: Viscount Eccles, whose speech during the debate on the Second Reading of the Bill in autumn 1987 was so salutary in setting the Lords on course to remove discrimination against 'commercial research' from fair dealing; and Lord Ardwick and Lord Lloyd of Kilgerran who found the time to propose several of our amendments. Lord Lloyd of Kilgerran later became President of Aslib. I am very pleased to have memories of witnessing the proceedings at first hand from the corner provided for expert advisers in the House of Lords 'in committee', and similarly later in a committee room during the House of Commons Standing Committee sessions. And the special skills and unfailing courtesy of the Patent Office team throughout the campaign are gratefully remembered.

Specifically for this volume, I wish to thank Denis Pilling of the British Library Document Supply Centre for sending documents to update me on legal deposit; Graham Gerrard of Computing Services at Loughborough University of Technology who, when I sought to test my flow-diagram of moral rights on an expert, kindly suggested an alternative 'decision-table' approach as less daunting; and Her Majesty's Stationery Office for permission to reproduce the transitional provisions and other extracts. Many thanks are also due to members of the Aslib editing and publishing team, for their meticulous care and helpful suggestions. Lastly but, as they so rightly say, by no means least – this book could not have been written without the patience and forbearance of my wife Irene, who is now breathing sighs of heartfelt relief at its completion.

Some approach Copyright in the belief that it is possible to be at once concise, unequivocal and unambiguous. My view is that these qualities are rarely found together in this complex subject with its plethora of provisos. I have tried, by means of approaches at different levels of detail, to make a guide not only for current practice but also to possible changes in future. After all, with electrocopying problems, European harmonisation of Copyright law, and licensing developments, there may be few dull moments for years to come!

Ray Wall, June 1993

References in the Text

Q refers to the Quick Reference Guide

Notes such as **(s3)**, **(s165)**, **(ss38-42)** mean sections of the Copyright, Designs and Patents Act 1988

Notes like **(2.17)** or **(16.27)** mean paragraphs of this volume

Notes like **A3/5.7** mean paragraphs in the appendices to this volume.

SI means Statutory Instrument (selectively listed in Appendix 2).

QUICK REFERENCE GUIDE

The outlines and summaries here are provided either as a reminder for those who do not need the background details provided later, or as an overview for those who intend to proceed to such details for further explanation. The Copyright, Designs and Patents Act 1988 is usually referred to in this volume as 'CDPA88' or just 'the Act'.

Q0 GENERAL NOTES

Permissions (Q3 and Q8)

The Copyright Designs and Patents Act 1988 begins with definitions and 'restricted acts'. These are followed by exceptions or 'acts permitted'. For Copyright, Q3 is an outline in the sequence of the Act itself, and Q8 is a summary arranged according to coverage of media categories. Database right overlaps and can override copyright permissions in respect of databases of any kind, summarized in Q13. Details appear in other parts of this book, and the relevant main paragraph is indicated in each case.

Effects of new database right

It is important to note at the outset that many of the CDPA88 copyright permissions may be overridden by the new 'database right'. CDPA88 itself contained no such thing as fair dealing in either of two major regimes: (a) electronic databases and the Internet, and (b) audiovisual materials. Nor are there any sets of rules or permissive guidelines for users of those regimes as yet, but certain agreements have been made, for example on stocking and lending sound recordings by public libraries (4.47). In respect of printed matter, the CDPA permissions still hold in respect of copyright, but do not cover the new database right, which notably includes fair dealing for research only when it does not have a 'commercial purpose'. The limited database right permissions are indicated in 3.28 et seq., commented upon in Appendix 3/5, and brief notes appear in Q13-14.

An advantage of database right permissions is that they apply to any format, electronic or printed, and fair dealing with databases for purposes other than commercial is permissible. A difficulty arises however from the coverage of all media and kinds of database, thus affecting many directories, handbooks, encyclopedias, anthologies, possibly even periodical issues, etc. as well as on- or off-line databases in the old sense. Any compilation, in any subject or medium, which is well-ordered (to put it simply) may be a database and entitled to database right if there has been substantial investment in its making. The reader will spot the need for definitions in the above, but some important definitions are not forthcoming from Government sources at present.

The UK's CDPA88 did not exclude 'commercial purposes' from 'research'. The EC 1996 Directive on extraction or re-utilisation of contents of databases prohibited commercial purposes (undefined). Infringement may occur if a substantial part or the whole is involved (similarly to copyright). Further new Directives on Reproduction Right and Communication to the Public are being drafted as this goes to press, but are most unlikely to be implemented before the year 2001 at the earliest. These may clarify some situations which have arisen with database right, but the discrimination against commercial purpose re databases may spread to all works due to publisher pressure.

New database right (Q13-14; 3.28; Appendix 3) is effective in the UK from 1 January 1998, when a difficult period of adjustment will begin, with results which may only be known precisely after several years of working with the new law. Under database right, there are no equivalents to the UK traditional permissions in CDPA88 ss28, 30 to 44, and 51 to 76. However, wherever a permission does not involve extraction or re-utilisation, the existing copyright permission will apply to a database. Putting this another way: unless care is taken, copying of a substantial part from a compilation under a copyright permission might cause infringement of database right, since it is 'extraction'.

It is recommended that users continue following the traditional 'norms' in this book in respect of all works which are not compilations known to qualify for database right, but bear in mind that any well-ordered compilation may be claimed to be a database. The situation should be monitored as far as possible through professional associations.

Publishers and producers, etc. will need time to adjust as well as users, and it is likely that tolerant attitudes will prevail. In a period of uncertainty, it is inevitable that many information services and libraries will simply opt to apply CDPA88 copyright permissions as they stood in 1997, until clarity emerges. It is conceivable, but impossible to guarantee, that most or all of the copyright permissions described in this book may become accepted by rights owner representatives as less than 'substantial parts', thus preserving them even for database copies for commercial purpose. However, profit-based organisations should seek some form of licensing anyway, as should be clear from 8.11.

In the copyright permissions chapters 5, 6, 7 and 9, attention will be drawn to any comparable database right permission or exception which may exist; otherwise the details of database right appear in chapters 2, 3, 4 plus some comments in Appendix 3/5.

Q1 COPYRIGHT MATERIALS

Copyright materials are by	
CREATORS *of content*	PRODUCERS *of physical formats*
Examples are	
writers and artists; photographers, composers, painters, database compilers	publishers, sound recording and film/video companies, broadcasters, computer disc producers
Fixed by	
manuscript, print, 3-D craft object (including electronic writing of text)	printed text layout, recordings (but not electronic writing)
For periods of copyright protection of	
creator's lifetime + 70 years	25 years, publishers; 50 others
(see Q10, Q11 and Q12 for more details of copyright protection)	
Then all copiable as public domain	
But a database, as a result of EC harmonisation, is additionally protected against extraction or re-utilisation of content for 15 years initially, but potentially perpetual. 'Database' can mean any organised compilation, paper or electronic, any medium, with copyright or noncopyright content (see Q13-14, 3.28 and Appendix 3)	
Some examples of materials less obviously copyright: arrangements of music, adaptations, translations, timetables, knitting patterns, notices, theatre programmes, bus tickets.	

Q2 RECOMMENDED PHOTOCOPY LIMITS: research or private study, including guidelines *(see Q0)*

N.B. The following also applies to printed databases.

Self-service or library copying service for 'research or private study' singles for anyone (including copying from a database but *not* for a commercial purpose, unless the extent is defensibly 'insubstantial'):

Periodicals

one copy of one article from an issue (unless a publisher's note shows availability of other articles or copies, e.g. quoting fees)

Books

up to 5 per cent or one complete chapter

Short books (e.g. without chapters), reports, standards, pamphlets

up to 10 per cent (not more than 20 pages or 2 if brief)

(If in doubt, ask a nonprofit based library to copy and decide CDPA88's 'reasonable proportion' of non-periodical items, as permitted to such libraries)

Poems, short stories

These are whole works, which require particular care, but: one anthology item up to 10 pages may be copied; and a poem, etc. embedded in a book chapter may be included

Illustrations and maps

up to 625 sq cm (A4 size) and up to 4 copies are allowed of an extract from an OS or OS-based map; any item which forms part of an extract as above; one copy of a photograph

Special to educational purposes

Slides or transparencies

one projectable copy, for instruction only, when purchase or hire or commercial production are not feasible

Exam questions/answers

any extent and multiple copies except music to perform

Other countries' works

treat like UK items

HMSO guidelines

For non-publishing purposes:

> single copies of the whole or part of an item from categories below, without further distribution;
>
> multiples of one complete chapter or equivalent, even if more than 30% of the whole, from an item in categories:
>
> > Parliamentary Papers, notably Hansard, House Business Papers, Command Papers, and Reports of Select Committees; Acts of Parliament; Statutory Instruments;
> >
> > Statutory Rules and Orders; Press Releases from official sources.

Other categories, or other purposes, permission required.

See also guidelines on Music if needed (ask a library).

Q3 OUTLINE OF LEGAL PERMISSIONS RE COPYRIGHT IN SEQUENCE OF CDPA88

Anyone, including any library, may also copy under any other permissions on behalf of another person, but see Q0. Libraries are subject to conditions, including a declaration (see 6). All statutory permissions override 'substantial part' considerations (4.32) and constitute a defence against infringement claims.

In the main text, any guideline should be found along with details of the legal permission. The computer programs entries come from SI 1992/3233, making amendments ss50A-C and 296A to the Act.

	Main paragraph number
'Fair dealing' concept	
research or private study including databases but not for a commercial purpose —	
original works, and published editions	5.6
criticism, review and news reporting	5.28
databases; extraction or re-utilisation as illustration for teaching or non-commercial research	*(general note)* 7
Incidental inclusion of copyright material	7.27
Education and instruction	
manual copying	7.1
making films or film sound-tracks	7.3
examination questions or answers	7.2
anthologies	7.6
playing, showing, performing (all works)	9.5
off-air recording	7.8
class multiples unless licence available	7.5
lending by educational establishments (new s36A)	4.39; 9.36

See also computer programs, below, and at end.

Nonprofit-based library or archive copying	
reliance on declarations	6.15
periodical articles for research or private study	6.9
non-periodical material for research or private study	6.11
copies for nonprofit-based library stocks	6.38
lending to public of books covered by Public Lending Right (new s40A) is permitted. Lending of existing stocks of nonprint materials (acquired before 1 December 1995) is unaffected. *(See also 4.44.)*	4.39; 9.36
archival or replacement copies	6.33; 6.35
unpublished works – research or private study	6.16
Copies of articles of cultural or historical importance	
For any library/archive	6.36
Public administration	
parliamentary and judicial proceedings	7.9
Royal Commission and statutory inquiries	7.10
material open to public inspection or on official register	7.11
material communicated to the Crown	7.12
public records	7.13
acts done under statutory authority	7.14
Computer programs	
back-up copies (new s50A)	7.16
decompilation or conversion (new s50B)	7.17
copying or adaptation (new s50C)	7.18
See also 7.19.	
Design copyright	
use of design documents and models	11.12
exploitation of design derived from artistic work	11.13
actions in reliance on registration of a design	11.14
typefaces	11.15
articles for producing material in a particular typeface	11.15
Other works	
electronic forms, transfer of copies	7.30
anonymous or pseudonymous works (assumed death of author or expiry of copyright)	7.28

recording of spoken words, whether written or
as sound recording (certain circumstances) 9.16
public reading or recitation 9.28
abstracts of scientific or technical articles
which accompany the articles 6.43
archival recording of unpublished songs
of unknown authorship (thus mainly folksongs) 9.22

Artistic works

representations of artistic works on public display
(drawings, photographs, etc.) 9.8
advertisements of sale of artistic works 7.24
subsequent works by the same artist 7.25
reconstruction of buildings (these being artistic works) 7.26

Lending to public, unless licensing scheme available

lending to the public of literary, dramatic, musical or artistic
works, sound recordings, or films: possible order by Secretary
of State if no certified licensing scheme available, subject to
payment of reasonable royalty (new s66) 4.44; 9.36
See also 4.39.
playing sound recordings to a non-profit club, society,
or other organisation 9.26

Broadcasts or cable programmes

incidental recording for purposes of the programmes 9.17
recording for supervision and control of the programmes 9.18
timeshift recording of a broadcast or cable programme
for private and domestic use 7.29
photographs of TV or cable programme screens 7.32
free public showing of broadcast or cable programme 9.27
reception of a broadcast and re-transmission in a
cable programme service 9.19
provision of subtitled copies of TV or cable
programmes to handicapped people 9.25
archival recording of broadcasts or cable programmes 9.23

Other permissions

adaptations (if permitted) of the above are also
covered by their permissions 7.33

moral rights, wherein please note that the nominated permissions are drawn from the above, and that none is peculiar to moral rights – but also note exceptions which amount to permissions 10
performers' and recording rights permissions 9.35
Crown use of designs for defence, etc. 11.16
computer programs: use of any equipment or means to observe, study, etc. a program (new s296A) 7.19
compulsory licensing: broadcasting – unlimited needle-time (by Broadcasting Act 1990) 9.14
cable re-transmission of broadcast from another EEA state: compulsory licensing (new s144A) 9.19

N.B. For other compulsory licensing comments see Appendix 3.

Publication right SI 1996/2967 Reg.16 affects unpublished works in which copyright has expired. Anyone in the EEA who publishes such materials for the first time in the EEA has a new 'publication right' which is equal to copyright (but no insertion point into the revised Act is stipulated in the SI). 4.51

Q4 PHOTOCOPYING OPTIONS

See Q0 notes.

Individual

Self-service: a person wanting to copy for himself or herself, for research or private study (legal basis is 'fair dealing', chapter 5), can use:

- Public library, or other public sector (i.e., nonprofit-based) library or archive – keep within copying extents in Q2 on notices beside machines (6.51); ask staff when in doubt. Use interlibrary service when item not in stock and only an extract required (otherwise recommend addition to stock).
- Company library – keep within copying extents in Q2 and on notices, plus any licences which may be held. Individuals – apply through library for interlibrary service when necessary, or buy copies from a licensed document supply agency.
- Licensed copyshop, whether self-service or not, keep within its regulations.
- Own home machine – keep to Q2, or use discretion responsibly on what should be 'fair' in the circumstances (5.29), avoiding in particular any copying to replace purchase when that is a viable option (i.e. availability and timescale) – and hold the copy for personal use only.

Staffed service: a person using an archive or library for staffed copying service for requests as per Q2:

> Ensure completion of valid declaration form (6.51) if the item is for research or private study. If for another permitted purpose, provide either a completed form as per 6.51 or some other kind of written certification of legitimate purpose and why purchase of an original is not an option. Make payment by whatever means is required when the service is nonprofit-based.

Requests in excess of norms: for extents or materials or numbers of copies not covered by known permissions or a licence:

- Check item, especially a periodical issue, for any helpful notes of extents, prices, etc. appearing at front or back, but only use if of UK origin (bank charges and delay problems).
- If item is of overseas origin, with or without such a note, consult CLARCS (Copyright Licensing Agency Rapid Clearance System, 8.13) if licensed, otherwise BL service or other document supply agency.

- Otherwise, phone or fax publisher for specific permission, or use faxed standard permission request form in 6.51. (If phone, get written confirmation for a substantial item.)

Nonprofit-based library

Subject to conditions in 6.13 and the prefatory note to Q2, a nonprofit-based staffed service can copy from written or printed matter when responding to requests for research or private study material, whether the requests are made on the spot or via another library of any kind (6.37). Can also copy a journal article or a whole book (subject to conditions) for the stock of another nonprofit-based library (6.35; 6.38), but cannot supplement its own stock by copying a borrowed item or an item already held, unless this is for archival or preservation purposes (6.33). However, can get a copy for its stock from any other kind of library, even of a whole work (6.38). Readers are strongly advised to follow precautions (6.31) when self-service copying machines are provided. See 15.28 concerning back-up photocopying service to a current awareness bulletin.

Profit-based library

Unless its parent body is licensed appropriately, this should limit regular staffed copying to in-house requests in respect of research or private study, for which 'fair dealing' (5.2) is the legal basis (6.18) but is no longer applicable to copying from a database (printed or electronic) for a commercial purpose. Otherwise, isolated extra-mural requests could be dealt with, also interlibrary requests from any UK source when a request contains a declaration (6.37; 6.51). Can also copy for the stock of a nonprofit-based library, even a whole work (subject of course to conditions), but must not receive a photocopy for its own stock unless permitted (6.38). Strongly advised to follow precautions (6.31) when providing self-service copying machines, unless licensed of course.

Cannot legally make one journal subscription serve for a number of far-flung sister establishments by photocopying key articles for them on a regular basis. *Cannot* legally provide back-up copying service to a current awareness bulletin extramurally, unless a holder of a 'document supply' licence, or has individual permission, or purchases copies if available as originals, or obtains photocopies from a document supply agency (8.10) or, if licensed, consults CLARCS (8.13) for every request for copying beyond licence terms of material in hand.

General

Whole works, e.g. maps, photographs beyond one copy for research or private study as allowed by guidelines, etc.: contact publisher for permission to copy an extract, or buy a whole work when an extract is useless (e.g. a knitting pattern, or computer program), or copy the whole work if permission obtained and payment made if wanted, when out of print but still in copyright.

Other needs in excess of Q2 or other permissions: contact publisher for permission. If not likely to be a regular type of requirement, tell publisher so in the first place; also CLA if the publisher refers the request to that agency. All firms which need to copy more or less regularly should consider licensing against the contingency of inadvertent multiple or excessive copying by any member of the organisation or by a visitor, provided the price is right.

For irregular needs there is always the option of buying copies from the British Library (8.10) or other document supply agency (6.47; 6.50), and either this or use of CLARCS (8.13) could prove a valid option to licensing when needs frequently exceed licensing or fair dealing norms, provided one can control actions of staff in self-service copying.

'Proxy' copying: any individual, or any archival or library service, can copy on behalf of an individual under any CDPA88 permissions or any guideline, subject to the conditions specified (and new database right). When copying under fair dealing for research or private study, only one copy may be made (except as permitted, e.g. OS maps allowance of up to four copies of small extracts). However, a staffed copying service is advised to obtain in advance a declaration or other written statement from the requester to certify the purpose of copying and why purchase is not an option, as mentioned already above.

Out of print material for which no current copyright owner can be traced: an individual could decide to copy even the whole work as fair dealing, whilst a nonprofit-based library wanting a stock copy could get any holding library to produce one (6.38). For copying a substantial part for a requester, a nonprofit-based library or archive could use the discretion implicit in the phrase 'reasonable proportion' of non-periodical material (6.11). It follows that other requesters should consult a nonprofit-based library when the publisher has gone out of business and the author (etc.) cannot be traced for permission.

Source details: All who copy should ensure that source details sufficient to identify the work and acknowledge its use, as well as to list it in a bibliography if necessary, are noted on copies. For permitted multiple copies, this means producing just one copy, augmenting any existing source details which may be shown, then running off the required number of copies.

Q5 EDUCATION: COPYRIGHT PERMISSIONS AND GUIDELINES

See Q0 notes.

	Main paragraph number
Copying of copyright material for instruction or education	
* Manual copying, any original work (instruction)	7.1
Examination questions or answers	7.2
* Instruction in making films or film soundtracks	7.3
Multiple copying (educational establishments)	7.5
Anthologies (educational establishments)	7.6
Slides and transparencies	7.7
Off-air recording (educational establishments)	7.8
Plus any copying under guidelines such as HMSO and any copying under licence	

** Copying must be done by person giving or receiving instruction.*

Computer programs	7.15
Permissions	7.16
Further computer program possibilities	7.21
Public playing, showing or performing; or lending	
Playing, showing or performing for educational establishments:	9.5
Lending *any kind* of material by educational establishments (new s36A);	4.39; 9.36
Video recordings	9.7
Artistic works	9.8
Moral rights	9.9
For instruction or education:	9.3
Instruction in making films, etc.	9.3
Examinations	9.4

N.B. Other provisions in CDPA88 reinforce governmental authority to impose compulsory licensing in respect of educational copying when suitable licensing schemes are not available (ss137-141). The user community has not so far deemed it necessary to approach the Secretary of State on this matter. Wider than education are the powers of the Monopolies and Mergers Commission arising from s144.

See also Q4 – Photocopying Options.

Q6 COPYRIGHT LICENSING OPTIONS SUMMARY

See Q0 notes.

Only names of organisations and broad purposes are given here, other information being in chapters 8 and 12.

Photocopying licences

Multiple copies in education; industry, commerce or professional groups; copyshops; and document supply agencies – Copyright Licensing Agency.

'Document supply' is a term used when a service is set up by a body which is not appropriately authorised by CDPA88, such as a firm wanting to run an extramural copying service; or when copying norms need to be exceeded on a regular basis as with the British Library's 'cleared copy' service (8.10).

Multiple copies of British Standards Specifications in education – British Standards Institution (8.21).

HMSO publications – publishing or multiple copying needs of unlicensed requesters, or for requirements beyond CLA terms – individual licensing or permission by HMSO (8.17).

Music in printed form has no licensing scheme. For needs not covered by a code of practice (6.27), contact publisher for permission as in Q4.

Maps – Ordnance Survey or OS-based maps are covered by OS licences (8.18-8.20).

Educational recording of broadcasts, etc. (8.25) – two schemes: Educational Recording Agency and Open University.

Playing, showing or performing (See Q7 for lending/rental.)

Film and video producers like to control their own rights, and public performance permission should be sought individually, unless in the case of a film it is known to be covered already for public showing.

Public performance (9.6). Music performance may require licensing by one or both of (a) and (b); or (a) and (c):

(a) Performing Right Society, acting for composers and music publishers, licenses any performance of music whether live or from a recording, during the period of copyright. Site or campus licences are available for TV, radio, hi-fi, etc. in public areas, with billing on annual returns. Those planning live concerts should ask PRS first (12.31).

(b) Phonographic Performance Ltd. PPL acts on behalf of recording companies and performers in respect of recorded music, including that which is used as background. Unless recordings have been hired from a company which includes royalty in its charge, a PPL licence is required for any public environment except a nonprofit-based organisation which is concerned with education, or social welfare, or has mainly charitable objectives, and devotes any admission charge solely to the organisation's purposes (9.26). A public sector academic establishment would not need a PPL licence for playing for an educational purpose unless public were present, but a firm would.

(c) Video Performance Ltd, same premises as PPL (12.31) covers music video recordings, such as pop.

N.B. An audience is to be regarded as 'public' if it is not 'private and domestic'. Educational establishment audiences are not regarded as public for educational purposes (9.5).

Re-recording of commercial sound recordings

For example, in preparation of a sound or video recording or as background for an educational presentation; plus broadcasting use – this needs to be licensed by the Mechanical Copyright Protection Society and PPL (see comparative treatment, 12.41).

Q7 AUDIOVISUAL MEDIA AND ELECTRONIC COPYRIGHT

See Q0 notes and Q13-14.

N.B. **Copying and lending/rental** only are covered here – for showing, playing or performing, see Q5 and Q6.
Computer programs: these are 'literary' regardless of physical format and are covered as such in the main text, and in Q4 as 'whole works'. As a result of EC harmonisation, some new permissions now exist (7.15-7.20).

Copying of sound or video recordings or films

Research or private study permissions *exclude* sound or video recordings and films. Hence there is no fair dealing for that purpose, nor any legal provision for library copying for research or private study because ss38 and 39 of the Act are couched in terms of copying from written or printed matter. But there is some fair dealing, for example for 'criticism or review' (5.28). There also other forms of permission, for example for public administration purposes (7.9). Thus libraries could copy on behalf of an individual under fair dealing, though *not* for research or private study, but should insist on a signed statement from the requester to certify the purpose and its coverage by the Act. The same applies to any other permission in the Act (Q8), unless the act of copying has to be confined to the requester himself, as in two cases in Education (Q5).

Broadcast programmes of course include many such media, and off-air recording is possible for education (Q5) and domestic timeshift (7.29).

Home taping of borrowed recordings is however illegal and to be discouraged wherever noticed. Tape levies are under EC consideration, but neither UK rights owners nor users currently regard them as fair (9.20).

Lending/rental right

New public lending or rental rights were established from 1 December 1996 (4.35 et seq.). 'Lending' is defined in terms of establishments accessible to the public, and these may charge provided the costs of service operation are not exceeded. Public 'rental' refers to loans for direct or indirect economic or commercial benefit; thus any other bodies making *any kind* of charge for loans will require licensing of 'rental' in respect of any materials, but can make loans only of books covered by Public Lending Right (PLR) without a licence. Accordingly, public and other nonprofit-based libraries and archives do not need a licence to lend books covered by PLR. However, public libraries are seeking licences to 'lend' (this to include their charges if not exceeding running costs) materials other than books, such as musical scores, CD-ROMs or other portable databases, and computer programs in electronic format. Also, public libraries need confirmation of an existing BPI arrangement in respect of sound recordings (4.47) and of the existing video position (4.47). Authors (and composers, etc.) and performers now have a right to royalty in the event of public lending, as well as the right to permit or refuse public lending/rental, and they may bring about changes. Anyone who may acquire a rental licence should note that, when an author or performer has transferred his right to a publisher/producing body, he is entitled to 'equitable remuneration' for rentals, but (if agreed) this can be a single sum for each work payable at the time of transfer.

The sound recording industry is said to be unlikely to license commercial rental. Video recordings have a lively commercial hire market and no licensing scheme, and are not currently concerned with limiting rental (4.47), but rights owners may require royalty for lending as noted above. Public rental or loan of computer programs is still not settled even 10 years after CDPA88 (4.45).

Electronic copyright

Discussion is still in progress on licensing possibilities for electrocopying, though any overall scheme seems unlikely until an Electronic Copyright Management System becomes established (3.56). Another possibility is central administration of a common form of licence allowing variant costs (Appendix 5). As a result of new database right, fair dealing applies to downloading (other than for commercial purpose) unless contrary to service contracts which may be individual to producers or hosts (Q13-14; 3.28; Appendix 3). In the absence of service contracts, users should assume ability to extract or download at least in order to summarise searches, and make a copy for files as well as a client.

As the 'Information Superhighway' comes closer, there is considerable activity not only in research on management of the Internet but also on multimedia copyright problems.

Q8 SUMMARY OF LEGAL COPYRIGHT PERMISSIONS GROUPED BY MEDIA SCOPE

N.B. Excludes database right permissions. See Q0 and Q13-14.

This item is mainly an overview and check for those readers who may already be familiar with copyright matters but, for others less familiar with this subject –

- When CDPA88 uses the word 'a work' without qualification, it covers original literary, dramatic, musical or artistic works, sound recordings, films, broadcasts or cable programmes, but should not be assumed to cover a physical format, such as a printed page or 'typographical arrangement' of a 'published edition', unless specifically stated. 'Original work' is used to mean literary, dramatic, musical or artistic works only.
- However, when the Act uses the phrase 'any copyright', this includes typographical arrangements along with every other form of copyright. The Act's phrases 'anything done' or 'any action' are even wider, including any right covered by the Act unless qualified by the context.
- The relevant paragraph numbers in the main text are given in parentheses.
- All permissions can be used as defences against infringement claims.
- The 'permitted acts' are grouped as follows to provide an alternative presentation to that of Q3, in the hope of stimulating progress towards deeper understanding of the ramifications. In Q3, compulsory licensing possibilities are included among permissions for convenience, but are excluded from Q8.

KEY to copyright kinds included in the permission groups

Permission re rights in:	*See Q8 paragraph number:*																		
	1	*2*	*3*	*4*	*5*	*6*	*7*	*8*	*9*	*10*	*11*	*12*	*13*	*14*	*15*	*16*	*17*	*18*	*19*
ORIGINAL WORKS																			
literary	•	•	•	•	•	•	•	•								•		•	•
computer programs	•	•	•	•	•	•	•	•	•					•				•	•
dramatic	•	•	•	•	•	•	•											•	•
musical	•	•	•	•	•	•												•	•
artistic	•	•	•		•	•										•	•	•	•
FORMATS																			
published (facsimile)	•		•	•														•	
sound recordings	•	•				•					•			•	•			•	
films, videos	•	•				•					•			•				•	
broadcasts	•	•									•	•	•						
cable services	•	•									•	•							
public performance or recording thereof	•									•									
public lending		•						•											
designs																•	•		
electronic forms																		•	
authorised adaptations																			•

Q8.1 Any action for the following purposes does not infringe:

- Incidental inclusion of any work in an artistic work, sound recording, film, broadcast or cable programme (7.27).
- Anything done for examination purposes – questions or answers – including multiple copies but excluding any reprographic copying of music for performance (7.2; 9.4).
- Parliamentary and judicial proceedings, excluding the copying of published reports on proceedings (7.9).
- Royal Commissions and statutory inquiries, excluding the copying of published reports on proceedings (7.10).
- Material open to public inspection or on official register: copying for members of the public (7.11).
- Public Records material which is open to public inspection: supply of copies (7.13).
- If export of an article of cultural or historical importance is illegal unless a copy is deposited in a suitable library or archive, a copy may be made and deposited (6.36).
- Acts done under statutory authority (7.14).

and, though possibly open to challenge on grounds of fairness:

- Fair dealing with any work for purposes of criticism or review, subject to acknowledgement (5.28).
- Fair dealing with any work other than a photograph for purposes of news reporting, subject to acknowledgement unless reported in a nonprint medium (5.31).

Q8.2 Actions which do not infringe the copyright in literary, dramatic or musical works, sound recordings, films, broadcasts or cable programmes:

N.B. this also includes 'artistic' because there is no right of showing for those works.

- Performing, playing or showing in an educational establishment for educational purposes to audiences of persons 'directly connected' with the establishment's activities (9.5).
- Lending of any kind of material by an educational establishment (9.37).

Q8.3 Actions which do not infringe any copyright in a written or otherwise recorded original literary, dramatic, musical or artistic work, or in published form as printed matter – but *not* other physical formats such as sound recordings or films, *nor* the copyright in broadcasts as services, or in cable programme services.

Fair dealing, never defined, and possibly challengeable on grounds of unfairness, permits copying for the following purposes:

- Research or private study (excluding multiple copying) (5.6); providing any library, or an individual on behalf of another, makes no more than one copy.

(See Q8.1 above for criticism or review or news reporting (5.28). Fair dealing is limited in respect of computer programs (5.5).

Education:

- Manual (non-reprographic) copying by teacher or student in the course of instruction (7.1).
- Anthologies of short extracts from published literary or dramatic works, including publication, subject to sufficient acknowedgement, etc. (7.6).
- Reprographic copying for classes from published literary, dramatic or musical works to a specified and very limited extent, unless licensing is available (7.5) (now available for the vast majority of needs).

Q8.4 Actions which do not infringe any copyright in a written or otherwise recorded original literary, dramatic, musical (not artistic) work, or in published form as printed matter – but *not* other physical formats such as sound recordings or films, *nor* the copyright in broadcasts as services, or in cable programme services:

Nonprofit-based library/archive copying (excluding artistic works) from written or printed matter only, including illustrations, subject to special conditions:

- Research or private study only, single copy of periodical article per issue (6.10) or reasonable proportion of non-periodical material (6.11). Reliance on declarations (6.15).
- Research or private study only, from unpublished works held by nonprofit-based libraries or archives, in whole or part (6.16).
- Copies for other library stocks (if they are nonprofit-based): single periodical article per issue or whole or part of a non-periodical item (6.38).
- Preservation purposes, from any item in the permanent collection kept mainly for reference purposes, in whole or part for own stock or another library's stock (if it is nonprofit-based) (6.33).

See also Q4.

Q8.5 Actions which do not infringe copyright in literary, dramatic, musical or artistic works (that is, original works only):

- Copying of anonymous or pseudonymous works, when it is reasonable to assume expiry of copyright: any action – but excluding Crown copyright works, and works of international organisations having longer copyright periods than 70 years (7.28).
- Crown use of original works: the Crown may copy or publish any literary, dramatic musical or artistic work communicated to it in the course of public business (7.12).

Q8.6 Actions which do not infringe copyright in literary, dramatic, musical or artistic works, sound recordings, or films:

- Incidental recording for broadcasts or cable programmes, when inclusion of a work is done under licence or by assignment of copyright (9.17).

Q8.7 Literary or dramatic works only:

- Public reading or recitation of a reasonable extract, subject to sufficient acknowledgement. Also making a sound recording of the extract, or broadcasting or including it in a cable programme service, subject to conditions (9.28).

Q8.8 Literary works only:

- Spoken words: written notes, or a direct sound recording in whole or part which has not been prohibited by the speaker or copyright owner, does not infringe for: news reporting; or inclusion in a broadcast or cable programme service (9.16).
- Abstracts on *scientific* or *technical* subjects published along with periodical articles can be copied or published if there is no licensing scheme available (6.43).
- Public lending by nonprofit-based libraries or archives of books only, when covered by Public Lending Right (4.39).

Q8.9 Computer programs (SI 1992/3233):

(a) back-up copies (7.16)
(b) 'decompilation' or conversion of a program language from lower to higher level; subject to conditions (7.17)
(c) copying or adaptation, subject to conditions (7.18)
(d) use of any device or means to study, observe or test a program (7.19). Contract terms cannot overrule (a), (b) or (d); also (c) in some cases.

Q8.10 Performances:

- Archival recording of a performance of an unpublished song may be made for an archive held by a designated body, subject to conditions (9.22).
- A copy of a recording of a performance acquired before 1 December 1996 is unaffected by new performance rights in SI 1996/2967.

Q8.11 Actions which do not infringe any copyright in a sound recording, film, broadcast or cable programme:

- Education or instruction: copying for instruction in making films or film soundtracks (7.3).

Q8.12 Actions which do not infringe copyright in broadcasts or cable programmes or their contents:

- Off-air recording by educational establishments in the absence of a licensing scheme (7.8).
- BBC, or IBA, or Cable Authority recordings of broadcasts or cable programmes of their own, or authorised by them, for the purposes of supervision and control (9.18).
- Photographs of television or cable programmes for private and domestic use (7.32).
- Timeshift recording of broadcast or cable programmes for private and domestic use (7.29).
- Free public showing or playing (9.27).
- Provision of subtitled copies of recordings for the disadvantaged by designated bodies (9.25).
- Archival recordings for a designated body (9.23).

Q8.13 Actions which do not infringe copyright in a broadcast from a UK location for reception and immediate re-transmission in a cable programme service:

- Inclusion does not infringe if required by the Cable and Broadcasting Acts, and if a satellite or encrypted transmission is not involved (9.19).

Q8.14 Lending to public of literary, dramatic, musical or artistic works:

- In the absence of licensing schemes, to be treated as licensed, subject to payment of reasonable royalty (4.44), if so required by order of the Secretary of State.

Q8.15 Playing of sound recordings:

- This is not an infringement for a nonprofit-based club or society or other organisation, having mainly charitable objects or concerned with the advancement of religion, education or social welfare, provided any admission charge is applied solely for the purposes of the organisation (9.26).

Q8.16 Actions in respect of design documents and models:

- Making an article to the design, or copying such an article, does not infringe (11.12). (This is because the Act now provides unregistered design right. The drawings and models are still copyright in themselves.)

Q8.17 Actions re artistic works only, including designs:

- Designs derived from artistic works: after 25 years from first marketing, making or copying articles to the design (11.13).
- Anything done in reliance on a design as having been registered under the Registered Design Act 1949 (11.14).
- Using a typeface design in the course of printing (11.15).
- After 25 years from first marketing, copying a typeface design (11.15).
- Sculptures, buildings, models for buildings and works of artistic craftsmanship on public display (which means paintings, drawings, etc. as well as objects) may be drawn or photographed or broadcast or included in a cable programme service (9.8).
- An artistic work may be copied to advertise it for sale (7.24).
- A copy of an artistic work by an author who is no longer the copyright owner does not infringe provided the main design is not repeated or imitated (7.25).
- Anything done for reconstruction of a building, including relevant drawings or plans, does not infringe (7.26).
- Crown use for defence, etc. (11.16).

Q8.18 Transference of an electronic form of a work:

- Permissions applicable under terms of purchase may be transferred to another person unless otherwise stated by the terms. This also applies where the original purchased copy is no longer usable and what is transferred is a further copy used in its place (7.30).

Q8.19 Adaptations:

- Any of the foregoing which is done in respect of an adaptation which has been made with due authorisation does not infringe copyright in the original work which was adapted (7.33).

N.B. Moral rights – the permissions designated in chapter 10 are drawn from those in Q8 above, and none is peculiar to moral rights – but also note that there are some exceptions which amount to permissions.

Q9 MORAL RIGHTS OUTLINE

The four rights described in chapter 10 subsist alongside copyright:

(a) Paternity right: the right to be identified as author (or director of a film), whether or not the current owner of copyright, of a work issued to or performed or exhibited in public (or other cognate actions). Lasts for the duration of copyright, but does not exist unless asserted by author or film director (10.9).

(b) Derogatory treatment of a work: right to object to this, lasting for the duration of copyright. Like (a), this right subsists in favour of the author or director whether or not he is the owner of copyright (10.12).

(c) False attribution: right *not* to suffer false attribution of a work. This lasts for life plus twenty years only (10.15).

(d) Privacy of photographs: right of a person commissioning copyright photographs or films *not* to have copies issued to the public, or exhibited or shown in public, or broadcast or included in a cable programme service. This right lasts for the duration of copyright, and subsists in favour of the commissioner whether or not he is the owner of copyright, as with (a) (10.16).

Other main points are:

(1) Moral rights cannot be assigned, but (a), (b) and (d) can be willed to someone.

(2) Infringement of the above rights is actionable as a breach of statutory duty.

(3) All the above rights may be waived.

(4) Each is subject to exceptions. There are also some permissions which are already listed in Q3 in respect of other contexts, and chapter 10 should be consulted for these permissions.

(5) These new additions to UK law will need to be borne in mind in a number of contexts, notably in assessing whether an action may be 'fair' in acting under fair dealing provisions.

Q10 DURATION OF AUTHOR'S COPYRIGHT

Q10.1 Duration of author's copyright in content of literary, dramatic and musical works, including copyright in the content of electronic records (excluding database right 3.28 et seq.)

Made (effective dates of Acts)			**Features of work**					**KEY to periods in Q10.2** (including possible *extension* or *revival* from EU changes) **death** or **publication** or **creation** year				
before 1/6/57	1/6/57 to 31/7/89	1/8/89 on-wards	publis-hed?	unpub-lished?	posthu-mously publis-hed?	known author?	anony-mous?	1924 or earlier	during 1925	1926-1944	during 1945	1946 or after
•				•		•		**11**	**10**	**13**	**12**	**14**
•			•			•		**11**	**10**	**13**	**12**	**14**
•			•		•	•		**2**	**10**	**4**	**3**	**5**
•				•			•	**1**	**1**	**1**	**1**	**1**
•			•				•	**2**	**10**	**4**	**3**	**5**
	•			•		•						**14/8***
	•		•			•						**14**
	•		•		•	•						**6**
	•			•			•					**8**
	•		•				•					**5**
		•		•		•						**14**
		•	•			•						**14**
		•	•		•	•						**6**
		•		•			•					**9/7****
		•	•				•					**7**

** 14, or 8 if deceased before 1/8/89 (CDPA88 commencement) and still unpublished.*
*** 9, or 7 if published within 70 years of creation.*

Q10.2 Duration of author's copyright: keys and periods

In the following, 'publication' date may also signify other means of making available to public, such as performance, especially in a case of first such action after author's death.

1. Copyright perpetual until 31/5/57
2. 50 years beyond *publication* year
3. 70 years beyond *publication* year after **extension** for 20 years from 1/1/96 when UK former 50-year copyright ended actually **on** 31/12/95 (see ch. 2.2)
4. 70 years beyond *publication* year after **revival** on 1/1/96 when former 50-year UK copyright ended before end of 1995 but work still copyright in another EEA state on 1/7/95 (see ch. 2.2)
5. 70 years beyond *publication* year
6. 70 years beyond *publication* year, *if* posthumous 50-year period of Copyright Act 1911 or Copyright Act 1956 began to run before 1/8/89
7. 70 years beyond *publication* year, if published within 70 years from creation
8. 70 years beyond 1989 (=2059)
9. 70 years beyond *creation* year
10. **Revival** for only 6 months, 1/1/96 to 30/6/96 when UK copyright ended before end of 1995 but work still copyright in another EEA state on 1/7/95
11. 50 years beyond author's *death* year
12. 70 years beyond author's *death* year, after **extension** from 1/1/96 for works ending UK's past norm of 50-year copyright actually **on** 31/12/95
13. 70 years beyond author's *death* year, after **revival** on 1/1/96 when UK's former 50-year copyright ended before 1995, but work still copyright in another EEA state on 1/7/95
14. 70 years beyond author's *death* year

Notes

1. Some artistic works made 1911 onwards are treated like the above, but earlier law affects surviving works from before 1/7/12 in respect of engravings, sculptures, paintings and drawings (but not photographs, see Q11).
2. Adaptations such as drama, translations, etc. count as publication — and for the latter read any means of 'making public' including performance.
3. If the 1988 Act allowed a later date than above, the *later* one applies *but* without the s57 provision on assumption of death of author (see 2.36).
4. The above reflects *only* the general situation and should be used with due regard to possible complexities (e.g. from EU harmonisation), which may need reference to legal authorities.
5. To use the above guidance, a copyright notice may help, of course: for example re a deceased author with a known or easily ascertainable death year.
6. When studying CDPA88 Schedule 1 (as revised) on transitional arrangements, there can be problems due to changes over time, whether in definitions, protection periods, or ownership, and help from experts may well be needed.
7. **All of Q10-Q12 are incidentally included as illustrations of difficulties in determination of duration, and form the background for proposals in Appendix 5. No responsibility can be taken for any reader's action, and checks with legal experts should be made when there is good reason (e.g. own publication needs).**

Q11 DURATION OF COPYRIGHT IN PHOTOGRAPHS

Q11.1 Duration of copyright in photographs; also Crown copyright in literary, dramatic or musical works *generally*, including Crown photographs

TAKEN	Features of work				Key to periods in Q11.2	Crown Copyright
	Publis-hed	*Unpub-lished*	*Author known*	*Anony-mous*		*(no revival or extension applies)*
1924 or earlier (CA11)	•	•	•	—	*a*	*h*
during 1925	•	•	*Owner of film was 'author', un-less commissioned for money, when commissioner was author*	—	*a/b*	*h*
1926 to 1944	•	•		—	*a*	*h*
during 1945	•	•		—	*c*	*h*
1946 to 30/5/57	•	•		—	*g*	*h*
1/6/57 to 31/7/89 (CA56)	•			—	*e*	*i*
		•		—	*d*	*j*
1/8/89 onwards (CDPA88)	•		•		*f*	*k*
		•	*Photographer*	•	*g*	**N/A**
	•			•	*e*	**N/A**
		•	•		*f*	*l*

Q11.2 Photographs, and Crown copyright periods including photographs

KEY

Periods

(a) 50 years beyond creation year
(b) **Revival** for only 6 months, 1/1/96 to 30/6/96 when UK copyright ended before end of 1995 but work still copyright in another EEA state on 1/7/95
(c) 70 years beyond *creation* year, after **extension** from 1/1/96 for works ending UK's past norm of 50-year copyright actually **on** 31/12/95
(d) 70 years beyond 1989 (=2059)
(e) 70 years beyond *publication* year
(f) 70 years beyond author's *death* year
(g) 70 years beyond *creation* year

Crown copyright periods (extension or revival does not apply)

(h) 50 years beyond *creation* year
(i) 50 years beyond *publication*
(j) 50 years beyond 1989 (=2039)
(k) 50 years beyond *publication* year if published within 75 years of creation
(l) 125 years beyond *creation* year

For Acts, period dates from end of year of Royal Assent.

Notes

1. In cases of revived copyright, the photographer is the owner if the former owner died before 1/8/89.
2. Film stills were defined as photographs up to 30/5/57. From 1/6/57, they are defined as films (treat as extracts) when taken from a continuous film sequence.
3. If CDPA88 allows later expiry than above, the later date applies.
4. No pre-1/7/12 (1912 Act commencement) photographs are still copyright.
5. This is only the general situation, and details can be complex.

See also the notes at the end of Q10.2. For example, there may be particular need for expert help in respect of foreign photographs.

Q12 RIGHTS OF EMPLOYERS AND JOURNALISTS AS EMPLOYEES under contract (4.2) – general situation only

Dates	First ownership of rights	Duration
before 1/7/12	***publisher or proprietor*** (of newspaper or other periodical) holds rights in the whole compilation, plus individual articles as separates	28 years beyond *publication*
	author (journalist) right to publish as *separates* reverts to author	*after* 28 years, publisher needed permission re separates
1/7/12 to 1/6/57	***author*** has right of *restraint* (only) against publication *otherwise* than in a newspaper or periodical	50 years beyond author's *death* year (see also Q10 for details of extension or revival of copyright, due to EU harmonisation)
1/7/57 to 31/7/89 (CA56)	**SPLIT:** ***employer*** holds reproduction rights in any periodical, including musical works	70 years beyond author's *death* year
	author holds all other rights (but not for music)	
1/8/89 onwards (CDPA88)	***employer, author not named,*** unless otherwise contracted	70 years beyond *creation* year, or 70 years beyond *publication* if published within 70 years of creation
	employer, author named	70 years beyond author's *death* year

The notes at the end of Q10.2 also apply to the above.

Q13 DATABASE RIGHT

The notes in Q13-14 follow on from Q0.

In compliance with EC harmonisation, the UK's new database right applies from 1 January 1998 (3.28; Appendix 3). An introduction to the effects has been given in Q0. The right is to be applied alongside copyright, which means that it can overrule a copyright permission unless that is repeated under database right.

A database is a compilation which contains a collection of independent works, data or other materials, which are arranged in a systematic or methodical way, and are individually accessible by electronic or other means. A simply arranged or 'sweat of brow' directory, for example, is not a database and is therefore not protected by database right, though it can nevertheless be protected under copyright as a compilation for the usual 'life plus 70 year' period (anomalous of the basic 15 years for database right). Content may be copyright or noncopyright, of any medium or multimedia, print or electronic format. Many publications as well as electronic databases are thus covered, e.g. organised directories, handbooks, periodical issues, etc.

The protection is against extraction or re-utilisation of items for 15 years initially, repeatable if updated significantly during that period, and so on with perpetual capability, even for noncopyright content. Similarly to copyright, infringement only occurs if a substantial part or the whole is involved, but that is to be assessed quantitatively and/or qualitatively.

Unlike a copyright work, a database need not be original but, in the event that it is original, will be copyright at compilation level as well as reflect any copyright which may subsist in items of content. However, it only qualifies for database *right* if there has been substantial investment in its making. The maker is the owner of the right.

Duration of rights in an existing database:

- A database created on or before 27 March 1996 (EC Directive was passed on that date), which is a copyright work immediately before commencement on 1 January 1998, continues to be copyright for the rest of its copyright term (author life plus 70 years, etc.).
- A database completed on or after 1 January 1983 which qualifies for database right will have protection for 15 years commencing 1 January 1998 in the first instance.

The licensing of database right is covered by Schedule 2 to the SI 1997/3032.

Q14 DATABASE RIGHT PERMISSIONS AND PROBLEMS OF ADJUSTMENT

Many copyright permissions are not repeated under database right. The only permissions relevant to database right are:

- fair dealing for research or private study, but not with a database for a commercial purpose (see 5.6);
- use of a substantial part for 'illustration for teaching and research', subject to fair dealing defence and indication of source; but notably no other educational permission;
- a 'lawful user' has a right to do anything *which is necessary for the purposes of exercising his or her right to use the database*; but this only means actions which his or her licence permits. However, a lawful user's right may not be overridden by some other contract.
- all 'public administration' copyright permissions are repeated under database right;
- any existing copyright permission which does *not* involve extraction or re-utilisation of parts of a database will apply to database right;
- anyone or any library may act on behalf of someone in respect of any permission which does apply (6.45);
- anyone may extract an 'insubstantial part', but repetitive extraction could be judged substantial. This may prove the only way to continue many of the existing permissions which apply under copyright, unless rights owners soon affirm them as involving insubstantial parts anyway.

Notably, there is no distinction between paper and electronic formats, hence any permission should apply to either, subject to 'lawful user' limits. An electronic database is a publication.

It may take some time before agreement can be reached (in the absence of statutory provision) on definitions. For example:

- what exactly is 'commercial purpose'?
- how does one distinguish between an ordinary compilation and a database, especially in printed matter? (For example, a sweat of brow compilation with

copyright for author life plus 70 years, compared with a database for 15 years from creation initially.)

— are rights owners prepared to recognise all or most existing permission re copyright as 'insubstantial parts' of databases? In particular, may the BCC copyright guidelines (Appendix 1/3) be affirmed re database right?
— otherwise, is it expected that all libraries, information services and firms must become licensed against the contingency of infringing database right, whether they extract or re-utilise or not?

Other problems are:

— noticing that a habitually-used permission continued under *copyright* is over-ridden by *database right* in respect of a database in hand or in access electronically;
— collecting day to day problems for notification to professional bodies and raising in connection with the expected three-year review of the Directive;
— monitoring the situation as notified through professional associations.

It is concluded that, when no specific guidance is to hand, it may well be simpler for the 'traditional' practices to be continued until a need for change is discovered or notified. See 5.6 and 6.4 for notes on fair dealing and library copying.

It is impossible to forecast the length of the adjustment period which will be required. Meanwhile, discretion is recommended, noting that publishers and producers also need adjustment to practices and time to prepare appropriate licensing. In the circumstances, rights owners may tolerate all but the worst excesses such as publication without permission. However, their actual views and new guidelines are being sought forthwith, principally through the LA/JCC Working Party on Copyright, but this may take some time. Looseleaf services such as the *Aslib guide to copyright* should be monitored by those with a special need to keep up to date, and professional advice should be sought where necessary.

1. INTRODUCTION

Main paragraph number

Aims of this book

1.1 Permissions

The principal aim of this book is to answer the main questions asked by all end-users of published copyright materials: 'What can I copy without asking anyone?' and 'How do I seek permission, or get a licence if need be?'. Those wanting just the basic facts about what can certainly be copied, with absolutely minimal background details, should go straight to the 'Quick reference guide' at the beginning of the volume, which aims to cover the main topics treated in the book.

Because the kinds of copyright materials and circumstances of their use are many and varied, copyright has become a somewhat convoluted subject. Many people appear to regard the special conditions attached to most permissions as a source of particular difficulty, but this kind of difficulty just has to be lived with. Even licensing has a set of detailed terms which must be followed. Attempts to simplify matters are nevertheless made in this book, mostly by providing summaries and notes on common problems of everyday practice. Quotations of actual phrases from the Act are preferred, with relevant section numbers, when simplification is considered undesirable or unnecessary.

This book covers the laws as amended to January 1998. So many changes have been made to the CDPA88 that, should a reader require 'the letter of the law' in more detail, he or she should consult a looseleaf service (e.g. the *Aslib guide to copyright* or an online database. Perhaps greater familiarity may not after all breed contempt, but might even engender respect for the skill of the drafters!

1.2 Background

Of course, some background details must be given in the main text of a volume of this kind. In giving background, the explanations will normally relegate controversial matters to other chapters. Likewise, a number of suggested solutions to specific problems are brought together in chapter 15.

Although not its main aim, this book attempts to include some information to interest and assist users of copyright materials who are also authors and publishers. These are liable to ask: 'How (and how well) is my work protected?'

The background details are provided in the hope that as many people as possible will take sufficient interest in the subject to understand how to behave in respect of copyright from day to day, and be forearmed against future attempts to change the law to the detriment of users. This takes rather more than just blindly following a list of do's and dont's. Also, it is recommended that every organisation involved in any aspect of communication and information should aim to have at least one staff member responsible for keeping up to date on copyright and serving as a first point of reference for colleagues.

It was also decided to expand a little on the outline on rights in performances in the first edition, because performers (as well as authors) have new rights in respect of lending/rental right.

1.3 Responsibility

The responsibility for any action taken must remain with the reader concerned, particularly as a number of points in this book are necessarily advisory rather than clear points of law (see 1.18).

Further help may be sought from texts in Appendix 1, or from reference to the current state of the Act, or by asking this author, or by consulting a member of the legal profession. Succeeding chapters will however indicate the degree of authority for copying permissions or 'allowances', and such notes are provided to assist decisions on everyday procedure.

Copyright is 'intellectual property'

1.4 A person who creates and records an original product of the mind becomes the first owner of 'intellectual property'. This term was first coined to cover literary, dramatic, musical and artistic works; designs of articles or devices; and inventions. The laws on intellectual property aim to protect an originator from unauthorised use or exploitation of his work or design or invention by someone else, though the protection lasts only for a limited period.

Why 'a person'? Because the law is built around individuals, not only in respect of obligations and rights but also penalties. United Kingdom law uses the word 'author' in its broadest sense, to apply to, say, not only a novelist but also a playwright, composer, photographer, artist, and so on. However, a provision relating to 'a body incorporated under the law...' (s154)' does appear among the Act's sections on 'qualification for protection' but this has been taken to mean only companies which are registered at Companies House (see 2.9). The law does not contain the librarian's much more general concept of corporate authorship by a body such as an institution or group of professionals. Now, in database right, a database maker may be a corporate body 'formed under the law of an EEA state'. Otherwise, any work originating through a corporate body which does not show responsibility of a personal author is protected as an 'anonymous work'.

Why say 'first owner'? Because intellectual property can change hands by assignment, whether wholly or partially. A novelist normally assigns to a publisher the right to reproduce copies of his or her work in return for payment, usually a 'royalty' which is a percentage of the sale price of the published book. Any other rights associated with the work, such as paperback or serialisation or film rights, can be sold separately if desired.

Why say the term 'intellectual property' was 'first coined'? Because nowadays the law gives rights of protection not only to originators but also to those who create physical formats for general distribution or sale, such as publishers, producers of audiovisual media, and providers of particular public services such as broadcasting and electronic databases. Rights are also given to performers.

1.5 This book focuses primarily upon written or printed matter, audiovisual media, and electronic media. Also included, though to a lesser extent, are designs and performances. Throughout this book, 'works' refers not only to original works but also physical formats such as sound recordings, videotapes, electronic databases, etc., in line with the approach adopted by the law. Readers who require a concise overview, or merely to know such essentials as copiable extents and purposes, are recommended to study the outlines and summaries at the beginning of this volume.

Nature of copyright

1.6 Copyright is concerned with original works and any forms in which they may be published or released or performed for others. There is slight overlap with what is known as 'design right', because design drawings and models are still protected by copyright. There is similar overlap with inventions which receive letters patent, because the documentation itself is protected as copyright, but patents are regarded as outside the scope of this volume.

The most frequently encountered kind of copyright is the right to copy or to authorise copying by others, whether from paper or an electronic database, or indeed any form of 'recorded information' – even a building. An author is not obliged to permit a publisher to make copies and sell them but, if permission is given, the author is entitled to benefit in accordance with terms agreed in a contract with the publisher. An author's work must accordingly be protected from copying or publication without permission, especially in ways which could damage its market.

Monopoly

1.7 In effect, an author is granted a monopoly. However, after a finite period, all copyright materials fall into the public domain and are usable without restriction for the betterment of research, education, or culture in general. This means that, unless some other means of control applies to the materials concerned, such as a contract, they can be used without permission and even re-published. The period of protection for authors of original works is related to lifetime: namely, life plus 70 years. Authors who produce physical formats like audiovisual media, other than films with a personal author, receive protection for those formats for a fixed period of 50 years -- except publishers, whose protection is limited to 25 years beyond the publication year. More details are given in later chapters.

1.8 The duration of copyright is therefore very important, but unfortunately it is rarely easy to determine whether an item is still protected when its period of copyright is linked to a lifetime. Conversely, it is no less important that the works of an author should be available with as few restrictions as possible in order to inform, educate and improve cultural levels. Accordingly, the law makes exceptions to copyright restrictions for particular purposes.

1.9 Under British law, copyright is said to 'subsist' in something because the right cannot exist by itself. Copyright is automatic, without any need for registration or claim, provided a work is 'fixed' or recorded in some form. There is however a system of legal deposit of copies of new publications with designated libraries of national standing for archival purposes, but this is separate from copyright. Although a copyright notice on a work is not essential to obtain protection in the UK itself, a notice is desirable for overseas protection in any remaining nations which have not yet signed or ratified international agreements on copyright. The specified form is known as a 'C-notice', consisting of a capital C within a circle, usually on the back of a title page, followed by the name of the copyright owner at the time of publication, plus the year – as on the back of the title page of this volume. By international agreement, a signatory nation must allow foreign materials at least as much protection as home-produced items.

Originality

1.10 A work must be original to be regarded as copyright, though its degree of originality may not be large. There seems to be no satisfactory way to define 'original' except through the courts in relation to specific items and circumstances. For example, timetables have been claimed to be copyright, though service operators would scarcely object if increased usage and profits could ensue from copying them, whereas publishers would object to loss of revenue from sale of their own copies. Works can of course overlap by coincidence, especially when reporting the news, and there is copyright in each report as a whole if not in the specific facts covered.

Questions are sometimes asked about book titles or characters, and company names. The latter are mostly outside the scope of this text, being subject to the law on trade marks and names (see 15.74), but it is believed that a case could possibly be based on copyright law, depending on exactly what the alleged infringer had 'copied' and why. Character names can cause quite complex cases to be fought and, if the characteristics or attributes of a fictitious character are also duplicated – whether by accident or design is immaterial – an infringement claim might well be upheld. There is no problem of course, if the original source is out of copyright, but the effects of revived or renewed copyright (2.2) must be borne in mind (for example, Toad from *Wind in the willows,* mentioned in 14.1). There would seem no harm in mentioning a character's name and even describing his or her attributes, as long as the latter are not ascribed to a new character without permission, though this would be a matter of degree.

Now that moral rights have been added to UK law (10), the risk of infringing these must be borne in mind as well as copyright per se. The use of a famous author's name for one's own work could offend not only on moral right grounds (false attribution, 10.2(c)) but might also lead to accusations of 'passing off' under common law. One should accordingly avoid using forms of name, or name-plus-title combinations, which could cause confusion to the public. With regard to book titles per se, infringement might be adjudged in respect of a long or otherwise uncommon title, especially of a well-known work such as a bestseller. However, use of the same title should not necessarily be ruled out: for example, a new book title *Little women*, though in danger if it were children's literature, should be safe enough as a scientific study of child development through adolescence!

1.11 In general, common facts are regarded as non-copyright in themselves – after all, anyone might otherwise claim to 'originate' a statement about such things as bibliographical details of publications. Care is necessary, nevertheless, and discretion must be applied to decide whether some facts such as statistics arising from research should be seen as integral with a whole copyright work, though those facts could still be quoted piecemeal, desirably with acknowledgement.

Ideas and copyright

1.12 It is commonly said that there is no copyright in ideas, but only in the form in which they are expressed. This tenet is true in general, and is a very desirable state of affairs for human progress. However, it should only be regarded as unchallengeable when an idea is interpretable as a concept from the real world which is capable of consideration separately from its context in order to help generate new concepts.

The totality of a group of related ideas should not be copied without permission or – even worse -- without acknowledgement, except within legal permissions or with licensing or specific rights-owner authority. Except for any real-life political allusions or satire which may be present, it is unlikely that the separate ideas in works of fantasy like those of Tolkien could be considered non-copyright. Nor is it likely that a paraphrase would survive litigation by an aggrieved author. The old adage about authorship still applies to most circumstances: that copying the work of one author is plagiarism, whilst copying the work of many is research.

Related rights to copyright

1.13 This term is used to cover rights which, whilst not concerned with copying and other copyright restrictions, apply to copyright materials and are linked to the duration of copyright. These rights include public rental or hire, public lending, moral rights, and 'neighbouring rights'. Some experts define as neighbouring rights those which they see as distinct from copyright, such as performing and broadcasting rights, recording rights and film distribution rights. The comprehensive approach adopted by UK statute, interlinked as it is with a background of contract law, makes the designation of neighbouring rights as a group largely unnecessary.

Protection of rights

1.14 Copyright and related rights are protected in the UK primarily by Act of Parliament, assisted by supplementary legislation in the form of Statutory Instruments containing special conditions or regulations or amendments to the Act under which they are generated. However, it would cause excessively complicated statutes to attempt coverage of all circumstances, and in the UK court decisions or 'case law' is seen as a means of enriching the legal framework. Case law however takes much time to build up, during which some ambiguities inevitably remain unresolved. It is perhaps preferable that the current statute aims to encourage recourse to contracts between parties to cover complexities, whether for detailed arrangements between an originator and a publisher (or producer, or recordist, etc.) or to license users to make copies, usually for non-publishing purposes. Copyright regulation methods are, broadly speaking, Law and -- for the want of a better term -- Quasi-law. The following is an outline, but this should not be taken as an indication of the arrangement of this volume.

Law and quasi-law

1.15 Legislation

Copyright, Designs and Patents Act 1988 (in force since 'commencement date' of 1 August 1989). This will be called 'CDPA88' or simply 'the Act' from this chapter onwards.

Regulations in association (Statutory Instruments), such as Copyright (Librarians and Archivists) (Copying of Copyright Materials) Regulations 1989, SI 1989/1212.

Council of Europe Directives which will require states to introduce additional national legislation. A harmonisation programme has begun with the aim of easing the operation of the Single Market. So far, computer software, public rental and lending, and protection against extraction from databases have been covered. One or two issues remain, such as home taping (in draft) and reprography. Directives must be followed by statutory instruments to adjust UK law accordingly. Later chapters, plus Appendix 3, incorporate such changes as have appeared in statutory instruments, and note the main effects of further expected changes.

1.16 Quasi-law

Contract: an 'agreement between parties' can override any part of statutory provisions on copyright, other than criminal liability in the event of infringement

Licensing, individual, for example: Ordnance Survey; British Standards Institution

Licensing, collective (known as 'schemes' in the 1988 Act when covering the works of more than one author), for example: by the Copyright Licensing Agency Ltd; Performing Right Society Ltd

Conditions of sale or hire (not always clearly contractual).

NB: Automatic charging, as in electronic systems, is a contractual arrangement.

1.17 Guidelines

- by rights owner representatives. Examples: the British Copyright Council; the Music Publishers' Association Ltd; British Photographers' Liaison Committee. Treat as authoritative when extending or clarifying legal permissions, but regard them as questionable when they seek to restrict actions to a greater extent than statute
- by individual publishers: HMSO; Ordnance Survey (ditto)
- by library or information service professional bodies: take as authoritative where in line with all above, otherwise treat as advisory. This book attempts a consolidation of the main guidelines
- Permissions printed on an item: of course, authoritative
- Restrictive phrases printed on an item: take as authoritative if they are reminders of legal rights and permissions, or when they are judged to be conditions of sale or hire
- Responses by individual rights owners to permission requests: obviously authoritative.

Approach adopted by CDPA88

1.18 Legal language

For far too long, the complexities of copyright have kept it almost an elitist topic. CDPA88 had as one of its declared aims the use of everyday language as far as possible, and this has certainly helped clarity compared with previous copyright statutes. But the need to avoid ambiguity and also produce the neat and elegant *multum in parvo* phrase inevitably causes difficulties for those unfamiliar with finding their way around legislation.

This volume attempts to avoid the worst pitfalls which this subject shares with many other legal areas. Even legal experts can at times miss provisos or semantic links with later sections of an Act and, being human, take risks when stripping down phraseology to make it more accessible for the reader.

The simplification of legal language, especially when its drafters have already gone as far as they think safe and reasonable in making it more user-friendly, is always fraught with the danger of inadvertently changing the meaning of legal provisions.

1.19 Restricted acts

After defining copyright materials, ownership and duration of copyright, CDPA88 sets out 'restricted acts' to define the exclusive rights of copyright owners. These are followed by exceptions or 'acts permitted', to be called 'permissions' in this volume.

1.20 Transitional provisions

There are extensive *transitional provisions and savings* in Schedule 1 to the Act, and some of these have been included in Q10 to Q12. Otherwise, because their nature would complicate the main text of this book, only a few examples of the provisions have been included. Anyone involved with problems affecting works in existence before CDPA88 came into force on 1 August 1989 should seek out Schedule 1 as amended.

Development of copyright

1.21 Whilst the history and development of copyright are generally excluded from this book, apart from the 'Landmarks' notes at the end of this chapter, a brief outline of the photocopy licensing controversy appears in Appendix 2, and several other fragments of history may be found. The bibliography in Appendix 1 contains a number of references which include considerable detail for those who may want it, including case law which is particularly avoided here owing to space limitations.

The new law has been said to be more liable to generate case law than past legislation on the subject, so future legal texts appear liable to expand at a greater rate than hitherto in successive editions.

Importance of copyright

1.22 Piracy

Without protection for copyright, unauthorised copying – regarded by rights owners as theft or even piracy – would be rife. A kind of intellectual anarchy would reign. Incentives to writers and publishers, and any others concerned with works and their physical formats, would diminish or disappear, along with economic benefits.

1.23 Balance

Copyright law tries to be even-handed both to rights owners and users, allowing the former to gain from their work and the latter to make appropriate use of it, hopefully for the good of society. A balancing Act may not be found witty by commercial publishers but does describe the result. The route from authors to publishers, booksellers, librarians, researchers, educators and back round to authors constitutes a 'communication loop'. It is essential to all progress that the loop be maintained, whilst ensuring that the economic incentive to participate suffers minimal damage. Therein lies one of the root causes of copyright law complexity. Others are the large range of kinds of copyright material, modes of utilisation, and available methods of copying without paying more than the cost of producing the copy. The protection of copyrights requires some flexibility in rights owners but, being fundamentally unpoliceable, ultimately depends on the honesty of users.

1.24 Some countries pay little attention to copyright, and these are to be found among the net importers of copyright materials. The UK is second only to the USA in the size of its export market for such materials. Copyright not only protects originators and publishers from potential loss of earnings – a very real loss where deliberate piracy occurs – but also encourages all concerned to create and publish further work. Both copyright itself, and flexibility in its protection in order to assist user-access, are equally essential to the whole process of creativity and to the cross-fertilisation of ideas which arises from communication.

Landmarks of copyright

1.25 The following may help to outline the origins and development of copyright law:

- Term 'copyright': first use uncertain; taken literally as 'right to copy'.
- In ancient times, that which mattered was what was said, not who said it. Growth of individualism is believed to date from about the 6th century BC in classical Greece: signing of works of art and poems. The right to make copies evolved in various societies as a means of controlling the flow of information. Linked with censorship at various times.
- Examples of extremes of control of information flow: Ancient China and Egypt. Contrast of community property approach in Bali.
- Ancient Jewish law involved economic returns for authors and their heirs. In Rome, contracts were drawn up between authors and publishers (scribes) and both benefited.
- Middle Ages: scribes in monasteries held virtual monopoly of production of copies.
- c.1436 Gutenberg (German) invented printing with movable types: explosion of printing followed.
- 1476 Caxton introduced printing into England; piracy rife.
- 1557 Stationers' Company: printers, bookbinders, booksellers – monopoly on printing and publishing, with copyright as publishers' right, until royal charter expired 1694, then considerable chaos and piracy.
- 1709 Statute of Queen Anne – protection against piracy of printed works – the first 'modern' copyright law anywhere.
- 1774 a House of Lords decision on a case changed copyright from publishers' right to authors' right.
- 1886 Berne Convention – rights of authors. 3 principles:
  1) national treatment – foreign works protected in each member state in same manner as country of origin.
  2) minimum standard of protection (content, scope, duration) must not be below that provided in the Convention
  3) automatic protection without registration or notice.

- 1952 Universal Copyright Convention – compromise to unify Berne Union with American system. A 'C notice' (©) was specified as required, principally for protection in the USA.
- 1956 Copyright Act, soon overtaken by technology.
- 1988 Copyright, Designs and Patents Act.

Modern copyright law has evolved from balancing the needs of users for access to and exchange of information with the rights of authors and publishers to financial benefit.

2. COPYRIGHT WORKS: DURATION AND AUTHORSHIP

What materials or media are copyright? How long does copyright last? These questions form the subject of this chapter and the next.

Kinds of copyright work

2.1 As summarised in Q1, copyright subsists in the following:

(a) original works: that is, the content of literary, dramatic, musical or artistic works (compilations, tables and computer programs are defined as 'literary'; photographs are 'artistic' irrespective of nature)
(b) sound recordings, films, broadcasts or cable programmes ('films' includes video recordings or any moving image, while 'cable programmes' include not only cable TV but also publicly accessible online electronic databases or audio information services
(c) the typographical arrangement of a 'published edition' (2.21) or printed pages, whether text or music or illustrations, etc.

The Act makes (a), (b) and (c) clearly copyright works. This has to be borne in mind when there is reference to 'literary, dramatic, musical or artistic works' – that is, original works – a reference which could be wrongly assumed to mean all physical forms of those works, like sound recordings, as well as original items.

Some have described (a) as the intellectual or 'creation' category, with (b) and (c) as 'production' categories. Despite the convenience of use in Q1, it has to be admitted that those terms, if not grey in themselves, might conceivably have a 'greying' effect on many a skilled and imaginative sound recordist, cinematographer or publisher.

Duration of copyright

2.2 Q10-12 provide summary charts on the essentials. The following are general remarks, for copyright duration is mentioned in later chapters in association with particular kinds of copyright material and related rights. Special provisions which apply to Crown and Parliamentary copyright are described in 2.44-2.52.

Duration of copyright is stated in complete calendar years, starting from the end of the year of an event, such as death of an author, and ending a fixed number of years later.

An EC Directive of 1993 on term of copyright was implemented in the UK by SI 1995/3297. A major change is the adoption of 70 years as the fixed period beyond an event (death of the author; creation or publication year). However:

> 'Where the country of origin of the work is not an EEA state and the author of the work is not a national of an EEA state, the duration of copyright is that to which the work is entitled in the country of origin, provided that does not exceed the period which would apply'

to works qualifying for the EEA period. This affects:

- original works, with or without a known personal author; and
- films *with* an identifiable personal author;

but *excludes* Crown or Parliamentary copyright (2.44) and that of international organisations (2.11).

There is an important retrospective effect. Works in which UK copyright expired before 31 December 1995 but were still protected by the laws of another EEA member state on 1 July 1995 receive either *extended* or *revived* copyright. (See 2.9 for meaning of EEA state.) The main example is Germany, where the period beyond an event has long been 70 years. Thus all UK-expired works which were still copyright in Germany on 1 July 1995 will receive revival periods of between 6 months (if the German fixed period ended in December 1995) and 20 years (1996-2016). Works in UK copyright on 31 December 1995 have extensions of 20 years added to the previously expected post mortem period, thus the works of an author who dies in 2050 will still be copyright until the end of 2120. These changes revive or extend the copyright of a great many works, for all personal authors who died during 1925 to 1945 might be involved. Fortunately, agreements made before the effective commencement date of 1 January 1996 are unaffected but, if a licensee or rights-purchaser has not secured coverage of prospective extensions or revivals of copyright, there may well need to be some re-negotiation by new authors or adapters with current copyright owners, for example, re *Wind in the Willows* (14.1).

Many people think the 70-year period is excessive, and indeed it could prove of little value for a lot of materials: for example, from computer programs through scientific or technical texts. As already in many respects, authors of popular fiction and their heirs seem likely to accrue the larger benefit.

This chapter is concerned with categories 2.1 (a) and (c), but only when printed or written (otherwise than electronically). Category (b), plus electronic versions of all three categories, are covered in chapter 3. Mention of duration may also be found in later chapters in association with particular kinds of work.

Accordingly, for 2.1(a) above, copyright protection now lasts for 70 years beyond the calendar year of the author's death when a personal author is known, so the event is the end of his year of decease. The post mortem period allows the heirs of a personal author to publish any unpublished works and benefit accordingly from those and from earlier publications. Duration continues to relate to author even when rights are sold or otherwise assigned to someone else. In joint authorship of a literary, dramatic, musical or artistic work, copyright duration is linked to the last death of any identifiable author as the event (s12). When no personal author is known, as in the case of corporate authorship, anonymous or pseudonymous works, duration is 70 years beyond the year of creation or, if published during that period, 70 years beyond the publication year (see 2.41). For most audiovisual materials in 2.1(b), the period is 50 years beyond the calendar year in which a work was first made or released or relayed, so the event relates to the work itself (ss13,14). However, a 70-year period applies to films with identifiable human authors. Further details appear in 3.2 et seq. For 2.1(c), copyright in a 'published edition' lasts for 25 years beyond the calendar year of first publication as the event (s15), as further described in 2.21. The above duration changes do not apply to Crown or Parliamentary copyright (see 2.44-2.52) or that of certain international organisations (2.11) which subsist by virtue of CDPA88 s168.

Recording of material

2.3 Copyright cannot subsist in works until they have been recorded in some way, not necessarily by the author personally. A secretary or other person responsible for recording a work is not the author. However, a conference rapporteur or news reporter may well have rights in his or her own particular account of events, but not in any content which is original to a person reported upon. It follows that anything unrecorded, such as many an after-dinner speech, is not copyright although regarded as a literary work (sometimes also 'dramatic', perhaps). Any item may have several forms, each of which is copyright. For a book, there will firstly be an unpublished manuscript (regarded as 'written' however produced), and secondly a published volume may come. A third possibility can be a reading or spoken version, performed in a broadcast or made into a sound recording such as a talking book. A fourth may be a dramatic version or a film. And so it goes on, with each format being copyright, frequently with different rights owners being involved.

There can be no copyright in an electronic record of text or 'electronic writing' in itself (s17). It is only a copy of a work, with no 'typographical arrangement' for which the Act makes an exception in giving a publisher copyright in printed matter. In other words, the law does not treat an electronic record of text like a publication, though there is protection for publicly accessible electronic services, as indicated in 3.18. Nevertheless, there is also protection for other electronic forms as physical formats, such as sound and video recordings where a format is copyright as well as its content.

Earlier comments about originality should be borne in mind in reading this chapter. Unless anyone challenges the point, any recorded product of mental effort should be regarded as copyright for the relevant period.

Definitions

2.4 Where CDPA88 definitions are considered sufficiently clear, extracts from them are quoted along with any comments considered desirable. Readers should note the Appendix 2/4 list of new sections. Those will not be present in a reader's own copy of the Act as published in 1988, hence the updated state may need to be consulted in one of the works in Appendix 1. Brief definitions of the main terms are drawn together in the Glossary at the end of this book.

2.5 Author

As with duration above, the following remarks are intended for general guidance. The authors of particular kinds of copyright materials are indicated later in this or other chapters.

Author: CDPA88 uses the term 'author' in its broadest sense, so that even a physical format like a sound recording or film has an 'author'. In general, the author is the person who creates an item. Exceptions apply to Crown copyright, the new category of Parliamentary copyright, and the copyright of certain international organisations.

Presumed author: when a person's name appears on a work, for example on a title page, that person is presumed to be the author unless indicated or proved otherwise (s104). When a title page contains a personal author but shows a C notice indicating copyright to be held by someone else as 'first owner', such as an employer or a professional body as publisher, the duration of copyright in the original work is nevertheless taken as related to the lifetime of the personal author.

Joint authorship: the Act takes 'joint authorship' to mean collaboration wherein the contribution of each of two or more authors is not distinct from the other contributions (s10).

2.6 Anonymous or pseudonymous work

If no personal author of an original work is indicated, or a pseudonym is used instead, the work is treated as 'anonymous or pseudonymous' and is copyright for 70 years beyond the year of creation if unpublished, or 70 years beyond year of making available to the public if published (or released, etc.) during the former 70-year period.

Separate considerations apply to Crown and Parliamentary copyright (4.7; 4.8).

There can be more than one kind of author concerned with a given copyright item, and among the more complex in terms of rights are broadcast programmes, each item carrying broadcaster's rights in the service as well as multiple rights in the content and its performance. An illustrated book may contain material in which the copyright belongs, at least initially, to an artist or photographer. As indicated already, the publisher has copyright of his own in the printed page, though this means the typographical arrangement of text and not illustrations, for those remain original artistic works.

2.7 Database maker

Where a name purporting to be that of the maker appeared on copies of the database as published, or on the database when it was made, the person whose name appeared shall be presumed, until the contrary is proved –

(a) to be the maker of the database, and
(b) not to have made it as an employee under contract (4.2), or the Crown or Crown servant (when Her Majesty is the maker of the database), and
(c) not to have made it jointly with another person.

2.8 Computer-generated works

These are unaffected by EC harmonisation. When a literary, dramatic, musical or artistic work is generated by computer, the work is not one of personal authorship, nor is it anonymous, and copyright ends 50 years after the calendar year in which the work was made. The 'author' of a computer-generated work, and therefore first owner (unless there is a contract of employment covering such activities) is the person by whom the arrangements necessary for the creation of the work are undertaken (s9).

Qualification for UK copyright

2.9 Broadly speaking, a work qualifies for copyright protection if

(a) the author is a qualifying person when the work is created, that is:
  - a British citizen or otherwise having nationality links (ss153-156); or
  - having a home or resident in the UK or another country covered by the Act; or
  - a body incorporated under UK law or that of another country to which the Act extends;

(b) the work was copyright under the 1956 Act immediately prior to the commencement of the 1988 Act on 1 August 1989;

(c) the work is first published in a qualifying country – the UK or another country to which the Act extends (13.10; 13.17).

In (a) above, 'a body incorporated' was the Act's only direct reference to authors other than persons (but see 2.10), and even this would seem to cover only companies registered at Companies House or overseas equivalents. Other corporate bodies such as institutions are not mentioned, although they can of course be 'authors' as well as publishers and thus be treatable as 'legal persons' in other contexts. It is recommended that such cases be treated in any event as 'anonymous or pseudonymous' when personal names are not indicated on an item. There can be special difficulties in considering transitional arrangements, not least with 'a body incorporated', because of variations in country coverage (and relevant boundaries) of qualification provisions over the years, and the date when a work was made may well determine who is 'author'. The situation is not helped either by variation in types of works which were, or were not, copyright under earlier legislation. Under the 1988 Act's definition of 'existing works' which qualify, some works from before the commencement of the 1911 Act cannot be copyright now because they were not copyright at the time they were made. With regard to countries or locations, the Act protects works made in England and Wales, Scotland and Northern Ireland. Coverage may be extended to any of the Channel Islands, the Isle of Man, or any colony. The Act is also extended by statutory instrument to other countries which give reciprocal protection to British works, and these countries are all signatories of international conventions (13). There are provisions concerning modifications by countries to which UK copyright has been extended, and concerning protection for citizens or works of other countries to which the Act has not been extended (ss157-162). Countries ceasing to be colonies may also be covered if so specified by statutory instrument. (See 2.2 re EC qualification re duration; 7.15 re EC and computer programs; and 3.28 re EC and database right.)

In short, qualification can be a complex matter for many reasons. Reference may be necessary at least to ss153-162 and associated statutory instruments, or to an expert. Even 'simultaneous publication' is by no means as straightforward as it may at first appear. Under SI 1995/3297, s15A and s172A have been added to CDPA88, defining 'country of origin' for the determination of duration, and summarised as follows:

(i) a Berne Convention country where first published there and not simultaneously published elsewhere;
(ii) a country which is the only Berne Convention country among two or more wherein first publication occurs simultaneously;
(iii) an EEA state if that is one of two or more Berne Convention countries in which first publication occurs simultaneously;
(iv) when none of the countries as indicated in (iv) is an EEA state, the country which has the shorter or shortest period of protection;
(v) for other than Berne Convention countries, whether a work is unpublished, first or simultaneously published
  - the country in which the maker of a film lives or has headquarters;
  - a Berne Convention country where an architectural and or artistic work is made;
  - in any other case, the country of which the author is a national.

A 'Berne Convention country' means one which is party to that Convention. 'Simultaneous publication' means publication within 30 days of first publication.

'EEA national' means a national of a state which is a party to the EEA Agreement of March 1993.

Qualification for database right

2.10 This only applies if, when databases became eligible for the new right (3.33), the maker (or joint makers) was –

(a) an individual who was a national of an EEA state or habitually resident within the EEA, or

(b) a body which was incorporated under the law of an EEA state and which ... had either its central administration or principal place of business within the EEA, or its registered office within the EEA and operations linked on an ongoing basis with the economy of an EEA state.

2.11 International organisations

In respect of certain international organisations, when neither qualification by authorship nor by country is associated with a work, copyright nevertheless subsists in it for 50 years from the end of the calendar year in which it was made (or longer if so specified in order to comply with international obligations). These organisations are unaffected by harmonisation. The organisation is first owner of copyright (s168). The organisations concerned can be designated by statutory instrument, and SI 1989/989 confers copyright protection on works originating with the United Nations, its specialised agencies or the Organisation of American States which would otherwise not enjoy copyright.

2.12 Folklore

There are also arrangements to cover folklore and the like of uncertain origin as unpublished and anonymous literary, dramatic, musical or artistic works (s169). Where there is evidence that any author qualifies by connection with a qualifying country outside the UK, copyright subsists in the work and a body in that country may be designated by statutory instrument to protect copyright.

2.13 Qualification in general

The provisions and arrangements for qualification are lengthy and complex. Those who may have a need for exhaustive treatment should study the legal manuals in the Bibliography, or the provisions directly in ss153-169 of the Act itself, plus relevant statutory instruments, assisted by legal advice if necessary.

Overseas works

2.14 Otherwise than as indicated above, users may find it easier to treat all works from overseas as though they are copyright in the UK, rather than explore the intricacies of international agreements and which nations are or were signatory to them at various times (13.9). Those who wish to explore further for themselves could use more detailed works such as that by Laddie et al. (App. 1/2), which includes in its 4.5 a 'quick guide' concerning the qualification of foreign works for British copyright. This also applies to publications of foreign governments, although US Government documents are mostly in the public domain as far as the USA itself is concerned (14.21).

Literary, dramatic and musical works (s3)

2.15 Literary work

This means any work, other than a dramatic or musical work, which is written, spoken or sung, and accordingly includes:

(a) a table or compilation other than a database
(b) a computer program
(c) preparatory design material for a computer program and
(d) a database.

Inclusions (a) and (b) were newly added to UK law by CDPA88; (c) was added by SI 1992/3233; and (d) by SI 1997/3032. This definition applies regardless of quality. A computer program remains a literary work even when stored electronically on tape or disc, etc. The inclusion of tables and compilations was welcomed as clarification long needed.

2.16 Compilations and databases

A compilation includes a directory, encyclopedia, anthology or collection, whether written or printed or in electronic form). A compilation which is (to put it simply) well-arranged could be seen as a 'database', newly defined as a result of an EC Directive on the legal protection of databases, now implemented by UK's SI 1997/3032. In database right (Q13-14) 'database' means a collection or compilation of works of any form (see 3.30 for literal definition). This includes print and nonprint, thus embracing text, still or moving images, sound and 'hard data' such as physical constants; but stops short of application to a collection of discrete items on shelves such as a 'library'. However, a 'package library' (for example of product information), or a library catalogue could be regarded as a database. A compilation has long had copyright protection at collection level, but this only applies to a database if it is the maker's own intellectual creation by virtue of the selection and arrangement of contents, whether those contents are themselves copyright or not. In other words, databases do not have to be original to be protected by database right, but they do have to be original to qualify for copyright protection as a whole at compilation level (like other copyright works). Infringement claims would be based upon the proportion of total items copied and/or the dependence of the copied extract on the selection and arrangement features of compilation. In order to be entitled to database right, a database must have involved substantial investment in its making.

From 1 January 1998, a new compilation which is definable as a database will only to be protected by copyright law if the *'selection or the arrangement of the contents'* are the author's *'own intellectual creation'*. Therefore it will not be possible in future to regard a database containing mere facts as copyright at compilation level, when little or no intellectual effort has been involved. Thus 'sweat of brow' copyright does not apply to databases, but copyright still does apply to compilations which do *not* qualify as databases for whatever reason (for the usual life plus 70 years, database right being anomalous at an initial 15 years only). The new right, which exists alongside copyright, can override its permissions, and is intended to protect *any* database against unauthorised extraction or re-utilisation of contents for 15 years beyond the year of recording. If published during that period, protection is for 15 years beyond the publication year. It is important to note that any *'substantial'* change, whether *'quantitative or qualitative'* in the content starts a new 15-year period, hence continuously updated databases could have perpetual protection even when the contents are not copyright. Databases made before 27 March 1996, and still copyright at the end of 1997, will continue to be copyright for 70 years beyond author's death year. However, a database completed on or after 1 January 1983 which qualifies for database right upon commencement of the new law on 1 January 1998 will *also* have protection under database right for 15 years beginning that date.

An author of an item of content in a compilation, such as a single chapter, will usually have assigned the right to publish to a compiler or editor, in return for a fee rather than a royalty on each copy sold. The content of a compilation may however be itself partially or wholly out of copyright as an original work. It should be noted that even an anthology of poems or essays by authors long deceased might now be claimed to be a database.

2.17 Computer programs

A computer program is clearly a literary work, with copyright vested normally in the programmer for 70 years beyond his or her death. However, if in employment as a programmer and his or her employer is first owner of the copyright as indicated in 4.2 and that employer is a corporate body, copyright lasts for 70 years beyond the year of creation or, if made available to the public during that period, 70 years beyond such publication or release. If the employed author were named as such on the item, copyright could last for the norm, that is, life plus 70 years.

SI 1992/3233 has extended the definition of literary work to include preparatory design material for a computer program and added certain permissions which do not apply to other literary material (7.16-7.22).

Since there is no copyright in an electronic record as such (3.12), a computer program remains a literary work even when in electronic form. When a program appears in a book, the publisher enjoys copyright in the published edition (2.22).

2.18 Dramatic work; and musical work (s3)

Dramatic work includes a work of dance or mime. A dramatico- musical work such as an opera has dramatic and musical copyright, plus literary copyright in the libretto, and these are just the 'original works' copyrights alone; to which may be added 'published edition', broadcasting and film rights.

2.19 Musical work means a work consisting of music, exclusive of any words or action intended to be sung, spoken or performed with the music. Thus sheet music containing song words is both literary and musical, whilst author's (composer's) rights during his or her life plus 70 years normally become shared by contract with a songwriter and any arranger. New arrangements have separate copyrights in the music but, if made from material still in copyright, would have required rights-owner permission for 'adaptation' (s21). This needs to be borne in mind when assessing whether an edition of a musical score for performance in public (like that of an opera long out of copyright as such) is covered by copyright.

2.20 It should be noted that definitions of copyright materials may be amplified by the definitions adopted by such bodies as the Performing Right Society, which requires much more detail than the above for the administration of performing rights. Such amplified definitions, although they may influence court decisions, especially if supported by case law already, have no legal force in themselves.

Published editions

2.21 The Act states that 'published edition' '*means a published edition of the whole or part of one or more literary, dramatic or musical works*' (s8(1)), thus excluding 'artistic'. This definition applies only in the context of a typographical arrangement. Therefore 'published edition' has been taken to only mean printed matter. The wording chosen has made irrelevant, at least at this point, the fact that the design of a typeface may itself be copyright. The '*whole or part*' and '*one or more ... works*' cover compilations and anthologies and later editions.

2.22 The author of a published edition is the publisher, who holds copyright for a fixed period of 25 years beyond the end of the calendar year of publication (s9(2)(d)), as outlined in 2.2. The Act's definitions of 'publication' and 'commercial publication' are given in their context in 4.17-4.19, but the meanings commonly understood will suffice pro tem. (It appears that screen display may be regarded as a typographical arrangement, and as part of a published edition (but should leave a publisher's 25 year right as confined to printed matter.)

2.23 Later editions

A publisher's copyright in a second or later published edition of a work only subsists in those parts which have not already appeared in the previous edition (s8(2)). Thus, at one end of the scale, an unrevised reprint does not give a publisher a renewed period of copyright, whilst at the other end of the scale a fully revised new edition will create a new 25-year period in the whole.

Because of the difficulties of extracting from a new edition that which may be perceived as no longer copyright, this is not regarded as having particular practical value to the user. But the provision does rule out completely any renewed period of publisher's copyright in a mere reprint, and renders progressively tenuous a publisher's own rights in new editions with only slight revisions. It would be difficult for a user to decide what might be regarded as no longer copyright by comparing editions. One must bear in mind the possibility that a publisher may have bought *all* rights and thus far outweigh his normal 25 years of potential benefit. Thus, by and large, the information user tends to rely on a publisher of material which contributes to the cultural, social and scientific corpus of knowledge to act responsibly when describing editions. Thus questions might only arise when a user had been refused copying permission in respect of a particular item and then found its claim to copyright to be somewhat insecure.

Artistic works (s4)

Firstly the term includes:

2.24 Graphic work

- This is any painting, drawing, diagram, map, chart or plan, or any engraving, etching, lithograph, woodcut or similar work, irrespective of artistic quality

2.25 Photographs

- This is a recording of light or other radiation on any medium on which an image is produced or from which an image may by any means be produced, and which is not part of a film thus including a negative, slide, or other transparency, or a microform. Thus film stills are to be treated as part of the film, and not as photographs.

2.26 Sculpture or collage

- This is a representation of an object in the round or in relief, created by moulding or carving, etc., and the term includes a cast or model made for the purposes of sculpture.

2.27 Secondly, 'artistic' applies also to a work of architecture being a building or a model for a building; and to a work of artistic craftsmanship.

2.28 Thirdly, a design may consist of or be derived from an artistic work, in which case the duration of copyright in the affected part of a work (or of course the whole) is reduced by commercial exploitation from author's life plus 70 years to 25 years beyond the year of first marketing (s52). This brings the protection period into line with the newly extended period provided under the Registered Designs Act 1949 as amended by CDPA88 (11.6).

Photographs and photographers

2.29 An important change in the 1988 Act is the treatment of photographers as *authors* in their own right, elegantly accomplished by the drafters of ss12 and 14 simply by omitting any specific mention of photographs. This change has long been sought by professional photographers, whose work used to belong to the commissioner of the work or to the owner of the film used. Accordingly, the usual duration of author's copyright applies – life plus 70 years – and the photographer is normally first owner (see Q11). A commission contract could however override the latter, for a photographer might accept a commission which was only offered subject to ownership of rights (4.5), though the duration would not change if the author remained personally identifiable in connection with the work. The same would apply to any other commissioned work bound by such terms, including portraits. There is another provision which can override photographer's copyright, namely contract of employment (4.2). A photographer employed as such, unless he or she has secured conditions of service otherwise, holds no copyright in the work done in the course of employment (s11), because copyright is vested in the employer as first owner. If the employer is a corporate body, the copyright period is taken to be that for anonymous works (2.6 and 2.34) unless a personal author becomes identifiable.

2.30 The omission of 'artistic' from 'published edition' has significance for photographs. Whilst typographical arrangements of literary, dramatic or musical works carry publisher's copyright, photographs are protected only as original works. Thus any plates or other artistic works in printed form, including drawings and maps, carry no publisher's copyright, but are simply copies of the master from which they are made, irrespective of how much effort may have been made by a publisher in the interim with plate preparation (see also next section below). Thus it is quite possible that a case could be based on a claim that a copy from a book illustration or map infringes the copyright in the master, whatever the form – slides or digital mapping included. This would apply whether the master is an original work of art, or a photograph or other representation of it used as master by a publisher. For example, a publisher does not create his own copyright when he photographs a work of art for printing.

Microforms

2.31 Whether microfilm, microfiche or microcard, microforms are not mentioned as such in the Act. However, they are effectively covered via two definitions:

(i) the definition of 'reprographic process', which includes the making of 'facsimile copies'; and
(ii) the definition of 'facsimile copy' which includes a *copy which is reduced or enlarged in scale*.

Following from (ii), a microform of printed matter may be copyright in several ways:

(a) If it is a part of a compilation – that is, the books or other items on it have been subjected to selection and arrangement rather than just the photographing of an entire set of originals – rights in the compilation will continue for 70 years beyond the compiler or editor's lifetime as author, but would probably be owned by the microform publishing firm as employer – as would be the case if there were no named personal author.
(b) Each frame or page of original represented may be considered a photograph – copyright duration as in (a).
(c) Any or all of the frames on a microform may in any event contain material which is still copyright, whether as original works or as typographical layouts in the published editions photographed.

Thus, for example, a collection on microform of selected documents of social importance may be covered by (a) even if all the documents are out of copyright, whilst a microform set of a newspaper may still be covered by (c).

2.32 Can a microform publisher claim infringement of his own copyright photograph when photocopies are made from a microform? Before 1988, at least, no microform publisher appears to have claimed rights in a microform as a photograph. As remarked in 2.30 in respect of plates in books, photographs are artistic works, and there is no such thing as publisher's copyright in the process as there is with a typographical arrangement, which the publisher himself or herself has devised and which results in rights in the published edition. Each microform, by whatever means it was produced, would be regarded as an original copyright photograph. Therefore, an infringement case based on that particular copyright would seem unlikely to succeed unless the defendant had copied the microform itself, that is, produced a duplicate microform. It is recommended that the content of microforms should be treated in the same way as the originals represented (6.29).

Unpublished literary, dramatic, musical or artistic works

2.33 If a personal author is known but an item remains unpublished, copyright lasts as usual for author's life plus 70 years. Thus the 'perpetual copyright' which used to be possible under previous law for works remaining unpublished during and after the author's lifetime has been removed.

2.34 Unpublished anonymous or pseudonymous works

Before the EC harmonisation described in 2.2, CDPA88 allowed copyright in an unpublished anonymous or pseudonymous work to continue indefinitely unless made available to the public, if ever, or unless it was reasonable to assume that the unknown author had been dead for 50 years (s57).Now, when the author is unknown, the new 70-year period (2.2) dates from the end of the year of creation. However, if during that period a work is made available to the public, copyright lasts for 70 years beyond the publication (or release, etc.) year. Any unauthorised action of making public does not count. This removes the 'perpetual' copyright which applied hitherto for an unpublished anonymous work, but such a work could nevertheless obtain a duration of somewhere between the 70-year minimum and the combined 140-year maximum if made public in the 70th year beyond creation. (This would seem more than fair if the aim is to equalise the situation with that of known authorship.) However, if the author becomes known before the expiry of the first 70 years or during the further period up to the possible total of 140, copyright duration becomes the norm of author's life plus 70 years.

It would suffice for one author to become known in a case of joint authorship. If the author becomes known after the first 70 years, there is no reinstatement of relationship to a lifetime and copyright has ended in the item.

2.35 In the context of literary, dramatic or musical works, 'made public' means – apart from publication, of course – public performance or broadcast or inclusion in a cable programme service such as an online database (3.18). Usually it is an employer or a publisher who is first owner of the 70-year right in the content of an anonymous work, as remarked earlier.

In the context of artistic works, 'made public' means public exhibition, or public showing of a film or video recording which includes the work, or inclusion in a broadcast or cable programme service.

2.36 In respect of an *unpublished* anonymous work created on or after 1 August 1989, it is important to note, from 2.33 and 2.34, that perpetual copyright no longer applies to either of: an unpublished work by a known author (now life plus 70 years); nor an anonymous unpublished work (now creation plus 70 years unless published during that period, when a further 70 year period dates from publication year).

2.37 However, the copyright in a computer-generated work ends 50 years after the year of creation, whether or not it is considered anonymous.

Transitional provisions

2.38 Each new piece of legislation creates an opportunity for updating or refining earlier provisions, and even for re-defining terms. Fortunately, re-definition is not made without bearing in mind the need to minimise confusion. Unfortunately, some re-defined terms or concepts do in fact cause complexity which inevitably leads to greater difficulties, for example in deciding whether a work might still be in copyright. Schedule 1 to the Act contains transitional provisions in respect of changes in the law. The extent of new provisions or revisions since the first edition has made the inclusion of Schedule 1 in this volume somewhat pointless, and one of the looseleaf authorities should be consulted by those wanting to see the details. CDPA88 came into force on 1 August 1989. Some of the transitional provisions are mentioned in this text, but they can be quite involved, and should be studied directly when problems arise.

2.39 With the aim of further assisting such study, Q10-Q13 contain summaries appertaining to the selected types of work named. It must be emphasized that these should be taken as covering only the general situations concerned, for details can alter cases. Not only photographers but also journalists in employment have suffered in the past, hence Q12.

Space forbids treatment of all transitional provisions in this way, and in any event the selection of the examples avoids some of the more involved cases, such as the performing right in music. From 10 August 1882, the commencement date of the Copyright (Musical Compositions) Act 1882, performing right could only subsist in published music if a phrase reserving that right were placed on the title page of all copies (see 3.41 of *Laddie et al.*, Appendix 1/2). Accordingly a musical work of that era (up to 1 July 1912, the commencement date of the 1911 Act) which shows no such reservation on published copies may have no performing, broadcasting or cable programme rights. However, the treatment of maps, charts and plans as literary works under the 1911 Act but artistic works under the 1956 and 1988 Acts should cause no trouble for those who perceive that Schedule 1(12)(6) effectively removes the earlier distinction.

Errors can be made by drafters: such as failure to notice the earlier removal of some countries from coverage when drafting a comparatively recent schedule which brought those countries back in, resulting in uncertainties re foreign works wherein the date of creation needs to be known as well as the place.

It should be noted, however, that supplementary legislation can change existing transitional arrangements: for example, extended or revived copyright (2.2) .

Extended copyright belongs to the owner immediately before 1 January 1996 (commencement of new regulations on duration in SI 1995/3297), namely film owner or his assignees, etc. (see example on photographs in 2.43). Other remarks on transitional provisions may appear later.

2.40 The new EC harmonisation term of copyright was mentioned in 2.34 on anonymous or pseudonymous, literary, dramatic, musical or artistic works. The pre-harmonisation situation is here given for comparison and emphasis, although it is built into Q10-12. Under Schedule 1 to CDPA88, anonymous or pseudonymous literary, dramatic, musical or artistic works, other than photographs, which were published and still copyright on 31 July 1989 were to continue to be copyright until the date at which this would have expired under the 1956 Act, namely 50 years beyond the year of publication.

Following EC harmonisation (2.2), all those works receive a 20-year extension if in copyright on 31 December 1995, or a revival period of 6 months to 20 years if still copyright under the laws of another member state on 1 July 1995, as could be the case for works published before the commencement of the 1956 Act. However, anonymous works published between the commencement dates of the 1956 and 1989 Acts were bound to be in copyright on 31 December 1995, amounting for those works to 'publication year plus 70 years' (Q10).

2.41 Such works, again other than photographs, which were in existence before the Act's commencement date of 1 August 1989 but unpublished, were given arbitrary treatment, namely a 50-year period of copyright from 1989 up to the end of 2039, which in effect cleared away many unpublished works of long standing whilst allowing rights owners a chance to publish and obtain benefit during that period. If the author became known before the end of that period, the usual rule of life plus 50 years was to be applied.

Following the EC harmonisation described in 2.2, the latter now becomes extended to life plus 70 years for works still copyright on 31 December 1995 (etc.), and the arbitrary extension to 2039 becomes 2059. Photographs were ostensibly omitted from this provision simply because, under previous law, the owner of the film used was the 'author', so the question of anonymity did not then arise. Since the harmonisation does not exclude photographs, the latter extension periods become applicable also to photographs.

2.42 The acts permitted on assumptions as to expiry of copyright or death of author (s57), already mentioned in 2.36, became modified in respect of works existing *before 1 August 1989* by a transitional provision, mainly as follows:

(a) photographs are omitted
(b) any rights conferred by the Copyright Act 1775 are omitted.

This last is immaterial since the universities which were accorded special privileges by that Act have made little or no use of them, and in any event another transitional provision drew those privileges to a close after 50 years beyond 1989, namely to the end of 2039 (Appendix 3.1(13)). It is assumed that the latter year would now be 2059 due to harmonisation (2.2). If duration under CDPA88 were found longer than the above for earlier works than 1 August 1989, the later date would apply but without any assumption of the unknown author's death.

2.43 Photographs: difficulties

A special difficulty arises with photographs because they are mostly prepared from re-usable negatives, so a librarian or archivist, when receiving a donated collection of photographs, cannot know how many other copies may have been made and located elsewhere (16.1). This is a difficulty shared with some kinds of unpublished document, such as a typed manuscript. Q11 covers the copyright duration for photographs, aiming to state the general situation from the possibly 'out of copyright' era onwards. The table has been expressed in precise terms, and the possibility of intrusion of finer points of law into specific litigation must always be borne in mind here as well as elsewhere. A foreign photograph could be an example, because variations over the years in the statutory provisions on qualification for UK copyright may well make it necessary to consult an expert on these matters.

Photographers gain any applicable revived copyright of between 6 months and 20 years, if the previous owner (owner of the film) has died before 1 January 1996 (see 2.39). SI 1996/2967 contained a '*Clarification of transitional provisions relating to pre-1989 photographs*' re who is to be regarded as author in deciding ownership of *revived* copyright (2.2), which can only exist after former copyright has expired. Revived copyright belongs to the person who *was* owner of copyright immediately before it expired, namely the owner of the film used or his beneficiaries or assignees, etc. However, when the former copyright owner has died before commencement of the SI on 1 January 1996, any revived copyright is vested in the *author* (SI 1995/3297(19)(2)(b). The author is now decided in accordance with s9 of CDPA88, namely, the creator or photographer. (This revises Schedule 1(10) which followed the law in force at the time the work was made.)

On the other hand, *extended* copyright in a photograph belongs to the person who owned it just before commencement of SI 1995/3297 on 1 January 1996 and, for pre-1 August 1989 photographs, that person is likely to be either the film owner (still) or beneficiaries or assignees, as noted in 2.39.

Crown and Parliamentary copyright: duration

2.44 In this context, the 'event' which starts a period of copyright is normally *not* the death of a personal author. As an exception, for a commissioned work (that is, commissioned before the event) where copyright remains with the author, duration would be life plus 70 years as is now the norm since harmonisation. Otherwise, the duration of copyright has no relationship to an author's lifetime, and the new 70-year period does not apply to Crown or Parliamentary copyright material.

2.45 Duration of Crown copyright

Protection, in respect of literary, dramatic, musical or artistic works, dates from the making of a work and lasts for 125 years beyond the year in which it was made – unless published commercially within the first 75 years, when protection continues for 50 years beyond the year of publication. So an unpublished Crown copyright work is copyright for over 125 years, whereas copyright in a published work could last for a minimum of 50 years and a maximum of 125 years (s163). The notes in Q11 effectively cover the essentials of Crown copyright duration; see 4.7 and 4.8 re Crown and Parliamentary authorship.

2.46 In respect of other kinds of copyright work, Crown copyright works are treated like others. Thus a Crown copyright sound recording or film would be protected until 50 years beyond the year in which it was made or, if released during that period, 50 years beyond the year when it was made. This gives a minimum of 50 years and a maximum of nearly 100 years, as with all other such works (3.5). Also similarly to other copyright works, the protection of a typographical layout of a published edition lasts for 25 years beyond the year of publication. The basis for that statement is s163(5), which is taken to mean that, where a category of work is excluded, that category should be treated like works other than those in Crown copyright. (It must be noted that some legal experts have taken the exclusion from s163(3) of sound recordings and films to mean that they are to be treated as they were under the 1956 Act, which would result in 50 years' protection beyond publication without reaching a theoretical 100-year maximum for a published sound recording which has remained unpublished for the first 50 years after it was made.

2.47 In joint authorship, Crown copyright applies only to that part of the work which was done by authors who were officers or servants of the Crown at the time the work was made.

2.48 Acts of Parliament and Measures of the General Synod of the Church of England: Crown copyright begins with Royal Assent and subsists for 50 years beyond the year of Assent (s164).

2.49 Duration of Parliamentary copyright

Since the 1988 Act, this covers works made by or under the direction or control of the House of Commons or the House of Lords, irrespective of the usual qualification for copyright protection – that is, regardless of where the work was made. In respect of literary, dramatic, musical or artistic works, copyright lasts for 50 years beyond the year in which the work was made (s165). However, Bills (below) have much shorter duration of copyright.

2.50 As may be specified in statutory instruments, the relevant provisions may be applied to works made by or under the direction or control of any other legislative body of another country to which the UK Act extends (see 2.10).

2.51 As with Crown copyright:

- in joint authorship, the description applies only to that part of the work which was done by authors who were acting on behalf of, or under the direction or control of, either House
- sound recordings, films, broadcasts, cable programmes are all treated as copyright in the usual manner (cf Crown, 2.46).

2.52 Bills: 'public', 'private', 'personal' – copyright ends upon either Royal Assent or, if Assent is not received, upon the withdrawal or rejection of the Bill or the end of the Session (s166). In respect of the House of Lords, rejection does not cause cessation of copyright until the end of the Session if it is possible nevertheless for the Bill to be presented for Royal Assent in that Session. The rights in the Copyright, etc. Bill of 1987 ceased with Royal Assent of the Act on 15 November 1988. (See House ownership comments in 4.9.) After cessation of copyright, the Act specifies that, unless a rejected Bill is reintroduced at a later date, no other copyright, or right in the nature of copyright subsists in a Bill, thus placing such a Bill in the public domain.

3. NONPRINT: AUDIOVISUAL MEDIA AND ELECTRONIC COPYRIGHT

General note on database right

Readers are requested to refer to **Q0** before proceeding with study of permissions chapters 5, 6, 7 and 9. Any permissions should be qualified by the details of database right (3.28) if not already specified herein.

Fair dealing and nonprint

3.1 Those to whom the term 'fair dealing' is quite new should note that slight reference to it has been made here in advance of its treatment in chapter 5. This assists the introduction of a special chapter on nonprint at this particular point. Reference could be made to the Glossary at the end for a brief definition, or the early paragraphs of chapter 5 could be consulted, before commencing this chapter. Although fair dealing has had very little application in this regime, relevant permissions do nevertheless exist and are described in later chapters, as reference to the outlines at the beginning of this volume should show. For similar reasons, some notes on 'infringement' appear in 3.46 in advance of the treatment given in chapter 4.

Sound recordings and films (s5)

3.2 A 'sound recording' means either a *recording of sounds from which those sounds may be reproduced, or a recording of the whole or any part of a literary, dramatic or musical work, from which sounds reproducing the work or part may be produced.* The medium used for recording is immaterial, as also is the method of sound reproduction or production. The definition therefore covers any kind of recording of signals which become sound when the record is accessed or played back

3.3 A 'film' means a *recording on any medium from which a moving image may by any means be produced.* This includes not only cinematographic films but also videotapes or video recordings of any kind. Similarly to the case of a published edition of printed matter, copyright does not subsist in a sound recording or film which is, or to the extent that it is, a copy taken from a previous sound recording or film.

3.4 The producing company's copyright warnings are frequently so small as to be illegible to most naked eyes, and access conditions for libraries or any other bodies should desirably warn against infringement by copying, and forbid playing to a public audience unless licensed as indicated in 4.43 and 9.6-9.7.

Authorship and copyright duration

3.5 The 'author' of a sound recording is the producer (s9(2) as revised by SI 1996/2967). The author of a film is the producer and principal director (joint authorship applies if these are not the same person). When a company is involved, as in many cases of at least sound recordings, any employment or other contractual relationships between actual recording companies, sound engineers, recordists, film producers or cinematographers do not affect the duration of copyright. For films with an identifiable personal author, duration has been increased (3.6). For sound recordings, or for films without a personal author, the duration is 50 years beyond the end of the calendar year in which the work is made or – if release occurs within 50 years of making – 50 years after the end of the calendar year of release. Thus, dating from its creation, the protection period of a sound recording, or of a film without a personal author (see below) can vary from 50 years up to a theoretical maximum of nearly 100 years if release does not occur until the last possible moment.

For a sound recording other than a film sound-track, 'release' means publishing, broadcasting or including in a cable programme service. For a film or film sound-track, 'release' means the first showing in public. (Any unauthorised acts do not count.) A sound track accompanying a film is treated as part of the film in respect of copyright.

3.6 Following the EC harmonisation indicated in 2.2, films with a personal author now have protection for 70 years beyond the end of the year of death. Under SI 1995/3297, the 70-year period is linked to the last to die of: principal director; author of screenplay; author of dialogue; or composer of music specially created for the film. If it is known that there is a personal author but the actual identity is unknown (treatable as an anonymous work), copyright expires 70 years beyond the year in which the film was made or, if the film is made available to the public during that period, 70 years beyond year of release. If an identity becomes known before the end of either 70-year period, the duration becomes related to death year as above. Unlike anonymous original works (2.34), the absence of known identity of a personal author does not qualify a film for any more than a fixed period of 50 years beyond year of making or release, like sound recordings (3.5). For a sound recording or film whose author is not an EEA national, duration is that which is relevant to the country of which the author is a national (2.10), provided the period does not exceed the period applicable above.

SI 1995/3297 has added a new provision s66A, on sound recordings and films, which repeats the substance of s57 (see 2.34) concerning assumption of expiry of copyright on author's death, but this excludes Crown copyright; also any copyright specified by an Order under s168 as longer than 70 years which originally vested in an international organisation.

3.7 Under transitional provisions of CDPA88, there is no copyright in a film as such which was made before 1 June 1957, when the Copyright Act 1956 came into force. However, a film made before then which was an original dramatic work as defined in the Copyright Act 1911 is to be treated as such under the 1988 Act as revised by SI 1995/3297 – that is, duration as per 3.6 for the film or for 'photographs forming part of the film', linked to the life of the author of the dramatic work.

The CDPA88 definition of 'photographs' per se (s4) clearly excludes an image which is *part of a film*. It is recommended that such photographs should accordingly be considered just that, which means that stills or video 'freeze-frames' are also considered parts of films. However, even an area within a frame might infringe if it were judged to be a substantial part, bearing in mind that this means significance of content as well as extent (4.32). Also, although there is fair dealing in photographs as artistic works, thus permitting single copies for research and private study, that does not extend to films. Under the Act itself, the only part of fair dealing which applies to films per se is s30 (5.28-5.31) (see also 7.32 on photographs for *private and domestic use* taken from TV and cable programmes). A new form of fair dealing is introduced under database right for 'illustration for teaching or research' (7, General note).

Broadcasts

3.8 'Broadcast' means a transmission by wireless telegraphy of visual images, sounds or other information which is capable of lawful reception by members of the public, or is transmitted for presentation to members of the public. 'Lawful reception' of encoded or encrypted transmissions is only possible when decoding means have been obtained with the authority of the person making the transmission or the person providing the contents.

Unlike Prestel (first British Telecom; later a firm called New Prestel; then Prestel Online; and subsequently 'Prestel Internet'), which is covered by the definition of 'cable programme service' as stated in 3.19 below, the UK has two teletext services which are broadcasts: namely, BBC's Ceefax and

ITV's Teletext on 3 and 4. The service is now owned by Scottish Telecom (a subsidiary of Scottish Power). Broadcasting anything or including it in a cable programme service (other than an electronic retrieval system) is a restricted act, but does not normally constitute publication (4.17).

As part of EC harmonisation, Directive EC 93/83 covers satellite broadcasting and cable re-transmission and was passed in September 1993. The UK implemented this by means of SI 1996/2967, effective from 1 December 1966. The aim is to make cross-border transmission copyright, whether via satellite or simultaneous cable re-transmission. Qualification for UK copyright (2.9) will depend on the country of origin of a transmssion. CDPA88 now has a new section 6A. This makes provisions regarding country of origin and the rights of authors, broadcasters, sound recording companies and performers. The details are excluded here, apart from noting that – for comparison with new lending/rental right provisions – sound recordists and performers will *share* a *single* equitable remuneration in respect of the broadcasting of sound recordings from a non-EEA state which fails to provide equivalent protection to that of the UK.

3.9 Author and copyright duration: broadcasts

The 'author' of a broadcast is either: the person transmitting the programme, if he has responsibility to any extent for its contents or any person providing the programme who makes with the person transmitting it the arrangements necessary for its transmission, or – in cases of relay and immediate re-transmission – the person concerned with the relayed broadcast. The duration of copyright in a broadcast is 50 years from the end of the calendar year in which the broadcast was made. Any repeats must be taken as having expired at the same time as the first broadcast.

3.10 In a broadcast, 'programme' refers to any item included, and 'relay' includes cable or other telecommunication system relay for re- transmission. Cable programme services which are not radio or television are electronic retrieval systems of one kind or another which are relayed via the telephone network (3.13). Copyright in the actual content of a programme, whether broadcast or cable, may well be current, and performing rights may also be involved in respect of live performances -- all these would add to the complexity of copyright problems for service providers. Possibly this is why the Act eases the way for broadcasting or cable programme service providers (9.17-9.19).

The Act's transitional provisions state that broadcasts made before 1 June 1957, when the 1956 Act came into force, are not copyright as such.

Electronic copyright

3.11 The term 'electronic copyright' should be regarded merely as a convenient heading to embrace electronic databases and their usage relevant to copyright. Thus an offline electronic database such as a diskette or CD-ROM, and online electronic databases, are covered by the term. Some regard 'electronic copyright' as embracing computer programs as well but, as those are 'literary works' whether in hard copy or diskette, etc., they are treated in 2.17, with permissions in 7.15 to 7.20.

As noted earlier, there is no copyright in an electronic form of record in itself, which is merely 'electronic writing'. However, a computer file embraces whatever copyright may subsist in the items included, and there is also copyright in the compilation as a whole, plus database right where applicable (3.28). The Act's definition of 'copying' includes storing the work in any medium by electronic means (s17). Aspects of 'electrocopying are explored in 3.45 et seq. Even the keying in of content or the scanning in of typography of copyright abstracts selected from a published abstracting service, or from printout from an electronic database, is copying which could infringe rights, and moreover amounts to multiple copying capability. Keying in non-copyright material such as an author's abstract (6.43; 15.4) along with the factual bibliographic details of a journal article did not infringe before database right came into force (3.28) but now could only be done with an insubstantial part, or if a database did not qualify for database right. Thus any developments towards licensing in respect of author abstracts should be monitored. Automatic charging was listed in 1.16 as coverable by contract. In theory, provided the rates were agreed also, there could at some future date be an end to copyright usage confusion (App. 5/7). When the majority of the 'current corpus' of knowledge becomes available in digital format, access could always be through an electronic bibliographic database and be traced from then on. This is not possible at present although ECMS developments (3.55) and digitisation progammes edge ever nearer to such a future.

Online databases as cable programme services

3.12 A 'cable programme' means any item included in a cable programme service, and 'cable programme service' means a service mainly for sending visual images, sounds or other information via a public telecommunications system otherwise than by wireless telegraphy for reception at two or more places (s7). This brings to mind audio information systems by telephone, cable television, teletext services, and electronic databases, but the wording of s7 avoids the latter word and appears from its lack of precision to aim at hospitality to future legislative policy as well as technical developments. This provision has not been amended in the UK implementation of the EC Directive on the legal protection of databases (3.27), hence this kind of copyright could be seen as overlapping database right at present.

3.13 Exceptions to definition of 'cable programme service'

By no means all cable services are covered by the definition of 'cable programme service' which specifically makes exceptions as follows – and these have no copyright as services:

- systems where there is communication between the receiver and the service providers or other receivers for purposes other than operation or control of the service
- services which are private, or domestic, or otherwise linked by a non-public telecommunications system
- services (or parts of services) which are run for persons providing broadcast or cable programme services or providing the programmes for inclusion.

The exceptions are subject to amendment by order of the Secretary of State, by means of statutory instrument.

This complex area has another exception, for copyright does not subsist in a cable programme if it is part of the service by virtue of reception and immediate re-transmission of a broadcast, or if the programme infringes copyright in another cable programme or broadcast (s7(6)). The possibility of a new 'transmission right' has been mooted. This would aim to give copyright protection to all forms of cable programme service and not just those services which are publicly accessible by a telecommunication system and are non-interactive (CDPA88 s7), thus incidentally overcoming the difficulty of defining the latter term. It is considered that revision of s7 may follow not long after the new database right (3.28). In the UK, the kinds of cable programme service covered by s7 (see 3.12; 3.18) already have a form of transmission right comparable with that of broadcast programmes. Also in the UK another, more general, form of transmission right is provided by CDPA88 s17(6), under which 'copying' in relation to any description of work includes the making of copies which are transient or are incidental to some other use of the work. Thus unauthorised transmission by means of a computer and/or telecommunication system can infringe. ('Copying' includes 'electronic writing' according to s17(2).) Moreover, s298 clearly affords a transmission right (*Rights and remedies... unauthorised reception of transmissions*). However, a transmission right may yet form part of WIPO revision of Berne (13.2) as well as EC harmonisation.

3.14 Author and copyright duration: cable programmes

The 'author' of a cable programme is the person providing the cable programme service in which the programme is included, and that person holds copyright for 50 years after the end of the calendar year in which the programme was included in a cable programme service. Any repeats must be taken as expiring at the same time as the first inclusion (s14).

3.15 Content of a cable programme

Any item can become a cable programme, and each item may well be copyright in itself as a literary work, such as the full text of a journal article. Any royalty arrangements between the author of a cable programme and the author of such an article are of course matters for contract between them and do not affect the user of the service directly.

Databases and downloading

3.16 An electronic record of a literary work, to repeat in this context, is only a copy of that work and not, like the published edition of a book, another copyright work in itself. In other words, such an electronic record is a literary work, and is theoretically subject to fair dealing in view of the lack of distinction between electronic and print formats in the new database right (3.28). Why only theoretically? Firstly, because in practice there is a first hurdle in front of an online database which prevents fair dealing: namely the service contract for database users which limits downloading for printout or any other reason to specified extents and particular purposes, and a 'lawful user' of a database is subject to such a contract. However, weighing the definitions of 'substantial' and 'insubstantial' parts under database right may make possible a clearer assessment of what may be done without lawful user rights. Secondly, a form of copyright in the service itself could in theory be claimed by a database producer (see 3.18). Thirdly, fair dealing does not apply to database right except as indicated in 3.40 (see also 5.6; 6.4).

3.17 Before revision in consequence of SI 1997/3032 the Act did not even mention 'databases', although there are some references to an electronic retrieval system as clearly being included in the term 'cable programme services' in s175 which defines 'publication'. The wording on cable programme services seems deliberately designed to allow for future technological developments. Some have reported their uncertainty about the coverage of databases by that wording. The interpretation of s7(2)(a) followed in the previous edition of this text as a result of studying drafters'notes of 1987 is that online electronic databases which are non-interactive (except for control of search, etc.), and which are accessible via a public telecomunications system, are 'cable programme services' . The viability of such a interpretation was, on enquiry, acknowledged by the Patent Office without comment, but at that time it appeared that rights owners would only claim rights in a database as a 'compilation'. Now, the provisions of new database right must be given preference over the latter interpretation.

3.18 Service copyright in online databases

However, for so long as s7 remains unamended, all online electronic databases, whether bibliographic or hard data, which are publicly accessible via a telecommunication system, and non-interactive except for 'operation or control' as above, will remain capable of being regarded as cable programme services. Accordingly it is considered that, comparably with a broadcast, a form of service copyright subsists. This would overlap published edition copyright, which is now taken to subsist in databases. The period of copyright applies to a cable programme and, as stated in 3.15, lasts for 50 years beyond the end of the year of first inclusion of the programme in a cable programme service (s14). For 'cable programme' in this context, unlike cable television, read 'any item', from a bibliographic record to a full text journal article.

It is this form of service copyright which *might* be usable as basis for an infringement claim against someone who habitually assumed fair dealing provisions to be applicable in this context. It is such uncertainty which suggests caution, despite the database producers' apparent lack of interest in this form of right and preference for control by service contract. However, now that database right has been implemented in the UK (3.27), it seems possible that no use at all may be made of the feature and that future amendment of CDPA88 may omit the relevant sections.

3.19 Owing to a transitional provision of the Act, there is no service protection for items included in a cable programme service before 1 January 1985, when the Cable and Broadcasting Act 1984 came into force. Nor is there any service copyright in repeats (s14). Thus only items (cable programmes) put into a database on or after 1 January 1985 have copyright in the service for 50 years beyond the year of first inclusion in a cable programme service.

3.20 However, this is immaterial to users who honour their contracts and download only as permitted. In any event, one cannot assume, even when bibliographical details show publication earlier than 1985, that the details were necessarily input earlier than 1 January 1985. This would require time-stamping of individual records, and such information is not normally capable of display by a user but could be made so.

3.21 Despite all this, uncertainty has persisted in some quarters about whether the Act covers online databases. Producers remain uncomfortable without service contracts which allow them to impose their own rules, which would now apply also to 'lawful user' rights under database right. The new law described in 3.27 et seq. is designed to form a 'level playing field' for copyright media in the Common Market, thus ending some kinds of uncertainty across Europe. However, there appears to be some way to go before clarity emerges and satisfactory regular practice develops, which seems unlikely without an ECMS (3.55). No database producer has yet claimed a 'service right' under s7 and it would seem to be ignored by legislators as well as rights owners.

3.22 Databases as copyright compilations

All databases, whether electronic or manual, are clearly 'compilations', included in the definition of 'literary works' by CDPA88 (s3), but that definition only affects copyright in the compilation. There may also, of course, be current copyright in each non-factual item included, possibly of various ownership and authorship. If a non-electronic or manual database is published, such as a directory, there is also copyright in the typographical arrangement of the published edition. The new law on extraction or re-utilisation of material from databases (3.28) makes it possible for many kinds of compilation, whether paper or electronic, to be considered 'databases'. Such permissions as relate to extraction can be taken to apply not only to printed directories, bibliographies, anthologies, etc but also to electronic formats. It is important to note that the former CDPA88 permissions ss30-44 and 51-76 must be considered overruled when database right applies.

3.23 Print-out

CDPA88 makes no distinction between paper and electronic 'writing', and an electronic database is a publication. Nevertheless, it remains unclear at present as to whether, in the absence of relevant case law, print-out from an electronic database could legally be claimed as the producer's copyright as a 'typographical layout'. It has been said that, although it is the producer's software which controls printing and its layout, the equipment and its local control are in the hands of the user (cf HTML, 15.47). Under the new database right the position is clear, since it applies to any format of database as indicated above and in 3.28, and permission to extract or re-utilise ignores any question of typographical layout.

3.24 Offline or 'portable' databases

CD-ROM, diskette, or tape are outside the definition of 'cable programme service' and therefore have no kind of copyright in the service – but they are covered by database right, and 3.28 should be studied. Under copyright provisions alone, it has been possible to regard a one-off or 'stand-alone' item such as a CD-ROM or diskette or tape as copiable – as hard copy only – to a similar extent as permitted for printed matter in respect of textual and associated image content only. This has been on the basis of fair dealing in the original works which form its contents, since there is no copyright in an electronic record as such. Therefore, it was believed, 'electrocopying' problems should not arise for copying within norms, provided a user does not take too large a proportion of a compilation. However, most kinds of compilation are now 'databases', whether paper or electronic (on or offline), and may qualify for database right. These are now protected against extraction or re-utilisation of individual records if there has been substantial investment. The definition of databases (3.29) rules out simple 'sweat-of-brow' compilations but those remain protected by copyright at compilation level for the usual term.) It must be noted that 'commercial purpose' has been removed from fair dealing in respect of a database under the new law. The former fair dealing situation should however continue to apply, at least until further possible EC revisions, in respect of a stand-alone database which is not under contract and which was created before 1 January 1983. It should be borne in mind that there is no fair dealing under copyright in sound or moving images, or in computer programs in their electronic format. Database right may apply as well as copyright. Fair dealing for research or private study now seems clear under the new law, but only in relation to copyright and excluding media not covered by s29. Although there is no infringement unless a substantial part or the whole is copied, 'substantial' can mean significance of an extract as well as extent, under both copyright and database right. Since there are no copyright permissions for audiovisual media, anything more than an 'insubstantial part' of a multimedia offline item such as a CD-ROM or CD-i should not be copied without permission, such as contract or a producer's note on or accompanying the item, or resulting from permission request.

3.25 Care has always been needed to avoid copying an unfair proportion of a compilation such as a directory, bibliography, abstracting journal, etc. Any producer's notices or contracts must be studied before electrocopying, not least because they may even contain helpful guidance in the new climate of database right. Many one-off CD-ROMs have a notice similar to that found on books (12.16), though without following the more recently favoured format used by the BCC (12.17). Such a notice does not in itself represent a contract any more than it does when found on a book. However, there seems to be nothing to hinder a producer from selling stand-alone items under conditions of sale which must be warranted as seen and signed before purchase and therefore could be claimed as contractual (see 12.18). An item which is not 'stand-alone', but updated by a subscription service that substitutes new CD-ROMs or etc for those held, may show restrictions on copying on either the subscription form itself or in a separate service contract. All contracts must of course be honoured, any shortfall in the satisfaction of needs being raised with the producer. Again, database right may also apply. However, offline databases have long been subject to even more stringent restrictions than online databases.

Why 'even more'? Some producers have at times showed some confusion about 'third-party usage'. Online producers should already know – or should be informed – that an information officer or 'information intermediary' provides a service which is being paid for, wherever the client may be located, and that any charge made is primarily for professional search expertise. Producers must also be aware of the shop-window effect of 'broker' or library subscriptions. But CD-ROM and other portable database producers fear a situation wherein one subscriber could serve a wide area without any extra revenue coming in, and may wish to prohibit or restrict use for external enquiries. Such a 'single-purchase' situation would seem most unlikely in practice. In contrast, hard copy sources such as directories have been used for many years in libraries to answer enquiries from just about anywhere and anyone, and under database right these actions will either need licensing, or be limited to insubstantial parts.

It is only to be expected that producers wish to impose restrictions on external use of a CD-ROM in respect of multiple copies, or lengthy extents, of printouts; and of transfer to other databases. The producers' concerns are particularly relevant to networking and, where licences for networking are available, they tend to be priced accordingly. Users nevertheless need stability as well as reasonableness of cost and contractual terms in licences, and understanding from rights owners of their daily service needs. The EUSIDIC Guidelines of 1989 (The European Association of Information Dissemination Centres) was an early unsuccessful attempt to regularise the situation. However, EBLIDA (12.39 and App. 4/3) has recently developed some standard headings for contracts and other recommendations, and projects like IMPRIMATUR should be fruitful (3.58).

3.26 Contracts and cable programmes

So what help is all this to an information user who is bound by the terms of a service contract in any event? None at all if the contract is clearly against any downloading without permission. But it would appear that a user who is not bound by a clear contract – whether or not the database producers claim a form of service protection – could provide a strong defence, if need be, for the recording of cable programmes for several kinds of purpose when neither copyright nor database right restricts this action:

- statutory permissions which are general – 'anything' does not infringe – such as parliamentary or judicial proceedings (s45)
- time-shift for private and domestic purposes (s70)
- educational establishment use in the absence of a collective licensing scheme (s35).

The present collective licensing arrangements for educational off- air recording relate only to broadcasts and cable television.

It must be emphasised that, having signed a contract, a user must abide by it and the downloading permissions should be found in the contract – if not, the producer should be asked. But there should be no hesitation in complaining about terms which seem unjustifiable or unfair, preferably to a user's professional body before signing.

Under database right a 'lawful user' (effectively having a contract upon purchase) has rights which cannot be overridden by other contracts.

Legal protection of databases

3.27 Apart from an obvious preference for service contracts, so unfortunately without a common standard so far, much attention was naturally paid by UK database producers to the various drafts of this Directive 96/9/EC in the run-up to its passage by the European Parliament in March 1996. It was expected that the UK would take advantage of the leeway allowed to member states in certain areas, and in particular that some form of fair dealing concept may be preserved; but excluding 'commercial purpose' since this is prohibited by the Directive. The publishers and database producers consider the new law to be essential for the protection of investment in database development and operation.

In August 1997 a draft SI emerged with a stated commencement date of 1 January 1998, thus demonstrating UK compliance with the Directive's deadline. The SI may lead to an unusual amount of litigation and ultimately depend more on case law than other areas of rights. The draft was passed in December 1997 as SI 1997/3032.

Changes to CDPA88 are minimal, for the new provisions constitute a piece of 'stand-alone' legislation to be applied alongside copyright and without prejudice to copyright. Extensive extracts from the SI appear in Appendix 3 along with comments on selected provisions. Readers should bear in mind that the assessments and comments made by this author may need verification in the light of several years of working with the new situation. The aim of the SI is of course to implement the Directive's provisions, and they are closely followed. Brief notes have appeared in Q13-14, and an outine of the provisions follows below.

3.28 Outline of database right provisions

Database right is to be applied alongside, and without prejudice to, copyright in a compilation as a whole or in its individual items of content. Both non-electronic and electronic formats can be covered by the new right, also both copyright and noncopyright items of content. The new law protects rights owners against unauthorised extraction or re-utilisation of the whole or substantial parts of database contents. The law applies only to collections of EEA origin but, since it applies both to print and electronic formats, the range of affected materials can include printed directories, handbooks, encyclopedias, anthologies, etc. as well as any electronic versions thereof which may exist. Even every single issue of a periodical might be claimed to be a 'database' qualifying for database right. There are two areas: firstly copyright at compilation level; and secondly EC's *sui generis* right, which is now to be called 'database right' in the UK. Subject to the notes on transitional provisions under duration below, the SI's *Regulations apply to databases before or after commencement* (1 January 1998).

3.29 Database definition

A database is a publication, whether print or electronic. The SI adds the definition of database to s3 of the Act: a compilation is to be seen as a 'database' if it contains:

> *'a collection of independent works, data or other materials which –*
> *(a) are arranged in a systematic or methodical way, and*
> *(b) are individually accessible by electronic or other means.'*

Then, and only then, provided the selection *or* arrangement of contents constitutes *the author's own intellectual creation*, the database constitutes an original work and is accordingly protected as a whole under copyright, possibly as well as under database right. The definition rules out, at least as a 'database', a mere 'sweat of brow' compilation such as a simple alphabetical telephone directory. However, there is a wide range of well arranged compilations which could qualify as databases. A database will have 'database right' irrespective of copyright in contents or in a compilation as a whole, provided *there has been substantial investment in obtaining verifying or presenting the contents of the database.* A 15-year duration, repeatable when substantial updating occurs, makes possible a perpetual monopoly in a collection of noncopyright records, such as bibliographical details or data such as physical constants.

3.30 Copyright in a database

In CDPA88 s3, a compilation is a 'literary work', long regarded as copyright as a whole if original and meeting other qualification requirements in the usual way, subject to existing case law. This situation, with duration of 70 years beyond author's death year, will continue in respect of copyright in a compilation which is *not* a database. This will include any simple 'sweat of brow'compilations which do not qualify as databases, so producing an anomaly because a specially ordered arrangement of the same information gets only 15 years' initial protection under database right. There may be few compilations remaining in this category. It is assumed that no-one would claim a set of collected works of one author to be a compilation; or indeed a collection on library shelves, though a 'package library' (for example, product information service) is very probably a database. A database which is not 'original' because it is not the author's own intellectual creation in respect of the selection *or* arrangement of contents, will have no copyright as a whole. Nevertheless, a non-original database may contain items of content which are copyright in themselves, and will in any event qualify for database right in respect of extraction or re-utilisation of contents, when substantial investment has been involved, as noted below.

3.31 Database right

A database *only* qualifies for database right if it was made:

- by one or more nationals or habitual residents of an EEA state (see 2.10), or
- by a body incorporated under the law of an EEA state and having its registered office or central administration , or principal place of business within the EEA.

The right however applies whether or not the database *or* any of its contents are copyright works. From an earlier note above, the traditional 'originality' requirement for copyright (at compilation level in this context) will not apply to databases unless the selection and arrangement of contents constitutes the author's *'own intellectual creation'*. Although any well ordered compilation may qualify as a database, the right itself will *only* subsist in a database *'if there has been substantial investment in obtaining, verifying or presenting the contents of the database'*. 'Substantial', where applied to an investment, or to extraction or re-utilisation, means *'substantial in terms of quantity or quality or a combination of both'*.

3.32 Extraction or re-utilisation

The right protects a *maker* of a database against infringement through the extraction *or* re-utilisation of all or a substantial part of the contents. The *'repeated and systematic extraction or re-utilisation of insubstantial parts of the contents of a database may amount to ... a substantial part of those contents'*. 'Extraction' means *'the permanent or temporary transfer of ... contents to another medium by any means or in any form'*. This should be taken as meaning anything from copying manually, through photocopying, to scanning-in printed matter or downloading to or from electronic format. It should be noted that 'extraction' need not involve the public.

'Re-utilisation' means *making those contents available to the public by any means*. Noting the word 'or' between extraction and re-utilisation, the latter could infringe through lending to the public of a printed directory (etc) or a CD, which appear to be what are meant by 'any means', but the SI makes an exception for establishments accessible to the public as in 4.35. Making a database available for on-the-spot reference use is excepted from database right but, as there is no relevant exception for viewing on screen, 'use' may not cover print-out or downloading to another file and such actions could constitute extraction or re-utilisation.

3.33 Maker of a database

This *means the person who takes the initiative in making a database and assumes the risk of investing in its making* ... subject to customary provisions regarding 'course of employment'; Her Majesty as a maker; and joint makers. The maker is first owner of database right. (Note from this that, apparently, the maker of a database having origin in an existing compilation need not be the same as the author of the compilation.) Where a name appears on a published database and purports to be that of a maker, that name is presumed to be that of the maker and that the database was not made in the course of employment etc.

3.34 Duration of database right

A database will have 'database right' irrespective of copyright in contents or in a compilation as a whole, provided there has been *substantial investment in obtaining verifying or presenting the contents of the database*. The right expires 15 years beyond the year of making but, when made available to public before the end of that period, duration continues until 15 years beyond the year of making available. However:

> 'Any substantial change to the contents of a database, including a substantial change resulting from the accumulation of successive additions, deletions or alterations, which would result in the database being considered to be a substantial new investment shall qualify the database resulting from that investment for its own term of protection'

– that is, another 15 years. As a transitional copyright provision, where a database was completed on or after 1 January 1983 *and* begins to qualify for database right on 1 January 1998, database right subsists for 15 years commencing on that date.This provision makes possible a perpetual monopoly not only in copyright items of content but also in noncopyright records, like bibliographical details or data such as physical constants.

3.35 Duration of copyright in a database

As a transitional database right provision, where a database:

(a) *was created on or before 27th March 1996, and*
(b) *is a copyright work immediately before commencement* (1 January 1998), *copyright shall continue to subsist in the database for the remainder of its copyright term* (under CDPA88 s12).

Existing databases completed on or after 1 January 1983 will commence an initial 15 years' protection on 1 January 1998.

The new law applies only to collections of EEA origin but, since it applies both to print and electronic formats, the range of affected materials includes printed directories, handbooks, encyclopedias, anthologies, etc. as well as any electronic versions thereof which may exist. Even every single issue of a periodical could theoretically be considered a 'database' qualifying for database right. Unless a single article per issue can be proved not to be a substantial part – or acknowledged in guidelines as such – might publishers press for licensing coverage of the massive number of single articles copied from printed matter in a commercial environment? The Government has effectively reversed the removal of discrimination against 'commercial research' in fair dealing for research or private study from the Copyright etc Bill, following lobbying during 1987/88, though only in respect of databases so far. Lobbying was vigorous not only because of definition problems but also because of forecasts of economic damage to industry, and that danger now again looms on the horizon.

3.36 'Lawful user' under copyright

A person who has a right to use a database by virtue of a licence or otherwise is a 'lawful user'. No infringement can arise from his use for the purposes of exercising his right to use the database as a whole, which in this context would mean the *proportion* of the database affected. Like the computer programs provision (7.16), the argument is quite 'circular' but at least cannot be overridden by contract. It is recommended that further definition should be sought by user groups.

3.37 'Lawful user' under database right

A 'circular statement' applies here also: *'any person who (whether under a licence to do any of the acts restricted by any database in the database or otherwise) has a right to use the database'*. Other contracts cannot override the rights of a lawful user.

3.38 Permissions under copyright and/or database right

It has been noted above that the extraction or re-utilisation of *insubstantial parts* will not infringe, subject to the proviso about repetitive action. An important point is the retention of fair dealing for research and private study at least for non-commercial purposes. This is to be noted in conjunction with the absence of any distinction in the SI between electronic formats and printed matter, hence electronic formats can also be copied under fair dealing unless governed by contract such as a licence for a lawful user. The same would apply to insubstantial items of parts of a database under Reg.16 of the draft. In the absence of contract, there is nothing in the law to prevent downloading of an insubstantial part of contents under Reg. 16 by anyone at all, for any purpose. Otherwise the draft SI closely follows the Directive in allowing only very minimal exceptions to database right such as the existing CDPA88 permissions for 'public administration' (ss45-50). (See also 3.40; 5.6; 6.4; and 7 General note.)

In April 1997, the Library and Information Commission (based with the British Library at 2 Sheraton Street, London W1V 4BH) issued a report which moots the setting up of a Public Library Networking Agency, with appropriate recompense to rights owners (see Appendix 4/6).

3.39 Fair dealing under copyright

Changes to fair dealing for research or private study are made: firstly, to require that source database be indicated; and secondly to exclude 'commercial purpose' in respect of a database. 'Commercial purpose' is not defined. No such discrimination is applied to the other fair dealing provisions in CDPA88 (criticism; news reporting; incidental inclusion; ss30-31). Note that there is no distinction between print and electronic formats under database right. Previously this was regarded as theoretical.

3.40 Permissions/exceptions under database right

There is an exception in respect of teaching or research, again merely as allowed by the Directive:

> '... Database right in a database which has been made available to the public in any manner is not infringed by fair dealing with a substantial part of its contents by a lawful user of the database for the purposes of illustration for teaching or research, other than teaching or research for a commercial purpose, but only by a lawful user and subject to ackowledgement of source.'

However, the word 'illustration' makes this absolutely minimal despite the word 'substantial'. Indeed it is difficult to see why it was mentioned since lawful user action should apply, but it does at least allow illustrative use of 'substantial parts' subject to a fair dealing test. It has the serious snag of excluding commercially-based organisations. Profit-based 'educational establishments' have previously avoided discrimination under copyright, it having been confirmed by DES in 1989 that the term applied to any establishment however funded, and the new effects are not yet known. Notably, other educational permissions such as examination questions/answers are conspicuous by their absence, but might be covered by 'lawful user' licence or by selecting only parts which could be defensible as 'insubstantial'. Similar comments apply to other permissions, including some which were deliberately inserted in 1987/88 to help the disadvantaged members of the public.

3.41 As noted above, public administration copyright permissions are reflected for databases in the SI. No attempt has been made under database right to reflect or delete other existing CDPA88 copyright permissions. Therefore, existing ss29-44 and 51-76 are still relevant to material other than databases. Also, those and indeed any other action which does not involve extraction or re-utiisation is permissible under database right, and the deliberate absence of any distinction between electronic and print formats is important. In all cases, however, it must be remembered that the contents themselves may be copyright, and that copying should not exceed a substantial part of the whole compilation., Otherwise, in practice database right will override any copyright permission when the two are in conflict, and inhibit *extraction or re-utilisation* of substantial parts (or of insubstantial parts taken repetitively, which together could make up a substantial part). New imminent Directives may cause further limitations ('Reproduction right'; and 'Communication to the public right') when SIs duly appear in about two years' time (at the earliest). The omission of traditional copyright permissions under database right as indicated could affect all copying (4.12-4.15); issue to the public, publication and commercial publication (4.17); plus any of the actions listed in 4.20 which involve extraction or re-utilisation of substantial parts from a database (the other 4.20 actions should be unaffected).

3.42 Anyone or any library may act on behalf of someone in respect of any permission or exception under copyright and/or database right unless overridden by the latter. Difficulties may arise from uncertainty as to definitions, for example 'substantial'. However, 'lawful user' licences may be sufficiently specific. Nevertheless, because printed matter is involved as well as electronic formats, even nonprofit-based information services and libraries may feel obliged to seek licensing against the contingency of infringement with printed compilations which may be definable as databases. Licensing is governed by a Schedule 2 to the SI and subject to arbitration by the Copyright Tribunal, reflecting the provisions re copyright in CDPA88.

3.43 Adjustment

Above are some very sweeping changes for which no adjustment time has so far been allowed. If publishers were agreeable to extend their guidelines to cover the traditional permissions at least in respect of printed databases, the effects might not be too serious, but the interim could be difficult. For electronic formats, service contracts will continue to 'rule', with a hope of increasing standardisation (App. 4). In respect of non-electronic formats, users may well be left to decide whether just to carry on until told that they may be infringing and then seek advice; or actively seek licensing forthwith. The latter has always been recommended by this author for commercially-based firms as a precaution against inadvertent but excessive copying, and should also apply without doubt to anyone wishing to publish. The former group who may just carry on pro tem will learn from information service or library notices or staff or their professional bodies or a looseleaf service such as the *Aslib guide to copyright* about any changes in copying norms. Meanwhile, this author commends careful action and cognisance of professional organisation meetings to discuss issues, bearing in mind that rights owners themselves will be taking time to adjust and certainly too busy, even if so inclined, to lie in wait to catch anyone out!

3.44 Infringement

A number of database matters are included in the above. Other situations follow.

Setting aside for a moment the risk of breaching a service contract and at least being barred from service, in what ways might the average day to day user be currently in danger of infringing the rights provided by the 1988 Act itself? The following are just the more common examples in respect of either on- or offline electronic databases:

(a) Making multiple copies of a printout. However, unless specifically prohibited under contract, a file copy could be taken by a library as well as the copy supplied to an enquirer.

(b) Supplying a copy to an enquirer for some purpose not covered by fair dealing or other relevant statutory permissions (including database right). Contract may however extend some permissions and not just limit user actions even more than statute.
(c) Supplying large segments of a compilation, thus exceeding coverage of a specific enquiry, and becoming open to accusations of infringement of copyright in the compilation.
(d) Downloading for input to another database of a 'substantial part' or more of the items in an electronic database, bearing in mind that in this context a court could see successive inputs from the same service as additive to make up a substantial part (4.32). Since the definition of the latter is somewhat elastic and involves significance to the user's purpose as well as to the extent of an item, no user should imagine that any extent of downloading without contractual coverage would not be open to challenge by rights owners, unless covered by 'lawful user' rights under database right..

However, it is appropriate now to move on to 'electrocopying' below.

Electrocopying in general

3.45 Electrocopying, some kinds of which have been covered above, has been a major concern for the information industry for some years. According to the International Federation of Reproduction Rights Organisations (IFRRO), the term covers any or all of the activities below. When written they apparently referred to literary material, but now should be seen as extending into other possible contexts of infringement of rights by electronic means. The cause is a copyright owner's underlying fear of loss of control of rights in the presence of digitization, for example of a musical performance. The foregoing description of the new database right should be taken in conjunction with these notes. The following electrocopying activities could be in danger of accusations of infringement unless permitted by service contract, or as lawful user, or otherwise:

(a) keying-in or machine-scanning of publications to make or augment a database
(b) downloading from an online or offline database to form or augment another database
(c) transfer of data from one database to another
(d) manipulation of data to make different files and/or publications

(e) print-out or publication, either reproducing original input or manipulated information
(f) networking – in other words, potentially a complex version of at least (b) to (e).

3.46 Protection against electrocopying is reinforced by the Act's inclusion of electronic storage, and even transient or temporary copies (s17(6)), in the restricted act of copying.

For that reason anyone who may claim that copying an electronic journal article is the same as copying the printed matter, should beware – unless of course their actions are covered by permission or service contract. Any of (a) to (f) can at present be done only under specific service contract with a database producer, subject to variation in terms and prices. It goes without saying that on-demand publishing of any kind can only be done under contract. In Appendix 4, work towards a standard form of contract or licence is reported, useful at least until an agreed ECMS can be developed which must inevitably cover contractual concerns held by rights owners in common. Hence a fully-fledged central registry with wider functions than co-ordinating contracts is preferred (Appendix 5/2).The Publishers' Association and the International Publishers' Association have had electrocopying problems under review for several years, Alarm spread rapidly to Europe during the 1980s after publishers in the USA were reported to have become concerned about an 'electronic corridor', through which a large number of US colleges were receiving full text journal articles without using any system of royalty payment. The explosion of Internet development and its use worldwide has since occurred, and considerable effort and research funding are being applied towards generally acceptable solutions to copyright problems.

Internet and e-mail

3.47 Descriptions of electronic mail, Internet and the usage of World Wide Web sites and bulletin boards are in general outside the scope of this book, being covered extensively in numerous other publications. In those – especially earlier texts – the absence of reference to copyright and moral rights was taken by some as symptomatic of the situation. The problem in this text is: 'How to focus on selected fine threads in an increasingly rich and multi-coloured tapestry?' – moreover, whilst it is still being woven – and yet show enough background to place points in context. In essence, all 'electronic copyright' concerns are represented by 'electrocopying' actions listed in 3.45 above, which suggests that any one of those may be applied as a test to determine whether infringement would occur in any situation. However, a summary of current rights-owner aims in respect of electronic copyright is here proposed as:

(a) protection to be as safe as possible in situations wherein illegal copying is all too easy;
(b) maximum control of rights: that is, of any permissions or licensing;
(c) consensus – at long last, the obvious lack of consensus on how to tackle electronic copyright problems has become recognised, but the answers will probably not be as simple as 'a,b,c' unless rights owners *first* agree to act under an agreed general control structure.

For (a), the popular means of copy-protection may well turn out to be encryption, especially for cross-border protection against piracy, though any method can be at best a deterrent for the majority of potential infringers rather than experienced hackers (it being hoped that they will some day reduce to a minority).

For (b), it is suggested that rights-owners might do better to seek control of the essentials only: namely, variation in charges for various uses (whilst treating all users for a given purpose in an equitable manner); and be more ready to accept an agreed common form of service contract on all other aspects. For (c), it seems increasingly obvious to the writer that further progress towards proper management of copyright may only be made if a national agency were established (Appendix 5/2).

3.48 User aims

Users and information professionals on their behalf have aims such as:

(i) online databases and CD-ROMs with predictable contractual terms instead of the current variation per supplier, and cheaper and more readily permitted networking;
(ii) maximal ease of exchanging electronic files with minimal bars on copyright and cost grounds;
(iii) sufficient flexibility to allow some clearly defined free actions, including single copies from electronic journals for research or private study, comparably with hard copy; browsing databases; and building up a local database or 'intranet'.

In respect of (i), the question of contract terms is dealt with in 12.

For (ii), compatibility in file formats is needed, plus more readiness by rights owners to permit passing on materials, especially between recipient organizations of a comparable type. In respect of (iii), the term 'intranet' would probably have evolved anyway, but is now big business as *Intranet*, described as a secure Web-enabled information system and the subject of *Intranet Expo 1997* at London's Olympia in April 1997. More generally for (iii), some provisions approaching those of the UK, including fair dealing for any kind of research, should be built into Berne; also, an 'access right' should be created for users in respect of viewing any materials already published or released. The contributions to Parliamentary lobbying in late 1987 and their subsequent debate, especially in the House of Lords, should be taken as conclusive evidence that fair dealing is accepted to be an essential concept. In the hard copy regime, where the problems of keeping track of small amounts copied, paying for them whether by time-consuming sampling or piecemeal would be administratively expensive and could seriously hinder research. In the electronic regime, where charging is automatic and, as has been said before, 'invisible' until the bills arrive, whether fair dealing is still provable as necessary would depend very much on the fee per copy required by rights owners, and whether it is an arbitrated standard fee. No user (bearing in mind that authors form the largest proportion of users of 'serious' literature and already regard their research as unfairly restricted by copyright) considers himself able to afford more for copying than at present. Moreover, as argued from 1987 onwards on behalf of users, ideally there should be no discrimination in fair dealing against 'commercial research' since that is regarded as virtually impossible to define (except in retrospect, which would seem ridiculous).

3.49 The Internet and copyright

Users of the Internet enjoyed an initial flush of enthusiasm during which many apparently formed the belief that items on the Net were put there as offerings for general use or 'public domain' works. This impression is believed to have grown partly:

- as a result of familiarity with e-mail and bulletin board use, for few of the public realise that even items of correspondence are copyright and subject to moral rights;
- from the fact that all US Government publications, apart from contractual documents, are published into the public domain and are included in the Net extensively;

- from the absence of general rules for Internet users as to marking items with copyright notices; and
- from an unfortunate assumption of 'implied licence' to copy in the absence of any words to the contrary.

Accordingly, enquirers to this author have been advised on the following lines pending the appearance of official rules:

1. No 'implied licence' should be assumed by a person for anything other than correspondence to himself, or for individual facts. Netizens should remember that copyright is automatic, and the absence of any mention of it should certainly not be taken as indicating the irrelevance of copyright considerations. Although discussion group contributions and bulletin board items seem most unlikely to be subjected to infringement claims by originators, the need for care should be borne in mind when passing on extensive or important items or indeed **any** data, other than individual facts, reported by someone else, even in e-mail. Only when it is known that material is in the public domain, such as most US Government publications (excluding contractual documents with industry), may these recommendations be inapplicable. Even so, source should always be cited.
2. Permission should be sought via the database provider or publisher before inputting – or passing on –information, whether marked or not, which *could* be someone else's copyright, and the position should be made clear –
   (a) if copyright is confirmed by the database provider or publisher as current, by words such as either:
      – *'permission given by ... but rights otherwise reserved, 1997'* (i.e. if published 1997, otherwise the appropriate year, or
      – when a 'C-notice' appears on a printed item being digitised with permission, such as '© by J. Smith, 1996', put in the same statement. If, as is usual the equipment does not readily allow the insertion of a © symbol, put *Copyright by J. Smith, 1996* (see 13.9) or in the form on the item itself (see (4) below), and add a phrase such as *'included by permission'*;
   (b) if an item on-screen is to be transferred to someone else and the item is marked as copyright or suspected to be copyright:
      – seek permission as in (a), because any permission noted by the original contributor to the Net cannot be taken as general and should be replaced by a new phrase as above;

   - when the item is your own but is to be in the public domain, state *copyright-free* or *copyright waived.*
3. Few netizens appear to have spared the time to read prefatory notes on service. For example, America OnLine (AOL) has an extensive statement on 'Rights and responsibilities' including ' You agree only to upload/transmit through AOL content that is not subject to any rights...'. When wishing to copy from the Net, always look for some kind of copyright notice and act accordingly. 'Home-made' notices began to appear before long, such as 'this frame should not be copied without permission of ... ' or even 'please do not copy this without asking ...'.
4. The standard 'circle-C' symbol (©) ceased to be essential for overseas protection when the USA joined the Berne Union in 1988, with the exception of one or two nations still bound only via treaty with the USA. The symbol nevertheless continues to be used in printed matter because it has become the custom to show the originator and date in this way, being as yet still current under the Universal Copyright Convention in any event. Hence the recommendations in 2(a) above.
5. When inputting one's own material for which protection is desired, state either C symbol etc if that is available; or the word 'copyright' in full, etc (as 13.9); or *All rights reserved by ...* (the author and year – unless contracted otherwise with a publisher, when use a phrase such as *All rights reserved by Aslib,*plus year). In other words, if trespass is to be avoided, fence your property – or hedge your bets. That works both ways, of course, and at present a possible defence against an infringement claim might be the absence of any indication of copyright holder and date. It would be somewhat pointless to attempt such a defence, however, if significant commercial use had been made of copied items.
6. However, if no rights are required, state *copyright-free* as per (2)(b) above. (See also 12.29 on avoidance of signing away electronic rights.)
7. A proviso to (5) is that, if considering input of one's own item and it is worth maximum protection, it could be wiser to refrain from putting it on the Internet until the current 'free-for-all' attitudes fade. (See also 3.39.)
8. Links: bibliographic details plus a Web address are no more than ordinary citations, as found in printed matter. The acid test is whether one is *copying* a substantial part without permission, Therefore a link which automatically brings up the text (or etc) of a reference gleaned prevously from elsewhere (having in any event been downloaded with questionable legality?), is undoubtedly 'copying'.

9. The restrictions created by database right (3.28) should be noted. This is by no means an attempt to lay down rules which ought to be drafted by a suitable panel when an appropriate ECMS nears operation, but merely to offer provisional guidance meanwhile for any who may wish to avoid accusations of infringement, or to discourage infringement of their own rights. That being said, it must be remarked that no set of rules can be a complete substitute for common sense and discretion. Nor, indeed – and unfortunately – no marking of an item can prevent someone from infringing. Opinions are bound to differ until such time as authoritative rules emerge. Those who wish to delve deeper and consider alternatives could refer to items in two brief bibiliographies: *Citing electronic references* and an American one *Citing electronic sites;* both in *Audiovisual Librarian: Multimedia Information,* vol. 22(2), May 1996, p107 and 108-109 respectively. Mentioned as possibly 'the standard' and cited in both is: *Electronic style: a guide to citing electronic information,* revised edition, by Xia Li and Nancy Crane, Westport, CT., Mecklermedia, 1996. Pressure for general rules may well increase as large commercial producers find their ownership being increasingly ignored by 'netizens' . Of possible help in respect of clearance, especially for educational needs, is *Copyright guidelines for the Teaching and Learning Technology Programme*, Bristol, TLTP Advisory Group, 1994, 32 pages (App. 1/3).

3.50 Moral rights and the Net

Moral rights (10) may be found to be even more readily overlooked. Three of the four rights last for the duration of copyright, now author's life plus 70 years. Only one, the right not to suffer false attribution, lasts for life plus 20 years. These rights cannot be assigned but can be waived. Those who may be involved in preparing surveys or summaries should note that the act of misquoting, or quoting into an unfortunate or misleading context, can infringe the right of an author not to suffer derogatory treatment of works. One – the right to be identified as author – does not exist unless asserted and unless publication is commercial or, for recordings or films, issued to the public (in the UK, this includes *an electronic retrieval system* (s175)). It is becoming customary for authors to assert paternity right by means of a statement on a title page as far as printed matter is concerned. It should be borne in mind that moral rights have not yet been harmonised by the EC, and that changes may be made when that occurs. Many apparently do not realise that paternity right can also, and more commonly, be asserted by a written statement from an author to the publisher or producer, and such a statement remains 'invisible' to users. Therefore, since it is impossible to know for certain whether an author wants to assert his 'paternity right' or not, the author or the current copyright owner should be asked whether an intended action is acceptable whenever there is any doubt.

'Electronic library' concept

3.51 An electronic library is taken to mean one which makes maximal use of electronic systems for information acquisition, storage, retrieval, and supply whether locally or remotely. For such a library to operate, it must include some effective and efficient means of managing copyright. Moreover, as the Internet matures, it increasingly demonstrates the pressing need for copyright management to be incorporated. If there is to be a successful international 'Information Superhighway', an acceptable *global* Electronic Copyright Management System (3.55) will be needed, but may need to be preceded by regional systems pro term. It is time for maximal collaboration, of course: the past controversy over photocopying and hard copy licensing, which has continued throughout the 1980s and 1990s so far, should be forgotten. Creators of recorded information, the producers of physical formats, the distributors and market outlets, the libraries and individual purchasers, and the end-users, are all chasing around the same communication/information circle. Authors (now or in future) form the majority of users and therefore underpin producers, but an over-energetic quest for profits can hinder authors and thus weaken a producer's own foundations. Piracy will always be present and can only be minimised, for there can be no absolutely reliable means of policing without disproportionate cost. Nothing endangers respect for copyright in users more than over-complicated rules, delays, seemingly unfair barriers and unjustified charges, and some people may think there is still some way to go in adjustment of rights-owner attitudes and behaviour patterns. This would seem an essential prelude to better observance of law by users who perceive it to be both clear and fair. Closer to home for publishers is another need, namely one for consensus, so conspicuously absent until quite recently (Appendix 4).

3.52 Many users of external databases like the simplicity arising from virtual invisibility of royalties – that is, until the bill arrives. Many features of an electronic library are now completely commonplace, and some are held in common with the book trade and publishing industry. The copyright elements which most require investigation from user viewpoints are suggested currently as:

- improved access to comprehensive digitized bibliographic information;
- on-the-spot digitization of some materials, or use of an external service, with readily transferable formats;
- electronic document delivery (6.50) without separate permission-seeking, including interlibrary loan;
- the ability to compile an intranet or LAN with as few copyright restrictions as possible – including growth via compulsory sale of non-copyright records, if achievable (Appendix 3/5);
- interaction between users and information professionals for best access and search success; and, to support the aims and satisfy the rights owners,
- study of usage patterns; and experiments in the management of copyright in particular environments for tracing and charging purposes.

3.53 Digitisation of materials

An electronic library aims to harness technology towards the utilization of all available information, whether stored near or far. Thus such a library is not solely a 'digitised collection' although it should of course incorporate as much information in digital form as possible. In time, all publications available in hard copy should also be issued in an electronic format suitable for user access, clear of control characters, etc. The backlog is a major problem, as always since the beginning of automation in libraries via cataloguing and other 'housekeeping' systems. The Institute for Scientific Information announced in 1995 its pilot sites for an Electronic Library Project: Brookhaven National Laboratories, Lehigh University, and, in the UK, University College London and Glaxo Research and Development. One of the UK's electronic library or 'eLib' projects, a list of which is mentioned in 6.49, provides a service (Digitization Centre, University of Hertfordshire 1996 for two years initially) to other eLib projects. There are of course no copyright clearance problems in digitising material out of copyright.

As might be expected, neither the 'electronic' nor the 'digital' library yet exists as a total entity. A US Digital Library Project announced in 1991 by the Corporation for National Research Initiatives includes the concept of a multimedia 'online scientific library' as a 'consortium of universities and publishers'. Various special collections have been put into digital form, for example in Carnegie Mellon University; Case Western Reserve University, Columbia University Law School, and the Kent Law Library in the University of Illinois. The extent of permission from rights owners for digitising copyright material will continue to be subject to contractual restrictions until an ECMS (3.55) is in operation.

3.54 Image digitisation

Images can involve more problems of copyright clearance than text.The BL's 'Pix' database of digitized images possibly involves more problems of copyright clearance than text. Perhaps of use in this context, Highwater FBI Limited (of Cheltenham) has developed a means of copyright protection for digital images. This:

> 'reinforces the originator's copyright by providing a hidden identifier or 'fingerprint' within the digital image ... detectable only with the originator's copy of ... decoder software, the fingerprints travel everywhere with the image data.. major advantage over watermarking and encryption simply because the fingerprint remains in place...'

despite manipulation, duplication, etc. Also, the famous photographic archive in Florence: Fratelli Alinari, will incorporate the High Water Signum SureSign fingerprinting technology into its digital systems during 1997, in work for IMPRIMATUR.

MIDRIB is a two-year eLib project announced in May 1996 involving Bristol University, St. George's Hospital Bristol and the Wellcome Trust; images of interest in medical, dentistry and veterinary education will be accessible, and each images has a logo to identify ownership. Public availability is of course desirable when copyright problems have been solved. Meanwhile, images go via SuperJanet to all British medical schools. The BL's PIX or Electronic Photo-viewing System is to digitise a portion of the massive number of images held by the BL. The Bibliotheque Nationale also has a digitisation project involving images. The French work is described in *The audiovisual progamme of the National Library of France,* by G. Grunberg, in *The Audiovisual Librarian: Multimedia Information* (Aslib Multimedia Group and Library Association Audiovisual Group), vol. 23(1), February 1997.

The BL's sweeping *Digital Library Development Programme* announced at in the autumn 1996 issue (number 15) of the BL's Research and Innovation Centre Research Bulletin, *will consist of a critical mass of digitally held documents, still images, moving images, sound, and any combination of these ... made available ... anywhere in the world.* Interest is wide: the G-7 countries have agreed to sponsor electronic library projects within their pilot projects towards the Information Society. Further reference to electronic library developments, all necessarily including some degree of ECMS experimentation, appears in 6.49.

3.55 Electronic Copyright Management System (ECMS)

Management system software should be able to track or monitor usage and distribution of an item, license and charge royalties where necessary. Such functions are among the aims of the IPA/STM Group, which also believes that an ECMS should help to identify copyright owners and assist the administration of international trade matters. Projects have shown that rights ownership and usage can be traced through every access to enable the system to function as desired. Alternatively, the market could simply operate in a manner analogous to that for printed matter, using encryption. Which procedure might ultimately – that is, in a global system – be the more suitable for producers and users is by no means clear, and both methods may well be combined. Infringement could ensue not only through electrocopying per se but also by adaptation or plagiarism, but the building of an electronic 'corpus of knowledge' with authority would seem to need highly complex and expensive tracing, as well as extensive intellectual interference or human monitoring, and thus cannot be foreseen at present. Whatever cheaper or temporary approach might be chosen until a global system emerges, it will be essential to address materials uniquely to specific users, make charges, and construct an archive file.

A US experiment called NetRelease, announced in 1994, might be seen as illustrating the problem of achieving consensus among publishers. After putting a brief description on the Internet without seeking payment, access to the full text is only permitted in return for a lump sum royalty, payable in advance, as agreed between the requestor and the author or publisher. One basis alone – the time taken to achieve access – would seem to make such a notion non-viable, although it is of interest. Whatever ECMS is developed, it must allow consultation of *all* published sources on a comparable basis and with maximum speed.

3.56 ECMS research examples

Some examples of significance for the UK now follow:

CITED and COPYCAT

Copyright in Transmitted Electronic Documents was funded by the EC as part of the second wave of ESPRIT research projects. The partners were from Belgium, France, Germany, Netherlands, and the UK, comprising electronic publishers, a computer manufacturer, The British Library (BL), a barrister, security and software specialists and experts in databases and networking. The aims were to explore the problems of electronically stored information and develop means of protection and royalty payment. The whole range of digitally stored data is involved, including audiovisual data as well as text. The *CITED final report*, September 1994 (ISBN 0 7123 2115 2) and available through the BL, contains key papers on various parts of the project, including a description of a future electronic library and detailed guidelines and examples of the actual working of the experimental system devised. The report proposes a EU agency to control 'CITEDization' but admits that expense may cause recourse to standards instead, such as: file structure, document identifiers, passwords, encryption, etc. Soon after completion, CITED became the 'umbrella' for COPICAT (Copyright Ownership, Protection for Computer-Assisted Training. also ESPRIT) on material for educational purposes, especially multimedia, using encryption.

There seems no doubt now of the key role of standardisation in progress towards a satisfactory ECMS. The CEC's *Communication from the Commission to the Council and the European Parliament on 'Standardisation and the global information society: the European approach'* (COM (96) 359 final, 24.7.96) calls for more work on standardisation, particularly on *technical identification and protection schemes.*

3.57 *Identifier*

Publishers of the STM Group, led by Springer-Verlag, have made a worldwide survey of document identifiers and means of measuring ('metering') document use. In 1995 they mooted the introduction of a Publishing Item Identifier (PII). In January 1996, it was announced that a 17-digit identifier would henceforth be used in journal issues from Elsevier Science and a number of other science or technology publishers in *Information World Review* of June 1995. The latter aim of unique identification will necessarily form part of EC projects COPEARMS and IMPRIMATUR.

3.58 *IMPRIMATUR*

The Intellectual Multimedia Property Rights Model and Terminology for Universal Reference project is studying the unification of the world's electronic copyright laws (cf digital fingerprinting of images, 3.54) and seeks to meet the challenge of multimedia rights clearance in networks. IMPRIMATUR will seek agreements on identification data numbers for electronic intellectual property rights, similar to the ISBN identifier for books and examine legal issues. An experimental server is being set up in the

University of Florence, and partners will communicate with it via e-mail. In order to test complexity of issues, all messages will be treated as copyright and may not, it is said, be *bounced on the next person without prior permission*, the purpose being to simulate a trading system. Participants include representatives of: publishing and information industries, the BL, ALCS, 'technology suppliers' like software houses, EUSIDIC, the universities of Florence and Imperial College London, plus international observers from the US Interactive Multimedia Association and the Japanese Institute of Intellectual Property. The project will also explore how consensus might be achieved.

Another international project is closer to 'home' in one sense at least. Under an EU/Australia treaty on research and technical development, IMPRIMATUR is to be linked with Australia's PROPAGATE project for the proection of digital multimedia property on the Internet. (IMPRIMATUR address: 8 Bedford Square, London WC1B 3RA.)

3.59 *COPEARMS*

Working closely with the foregoing, COPEARMS (Coordinating Project for an Electronic Authors' Rights Management System) is an EC project which follows on from CITED, aiming to develop and implement standards for the operation of global electronic copyright management. The first need is standard identifiers. IFLA is a prime partner in promoting and publicising the project via special interest groups and workshops. The partners are able to offer help to electronic library projects by establishing a CITED-based ECMS within a project. A major international ECMS conference is due in November 1997, and COPEARMS ends in December 1998. A COPEARMS Web site is now on IFLANET: *http://www.nlcbnc.ca/ifla/VI/2/p5/proj5.htm*

'Ups and downs' of the Net

3.60 To digress in providing background, every new human development is well known to have its good side and its bad. There is rising concern about the need to police pornography on the Net, for example, plus the continuing free but illegal distribution around the world of computer games. The Safety-Net Foundation, set up by ISPA (Internet Service Providers' Association) and LINX (London Internet Exchange), has a hot-line for users to report illegal material. Interests may expand to embrace copyright infringement, especially as ECMS development proceeds (perhaps like CLA's 'Copywatch in 8.10). Concern may also grow about the clogging of Net space and the problem of panning the gold from among a mass of dross. Not surprisingly there is a waste of manhours from the floating of casual or leisure communications, or piecemeal questions to all and sundry. Asking in effect 'Is there somebody out there?' or believing 'The truth is out there' principle may well bring results of a kind, but which of those is authoritative and therefore safe to follow? Few experts can spare time to give detailed answers on the Net as well as write for publication and/or giving lectures, and keep up to date on the changing legal scene. The dangers of over-simplification and brevity have been mentioned in the preface. Experts who would like to reply, but find it impossible for various reasons, may well regard the excessively brief answers of others, including copyright matters, as 'net-bites' – as irritating as the other kind and present all year round!

Many questions, especially copyright problems, are best raised *after* reading the published sources, not before or without reading them at all. A visit to a library could prove more fruitful and considerably more authoritative. However, it is encouraging to find, particularly when questions are in advance of published sources or accepted practice, that at least people are 'talking', so to say, about copyright – however arguable some answers may be. Many 'downside' aspects should fade with increasing Net usage as well as the maturity of the first wave of users.

'Upside' examples are more obvious – first, the enormous and rapidly increasing inclusion of information from many sources, including specialists themselves when they take time to input directly and in advance of the literature; second, publication directly on to the Net, though the dangers of loss of publisher refereeing, general source authority, plus marketing facilities, should be remembered. There are of course moves which aim to provide a means of peer review in electronic media. Some individual authors desiring economic benefit from their copyright may prefer to avoid direct input until some form of ECMS is in use. Third, education and hands-on experience in the use of computer networks, and in 'socialising' or humanising a mechanical system, even to the extent of founding friendships far afield by young netizens; fourth, the movement towards multimedia inclusion on a large scale in the Information Superhighway; fifth, the moves towards encryption, which can allow specific addressing as well as policing.

3.61 Government concern about computer system security is evident. The DTI, NCC, ICL and ITSEC published *The 1996 information security breaches survey*, of which a free summary is available from the National Computing

Centre. Several other DTI publications of 1996 are also of importance (see *Basic information security*, by the DTI Information Security Policy Group, in *Managing Information,* vol. 3(11), p38-39. A survey by Kable Ltd, published in 1996, on Civil Service use of the Internet reveals that *poor security is the main reason that stops government organizations from using it.* (The cost of dishonesty of all kinds grows ever greater, it seems.)

Vigilance is essential, especially in respect of the virus problem. As will be recognized, there can be no substitute for honesty in all users and fairness of providers, plus the application of discretion and common sense. The capacity limitations of the system may nevertheless require some means of registering the rights ownership of all those who are entitled to publish on the Net, enabling unauthorised access for input purposes to be barred by the software (see also 3.68 re central registry).

Encryption

3.62 When first mooted, encryption aroused as much caution, even opposition, as technical methods of copy-prevention have in the non-electronic regime. It is however difficult to envisage just how large copyright works can be protected in any other way when accessible in digitized form. The possibility of several layers, or shells, of encryption has been considered, possibly aided by COPYCAT research (3.38), but there appear to be many technical problems related to security of keys.

It is unclear in theory how the encryption key itself could be safely communicated except by traditional mail. It is this very complexity which many information professionals find off-putting at present. This attitude should change when it proves possible for every encryption-related action to be entirely hidden from a user. (See also image fingerprinting, 3.54.) In practice, however, Oxford University Press began in 1996 to sell encrypted copies of selected textbooks or individual chapters, held in Acrobat PDF (Portable Document Format) files. These are made only readable by a special version of the Acrobat reader, from which encryption software is downloaded along with the material itself. Protection is said to arise because the software will only run on the special reader (e-mail details: *peacockt@oup.co.uk*). More recently Aslib has announced provision of access to, for example, its quarterly journal *Program - electronic library and information systems* via the Web in Adobe Acrobat to hard copy subscribers only.

Electronic publishing and document delivery

3.63 If there ever was any clear demarcation between electronic publishing, on-demand publishing, and document delivery, they should now be seen as overlapping concepts. Publishing directly on to the Net has become common. Electronic full text, and contents-listing, have grown at speed in the last few years, and electronic journals, whether in CD-ROM or network or online, are now numerous. In many cases, including Aslib's journal, *Program*, such publications may be available in hard copy as well as in electronic format. For example, Elsevier plus nine US universities ran TULIP – the Universities Licensing Program – during 1991 to 1995 as an investigation of the digital library environment of journal information. Some 43 Elsevier and Pergamon journals on materials science were made available by networked delivery via Engineering Information to desktops as full text or scanned page images. In 1995 this became Elsevier Electronic Subscriptions (EES), expanding to a full service in 1996 on 1200 journals, available in electronic format instead of or in addition to paper copy. TULIP produced its final report in 1996, available from Elsevier Science (*http://elsevier.nl/locate/tulip*).

Springer-Verlag has RED SAGE – Bell Laboratories 'Right Pages' plus UCAL San Francisco – which tests licensing and tracking systems. In the UK, a number of eLib projects are relevant (6.49), including the SuperJournal project which will experimentally provide a cluster of electronic journals in a given subject area.

The STM Group has been reported (IPA Bulletin, no.2, 1994, p5) as seeing its market breakdown as: broad subsets (CD-ROM, Online, tapes) for information services and corporate users, etc.; large quantities of data (CD-ROM, Online, tapes) for end-users of information services; small quantitites of data (CD-ROM, diskettes) for individual end-users. Document delivery is treated further in in the information service and library context in 6.47-6.50.

On-demand publishing

3.64 This is believed to have an increasing role for some uses. It is assumed that 'on-demand publishing' is normally regarded as a separate endeavour from supply by a licensed agency of an individual document copied from a published original. It is difficult to see how on-demand publishing of journal articles can be cost-effective in the face of notable growth in such licensed document supply agencies (6.50). Esoteric material requiring search, or material with special illustration production or difficult clearance problems not solvable by a supply agency is an exception. However, it is believed that there could be considerable growth in the preparation of anthologies, or search results, brought together and made available in hard copy regardless of source format. Many papers or book chapters are highly illustration-dependent and replication, whether from full electronic text or hard copy, can cause difficulties for some document delivery services. On-demand production should have little difficulty in overcoming the illustration problem with present equipment, *provided* there can be access directly either to originals or to a database containing reliable image data. However, protection of on-demand publishing is under discussion by the CEC.

University libraries find it administratively time-consuming to obtain clearance for collections or 'study packs' of extracts, articles, or book chapters required outside ordinary licensing. Some tend to leave the matter to departments with resultant variation in attention and continuity, etc., and central control should be preferred. Some eLib projects (6.49) are investigating the internal or 'intranet' possibilities of a campus collection in electronic form, but it is believd that a very long time will elapse before printed matter will lose its appeal, if ever. Hence a student, it is suggested, should not only have access to a valuable hard copy 'short loan' or 'reserve collection' of high-use material, and possibly a shared electronic store which preferably covers a number of institutions, but also possess his or her own copy of a hard copy collection of the more important papers or book chapters, supplied at the start of every course or option. Obviously some subjects would lose out comparatively, such as history or literature, but in general higher education is too expensive to waste time in repetitively looking for required reading in a busy library and finding that, despite the library's purchase of extra copies, all are out on loan and reservation is the only option. However, it may be that, if libraries were to accept a coordinating role on requests, even across various establishments, on-demand publishing could be a solution, especially as it would leave all clearance problems for informed and experienced attention centrally.

Multimedia and the 'Information Superhighway'

3.65 The Superhighway cannot exist without improvements in the technical system of the Internet. Carrying capacity and speed of response are problems with which all Net users must be familiar, especially in afternoons when searching US databases which by then are in heavy demand-contention as American daytime use begins. It is claimed that large online databases are increasingly turning towards Internet availability. No matter what expansions may be made, will they be sufficient if usage continues to grow at its present rate or even faster, with continuation of lax attitudes to copyright? The publishing industry may choose what it may regard as the ultimate solution, as mentioned above, namely more recourse to broadcasting for some services, and extensive use of encryption for others.

3.66 The definition of 'multimedia' by the US Department of Commerce/International Trade Administration is as follows (from *US Industrial Outlook 1994* and quoted in *The value of integrated access to print and AV collections,* by W. Storm, *IASA Journal* no. 7, May 1996 p53-67):

> 'Multimedia is a broadly defined cornucopia of technologies designed to combine full-motion video, animation, still pictures, voice, music, graphics, and text into a fully integrated and interactive system. These new integrated capabilities bring computers a step closer to realizing their enormous potential. Potential uses include training, education, publishing, entertainment, voice and video mail teleconferencing, public information, and document imaging and archival systems... Multimedia products blur the lines between several formerly distinct products and industries: computers, software, consumer electronics, communications, publishing and entertainment. Computer communications and entertainment companies that have joined efforts in the last 24 months include Time Warner and US West; IBM, Apple and Toshiba; and Time Warner and Telecommunications Inc. Two aspects ... are worth noting... First as expected the alliances cut across industries. Second, many alliances are international, signalling that the production of multimedia products will be global from the start.'

Some information professionals with long experience of information retrieval systems may find such a definition fulsome, perhaps believing that most multimedia, for some time to come, will be simply be 'mixed media' plus sophisticated retrieval software. (Before too long it should be possible to retrieve instantly a quick burst of Mozart to illustrate a point about infant prodigies in a psychology work, or provide musical or video accompaniment of choice; though this writer knows of no such system as yet.) However, although a relationship is obvious, a mixture of discrete individual media (media packs or kits, such as those for instruction, see 15.52) should remain simpler. The term 'multimedia' should never be used to cover media packs, unless of course they become digitized into multimedia per se. The key differences from media packs are: firstly the common, single digital format including any kind of data whether text, sound or images; and secondly the software for access and 'navigation' among the contents.

Multimedia will naturally increase the capacity problems of the Internet more than ever, though with broadcasting the transmission bandwidth problems are at least familiar. Much has been made in discussions of the contractual problems, and some mention of these is made in chapter 8. Yet, after all, the BBC has for many years been coping with problems of a similar nature. Dealing with a wide range of rights owners and types of media, in various national legal frameworks, will be necessary with multimedia cross-border service on the Superhighway, and here again the BBC has experience of such dealing.

3.67 So what is different? One factor, perhaps, is that the BBC constitutes its own central unit for contractual dealings, whereas there is no such unit to facilitate the placing of multimedia on to the Highway. As a result, rights owners have in the BBC just one focal body, thus knowing who to trust – supported by contract – not to infringe, or who to blame if infringement occurs. The BBC also has experience in the problems of tracing ownership, which can change so much, especially outside the regime of academic materials, and even more specially in respect of overseas materials. Each element in a multimedia programme may have its own rights, including performing rights, plus copyright in the programme as a compilation. In the EC, database rights could further complicate the situation. There is also a danger of unwitting secondary infringement through the (locally) legal incorporation of a work into a service and then supplying service to a country in which that incorporation is an illegal act. The rapid growth of the World Wide Web for storing and accessing documents in hypertext format is notable as the start of the Superhighway. Doubtless multimedia with full moving image/sound capabilities will be incorporated as soon as technically and legally possible. However, there may well be a perpetual problem of what and when to relegate to separate archival systems.

Central registry

3.68 Were a central registry to be set up as part of a national agency (Appendix 5/2), it could not only negotiate on behalf of clients but also effect control of authorisation to input encrypted copyright material on to the Highway, thus helping with policing and reducing the Net's tendency to accumulate space-eating rubbish. Because so many different publishers and producers will be involved, standard contracts, including one on multimedia, would seem to be essential (see 12.29). In Appendix 1/8 are listed some 'Steps towards the Highway', or documents/events of importance in recent years, and several are relevant to multimedia. The Government reports listed there are more examples of considerable official interest. In particular, in 1996 the EC published an extensive 'practical guide' to copyright law and problems for multimedia producers, and this publication is also of more general interest (Appendix 1/7). If there is to be a really Superhighway, why cannot past protagonists from the era of photocopying controversy work towards a system regulated as much by honesty, fairness, and mutual respect for rights and needs, as by statute and contract? However, this could be an impossible dream in such an economically competitive area as this, described by an EC White Paper on *Growth, competitiveness, employment: the challenges and ways forward into the 21st century* in the following terms:

> 'The dawning of a multimedia world represents a radical change comparable with the first industrial revolution'.

4. RIGHTS OF OWNERSHIP: COPYRIGHT, DATABASE RIGHT

Restricted acts and permitted acts

Note on scope:

This chapter is concerned with ownership rights other than those covered in chapter 3, the prefatory note of which may be relevant here also, and includes the new lending/rental and database rights. The latter, however, is treated as a whole in 3.28 et seq., outlined in Q0 and Q13-14, and commented on in Appendix 3/5.

4.1 The law's main approach is to define a number of kinds of protection, or forms of right, as 'restricted acts' (4.10 below). These are followed by exceptions to those rights, which result in a number of 'permitted acts' as listed in the outlines at the front of this volume and detailed in chapter 5 onwards. The first requirement here is to discuss the ownership of rights.

First owner

4.2 It is considered neither appropriate nor convenient to split all treatments of ownership from authorship. Other chapters, especially 2 and 3, necessarily refer to ownership of rights because this is bound up with authorship. Exceptionally, this chapter contains separate treatment of 'first owner' in respect of commissioning, Crown copyright and Parliamentary copyright (4.5-4.8).

Recapitulating the essentials in a different manner here, the ownership of copyright is normally vested initially in the author (writer, composer, etc.) as first owner. Why only normally? Firstly because, when an employee makes a literary, dramatic, musical or artistic work in the course of his employment under a contract of employment or apprenticeship, the first owner of any copyright in the work is the employer, unless there is any agreement to the contrary (s11). Secondly, when a work names no personal author, or gives an unidentifiable pseudonym, it is treated as anonymous. In this case the first owner may be a publisher, if the author has assigned his rights to that publisher and failed to assert his moral right to be identified as author (10.9). Otherwise, there is no first owner, and no publication would occur until it became reasonable to assume that copyright had expired (7.28).

The CDPA88 term 'first owner' reflects the fact that copyright can be assigned or sold in whole or part, or leased, or gifted, and this refers also to separate rights in the same item, such as book rights, film rights, serialisation rights, and so on.

The rights in this book form an example. At present, Aslib is permitted by contract exclusively to publish this material in book form in return for providing the author with royalties on sales. This book generates for Aslib itself a copyright in the typographical layout for 25 years. But the author has retained ownership of the copyright in all the content and could publish it in other forms or use it as a basis for other works, if so desired, as indeed could any heirs for 70 years after his death.

The first owner of database right is the maker, that is, '*the person who takes the initiative in making a database and assumes the risk of investing in its making*'. At least until there has been more experience of working with database right, there may be uncertainty regarding just who is the maker of a given database. Meanwhile, users will feel it reasonable to regard a person named as a compiler or editor as the maker, unless the making is known to have occurred by such a person in the course of employment, when the employer shall be regarded as the maker subject to any agreement to the contrary. Database right is a property right which only subsists if there has been a *substantial investment in obtaining, verifyng or presenting the contents of the database*. 'Investment' can include any kind, *whether of financial, human or technical resources.*

Dealings

4.3 The Act uses the term 'dealings' to mean assignment of rights, whether for payment or otherwise. For a best-selling novel, other procedures than a simple licence to publish would be worth considering (ss90-95). The author, if copyright ownership had been retained, could sell separately the film and/or serialisation rights. The owner could also sell or give someone an exclusive licence to make an adaptation or re-publish extracts or the whole of the content. Publishing agreements, of course, are best drawn up by experts. The owner could bequeath rights in specific works to beneficiaries of a will, including moral rights. When unpublished or unmarketed materials change hands by will, the beneficiary also owns copyright, provided there is no evidence to the contrary (s93). For example, the deceased might have specifically excluded copyright from the bequest, or evidence might be found that the author had assigned all rights in a specific work to someone else, or at some time past he might have assigned all future rights to someone in respect of works not yet written (s91). For databases, ss90-93 apply to database right as much as to copyright.

Shared ownership

4.4 In shared ownership whether after assignment or otherwise, the relevant people may be differently involved in respect of rights. So, for a particular purpose, the rights owner is taken to be the person whose entitlement applies to that purpose. For databases made jointly, the new law states that the 'maker' of a database is to be taken as a reference to all the makers of the database. Where authorship or making is joint in a whole work or a database, any licence would require the agreement of all authors (s173) or all makers of a database.

Commissioned works

4.5 CDPA88 removed provisions under earlier law whereby the commissioner of a photograph, portrait or engraving was first owner of copyright. For example, as remarked in 2.29, a photographer is now an author, on equal terms with, say, a journalist. The photographer as author is now also the first owner, unless a contract is made to the contrary. Works not yet completed at the time of commencement of the new Act on 1 August 1989 are governed by the earlier law, as indeed are all works which existed on 31 July 1989. The new law has however created a relevant moral right about photographs only: that a commissioner for private and domestic purposes has a form of a negative right, namely to object to the public display, showing or exhibition of photographs made under the commission (10.16).

4.6 A commission must pre-date the work. When a commissioner needs to have first ownership, this must be clearly written into the commissioning contract, for example:

> 'Copyright, and any other rights in the nature of copyright, in materials produced in accordance with or arising out of this agreement shall vest in the person who commissioned the work or works.'

Of course, the author might not accept such a commission, especially when possessed of well-known expertise. Then, either an alternative author would need to be sought, or some contractual compromise be worked out to the satisfaction of commissioner and author. The only references to commissioning in CDPA88, apart from transitional provisions, concern designs (ss215; 219).

Crown copyright

4.7 As indicated in 2.45, this is not limited by the usual qualifications for protection, and has a long fixed duration independent of an author's life. Her Majesty is first owner of copyright in a work made by her or by an officer or servant of the Crown in the course of his duties (s163) and similarly first owner of a database so made. This includes any civil servant and therefore any member of a government department who creates a work as part of his job. It excludes material created by someone else who is acting under the direction or control of a government department but is not himself an officer or servant of the Crown. A provision of earlier law that Crown copyright would subsist in every original work made by or under the direction or control of Her Majesty or a government department has been removed by the new law. Those with government research contracts made before 1 August 1989 should ascertain who is first owner of materials arising out of the work, since those contracts would not have needed to specify Crown ownership although it would have subsisted. Of course, those with ongoing research contracts of any date or sponsor should always be aware of the copyright situation. The remarks on commissioned works in 4.6 above therefore apply here also, replacing the last words of the suggested clause with 'shall vest in the Crown'.

Parliamentary copyright

4.8 As described in 2.49, this new provision accords rights in respect of works made by or under the direction or control of either House (s165). As with Crown copyright, a work can be Parliamentary copyright irrespective of the usual qualifications for protection (s153). The House concerned is first owner of copyright in a work made by an officer or employee in the course of his duties, and any sound recording, film, live broadcast or live cable programme of the proceedings of the House. This can be the case when works have been commissioned, since similar wording to that which used to apply to Crown Copyright is employed here. However, works are not automatically regarded as 'made by or under the direction or control' of a House just because they were commissioned by the House (s165(4)) – therefore a commissioning contract, similar to Crown Copyright, should preferably specify copyright ownership.

Also similiarly to Crown Copyright, a work of joint authorship can be only partially Parliamentary copyright if not all the authors were under the direction or control of a House.

4.9 Bills

Public Bill

The first owner of copyright is the House into which the Bill was first introduced by handing in the text. Thus rights in the Copyright (etc.) Bill 1987 were first owned by the House of Lords, then jointly owned by both Houses when the Bill went to the Commons early in 1988; but the rights ceased with Royal Assent of the Act on 15 November 1988.

Private Bill

Both Houses share ownership from the time of first deposit in either House.

Personal Bill

Copyright dates from the First Reading in the House of Lords and that House is first owner of rights, which then become jointly owned by both Houses when the Bill goes to the House of Commons.

Rights of copyright owners

4.10 CDPA88, as mentioned earlier, specifies restricted acts. These in effect define exclusive rights, that is rights which only the owner may control for the duration of copyright.

Only the owner may do or authorise the following, apart from any exceptions or permissions given by the Act:

(a) copy the work
(b) issue copies to the public, by publishing it or other means
(c) rent or lend the work to the public (4.35 et seq.)
(d) perform, show or play the work in public
(e) broadcast the work or include it in a cable programme service (of which more later)
(f) adapt the work or do any of the above in relation to an adaptation.

Infringement: general

4.11 Copyright law aims to protect intellectual property, but how can copyright itself be protected? The police can be called to seek out a burglar or car thief, etc., but is this a remedy for properties like copyright? To the surprise of some readers, the answer is 'yes' in respect of deliberate infringement for profit (4.29).

Just as litigation is the only recourse for anyone suffering damage to honour or reputation, so the courts provide the only means for a copyright owner to seek redress or 'remedies' for infringement. Some notes on infringement have already appeared in the context of nonprint media (3.29). The five exclusive rights or 'restricted acts' above are those actions which could infringe copyright unless otherwise permitted or licensed. Infringement of database right occurs if a person extracts or re-utlises all or a substantial part of the contents. The 'repeated and systematic' extraction, etc may amount to a substantial part.

Restricted acts: definitions

The definitions are as follows, relevant to 4.10(a) to (f)

4.12 Copying a work (4.10(a))

This means reproducing it in any material form, irrespective of dimensional changes (s17). Copying includes storing a work electronically, and includes transient copying such as that which would arise when inputting a work to a computer-based system in order to produce an adaptation.

However, as indicated earlier, this does not mean that an electronic form of record of text would be copyright in itself, as if it were a typographical arrangement on a printed page. Electronic records of text do not carry copyright in themselves, unlike a published edition of a book, but they do of course carry the copyright in the work represented.

4.13 Computer programs

In fact, storing a work electronically is tantamount to providing a means of making multiple copies (s17(2)), and even transient copying infringes (s17(6)). The unauthorised keying-in of a hard copy program would therefore infringe if a substantial part or more were affected, which would apply to virtually all situations with programs in printed form. Unauthorised reading-in of a computer program in electronic format would likewise infringe as far as the Act is concerned. Unauthorised adaptations, including translations, infringe copyright (s21), and 'translation' includes the conversion of a program from one programming or machine language into another, otherwise than incidentally when running the program. Nevertheless, a form of fair dealing may be applicable, arising from some permissions in SI 1992/3233 which came into force concerning programs made before or after 1 January 1993 unless modified by contract before that date (7.15-7.20). (See also 4.45).

4.14 Reprography

In respect of a 'published edition', copying includes making a facsimile copy of the typographical arrangement, for example by reprography. A 'reprographic process' is in fact defined as a means for making facsimile copies, or a process which involves a photocopier or other machine for making multiple copies, and includes copying by electronic means when a work is held electronically (s178).

A 'facsimile copy' includes a copy which is reduced or enlarged in scale (s178) and therefore covers microforms as indicated previously (2.31).

In respect of an artistic work, copying includes a three-dimensional copy of a two-dimensional work and vice versa. In respect of films, television broadcasts or cable programmes, copying includes making a photograph of any image.

4.15 Databases: extraction/re-utilisation

In SI 1997/3032, 'extraction' is defined in relation to contents as:

> the permanent or temporary transfer of those contents to another medium by any means or in any form.

'Re-utilisation' means:

> making those contents available to the public by any means.

In short, extraction is simply copying of any kind or form; whereas re-utilisation implies placing a copied extract (or the whole) in another context and making it available to the public, thus implying permission for using 'insubstantial parts'.

Infringement could be claimed if either or both actions occur in respect of all or a 'substantial part' of the contents. However, as remarked elsewhere, the repeated and systematic extraction of such parts may amount to a substantial part. Actions under agreements made before 1 January 1998 are unaffected by the new law, but otherwise, the law can be applied to databases made before or after commencement.

4.16 Infringing copy

An 'infringing copy' is one which has been made from a copyright work without authorisation of some kind. (s27). The phrase 'primary infringement' is not used in the Act, which only specifies 'secondary'. However, 'primary' could be applied to any action taken without permission in respect of any of the restricted acts (4.12-4.26) involving more than a substantial part.

When a copy has been made with permission for a particular purpose, such as research or private study, 'infringing copy' *includes* (s27) such a copy used for one of the purposes covered by the following sections of CDPA88: 32(5), copies for instruction or examination; 35(3), recordings by educational establishments for educational purposes;36(5), reprographic copying by educational establishments for the purposes of instruction; 37(3)(b), copies made by a librarian or archivist in reliance on a false declaration' 56(2), further copies, adaptations, etc of work in electronic form retained on transfer of principal work; 63(2), copies made for purposes of advertising artistic work for sale; 68(4), copies made for purpose of broadcast or cable programme, or any provision of an order under section 141 (statutory licence for certain reprographic copying by educational establishments.

Notes on 'secondary infringement' appear in 4.27-4.28. For example, when an imported copy of a work would have infringed if it had been made in the UK, or would have breached an exclusive licence or contract about the work, the copy is an infringing copy.

4.17 Issue to public, publication and commercial publication (4.10(b))

The definition of 'issue to the public' in s18 of CDPA88 is very important, not least because it is a major 'restricted act', now also known as the 'distribution right'. 'Issue to the public' covers the first act of putting copies into circulation, not just in the UK but anywhere else, and not later distribution of those copies or later importation of such copies. Unauthorised rental or lending would infringe this right. Reg. 9 of SI 1996/2967amends the definition, changing references to 'UK' to 'EEA' (European Economic Area), and adds a new s18A on rental/lending right (4.35 et seq. below). ('Copies' includes the original.)

4.18 'Publication' is a form of 'issue of copies to the public'. For literary, dramatic, musical or artistic works, the term includes making available via an electronic retrieval system (s175). Physical formats – sound recordings and films – are not so published, nor does such

4.19 'Commercial publication' means issue of literary etc. works to the public:

- when copies have been made in advance of orders and are generally available to the public, or
- making a literary etc. work available to the public via an electronic retrieval system.

4.20 Excluded from 'publication' are,

1. for literary, dramatic or musical works:
- performing a work, or
- broadcasting or including it in a cable programme service other than an electronic retrieval system;

2. for artistic works:
- exhibiting the work
- issue to the public of graphic representations (drawings, photographs, etc.) of a building or model for a building, a sculpture, or a work of artistic craftsmanship
- issue to the public of copies of a film including the work
- broadcasting the work or including it in a cable programme service other than an electronic retrieval system;

3. for sound recordings or films and videos:
- playing or showing the work in public
- broadcasting the work or including it in a cable programme service.

However, although the latter do not constitute 'publication, they *do* constitute 'making available to the public' (s12) and can affect the duration of copyright in respect of anonymous works (2.33-2.36) in the following manner.

If a novel by a known author were first to be broadcast from the author's manuscript, for example by reading in parts, this would *not* be publication. But the broadcasting organisation would have copyright in the broadcast for 50 years and there would be performing right in the actual reading. However, if the novel were anonymous, broadcasting counts as making available to the public, and copyright in the novel itself, as well as in the broadcast, would then expire 70 years beyond the year of broadcast (s12(2) as revised by SI 1995/3297).

However, whether or not anonymous, periodical articles which were first made available to the public in an electronic retrieval system are commercially published from that time. This starts a copyright period of 50 years for the database producer (as a cable programme service), earlier than a publisher's copyright for 25 years if hard copy is later issued. Thus an 'electronic journal' is commercially published. (Any authors' rights in the content at life plus 70 years are of course unaffected by this.)

4.21 Rent or lend the work to the public (4.10(c))

Newly defined as a restricted act (s18A, 4.35 et seq. and 9.37).

4.22 Performing, showing or playing the work in public (4.10(d)

This includes delivery in the case of lectures, addresses, speeches and sermons, and in general includes '*any mode of visual or acoustic presentation, including ... sound recording, film, broadcast or cable programme...*' (s19).

In respect of (d), the difference between *performing* and *performance* should be noted. 'Performing, showing or playing' refers to performance in public of a copyright work by whatever means, and is an exclusive right under Part I (Copyright) of the Act to permit or prohibit, like other restricted acts. 'Performance' relates (a) to a live performer's exclusive right under Part II of the Act to give consent to the recording of his performance; and (b) to his right to benefit from commercial production and sale, etc. of copies of recordings. The rights of a live performer are called 'rights in performances' but, in respect of (a), note that a live performance is *not* copyright unless and until recorded. Thus there appears to be nothing in the Act to indicate that closely imitating another performer's style would infringe copyright, but copying his content – the songs or jokes or catchphrases etc – could well infringe. Note further that, when a copyright work is repeatedly performed live by different performers, each successive performer acquires the above rights in his own performance. (See 9.37 on permissions.)

4.23 Broadcasting the work or including it in a cable programme service (4.10(e))

This is a restricted act in respect of literary, dramatic, musical or artistic works; audiovisual media; and broadcasts or cable programmes. Copyright in broadcasting etc as services has been described in 3.8 et seq., and 3.14 on a mooted transmission right. (See also 4.21.)

A 'broadcast' is defined as a wireless transmission of images , sounds, etc which is:

> capable of being lawfully received by members of the public, or is transmitted for presentation to members of the public.

An encrypted transmission can only be *lawfully received* by members of the public when decoding equipment has been made available to them with the authority of the broadcasters or the provider of the content (s6(2)). Safeguards re satellite broadcasting are introduced by SI 1996/2967 Reg. 6, and Reg. 7 provides for *compulsory collective administration of certain cable re-transmission rights.*

4.24 Making an adaptation of the work or doing any of the foregoing in relation to an adaptation (s21) (4.10(f))

In respect of a literary, dramatic or musical work, this includes:

1) translation of the work
2) converting a literary work into a dramatic version or vice versa
3) producing a serial version, or a pictorial version
4) making an arrangement or transcription of a musical work.

In 1) 'translation' includes the conversion of computer programming languages or codes, otherwise than incidental conversion in the course of running a program. Examples of 3) are: a children's picture book based on text; or a cartoon version of a detective story.

4.25 Artistic works are excluded from this restricted act. Possibly the restriction of copying under (a) is as much as may be found desirable or necessary, after singling out a case of copying in three or two dimensions as noted above.

4.26 The fact that a work is an adaptation does not automatically mean that copying of the work has occurred: aspects of copying would require assessment.

Secondary infringement

4.27 This can arise when, again without licence from the rights owner, a person takes an action and knows or has reason to believe that infringement is or will be involved. Information users are unlikely to be affected, but those interested should study ss22-26 of the Act. The main restricted acts are:

- possessing or dealing with an infringing copy or a means of making infringing copies (4.16)
- transmission otherwise by broadcast or cable programme for a receiver in the UK or elsewhere to use for making infringing copies
- permitting use of premises or apparatus for infringing performances.

4.28 Only the first of these calls for particular comment as far as most users are concerned: namely, 'a means of making infringing copies'. Some users have read this as a possible basis for prohibiting photocopying machines, but this is not the case. The Act's wording refers to an article specifically designed or adapted for making copies of that work (s24). CDPA88 dropped the 1956 Act's reference to a 'plate' in order to make the new wording cover all articles specifically designed or adapted for making copies of a particular work and this clearly implies actual plates or masters for a particular item.

Infringement 'remedies' or penalties: criminal or civil liability

4.29 Those who infringe the rights in the Act by doing any of the above 'restricted acts' without authorisation may be *criminally* liable for punitive damages or imprisonment. Infringement can be very serious in cases of deliberate infringement for profit, called 'piracy' by rights owners. Piracy of sound or video tapes and their distribution or sale, for example, or another action aimed at commercial gain, could be expected to invoke the consideration of such penalties. Also in respect of piracy in audiovisual recordings, the Act gives rights to the copyright owner against anyone dealing in electronic devices designed to circumvent any 'copy-protection' methods which may have been incorporated into a recording (s296). Similar protection is given to broadcasts or cable services consisting of 'encrypted' (encoded) transmissions (ss297; 298). CDPA88 uses the phrase *criminal liability* for the first time in UK copyright law, although it has been possible in the past for civil actions to result in prison sentences.

Under database right (3.28), some rights and remedies sections of CDPA88 under copyright, namely ss96-98 (rights and remedies of copyright owners) and ss101-102 (rights and remedis of exclusive licensee), apply similarly under the new right. Unlike copyright, there is no section which relates to 'criminal liability', but this should not be taken as a sign of less stringent remedies for database infringements. Provisions as to licensing of database right are set out in Schedule 2 to SI 1997/3032, which extends certain authority in to the Copyright Tribunal in respect of licensing schemes and licensing bodies, provided *the Tribunal is satisfied that the organisation is reasonably representative of the class of persons which it claims to represent.*

4.30 Civil liability

In most cases, however, especially where deliberate infringement for profit is not involved, a penalty might consist of an injunction forbidding further infringement, a court order to send all infringing copies to the rights owners, and an award of damages, usually better settled out of court. The details regarding penalties should be studied directly in the Act by anyone in danger of infringing (ss107-115). Those at risk of infringement should note that a senior staff member can be made personally liable (s110). Thus, a company director who deliberately allows his firm to continue infringing copyright by excessive photocopying, for example, after turning down a licensing offer, might find himself arrested without warning.

4.31 Rights owners are unlikely to prosecute, say, a student who steps over the mark on copying, but might be interested in bringing a test case in respect of instances of copying in a firm which exceed rights- owner norms of fair or reasonable copying extents. It is recommended that all users should keep within the limits given in this volume and other guidelines, for laxity can spread like a computer virus or a rabble-rousing slogan and undermine any code of conduct, whether based on ethics or law. Basically, as remarked in 1.23, copyright depends on individual honesty. So a user who might consider infringement for private use, on the basis that no-one would ever know, should give due thought to what could happen to the copy later and put himself in the position of a copyright owner. When using self-service copying equipment it is in any event essential to follow the guidance given by notices or staff about copiable extents, otherwise the organisation concerned could be at risk of sharing blame if litigation ensued (6.31).

4.32 Substantial part

An action cannot infringe unless it involves the whole or a 'substantial part', which it is not possible to define except in relation to a particular work and the circumstances involved (ss16,17). Case law already exists, however, establishing that 'substantial' relates not only to extent but also to the significance of content. It was remarked in the House of Lords during passage of CDPA88 that only one single note of a song might be judged a 'substantial part' if it called to mind the entire song and were used in a commercial advertisement. Similarly, a precis which made it unnecessary to consult the work itself in order to grasp the essential content could be subject to challenge by rights owners.

Any permission in the Act (chapters 5, 6, 7, 9) removes the necessity for a user to limit his action to less than a substantial part, whatever he may think that is in a particular set of circumstances. The permissions really constitute allowable defences in the event of infringement claims.

Under database right, the terms 'substantial' or 'insubstantial' parts are used. Like 'substantial part' under copyright, no attempt is made to set statutory limits (for similar reasons). Unlike copyright, the user may be able to reach discretionary decisions by weighing the two terms when seeking to extract or re-utilise parts of databases. However, both are to be defined 'quantitatively or qualitatively', which has long been the situation for copyright anyway under case law.

Other rights and remedies

4.33 Several CDPA88 provisions relate to rights and remedies in fraud situations: devices designed to circumvent technical means of copy-protection (s296); fraudulent reception of broadcasts of cable programmes (ss297-299); fraudulent application or use of a trade mark (s300). The second of these could apply, for example, to the use of an online database without due payment. The last relevant section of the Act affects rights indirectly, for it provides for financial assistance to certain international bodies having functions relating to trade marks or other intellectual property (s302), on which nothing further will appear in this volume. A special right is conferred on the Hospital for Sick Children (s301), further remarked upon in 14.2. Otherwise, the major rights of rental and lending follow below in 4.35 et seq.

Lawful user

4.34 Before SI 1992/3233 in implementation of a EC Directive on computer software, there were no 'rights' as such for users, only permissions or exceptions in respect of restrictions. The policy re computer programs (7.16-7.18) has been followed under the new database right arising from SI 1997/3032, wherein a 'lawful user' is defined to mean 'any person ... who has a right to use the database' – not a helpful decision at present in this context

(Appendix 3/5). The rights of a lawful user, under an agreement, to use a database which has been 'made available to the public in any manner' cannot be overridden by any term in the agreement which purports to prevent the lawful user from exercising his rights in a way which does not infringe any database right subsisting in the database. Similar provisions re copyright in a database (that is, at compilation level) are made by insertion of new ss50D and 296B.

Rental and lending

4.35 The law made by CDPA88 concerning the rental or lending of copyright works *to the public* has been revised by SI 1996/2967. Under this, effective 1 December 1996 in implementation of a 1992 EC Directive, rental right no longer covers only sound recordings, films and computer programs, and public lending right is no longer confined to books. The extensions are all made by means of CDPA88 amendments without changing the Public Lending Right Act 1979. The rights to permit or disallow rental/lending belong to authors of original works, to recording and film companies in respect of physical formats, and to performers in respect of fixations of their live performances. Publishers of printed matter, although 'authors of typographical arrangements' in other respects, hold no rental/lending right except when transferred to them by authors of original works. The lending of books to the public is unaffected, being regarded as covered by existing Public Lending Right law (4.48; 14.8).

Lending to the public of other materials, categorised in 4.38 below, will require public libraries to seek licences, but such action is no longer to be defined as 'rental' unless charges result in returns which exceed administrative costs of the service. The new law has ramifications in respect of rights in performances and further details follow.

4.36 Rental definition

The definition of 'rental' per se, as laid down in CDPA88(s178), is unchanged:

'rental' means any arrangement under which a copy of a work is made available –

(a) for payment (in money or money's worth), or
(b) in the course of a business, as part of services or amenities for which payment is made, on terms that it will or may be returned.

'Money's worth' in the above definition of rental per se includes payment via a subscription for library service or club membership. It should be noted that this defines 'rental' per se and not the restricted act of 'rental to the public' below, and that it does not mention profit or administrative charges. Hence *any* payment of this kind may be regarded as 'rental' unless otherwise agreed or permitted by statute in particular contexts. Public library loans of recordings, films and computer programs in electronic format were to be regarded by CDPA88 as 'rental' even if only an administrative charge were made. Licences will continue to be necessary for lending (or rental where the profit regime is entered) of materials other than books (including computer programs in electronic form).

The lending of books by public libraries, and by other nonprofit-based libraries or archives accessible to public, is permitted (4.39) owing to the existence of Public Lending Right. A definition of 'lending' to public is now provided, and permissions indicate no change in library lending of books containing printed text and illustrations thereof. Of libraries and archives as a whole, only public libraries are affected by the newly extended rights in respect of lending non-book materials. However, any organisation intent on rental will need licensing.

Until 1 December 1996, any royalties from rental of sound recordings, films or computer programs would have been due to the recording or software companies as 'authors' of those formats, leaving authors of the original works to negotiate a share by contract. Similarly, performers would have needed to seek, had the sound recording and other industries arranged for commercial rental to be licensed at all, a share of any rental income in their contracts with recording companies. Such contractual arrangements may well still arise in some form or another, whether incorporating or separate from new unwaivable rights of personal authors (4.40) and performers (4.42) to 'equitable remuneration' in respect of rental/lending.

4.37 Definitions of rental/lending right

In order to be at risk of infringement, the *public* must be involved. From new s18A of the Act:

> '"rental" means making a copy of the work available for use, on terms that it will or may be returned, for direct or indirect economic or commercial advantage, [and] 'lending' means making a copy of the work available for use, on terms that it will or may be returned, otherwise than for direct or indirect economic advantage, through an establishment which is accessible to the public.'

This applies also under database right, where making available a copy of a database on such terms will not constitute 'extraction or re-utilisation' of contents. 'Lending' excludes making available between establishments which are publicly accessible, being regarded as non-public lending. When any payment to such an establishment does not exceed operating costs, there is considered to be no economic or commercial advantage to that establishment (cf 6.3 on profit). Any publicly accessible establishment which derived an income for loans to public in excess of operating costs would be practising 'rental' and require licensing, as indeed would any other organisation making any charge at all for loans to public.

Both 'rental' and 'lending' *exclude* 'making available for the purpose of public performance, playing or showing in public, broadcasting or inclusion in a cable programme service' (these being covered in other ways in any case); 'exhibition in public; or reference use on the spot'.

Under database right, however, the provision concerning lending above is not repeated as applicable to reference use, the implication being that reference users are capable of extraction etc, and must be governed by database right provisions.

It should be noted that: any clientele other than a domestic or quasi-domestic group should be taken as 'public' – unless the Act (e.g. s34) or a contract defines 'public' differently. rental to the public does not, unlike 'lending', have to be through an establishment which is accessible to the public; loans to the public become 'rental' for any establishment when payments exceed operating costs and result in economic or commercial advantage; any person or organisation not covered by statutory permission will need licensing of some kind or other; and that no rental is permissible without licence.

For an updated Schedule 1 CDPA88 on transitional provisions and savings, readers should refer to the *Aslib guide to copyright* (Appendix 1/2) or another reference work which keeps continuously up to date. Materials acquired before 1 December 1996 for public rental or lending are unaffected, thus library stocks then existing are unaffected. Nothing in the new Regulations affects an agreement made before 19 November 1992, nor can pursuance of such an agreement be regarded as *infringement of any new right* included, other than a right to equitable remuneration.

4.38 Authorisation of rental/lending

Now, authors of original literary, dramatic, musical or artistic works have an exclusive right either to authorise or to prohibit rental/lending to the public, whatever the physical format of those works. Producers of audio-visual materials also have this control in respect of the formats they produce. Performers can either authorise or prohibit the rental/lending of fixations of their live performances. However, both the authors and the performers are subject to certain legal permissions built into the SI.

Otherwise than by permission or licence, rental or lending to the public of the following will infringe unless statutorily permitted, and this is taken as referring to the whole period of copyright:

i) films, videos and sound recordings (but note that a film/video, when it has an identifiable personal author, now has the norm of author's life plus 70 years, whereas sound recordings remain at 50-100 years along with other films);
ii) literary, dramatic or musical works – duration is life plus 70 years (it is suggested that this category be taken as including written or printed formats – including electronic 'writing' of musical scores and computer programs; recordings of performances being in category (i)).
iii) artistic works – duration 70 years, but rental does not apply to a building or model for one; or a *work of applied art* – suggested as meaning a sculpture, craft item or other work for which public display is inherent. (Artistic works have no right of showing or performance as such (s19).)

In (i), note that a film director or sound recordist to whom rental/lending right has been transferred by an author and/or performer will also be entitled to his own rental royalty as 'author' of the format. This overlaps the right of an author of content, or a performer, to equitable remuneration for rental/lending of recordings and films (4.40) in the event of such transfer.

In respect of (ii), note that the rental of computer programs is no longer mentioned specifically by the SI, since authors of any kind now have rental/lending rights, and a computer programmer's work is 'literary' regardless of physical form, an electronic format being merely 'writing'. Compared with the pre-SI situation, it is the author who now has first right to remuneration for rental and not a software house which produces copies. Similarly, the 50-year period which formerly applied can be considered removed, since the author's rental right applies for the copyright norm of life plus 70 years.

4.39 Permitted lending

Permissions are specified in respect of lending by nonprofit-based libraries and educational establishments, as follows. In addition, any statutory permission which allows *any* action for certain purposes (such as judiciary proceedings, 7.9) will apply here also. Permissions are also concisely stated in 9.36.

Educational establishments

Lending of *any kind* of work to the public does not infringe copyright. This should not be taken as applying also to rental to public. However, classes in educational establishments are not defined in other contexts (e.g. playing or showing, 9.5) as 'public' audiences. Nor is it clear why those establishments should be thought to be 'open to public' in this context and thus invoke the definition of 'lending'. Pending possible future clarification, educational establishments are recommended to avoid 'rental' (which means making any charge at all) to non-students of theirs (see 15.79). (New s36A; see also note about permission re performers' rights in 4.41.)

Public libraries

New s40A provides that '*Copyright in a work of any description is not infringed by the lending of a book by a public library if the book is within the public lending right scheme*' (SI 1982/719, as amended). In this context a 'book' is defined by Regulation 11 of SI 1996/2967 as follows:

> 'a book is within the public lending right scheme if it is a book within the meaning of the provisions of the scheme relating to eligibility, whether or not it is in fact eligible.'

The above words about 'eligibility' are clearly unclear! It is suggested that the sentence be taken to mean that, for the purposes of rental/lending rights, *all* books of text and accompanying illustrations are to be considered eligible for this permission, whether or not they accord with PLR eligibility details. The definition of PLR-eligibility is itself rather limited (4.45).

Nonprofit-based libraries or archives other than public libraries

New s40A is interpreted to permit the lending of any kind of work. Thus such services will only require licences if they make charges *for loans to public* which exceed operating costs, and therefore enter the rental right regime.

A saving is made concerning copies acquired before 1 December 1996; see end of 4.37 above. A note on permission also appears as 9.36.

4.40 Transfer of rental right by author: equitable remuneration (sound recordings or films)

Upon transfer of rental right by an author (or composer, etc) to a recording company or film company, a *right of equitable remuneration* is retained by the author (new s93B) in the event of *rental* of a sound recording or film (including video). This new right cannot be overridden by contract, cannot be waived and cannot be assigned by the author except to a collecting society, but can be bequeathed or sold on as property, after which it may be assigned or otherwise further transmitted by the holder. The authors concerned are described as *the author of a literary, dramatic, musical or artistic work* and the principal director of a film.

Equitable remuneration must be paid by the current holder of rental right via the collecting society which acts on an author's behalf. The remuneration rate is subject to arbitration by the Copyright Tribunal (new s93C). However, the SI states that a single payment, made at the time of transfer of rental right, would not be considered inequitable. Because of statutory backing, the effect is that the equitable remuneration will be the minimum benefit to be received which cannot be negotiated away. Note that there is no such thing as equitable remuneration right when rental right for other media is transferred, any benefit being subject only to contractual arrangements between an author and a producing body.

In the video hire industry, the producing companies have long practised 'up-front' pricing to cover rental royalties in advance, through a single sum added into the purchase price. The extent to which authors (script writers, composers, artists, etc) may be found amenable to continuing this method is unknown at this time, but some might do so if contracts with producing companies gave appropriate recompense. However, this situation could become further complicated if performers were to insist on market limitations in contracts in consequence of their own new rights.

Performers' rights

4.41 A performer already has the right to refuse consent for a recording of his live performance, and this is now styled his *reproduction right*. The SI has extended and formalised performers' rights in various ways. A performer's consent in contract to the making and issue of copies for the public is now styled *distribution right* whereby he can *authorise or prohibit the issue of* *copies to the public* (new s182B). The performer's consent is also needed for lending or rental of copies to the public.

The *lending* (but not rental) of copies of a recording of a performance by educational establishments, or by nonprofit-based libraries/archives *other than public libraries*, will not infringe performers' Part II rights by virtue of new ss 6A, 6B and 14A in CDPA88, Schedule 2 (see 4.37 above for Part I copyright permissions). The effect is to exclude any statutory basis for a performer to benefit from *lending* by library/archival services except those controlled by local authorities. It should be noted further that:

(a) SI 1996/2967 also adds to CDPA88 a new Schedule 2A on *Licensing of performers' property rights:*
(b) A copy of a recording of a performance which has been acquired before 1 December 1996 is unaffected by any new right in a performance covered by that SI.

4.42 Equitable remuneration – performers

A performer may be expected to transfer his rental/lending right for copies of recordings of his performances to an audiovisual recording or cinema film company. He nevertheless retains an unwaivable right to *equitable remuneration* in the event of *rental*, excluding copies rented or loaned for public performance, etc (4.37). That remuneration is payable by the current copyright owner or transferee of rental right and payment by a single sum is possible. The equitable remuneration right may only be assigned to a collecting society for the purposes of enforcement.

However, equitable remuneration is specified as applicable *only* to rental right transfers of sound recordings or films made on or after 1 April 1997. There is also a provision whereby rentals after that date of sound recordings or films made under agreements in force before 1 July 1994 do not carry equitable remuneration entitlement, unless the right-holder has before 1 January 1997 notified the person liable to pay that he intends to exercise the right. As the SI became available only at the beginning of December 1996, this allowed only a month for performers to realise the situation and act accordingly, hence there was considerable protest (such as that reported as '*The great video diddle: stars hit out at ministers over backdated fees*' in the *Daily Express* of 20 December 1996.The duration of all a performer's rights in fixations of his performances is taken as coincident with copyright duration in sound recordings, namely 50 years (s191) (see Appendix 3/4 re Spoken Word Association).

4.43 Public performance

Additionally to rental/lending right, a performer also has a right to equitable remuneration for the *exploitation* (by public performance, broadcast or cable programme service) of sound recordings of his live performances (films/videos are not mentioned, being artistic works omitted from s19 and having no showing/performing right), payable by the owner of copyright in the sound recording. Thus the SI formalises the entitlement of performers to equitable remuneration for such public performances (new s182D) of sound recordings. It will be for performers, recording companies and existing collecting societies, especially PPL (9.6) as already mentioned above, to seek equitable arrangements (more or less as at present, except that an individual performer now has statutory backing). (Note that rental for the purposes of public performance is excluded from rental right (4.36)).

Licensing of rental/lending

4.44 Note that 'lending' is defined in 4.36 *only* in terms of access to a nonprofit-based service by an establishment *which is accessible to the public*. That phrase is taken to include *any* nonprofit-based library or archive which is open to, or provides service usable by, members of the public. However, for emphasis, it is clear that *all materials rented* to the public will require licensing coverage.

It is when publicly accessible services charge for lending, and could be defined as operating for economic or commercial advantage, that their actions become 'rental'. Moreover, because of the definition of rental per se in 4.35, the absence of such advantage would need to be demonstrated by a prospective service provider, hence it behoves any service or person making any kind of charge for loans to approach rights owners and discuss possible licensing needs.

Publicly accessible services may seek compulsory licensing of 'lending' if it is not available satisfactorily in any other way. The Secretary of State may make an order that various categories of work shall be treated as licensed *subject only to the payment of such reasonable royalty or other payment as may be agreed or determined in default of agreement by the Copyright Tribunal* (s66 as revised), unless a *certified licensing scheme* is available. No advantage has been taken by libraries (for example, in respect of computer programs in electronic form (4.45)) of an earlier and similar provision during the lengthy period since the Act came into force. However, this provision was obviously intended to encourage collective licensing. Public libraries will find it necessary to seek licences or general permission in order to lend the following:

- musical scores;
- sound recordings (confirmation or modification of present 'free' licence, 4.47);
- video recordings (unless present up-front pricing can continue, 4.47);
- maps;
- offline or 'portable' databases (tape; CD-ROM; CD-i);
- computer programs in electronic form..

For musical scores, discussion is under way with the Music Publishers' Association.

For databases:

> 'the making of a copy of a database available on terms that it will or may be returned otherwise than for direct or indirect economic or commercial advantage, through an establishment which is accessible to the public, shall not be taken . to constitute extraction or re-utilisation of the contents of the database' (SI 1997/3032).

The establishment of database right may hasten the possibility of collective licensing.

For computer programs in electronic format, collective licence availability seems unlikely at present, but progress may be checked from time to time with the LA/JCC/WPC Secretariat, as mentioned in 4.47. CD-ROMs naturally include the programs necessary for access to and use of content. A lending service involving a compilation of CD-ROMS was launched in 1995 via a number of public libraries. Known as the *CD-ROMs-to-lend* service, it was initiated by an independent firm called Rameses with more than 300 CD-ROMs. The selection includes some reference works, educational software, multimedia books, guides to languages and literature, software compilations, plus some image material and games.

Computer programs and rental/lending

4.45 A note appears at the end of 4.35 above concerning changes in the treatment of computer programs in respect of rental/lending. It should be remembered that programs may be printed and appear in books, when they are treatable as books in respect of rental/lending (see 4.13) and covered by nonprofit-based library/archive lending permissions. At various times, interest has been expressed by public libraries in lending computer programs in electronic form, especially educational software and games, but CDPA88 made electronic forms subject to licensing for 50 years (the kind of lending was not then distinguished from 'rental') and no licence was obtainable from the software industry. Public libraries and academic establishments could at any time since August 1989 have asked the Secretary of State to act as specified by s66 and make an order to impose a form of licensing where none exists, but this was not done. In any event, enthusiasm has inevitably been tempered, at least in locations accessible to the public, by fear of computer viruses. The Computer Misuse Act, 1990 has however outlawed the insertion of viruses as well as hacking, and transgressors motivated by malice or mischief might be deterred since their identities would be recorded against given periods of loan.

Enthusiasm was also tempered by the issue of programs in shrink-wrap packaging which forbade loan as well as duplication. In view of the special vulnerability of software, and although the contractual authenticity of this method appears to be in doubt (12.18), it is recommended that the software house's requirement be honoured. (See also software inclusion in Rameses in 4.40; CHEST and ESPA licensing for educational use in 8.23 and 8.24.) However, the prohibition of duplication is now overridden to some extent in respect of back-up copies (7.16 and s296A), and lending among staff in the same location should naturally be considered allowable as long as unauthorised duplication does not arise.

In discussion with representatives of the computer software industry, concern was expressed at the great damage brought upon software houses by illegal copying of games and educational programs (8.23), particularly via a phenomenon which could be called 'communication by computer' worldwide. However it appeared possible that an action which might be licensed (whether free or in return for royalties has not been explored) could be the provision of a collection of demonstration programs for use at a library's workstations. The industry, it was said, would be unlikely to license any other body for rental purposes. Technical means of preventing unauthorised copying, or 'copy-protection devices' (s296), continue to be researched. Thus the scene could change, and not only for the latter reason but because programmers might choose to seek rental/lending royalty or equitable remuneration in lieu thereof.

'Open for Learning'

4.46 Meanwhile, although the general public library licensing situation has not improved, it is still possible to approach individual software publishers for specific arrangements. An example is the 'Open for Learning' project for the establishment of support units for further education, started with Department of Education funding and reported in the first edition of this book as involving Birmingham and a number of other public libraries. The inclusion of computer programs in multimedia learning packages was, and still is, an important aim. The concern about viruses is reduced by checking each returned item. It is believed that the range of publishers who have agreed to sell for public loan has increased significantly since the initial dozen in the early 1990s.

Rental/lending of recordings and ciné films

4.47 Discussions with the recording industry, initially and principally with the British Phonographic Industry Limited, led to a 'free licence' for nonprofit based libraries to lend sound recordings, which is subject to some limitations on numbers put into stock. Limitations on numbers purchased would no longer apply unless kept in the licence so as to offset advantages such as removal of any need to pay piecemeal for every loan event. The inalienable right to equitable remuneration would be handled only between producing bodies and collecting societies. The sound recording industry may however continue its previous reluctance to permit licensing of any other bodies than nonprofit-based libraries for loan of sound recordings, fearing piracy through home recording (but see EC possible tape levy, 8.37).

At the time of writing, no changes have been announced in the BPI's 'free licence', and Library Association representatives of the JCC/WPC have already begun discussions with several organisations. These include, among others, BPI, the Spoken Word Publishers Association, and a new ad hoc group called the Unabridged Audio Publishers Association.

On the other hand, enquiries to the British Video Association in 1988 revealed a preference to cover commercial video hire service royalty needs by means of single 'up-front' additions to purchase prices; and also no desire to introduce licensing at that time. Public library loan services were to be regarded no differently from commercial hire outlets in respect of purchase prices, even for cheap supermarket 'sell-through' copies. This situation should henceforth be watched for changes, of course. The status of the agreement with BPI, and of progress with spoken word and other associations, can be ascertained from the Secretariat of the JCC/WPC at LA headquarters (12.33), which will keep local authorities duly informed of progress or changes.

Ciné films hired from an agency should already include a royalty in the charge. Users intending public performance should desirably inform the hire source. If necessary, the permission of the producing company should be sought via the national distributor. Unless contracted otherwise (including conditions of sale known before the event) the purchaser of a copy of a film could lend it to someone else free of charge, providing that purchaser is not an unlicensed public library.

Public Lending Right Act 1979

4.48 Under the above Act, the UK set up a central means of gathering public library loan records for books, and paying a small sum per loan to personal authors in accordance with the number of loans in a given year. Payment is made only to authors who have registered their wish to receive it. The number of loans is based on sampling: for example, in 1989 some 30 service points were selected from eight regions. Rotation is mostly one or two years for service points and three years for an authority, though four years has been the period for some areas where there is a shortage of suitably computerised service points. The money for payments to authors comes from the Treasury and not from public library funds.

Libraries under local authority control are considered 'public libraries'. Those required to engage in sampling which needed assistance to automate their loan systems received Government grants. Statistics and payment are exchanged between the UK and several countries, particularly elsewhere in Europe. By recompensing authors, lending right should in theory encourage authorship. In practice, however, the largest payments – indeed, the only worthwhile payments, according to some complainants – go to authors of bestsellers who have already been compensated by the market for their efforts, since their works are those most loaned. PLR sampling has been improved by allowing the collection of data from all computerised service points in each designated authority. Possible extensions of PLR to reference books, academic texts, and school loans have been discussed. Meanwhile the eligibility limits expressed in SI 1982/719 (as amended) still apply, as follows.

4.49 Eligibility of books for PLR

Some notes have already been made in 4.39 above. The following details have been taken from SI 1982/719 *Public Lending Right Scheme 1982 (Commencement Order 1982)*, as amended:

(1) *Eligible persons* = human authors (writers, translators, illustrators (including an author of a photograph), and an editor or compiler who has contributed more than ten per cent or ten pages of the contents **or** is entitled to royalty from publishers) provided they satisfy the qualification requirements for British copyright.
(2) *Eligible books* (each volume of a multi-volume work, and each new edition, is treated as a separate book) = printed and bound publications (including paper-back editions).)

Provided that 'book' **does not include** a book –

(a) bearing, in lieu of the name of an author who is a natural person, the name of a body corporate or an unincorporated association;
(b) (this excluded a book with four or more authors, but was deleted by SI 1991/2618)
(c) which is wholly or mainly a musical score;
(d) the copyright of which is vested in the Crown;
(e) which has not been offered for sale to the public; or
(f) a serial publication including, without prejudice to the generality of that expression, a newspaper, magazine, journal or periodical.
(g) in respect of which an application for first registration of Public Lending Right has not been made before 30 June 1991 and which does not have an International Standard Book Number.

The specification of personal authors in (a) is appropriately in line with the Berne tradition which the EC Directive follows. In practice all member states must apply sensible limits as to materials, and the PLR definitions above seem sensible enough, at least in respect of 'books' with personal authors, and should be acceptable as indicating UK compliance with the EC Directive (but see comments in 4.50 below).

Although nonprofit-based services are ostensibly well covered by permissions, a figurative question mark has to remain against the definition of eligibility in 4.37(i) above until clarification arises in the course of events. Maps are not mentioned but are in any event rarely lent by public libraries. An individual map is clearly not a 'printed and bound publication' and is therefore excluded, but the situation regarding atlases and map handbooks is not at all clear. Until clarification may occur, it is suggested that *any* item in book form **other than a musical score or a volume of maps** be regarded as covered by the above permission. The exclusion of musical scores, even when bound in book form, is considered serious (4.44). Reference use is unaffected for both maps and music (4.37).

Comments on rental/lending right

4.50 It should be noted that, unlike the PLR situation, the SI does not specify that the payment of royalties for rental or lending *must* be made per event. In the rental situation, however, the reference to the possibility of a single payment for equitable remuneration in respect of sound recordings and films implies that a relationship between number of rental events and the sum due might conceivably be sought by authors and performers as a condition of agreement to public rental/lending. A PLR-type system would in theory result in annual payments, ranging from very small to significant, to individual authors and performers, whose address etc details would need to be held on a updated file. In practice, such a system would be prohibitively expensive, and indeed could only be achieved if the PLR system were extended in order to sample loans of other materials as well as books, and pay out of PLR funding via the existing collecting societies rather than direct to individuals. Otherwise, library systems would require the expensive local replication of data-gathering arrangements right across the nation, as well as payment out of beleaguered funds at the mercy of variable local control. Not surprisingly, however, the government has expressed no interest at this time in expanding the PLR scheme in such a manner.

It is suggested that the achievement of cost-effective arrangements for rental/lending right would depend largely on the relevant industrial associations, who would need to encourage individual producing companies to provide, and authors/performers to accept, equitable remuneration as a single payment on transfer of rental/lending right in sound recordings and films. For other media, sharing of rental royalties will depend as usual on contracts between producing bodies and authors. The Copyright Tribunal – if approached for arbitration – would consider not only royalty or equitable remuneration amounts but also method of payment. This would suggest the possibility of a ruling in favour of single payments. This practice should be preferred by all involved, since otherwise the expenses of collecting societies, plus the administrative costs to services of setting up and running internal arrangements for gathering payment from clients (whether by sample or per rental/loan event), could well be disproportionate and reduce benefits to rights holders. In particular, an intolerable burden could be placed on public libraries perpetually short of staff and funds.

If one takes literally the definition of 'eligibility' in the PLR scheme, the number found ineligible for PLR (and therefore for the permissions in 4.39 above) may prove to be quite large. For example, works without a personal author or otherwise excluded on authorship grounds could themselves form a significant proportion (but see suggested interpretation of eligibility, 4.49.) Pending clarification, it is suggested that a similar ordering practice to one recommended in another context some years ago be adopted by any nonprofit-based service manager who may be in doubt – namely, placing a clear phrase on each loan stock order stating: 'This order is placed on the understanding that the materials concerned may be added to stock for lending to the public', and report any negative response to the relevant professional body.

As the law now stands, it is to be hoped that all the producing companies, if not also the individual authors and performers, may see the end-result danger of losing the 'shop-window' at present provided by public lending services. If so, assignment of rights to producing companies, and payment to them of a single figure 'up-front' in a purchase price to cover remuneration rights, could prove to be the most economical procedure. The video companies which already use an up-front figure within the purchase price may be the more ready to expand the procedure, as indicated earlier. It has become apparent that neither the sound nor video industrial bodies (BPI and BVA) seem particularly anxious to go to the expense of setting up licensing schemes for these purposes. Difficulties and unfortunate variations may well arise from the freedom of action and decision now open to authors and performers, although they would seem likely to see the dangers in choosing a self-defeating manouevre.

Because some points may become 'issues', a summary and overview appears separately in Appendix 3/4.

Publication right

4.51 In addition to the foregoing, SI 1996/2967(16) creates a new 'publication right', equivalent to copyright, which applies to first publication of a work at a time when copyright has expired. Being intended as a 'stand-alone' right, the SI leaves the details without a section number for insertion into CDPA88. Hence it has been suggested that they be regarded as called 'after s8' and inserted accordingly (following an earlier example where a SI prescribed a section for insertion 'after 76').

This right belongs to '*a person who, after the expiry of copyright protection, publishes for the first time a previously unpublished work*'. The right expires 25 years beyond the end of the year of such first publication. A work can only qualify for protection if –

- first publication is in the EEA. and
- the publisher of the work is at the time of first publication a national of an EEA state.

In respect of this right, 'work' means '*a literary, dramatic, musical or artistic work or a film*'. Crown and Parliamentary copyright works are excluded from this provision.

The definition of 'publication' for this right is much wider than that in s175 of the Act (see 4.17-4.20):

(a) issue of copies to the public;
(b) making the work available by means of an electronic retrieval system

(these first two, at least, are in s175);

(c) rental or lending copies of the work to the public (4.35-4.45);
(d) performance, exhibition or showing of the work in public; or
(e) broadcasting the work or including it in a cable programme service.

SI 1996/2967 Reg. 17 lists the chapters of CDPA88 Part I which in general apply to publication right, and then lists exceptions and modifications. Notably, moral rights do not apply.

It is believed that this new right may provide incentives for publishing useful materials which are at present in private or public archives or libraries, for example a collection of unpublished photographs relating to an area or special event. However, this could only properly be done if the collection had not been on public display ((d) above).

Droit de suite: artists' resale right

4.52 A gifted artist may progress from 'doodles and daubs' with little or no gain to paintings which reflect his skills fully and which sell well as his fame spreads. After his death, those works can become highly prized and priced, and even the doodles, daubs, and rough preparatory sketches can also become greatly valued. Many a painting, bought for the proverbial song during the artist's lifetime, has been sold subsequently at enormous profit. The principle of France's *droit de suite* is that an artist or his heirs should be entitled to a share of profit when his work only gains recognition in late life or after death, and is sold for a substantially greater sum than he was paid. A draft EC Directive has been under consideration for some time, but has gained little support in the UK from those who see long-term difficulties and dangers. In anticipation of future debate, comments appear separately later (8.37).

Academic environment and copyright

4.53 Practice has long varied between universities and colleges concerning campus copyright matters, not only regarding students' work but also that of teaching and research staff. An academic establishment's regulations should include provisions concerning copyright, not only in respect of theses, dissertations and course-work but also computer programs and audiovisual material. In accepting a place under those regulations, a student becomes contractually bound to abide by them. Similarly, staff should be bound by staff conditions of service. Some establishments, at least in the past, have wanted full control and have interpreted both students and staff as employees (4.2), thus indicating the establishment to hold copyright from the outset. Most if not all universities, however, are believed nowadays to regard commercial publications, whether periodical articles or books, as the writer's own copyright, with internal written material such as lecture notes left as a 'grey area' wherein intention to publish commercially as work at a particular establishment should preferably be approved by a deparmental head.

4.54 Theses

There have been many years of confusion concerning theses or dissertations and the ownership of copyright in them. Some establishments have in the past regarded students as 'employees under contract', thus making the establishment the first owner of copyright. Many regard theses as 'semi-published' but possibly subject to commercial publication later. However, publication has no effect on authorship and first ownership of copyright, nor would there be much doubt nowadays that a student is the author and first owner or copyright in his *own* original work.

Most universities have nevertheless sought to control access to theses. Possibly the increased post mortem copyright period to 70 years, and the inception of moral rights in the 1988 Act, may focus more attention on the concept of some degree of control in addition to examination. Oxford and Cambridge libraries long allowed access to a thesis only in return for a declaration that it would be used solely with the library which had borrowed it for a reader, also that it would not be shown to anyone else, nor copied without permission.

4.55 Moratoria on access to theses

Student regulations are a means of controlling access to theses (research confidentiality; ongoing research; or similar 'sensitivity' reasons) at least for a 'moratorium' determined by a department head when a thesis is submitted. During a moratorium (three years used to be the minimum), it is fairly common to require the incorporation of a 'thesis access form' into all complete copies made. Such a form can include: classification (open, restricted or confidential); moratorium period if any; author/title and supervisor; research funding body if any; a statement for student's signature which specifically transfers control of both access and photocopying to the Librarian (open theses) or to the head of a named department and/or the research funding body (restricted or confidential theses). Columns for signature and date are included relating to anyone allowed access during a moratorium period. Via the regulations, therefore, it is seen as appropriate that a student should forego his right to control photocopying until or unless he publishes commercially. Such university control should avoid the strange situations which can arise of considerable waste of time in trying to trace an overseas student to get permission to copy. (Sometimes such permission has been granted subject to payment of an unreasonable sum!)

Most university libraries would nowadays only accept deposit of theses on condition that control is allocated as mentioned above. A funding body may require a moratorium even for an unclassified topic if it is 'sensitive', and this can be labelled 'restricted' rather than 'confidential', with a moratorium period which could be the funding body's decision. It is possible to produce catalogue entries and purely 'descriptive' abstracts which are themselves 'open' even if the thesis concerned is not. Moratoria are out of fashion for 'open' theses, and indeed the tendency is inceasingly towards open availability. UK doctoral theses have been microfilmed by the British Library since around 1972. Naturally it is desirable that open theses should contribute to the generally available corpus of knowledge. The BL will supply a copy of a PhD thesis to a requestor, this having been accepted by many universities as a suitable alternative to the Dissertation Abstracts proposal of University Microfilms Inc., which required formal assignment of copyright to that publisher. Incidentally a project was begun at Edinburgh University Library in 1996, entitled *The current production, management and use of theses in the UK: a survey*. Also, moves towards digitization.are represented by UTOG (University Thesis Online Group) comprising some 15 university representatives and the British Library.

When moratoria on access were the rule even for 'open' theses, many students are said to have found the enforced delay on commercial publication useful in allowing for second thoughts on conclusions or recommendations, better presentation, or expansion of coverage whilst indicating the thesis as the basis. It is desirable, however, and a courtesy in any event, for a supervisor and/or head of department to be consulted before going ahead with publication of a thesis, since other persons may have been involved and/or related work may be in progress. If research is under sponsorship, the student would need the approval of the sponsor before even approaching any publisher, or indeed of desk-top or electronic publishing on his own.

4.56 Audiovisual and electronic formats

Contributions by staff or students to an electronic database are also their own copyright, though some may have signed away their s7 rights (3.18) or (more usually) allowed them to be taken over by the database producer. University regulations, however, may regard audiovisual programmes, electronic databases and computer programs differently from other materials. In most cases they will have used campus facilities and contributions by other staff. Also, In 'going commercial', the question of proper copyright clearance for material included from other sources becomes highlighted, though this is certainly not to say that internally it could be overlooked. Errors of clearance could lead to blame falling on the institution for infringement. Lack of knowledge of moral rights could also lead to infringement claims.

The possibility of university interest in sharing commercial gain (and perhaps also discouraging clearance errors) can be covered by a 'catch-all' phrase in both student regulations and staff conditions of services, such as the following example. This is intended to make possible the sharing of gains or other intervention when desired, although such may rarely occur:

> The ownership of all apparatus or results and also patents, designs, copyrights, inventions or other intellectual property (including computer software but excluding books, journal articles and theses), whether individually or jointly developed or produced, relevant to and arising during the period of a student's studies with the University shall be vested in or deemed to be assigned to the University. Should the question of exploitation arise, the student shall be required to take all the necessary action to facilitate such exploitation and the University shall negotiate with the student as to whether he shall participate in the benefit thereof and, if so, on what terms.

Further EC harmonisation

4.57 Apart from rental right reported above (4.35 et seq.), there are other CEC plans. Most if not all of them arose in the context of Information Society considerations. Probably the more important to many users is the draft on reproduction right and right of communication to the public.

5. COPYRIGHT PERMISSIONS: FAIR DEALING INCLUDING GUIDELINES

General note on database right:

Readers are requested to refer to **Q0** before proceeding with study of permissions chapters 5, 6, 7 and 9. Any permissions should be qualified by the details of database right (3.28) if not already specified herein.

Scope of this chapter

The first of several chapters on permission, this details copyright exceptions or permissions outlined at the beginning of this volume.

Interpretation

5.1 When the Act uses the words 'a work' without qualification, the term covers any original literary, dramatic, musical or artistic work, sound recording, film, broadcast or cable programme, but should not be assumed to cover the printed page, or 'typographical arrangement' of a 'published edition', unless specifically stated. 'Original work' is used here to mean literary, dramatic, musical or artistic works only. However, when the Act uses the phrase 'any copyright', this includes typographical arrangements along with every other form of copyright. The Act's phrases 'anything done' or 'any action' are even wider, including any right covered by the Act unless qualified by the context.

Having laid down the 'restricted acts' which define exclusive rights for their owners, as described in previous chapters, the Act makes certain exceptions or exclusions from rights, normally called *permitted actions* which do not require any approach to a rights owner. Also, rights owners themselves or their representative bodies may publish guidelines for users of copyright materials in which permissions may be given. Furthermore, in licensing a user, a rights owner in effect provides permissions, subject of course to conditions which normally include payment or adherence to certain limits. In all, there are six kinds of copyright permission:

a) those in the Act as already indicated;
b) advisory statements given in guidelines produced by professional organisations representing user interests;
c) guidelines produced by or on behalf of rights owners, such as HMSO, giving specific permissions in respect of actions which they regard as reasonable;

d) notices found on published items, indicating copiable extents;
e) licence terms, whether collective or individual (see 12) and service contracts, for example for databases;
f) responses by rights owners to specific requests made by users, for example when guidelines or licences are unclear or considered unfairly restrictive for particular circumstances.

This chapter focuses on general permissions affecting individuals or libraries/archives or other organisations. Fair dealing now applies to databases, but only if extraction or re-utilisation of content is not for a 'commercial purpose'. Apart from the 'public administration' permissions plus one educational permission in chapter 7, existing copyright permissions are not reflected under database right. In chapter 6 on libraries/archives, additional permissions are incorporated in a survey of all relevant. The permissions chapters should be taken in conjunction, especially as some library permissions also apply to anyone (again, HMSO is an example). Some schemes of licensed copying are described in chapter 8, and copyright administration generally is outlined in chapter 12.

Fair dealing

5.2 The term 'fair dealing' has never been defined in law, due to the vast range of kinds of copyright material and modes of use. The word 'dealing' is not confined to trade contexts but is used in the broadest sense, so it can mean any action in respect of a copyright work. It is left to the courts to decide what may be 'fair' in particular infringement cases. In the USA, a term 'fair use' is defined on four bases, including the effect of copying on the potential market for a work. However, the US 'fair use' is often potentially applicable to all material and usage contexts.

The UK's 'fair dealing' specifies the permitted purposes of copying rather than effects, and is limited to particular materials and contexts. The US and UK concepts should never be regarded as equivalents, despite laxities which creep into common parlance. Within the relevant contexts, the UK's 'fair dealing' is normally regarded as a possible means of covering any action (within the permitted purposes) which should not unduly affect a rights owner's market. Unlike library copying permissions, which are specific and unchallengable, anything done under fair dealing is potentially subject to challenge by rights owners on grounds of fairness. It has been considered necessary to make brief references to the fair dealing concept in advance of the details given here (3.7; 3.17; 3.24; 3.38-3.40).

5.3 Fair dealing: lobbying results

One of the greatest successes of user-based lobbying during 1987 to 1988 was the preservation of the fair dealing concept. Not only was it preserved but also clarified at long last, after years of uncertainty as to whether it covered commercial ends within 'research or private study'. The case presented during lobbying drew together arguments which helped the House of Lords to remove the Bill's discrimination against 'commercial research' in fair dealing. This has not prevented some rights owners, since then, from attempting to absorb fair dealing into licensing. The Government expressed, early in 1988, its key reason for removing discrimination against commercial research in fair dealing from the Bill, namely the avoidance of excessive cost to industry because most copying is from periodicals and is covered by fair dealing. However, Government also expressed the belief that industry should expect to pay for nonfair dealing. The user community has never argued with that principle, but only with the methods and proposed levels of charging and the administrative costs anticipated.

To all users, fair dealing without discrimination against 'commercial research' has been regarded as a most important feature of CDPA88, providing the essential flexibility without which academic, industrial and cultural information worlds would have been in very considerable difficulties. Indeed, the whole basis of authorship and publishing could have been undermined.

5.4 Fair dealing purposes

The permitted purposes to which the 'fair dealing' concept (ss29, 30) can apply from 1 January 1998 are:

(a) From s29: research or private study – applicable to any original work, including artistic works, and including copying of a 'typographical arrangement' (printed page), but not to extraction or re-utilisation (by whatever means) of parts of databases for research having a commercial purpose;

(b) From s30:
    (i) criticism or review of any copyright work, or of a performance of a work, subject to sufficient acknowledgment;
    (ii) news reporting (i.e. current events) in respect of any copyright work except a photograph, subject to sufficient acknowledgment

when the news is being reported in written or printed form; provided neither (i) or (ii) involves the extraction or re-utilisation of the whole or a substantial part of a database, because s30 is not reflected under database right.

Within the permitted purposes, 'fair dealing' can range over all possible treatments of copyright material which otherwise might amount to infringement. Thus fair dealing under (a) could override considerations of the 'substantial part' which would otherwise infringe (4.32; 5.6). Under (a), copying is possible from a database for research or private study if the purpose is not commercial, or if the parts concerned are defensibly 'insubstantial' whatever the purpose.

Since the fair dealing concept is really only a permissible defence if taken to court for infringement, anything done under fair dealing obviously calls for the exercise of judgment. So it is advisable to take due note of any guidelines issued by rights-owner groups in order to indicate what they regard as 'fair'. The 'moral rights' in chapter 10 must also be borne in mind when considering whether a given action might be accepted as fair.

5.5 Computer programs

Since they remain literary material even when in an electronic format, computer programs are theoretically subject to fair dealing. This is clearly applicable to hard copy, though copying norms should be followed, which means only a percentage of the whole of a program, even when embedded in a book as a chapter, because it is nevertheless a whole work (6.39). The theory becomes questionable in respect of electronic formats:

(a) firstly, because it is not possible to make any kind of extract from a program as a whole work without reading it into a computer in entirety, which is itself a restricted act for any other purpose than using the program – even transient copies are copies (s17(6))

(b) secondly, because shrink-wrap conditions usually prohibit any kind of copying other than producing a working copy for the purchaser's own purposes and reading in for use (12.18). There is also s21 to be considered, which makes the production of adaptations a restricted act. Nevertheless, the fair dealing concept could conceivably override those provisions if a defence were soundly enough based to withstand a challenge in court. In short, the possible existence of fair dealing in computer programs could lead to some case law. However, there is one potential action which would now be ruled out as far as fair dealing is concerned, because SI 1992/3233 came into force on 1 January 1993. This arose from EC harmonisation of copyright law (13.12). It amends CDPA88 in a number of places. In fair dealing, 'decompilation' or conversion of a program language from lower to higher level is excluded from fair dealing, and so is any incidental copying in the course of such conversion. However, this is an instance of removal of a possible fair dealing interpretation in order to help users, because a new s50B permits decompilation by a lawful user, subject to specified conditions. Other permissions are also given (7.15-7.20).

Fair dealing for research or private study

5.6 The main points are:

(a) As indicated in 5.3, the 'research or private study' purpose is limited to literary, dramatic, musical or artistic works, and typographical arrangements. Because of that last phrase, it has so far been assumed that fair dealing does not apply to electronic formats of original works, nor to sound recordings or films. The new database right effectively confirms and underlines the Act's failure to mention 'databases' per se, nor makes any distinction between electronic writing and printed matter.

(b) It is now clear that fair dealing can apply to databases for research of private study but – as indicated in SI 1997/3032 – not for a commercial purpose unless allowed by contract. Whether revised publisher guidelines will indicate acceptance of the present advisory copiable extents as 'insubstantial' is not yet known, but such acceptance appears unlikely if their aim is to extend control by licensing.

(c) Extents of copying are not specified by the Act, and 'fairness' could be challenged in court. Anyone may extract or re-utilise insubstantial parts of a database without infringing copyright but could infringe database right unless a 'lawful user', that is, licensed (3.28 et seq.). However, the lawful user of a printed matter database (e.g. a directory or handbook) should become regarded simply as the purchaser.

N.B. The above should be considered in conjunction with 6.4 on library copying.

(d) The inclusion of 'artistic' is however important to people copying on behalf of others under fair dealing -- including staff of libraries or archives who are otherwise not permitted to copy artistic material, such as maps or photographs, under nonprofit-based library/archive copying provisions.

(e) Where rights-owner groups have issued guidelines as to what they themselves regard as fair or reasonable, these should be duly noted (5.3).

(f) Any person may copy on behalf of another but must not make more than one copy. Any library may also copy on behalf of an individual under fair dealing if only one copy is made for an enquirer. (The making of more than one copy would exceed the specific limits of library copying.) Otherwise, the number of copies is not specified when an individual copies for himself, but see self-service copying precautions in libraries (6.31). Whether any form of electrocopying is allowable as fair dealing is mentioned in 6.9.

For emphasis of 5.1, any kind of research is covered by copyright permissions, except research for commercial purposes in respect of copyright in databases, whether copying is from print or electronic compilations. In respect of copyright databases being accessed for other purposes, fair dealing for research or private study will now apply to extraction or re-utilisation of contents regardless of whether the database is on paper or in electronic format, but only insubstantial parts may be taken under database right unless by a lawful user.

An initial difficulty for users may be the need to adjust to the new meaning of 'database', which is now liable to embrace any compilation which is well-selected and arranged, whether print or nonprint of any kind. This would seem quite appropriate in principle. The difficulty arises from the removal at a stroke of most of the existing copyright permissions, for they do not apply to database right. (When rights owners produce guidelines, perhaps after the forthcoming Directive on Reproduction Right, these may reinforce some of the copyright permissions and/or clarify the situation for users. This would be helpful, since it is difficult to determine which databases carry database right, because any database may not qualify unless substantial investment has been made. Some rights owners are nevertheless still endeavouring to remove fair dealing altogether, so there are no guarantees.)

Databases which are original are copyright at compilation level, as well being liable to include copyright items, and the CDPA88 permissions will apply to all copyright aspects when database right provisions do not conflict. However, anyone can extract or re-utilise 'insubstantial parts' for any purpose, including commercial, but 'insubstantial' is to be defined qualitatively as well as quantitatively, thus emulating the copyright provisions regarding infringement. Also, a 'lawful user' (licensed or permitted through purchase or otherwise) of a database can use it for whatever purpose he or she is authorised without his or her 'lawful user's right' being overridden by other contracts.

5.7 Interpretation

Confusion has been reported due to the phrasing of s29(3)(a), hence it is quoted here and analysed in more detail than above, as follows:

> 29(3) 'Copying by a person other than the researcher or student himself is not fair dealing if – (a) in the case of a librarian, or a person acting on behalf of a librarian, he does anything which regulations under section 40 would not permit to be done under section 38 or 39 (articles or parts of published works: restriction on multiple copies of same material) ...'

Firstly, note the important colon after 'works' in the penultimate line above. Secondly, note that the kind of library is not specified, hence profit-based services are included. The main purpose of this subsection is in fact to transfer the multiple copying restrictions in ss38-40 copying permissions for nonprofit services to profit-based libraries also. It is clear from the BCC guidelines (App. 1/3) that it also has made this interpretation. The subsection also shows that, since artistic works are included in fair dealing but not in nonprofit-based library copying (6.4), the latter or any other kind of library (or indeed individual for himself or another) can copy from an artistic work under fair dealing, but should note the proviso about challengeability (5.2).

Having dealt with libraries in s29(3)(a), subsection (b) goes on to rule out the making by anyone else of more than one copy for another person (there is no stated limit on copies for himself). Hence it is quite clear that no-one or no kind of library may use fair dealing to get a second copy for an enquirer.

5.8 The specific unchallengeable permissions in ss38-39 have constituted safeguards for publishers against any nonprofit-based library exceeding its 'allowance' by using fair dealing to get a second copy from a literary, dramatic or musical work or a periodical article for an enquirer. Some librarians have erroneously concluded that, because of those specific permissions in ss38-39 and their confinement to research or private study, nonprofit-based libraries are effectively prohibited from copying under any other part of the Act. Since artistic works are excluded from ss38-39 but included in fair dealing, this would have meant that nonprofit-based libraries could not copy an artistic work, such as a map under fair dealing whereas a profit-based library could do so (noting that all its unlicensed copying actions are *only* under fair dealing). It would also have meant that the very archival or holding points for materials subject to permission in other sections of the Act (see Q3 and 6.45) , could not provide statutorily permitted copying service for any other purpose than research or private study, hence the permissions would have been quite pointless. The situation has changed with the inception of database right, because the specific extents covered by library/archive permissions to databases which qualify for database right do not apply (except insubstantial parts). Much will depend on rights-owner views as to the meaning of the latter.

5.9 Infringement of copyright

It should be noted in respect of all legal permissions that, when a copy has been made with permission for a given purpose and is then later used for another purpose for which the making of a copy is not specifically permitted, the copy becomes an infringing copy if it amounts to the whole or a 'substantial part' (4.32) of the original (see 4.16). There has been discussion as to whether a research or private study copy can be later donated to a library. The declaration required from a requester of a copy from a nonprofit-based library (6.51) includes:

> 2(b) 'I will not use the copy except for research or private study and will not supply a copy of it to another person.'

There are three points here: (a) note the words 'a *copy* of it', not the one held by the requester, hence other members of a research team could read the item; (b) but note however that this promise is preceded by the requester's warranty that he will not use the copy for any purpose other than research or private study; (c) although the list relevant to 'infringing copies' in 4.16 does not refer to fair dealing, it begins with a phrase containing 'includes', which might be taken as leaving the way open for other applications to be deemed infringing. Hence one view is that later donation to library stock of a copy made under either fair dealing or nonprofit-based library copying might render the declaration false, and accordingly make the copy an infringing one. An alternative view is that it is only the *making* of the copy which is restricted in respect of a given purpose and that, once made, a copy may be used for another purpose. The writer is unconvinced by the latter argument in general but, if a nonprofit-based library can in any event obtain a free copy from another library, for example under s41 (6.38), one copy only of a given item might in theory be accepted as a donation after first use for research or private study (a 'value judgment'!).

5.10 Advisory limits

The interpretation followed in this volume in respect of photocopying is to regard any individual who copies for himself for research or private study, regardless of location of the photocopying machine, as able to copy to the same limits as those which apply to staffed copying services in libraries and archives. In other words, it is recommended that reasonable limits be applied to fair dealing, and advisory limits are given later in this chapter. Then chapter 6 draws together the various guideline documents and takes them in conjunction with statutory permissions and fair dealing from this chapter. Chapter 7 goes on to describe other copying permissions, any of which could be done either by an individual for himself or by a library or archive on his behalf. Chapter 8 describes the licences which are available to extend the statutory copying limits. Then other permissions than copying are described in chapter 9: playing, showing or performing.

5.11 Research or private study: purpose

This is the best-known copying purpose and is common to both fair dealing and library or archive copying provisions, and this has led in the past to some confusion. The two provisions are really separate. Library/archive copying provisions have strict and specific limitations, whereas fair dealing – as already indicated above – has none, saving the prohibition of multiples when one individual copies on behalf of another individual, or when any library copies. Further comments will appear in the next chapter on another important difference, namely that between fair dealing and nonprofit-based library copying (6.9).

5.12 Research or private study: meaning

The phrase is frequently misquoted as 'research and private study' or 'private research and study'. It is important to keep the phrase as it stands in the Act. Even the word 'or' is significant because it signifies that an act of copying does not need to have both purposes at once. Also, the 'research' does not have to be private, and there is nothing to prevent an individual from lending or showing his photocopy, whether made under fair dealing or under library copying provisions, to a colleague. Furthermore, there is also nothing to prevent a colleague from proceeding to make his own copy under fair dealing – subject to the usual provisos about challengeability in court on fairness grounds. Although an individual signing a declaration to a library or archive staffed copying service is rightly expected to honour it to the letter, that letter does not prevent showing or loaning to colleagues but does forbid the recipient from making a copy of his copy to pass on to another person, as detailed later (6.17). 'Private study' has become accepted as excluding group or class study, and that is in fact the basis of photocopy licensing of multiple copying in the education sector. Otherwise, 'private' is quite broad in meaning and applies to any individual. It cannot imply its application only to pupils or students, for anyone of any age or circumstance can study anything – and 'study' also is broad in meaning, simply signifying in-depth consideration.

The 'research or private study' purpose embraces original literary, dramatic, musical or artistic works and 'published editions' or printed versions of those works. In database right, the phrase itself should relate to any format, print or nonprint, and any medium.

5.13 Periodical articles as fair dealing

A main concern for some publishers has long been the apparent 'unfairness' of single copies of journal articles. Users regard these mostly as 'convenience copies', or substitutes for actual reading, which would not be made at all if photocopying were impossible. In the user community it is well known, albeit regrettable, that many of the copied articles never get actually read, but remain in filing cabinets just in case until clear-out time on retirement. Since almost all the copying in industry and commerce is of single copies of journal articles, the cost of photocopy licensing in the private sector, it is believed, would be crippling if the British Copyright Council view were to be accepted. The BCC argues:

> The very fact that prescribed libraries alone are given the right to operate the library privileges and under very strict conditions, suggests strongly that fair dealing does not encompass in any way the copying of an entire article from a periodical.

There are several possible comments on this:

(a) nowhere has the Act laid down any limits for fair dealing, nor could it even hint at limits, for reasons already indicated
(b) in library copying, it is much more likely that the drafters merely sought to keep the only limits which they could dictate firmly – namely, for nonprofit-based library copying – within reasonable bounds for the sake of the rights owners.
(c) it seems unlikely that one article in an issue would be judged a 'substantial part' of the issue.

However, (c) is now weakened by the new position on databases. A periodical issue might be claimed to be a 'database'.

Bearing in mind the discrimination against commercial purpose in fair dealing with databases (above), the results for businesses cannot be foreseen at this time.

5.14 The Association of Learned and Professional Society Publishers (ALPSP) considered journal article copying to be fair dealing for research or private study and no doubt will continue so for media other than databases. It is regarded by this writer as inappropriate that special considerations should apply to fair dealing quantities as compared with 'library copying' quantities, since both kinds of copying are liable to be done in a library or archive by the same people, and confusion does not help the cause of copyright. Further, it has been suggested as unlikely that a court would rule any copying under fair dealing to be 'unfair' when it could be legally done on a person's behalf at the nearest public library in any event. The Library Association has taken the view in respect of copyright that one copy may be made of an article in an issue of a periodical under both fair dealing and library provisions of the Act.

5.15 Discretion

As indicated in 5.6 and elsewhere, fair dealing has no limits of copying save multiples. Discretion must therefore be applied in deciding whether the intended copying should be considered 'fair' to rights owners in the circumstances (5.29). Consequently, guidelines issued by rights-owner representatives are very important, since following them should at once satisfy rights owners and remove fear of infringement on the part of users. Nevertheless, circumstances arise wherein discretion is still required. For example, if a volume has been found to be out of print and unobtainable, few would bother to contest the fairness of copying by an individual for research or private study, though a rights owner might well object if a library copied the work for stock without permission.

5.16 Multiple copying

Whether an individual may consider it fair to make more than one copy for himself is left primarily to individual judgment, but neither an individual (nor any library, 5.6(f)) may copy on behalf of someone else if there is reason to believe that this will result in more than one copy – that is, multiple copying. The definition in library copying provisions should help here also: multiples are '*copies of substantially the same material to more than one person at substantially the same time and for substantially the same purpose*' (s40). It has become accepted that multiples for such purposes do not amount to 'private study'.

In the education sector, another term is encountered, namely 'systematic': rights owner representatives have called multiples 'systematic copying' when they are to be regarded as constructive multiple copying (8.1). Nevertheless, it is arguable that, if a group of students visits the library of another organisation where they are not specifically served as students but just as clients or members of the public, a court might regard it as fair dealing for each of them to take a single copy for himself on self-service equipment. However, the education sector is by no means concerned with contesting this point. Earlier it was remarked that due notice should be taken of rights-owner views on what copying is to be considered reasonable or fair. Several sets of guidelines exist, of which the most general in application is the following.

5.17 Guidelines

The British Copyright Council (Clark, Appendix 1/3) states the views of the Society of Authors, the Writers' Guild and the Publishers Association: that in general the following are considered fair dealing for research or private study copying by individuals. Some BCC views have been augmented as indicated.

Books and other non-periodical material

5.18
- one copy of a maximum of a complete chapter in a book, or one copy of a maximum otherwise of 5 per cent of a literary work. This means whichever is the greater may be copied. As this offers no guidance on short works without chapters, the advice repeated in the Library Association guides (App. 1/3) is:
- short books, reports, standards, pamphlets: up to 10 per cent if not more than 20 pages or 2 pages if brief.) Poems, essays, short stories, etc. It is however pointed out, in respect of anthologies and other cases of inclusion that poems, short stories, and other short literary works must be seen as whole works in themselves, and not as parts of volumes in which they may appear. In such cases of inclusion in volumes:
- one copy may be made of a short story or poem which does not exceed ten pages in length. Otherwise, the 5 per cent limit applies.

The BCC extents specifically exclude periodical articles (see 5.13), which the BCC regards as whole works in themselves, although it is mentioned that some journal publishers print permission in each issue for single copying of articles. However, the Association of Learned and Professional Society Publishers indicated a decade ago that it regarded the copying of single periodical articles as fair dealing (see also 5.21). No rights-owner guidance is yet available on database right.

Periodicals

5.19 When wishing to copy from any periodical, the issue should first be checked at front and back to see if there is any note indicating how copies can be made – and, if necessary, paid for – when the requirement exceeds the extent and single copy obtainable legally from a nonprofit-based library service. If the payment is to be made to an overseas address, this is not practical because the bank transfer charges would probably exceed the fee charged, but a photocopy could be requested via the nearest library from the British Library Document Supply Centre or another agency (6.47; 6.50) which is licensed to copy in excess of singles and more than the 'one article per issue' limit (8.10).

Illustrations

5.20 These are not mentioned by the BCC but it is suggested that, as is the case for nonprofit-based libraries, illustrations accompanying a work can be copied along with it by anyone. However, care should be taken in respect of artistic works such as photographs, the copying of which, if for use in isolation from accompanying text might amount to infringement of artistic copyright. (See 6.21; also 7.7 on transparencies for instruction.) As far as published material is concerned this is because, as mentioned elsewhere (2.21), the published edition in which a publisher has copyright excludes artistic works, as indeed do the specific unchallengable permissions for nonprofit-based libraries. Thus every plate is treatable as a whole work in itself and as a copy of the original from which the printer's medium was made.

Photographs

5.21 The British Photographers Liaison Committee guide (Appendix 1/4) allows a single copy of a photograph to be made by or on behalf of an individual under fair dealing for research or private study. The copying of segments or extracts or areas within a photograph may be considered less than fair by rights owners. This would apply especially if the quality of resolution were unrepresentative of the standard of the original. However, irrespective of resolution quality, CDPA88s29 on fair dealing covers the making of one copy by an individual, or any library on his behalf, of a complete photograph for 'research or private study'. In respect of segments or extracts as mentioned above, whose copying could endanger moral rights as well as copyright per se, rights owners would prefer the s29 phrase to be interpreted as relating to a person's own *private and domestic use*. Otherwise, a rights-owner statement which forbids copying of an item need not affect users governed by UK or similar law which gives relevant permissions, unless a user is controlled by contract. Also, it must be borne in mind that a collection of photographs may be a database. Any case of doubt should be the subject of a permission request, and that is usually forthcoming in respect of reasonable conditions.

British Standard Specifications

5.22 The British Standards Institution regards 10 percent as a reasonable extent to copy from a standard for research or private study. Standards other than those of the BSI are covered by the reference to 'standards' under 'short books' in the notice for display beside machines which appears at the end of this volume. The BSI does not wish the '2 pages if brief' proviso to apply to British Standards, since many are only of such length in toto.

Ordnance Survey maps

5.23 OS has confirmed a copying allowance of long standing: up to four copies of a limited extract from any OS or OS-based map may be made by an individual. The extract must not exceed 625 sq. cm. (roughly A4 size) at scale. In the absence of any other guidance, it is suggested that this limit should be applied to all other maps, since no other statement is available.

Her Majesty's Stationery Office publications

5.24 The more commonly needed guidelines on copying HMSO material appear in a letter addressed 'Dear Librarian' and two letters to 'Dear Publisher...'. HMSO guidelines can apply to individuals as much as to libraries or publishing firms, and the latest copy of each relevant documents should be kept to hand. A digest of the September 1996 Librarian letter is given later (6.24), and both Publisher letters of February 1997 are digested in 6.25. However, the latest state of these and other HMSO guidance documents can be found on the following web site: *http://www/hmso.gov.uk/copy.htm*. Reproduction is not allowed in respect of advertising, endorsement, or potentially libellous statements, nor unfair or misleading selection or undignified associations. Otherwise, the permissions are liberal enough to reflect recognition by HMSO of the extent of interest in and demand for copying Crown or Parliamentary documents. The publishing arm of HMSO was privatised in 1996 and became The Stationery Office, but the residual arm of HMSO will operate as part of the Cabinet Office in administering the republication rights of previously published Crown material.

Music

5.25 As with HMSO material above, it is considered best to include some notes in the next chapter about the Music Publishers' Association Ltd.'s pamphlet: *The code of fair practice* (Appendix 1/3), which applies both to individuals and organisations. The prohibitions in the code are quoted in 5.35 as examples of points to consider when judging fairness.

Can licensing absorb fair dealing or other statutory permissions?

5.27 Despite worries by users, it has never been shown that anyone can completely override fair dealing for research or private study by a licence, since it is a permission applicable to individuals who have lives which continue outside the organisation where they work. Moreover, for like reasons it is doubtful whether an employer can sign away a permission that applies to his individual members of staff, though he could guarantee to control copying and achieve a similar effect. Of course, the application of fair dealing could only be controlled in the workplace, and then only by conditions of service or limitation of access to photocopying equipment. Other statutory permission may prove capable of being absorbed or at least modified by licence, but this should be resisted unless adequate compensation is made in terms of licensed actions and reasonable cost.

Fair dealing for criticism, review, and news reporting (s30)

5.28 Criticism or review

For criticism or review, any copyright work, or a performance of a work, is covered.

This includes, for example, films and sound recordings. Any reproduction must be accompanied by *sufficient acknowledgment*. Copying or quoting a sufficient extent or significance to render consultation of the original unnecessary or less necessary would be unlikely to be judged 'fair' in court. Obviously it would be most unfair to include large quantities of a work, since serious harm could result to the rights owner's market, for which due recompense would probably be sought in the courts. This should be borne in mind not only by reviewers but also by the producer of an abstract, digest or precis: for example, a 'full' precis should only be published with permission.

5.29 Quotation limits

In 1958, the Society of Authors and the Publishers Association jointly agreed that while the limits of 'fair dealing' for the purpose of criticism or review must vary according to the circumstances, it would be a convenience to all concerned and save correspondence about short quotations for these purposes if a general understanding could be established for normal practice.

> They therefore ... would not regard it as 'unfair' if... a single extract of 400 words, or a series of extracts (of which none exceeded 300 words) to a total of 800 words were taken from prose copyright works, or... up to 40 lines from a poem, provided that this extract amounted to no more than one quarter of the poem.

(Quoted from *Photocopying and the law*, British Copyright Council, 1970 reprint of 1960s pamphlet; excluded from the Bibliography because it has been withdrawn in the light of new law and the inception of licensing. This particular statement, however, has not been revised and should still be followed in general as the only advice available, subject to possible review in the light of database right. Under database right, as indicated earlier, anyone may extract or re-utilise an insubstantial part of a database for any purpose without infringement, though deciding what might be accepted as 'insubstantial' will need assistance from rights-owner guidelines in due course, or from case law.

Discretion is important, however, in ensuring that a quotation is not excessive unless authorised, and particularly in seeking permission for any 'advertisement or marketing' applications irrespective of permitted use for 'criticism or review'. Moral rights must also be borne in mind: for example, a falsely credited or unrepresentative quotation could cause considerable offence and lead to litigation

5.30 Multiple copying, or publication, is not ruled out for criticism or review by CDPA88 provided sufficient acknowledgement is made. It is advised however that one should not assume this to be applicable to multiple copying or re-publication of any part of a printed page, because typographical arrangement is not specifically cleared for this purpose, unlike research or private study. However, the British Photographers' Liaison Committee guide (Appendix 1/3) accepts that a photograph may be reproduced for criticism or review, either on its own or as part of a compilation of several authors' works, provided that it is accompanied by a credit identifying the author and title, if any. Quotation for criticism or review is in any event legally subject to sufficient acknowledgment of source. Excessive quotation requirements – and any other purpose than the two specifically allowed – should be the subject of permission requests. Response to requests to newspapers may vary according to whether an item has an individual by-line.

5.31 News reporting

For news reporting, any copyright material other than a photograph is covered by the permission. This is subject to sufficient acknowledgment, but no acknowledgment need be made when news is reported by means of a sound or video recording, film, broadcast or cable programme. As with criticism or review, it is advised that, although multiple copying and even publication is included in respect of the content, this permission should not be taken to apply to multiple copying or re-publication of parts of printed pages.

General

5.32 It seems unlikely that rights owners would take action against an isolated individual whose need is clearly for research or private study, and who does not allow a copy to become an infringing copy by using it for certain other purpose not covered by a permission (see 4.16), and who has not copied an excessive amount in order to avoid purchase of readily available originals. But rights owners would probably not hesitate to take action against an organisation whose members infringed and which failed to take adequate steps to discourage infringement. The costs of litigation and associated staff time alone, even without a damages award, could be punitive as well as potentially disastrous for a corporate image. Individuals, or profit-based services on their behalf, wishing to copy under fair dealing are advised that the copiable extents applicable to non-profit based libraries should not be exceeded, wherever the copying takes place.

5.33 The library and information professional bodies take the view that the same allowances should apply both to individuals copying for themselves under fair dealing and to libraries. To have separate allowances for fair dealing on the one hand and library copying on the other hand would merely be a source of continual confusion which could militate against respect for copyright. This is why permitted extents are drawn together in the next chapter, and also summarised in Q2 and in a notice for display beside photocopiers (end of volume). For any greater needs, one must ask permission from or via the publisher or producer, or from the author if unpublished, or act in accordance with any licence or other contract which might be held. A note appears at the end of Q4 about annotation of photocopies with source details, both for acknowledgment purposes and future reference.

5.34 Overseas material

Overseas material should normally be treated in the same way as UK material unless it is known that an alternative action is feasible, for example if the source country is known to be non-signatory to the international conventions (13.10; 14.21) or non-EEA (2.2).

5.35 What is 'fair'?

Mention has already been made of the need to apply discretion or judgment, before deciding whether copying is appropriate in a given case. Because of the vast variation in circumstances and materials, no universal guidance can be given, but at least seven of the eight 'prohibitions' in the MPA code (Appendix 1/3) may be regarded as applicable to all copyright material and not just printed music:

1 Copying in order to evade the hire or purchase of music.
2. Copying works supplied on approval for inspection.
3 Copying whole works or complete movements.
4. Copying works which have been obtained on hire.
5. Copying from various publications to make anthologies.
6. Copying or making excerpts from publications which are clearly designed as 'consumables' in the course of study such as work- books, tutors, methods, exercises, standard test and answer sheets, and similar material.
7. Selling or hiring copies which have been made under the Permissions.

Some of these, or similar statements, can be found in collective licensing also, especially 3 and 6. Obviously, there can be no completely 'fair' procedure other than the purchase of originals if still in print – or the payment of royalty for every piecemeal requirement, which would be an impossible, or impossibly costly, administrative undertaking for rights owners as well as users.

5.36 Moral rights, newly introduced to the UK by CDPA88, now need to be borne in mind when considering fairness, as indicated briefly earlier in this chapter. The specific provisions for libraries in the next chapter transcend any consideration of fairness.

5.37 Like the Act itself, permission guidelines from copyright owners tread the narrow line between the entitlement of creators to benefit and the need of users to appropriate flexibility. Rights owners who, like the BCC, OS, HMSO and MPA, recognise essential user needs are liable to receive, more readily than others, the attention and compliance of user communities.

5.38 Copying on behalf of others

Lastly on fair dealing, it must be stated again for emphasis that anyone may act on behalf of another in respect of the actual production of permitted copies, including any kind of library whether profit-based or nonprofit-based. This ability to act on behalf of others is also considered to apply to almost all other copyright permissions in the Act, the only exceptions being found in copying for instruction (7.1; 7.3). Remarks on possible library involvement appear in 6.45.

6. LIBRARIES AND ARCHIVES COPYING: PERMISSIONS AND GUIDELINES

General note on database right

Readers are requested to refer to **Q0** before proceeding with study of permissions chapters 5, 6, 7 and 9. Any permissions should be qualified by the details of database right (3.28) if not already specified herein.

Note on scope of this chapter

Like the last chapter, this is not confined to the provisions of CDPA88, but also brings in rights-owner guidelines and the question of self-service copying in libraries or archives. Accordingly it should be read in conjunction with chapter 5. Because library staffs need to be informed of the needs of other departments which may publish from time to time and need to include extracts from official documents, the 'publisher' guidelines from Her Majesty's Stationery Office are included as well as those for libraries.

The Act refers in various places to *archives*. This is taken to be merely for avoidance of doubt, since an archive should surely be considered a library with a primarily archival purpose and not necessarily accessible to other than bona fide enquirers. In this text, 'library or archive' is the phrase used where it is thought that doubt may otherwise exist; but in most instances 'library' is intended to encompass 'archive' in respect of all copyright matters.

Database right regulations in SI 1997/3032 will require qualification and/or clarfication by means of rights-owner guidelines and further definitions. Similarly, unless an audiovisual item is absorbed into a database – whether the collection is mono- or multimedia – there are as yet no general sets of rules or permissive guidelines for users in respect of electronic databases or audiovisual recordings, although there are some agreements on particular matters which amount to 'free licences' and progress is being made with electronic guidelines (see App. 4). The Round Table for Audiovisual Research (members of UNESCO nongovernmental organisations concerned with audiovisual archives and libraries) recommended work towards AV guidelines as long ago as 1990. The suggestions would have provided some flexibility for libraries and archives, but the industries concerned do not appear to have arrived at decisions as yet.

Readers who require a concise approach, at least as a prelude to detail, may prefer to turn firstly to the outlines or summaries in the Quick Reference Section at the beginning of the volume.

Copying permission or authority

6.1 There can be various kinds of authority for copying in libraries and/or their parent organisations:

(a) statutory provisions about 'prescribed' libraries or archives (6.2), which are intended to relate only to staffed copying service
(b) guidelines from rights owners, on copying extents regarded as fair for both (a) and (c)
(c) fair dealing provisions, which cover self-service copying wherever done, and copying by anyone or any library on behalf of an individual under any other relevant permission
(d) copying under licence, whether individual (such as the Ordnance Survey, or 'lawful user' of a computer program or a database); or collective (such as the Copyright Licensing Agency)
(e) copying under specific permission, either printed on an item, such as a journal issue, or obtained direct from a publisher.

The staffed copying of (a) can include not only requests from clients but also interlibrary and certain other needs. The (b) to (d) kinds of authority are considered in conjunction with statutory provisions in the sections below.

6.2 Prescribed

To begin with, a certain word needs to be removed from the scene as far as this book is concerned – the word 'prescribed' – because the library and archive copying provisions (ss37-42) apply only to 'prescribed' services. Further words on those appear in SI 1989/1212, from which it can be seen that all UK and even some overseas libraries or archives are 'prescribed' in one way or another:

- only nonprofit-based UK libraries are prescribed as able to copy under ss38 and 39 in respect of periodical and book copying for individual requesters
- all UK libraries and archives may make and supply copies under s42 (archival copying) and 43 (unpublished works), and any UK nonprofit-based library or archive may receive for stock copies (including unpublished works) made for it under s41 or s42; but only individual requesters may receive copies of unpublished documents made under s43.

In the points above, the words 'nonprofit-based' have been substituted here for the Act's phrase 'not conducted for profit'. On the other hand, a profit-based library or archive is one which is established or conducted for profit or which forms part of, or is administered by, a body established or conducted for profit (SI 1989/1212).

6.3 Profit

No definition of 'established or conducted for profit' is provided, hence one was devised and has been adopted by the Library Association in its published series of guides (Appendix 1/3). It is suggested that this could serve at least until someone takes a definition to court and seek to establish it as authoritative. This might never happen, since the context of use of the phrase can vary considerably, like 'fair dealing'. For the purposes of advising users of copyright materials, the definition of 'established or conducted for profit' supplied for the LA guides is repeated here:

> 'The Act's phrase 'established or conducted for profit' applies to the parent organisation as well as to the services themselves, but the profit aim is not defined. It seems reasonable to assume that it means that the organisation or service concerned has the objective of attaining an excess of income over expenditure. The mere selling of services to recover a proportion of the expenditure, or even all the direct costs, without covering overheads and without making a true surplus would not be construed as 'established or conducted for profit'. If a service were split off as an independent business without subsidy, it would then become 'established or conducted for profit'. However, libraries in industry, commerce and professional practice (e.g. firms of architects, lawyers etc.) are clearly profit-based.'

In the circumstances, it is considered more convenient and possibly less confusing to think in terms of 'nonprofit-based' and 'profit-based' services, and the word 'prescribed' will be omitted from this book from here onwards. Also, as remarked in the prefatory note to this chapter, a far less clear distinction between libraries and archives than that implied by the Act has been adopted here. Any library can and usually does have archival functions, and any archive collects and makes available materials, often in a broadly similar way to a library. In any event, no separate definitions of 'library' or 'archive' are supplied by the Act. There is a list at the end of SI 1989/1212 of kinds of library which are 'prescribed'. These include: local public, national, academic, parliamentary or government department, and a last broad category. This lists the subject areas with which a library or its parent body may be involved, in terms which leave out no conceivable serious contenders. A similar list appears against any library outside the United Kingdom. In this text, there is accordingly no hesitation in dropping the word 'prescribed'. Moreover, from here onwards, when a 'library' is mentioned alone it should be borne in mind that the context may also apply to an archive which incorporates library functions and vice versa.

Some uncertainty continues about organisations describing themselves as charities, but it is suggested that registered charities could be regarded as nonprofit-based, regardless of their fund-raising methods.

Features of library/archive copying

6.4 Additionally to fair dealing, the Act's extent-related and specific permissions to nonprofit-based libraries or archives cover **copyright** in respect of:

(a) written or printed matter only, single copies only;
(b) research or private study copying for clients, whether on the spot or via another library
(c) interlibrary copying for stock
(d) archival copying for stock, on the spot or interlibrary;

and all copying is subject to conditions.

The interpretation in (a) is based on the Act's definition of 'published edition' only in the context of typographical arrangements (s8). The inception and presentation of database right regulations from January 1998 onwards effectively confirms the applicability of hard copy copyright permissions to the copyright in material in electronic formats, for no distinction is made between electronic writing and other means of recording intellectual property. This includes only original works, but not sound recordings or films. The latter may be included in a database, hence any database right permissions would cover those media as records as well as any text etc present. There are no database right permissions which apply to libraries or archives. There is under database right a fair dealing permission for research or private study purposes but this states only that such use will not infringe copyright, meaning the copyright in the compilation as a whole which forms the database and the items within it, but not the database right in the making of the database. With regard to research for a 'commercial purpose', however, 'anything' would not be fair dealing.

Database right reflects all the 'public administration' permissions relating to copyright, so a library could act under any of these permissions on behalf of a client, without itself being alawful user. It would however need to be part of a 'lawful user' organisation in order to act in respect of the database right permission to extract substantial parts (subject to consideration of fair dealing) for 'illustration for teaching or research', since the permission is limited to a lawful user. It is concluded therefore that, apart from public administration purposes and fair dealing for research or private study with hard copy databases or with any other written or printed materials, libraries will need coverage by licence for (b), (c) and (d) in respect of extraction or re-utlilisation from electronic databases: that is, appropriate 'lawful user' licences (see 3.28 et seq.); or else confine actions to 'insubstantial parts' which should not infringe either copyright or database right.

Although fair dealing includes 'artistic works' (s29), nonprofit-based library permissions do not. Also, although two out of three fair dealing purposes can involve nonprint media, the Act's nonprofit-based library copying permissions do not, which is why the first note above states only written or printed materials. However, both nonprofit-based and profit-based services can copy on behalf of someone under fair dealing provided multiple copies are not involved, or under a number of the other permissions which otherwise do not obviously affect libraries, some of which cover nonprint media. Anyone still in doubt should study s29 and note the reference to 'a library', to be interpreted as 'any library' as indicated in the British Copyright Council's pamphlet (Appendix 1/3). Certain of these matters will be amplified in the course of this chapter, but 5.6 has already made a comparison between fair dealing and library copying permissions and should be studied in conjunction.

6.5 Specific statutory permission

It should also be noted that, whilst library copying provisions share the 'research or private study' purpose with the fair dealing provisions (see 5.4), there is a very important difference. Whereas anything done under fair dealing which is a 'substantial part' (4.32) may be challenged by a rights owner, anything done under library copying by a nonprofit-based service is a clear statutory permission and, providing the specified conditions are followed, may not be challenged. It follows that a profit-based service which applies the 'library copying' extents in the Act can only do so under fair dealing, unless of course its parent body is appropriately licensed.

6.6 In other words, copying is possible by:

- nonprofit based libraries or archives in the public sector, such as state, academic and public libraries, under library copying provisions and under fair dealing. However, nonprofit-based libraries must not exceed –

when they copy for research or private study from printed matter (though not otherwise, see 6.45) – the permitted copying from periodicals, nonperiodical printed matter, and unpublished documents.

- profit-based libraries or information units or archives, such as those in firms and professional practices, or in commercial units made independent of but still associated with public sector bodies such as universities; under fair dealing provisions only or under other permissions in the Act on behalf of someone.

6.7 Accordingly, *both* nonprofit and profit-based libraries may:

(a) make single photocopies on behalf of individuals for research or private study under fair dealing provisions. In the case of nonprofit-based services, this is in addition to photocopying under library copying provisions, but fair dealing must not be used to exceed the extents and single copy limits, when copying from text. In the case of profit-based services, however, it should not be assumed that copying for extra-mural supply would be considered 'fair' (15.29). It is recommended that profit-based services should avoid copying for members of the public except as in (b).

(b) from published or unpublished material, make a copy in response to an interlibrary request made by an individual through any library for the purpose of research or private study (6.37).

(c) from published material, make a copy requested for the stock of a nonprofit-based library. (Profit-based libraries may make such stock copies, but cannot receive them without specific permission.)

(d) act on behalf of an enquirer in respect of either of the other two fair dealing purposes, criticism or review, and news reporting; or any other permission in Q3 and Q8 to supply copies of whatever kind of copyright material for specified purposes, not just written or printed matter.

6.8 It is emphasised that only nonprofit-based services are clearly and specifically authorised to make single copies of the extents permitted from *printed* databases without 'lawful user' or other licence, at least until database rights owners produce guidelines. Profit-based services should nevertheless regard themselves, it is recommended, as able to copy the same extents for research or private study purposes as those authorised for nonprofit-based libraries, provided the copying is done in response to individual requests, normally in-house – and not in association with a public service like a current awareness bulletin available extra-murally. However, profit-based libraries should be aware of the British Copyright Council view on periodical articles (5.14), also of the self-service copying precautions in 6.31. All information services and libraries should note that database right permissions do not reflect the foregoing statutory permission for nonprofit-based libraries, except in respect of insubstantial parts.

Research or private study: copying limits

6.9 This purpose is common to both library copying and fair dealing. The important difference between a nonprofit-based library copying under the relevant provisions and a profit-based service copying under fair dealing has been noted in 6.5. This writer recommends that neither scanning into a database, nor downloading for another database from an electronic file should be considered. The ECUP document in Appendix 4, covers the various ways in which information and library professionals are trying to preserve the flexibility of fair dealing and library copying in the face of pressure from publishers via WIPO to amend Berne (13.7). Many publishers have long recommended a suitable balance between rights-owner and user interests. Both 'fair dealing for research or private study', and 'nonprofit based library copying' permissions are believed to be confined to printed or written material. Downloading from an electronic format would result in a capability for multiple copying, and such actions should only be done if service contracts permit (not at present except in some electronic library research projects). Whether printout is allowable as fair dealing is another matter, but it is suggested that this may be done when there is no service contract to indicate the contrary. (See also electrocopying, 3.45). A nonprofit-based library or archive is legally permitted (ss37-40) subject to the conditions below, to make and supply a copy of:

- an article in a periodical, including illustrations accompanying the text or in the typographical arrangement (s38)
- from a published edition of non-periodical material, a reasonable proportion of a literary, dramatic or musical work (s39). (See below for advisory extents.) This includes illustrations accompanying the text or in the typographical arrangement
- the whole or part of an unpublished work in the collection, provided the rights owner has not forbidden copying (s43).

NB: In respect of databases, these permissions may now only apply if they involve an insubstantial part of database contents (3.28).

6.10 Articles

The Act's definition of an article is any item. A table of contents is an item. A number of small items can appear together, either on the same page or in several adjacent pages, such as items of news without individual authors, and neither the Act nor the rights owners give any guidance on these. However, the BCC has not demurred from advice in LA guidelines that such pieces may be regarded as one item when the total extract does not form an unreasonable proportion of the periodical issue. The BCC guidelines on nonprofit-based library copying affirm that: a single article from a periodical publication may be copied by a staffed service, but the BCC does not agree that the copying of periodical articles is fair dealing when done by self-service, which is contrary to the view taken by the Library Association and recommended here (see also 5.14 and 5.19).

The BCC view is that a periodical article is a 'whole work' – the rationale of this might be compared with the beginning of this paragraph above. Whether an article in a full-text electronic journal can be regarded as an article in a 'periodical' requires confirmation, though in theory it might be acceptable where there is no control via contract, provided transfer from one database to another does not occur without permission (such as lawful user licence).

6.11 Non-periodical materials

The Act's term reasonable proportion of non-periodical publications effectively allows discretion to the librarian to decide what may be considered 'reasonable' in particular circumstances, and this degree of flexibility should always be borne in mind. The BCC offered the suggestion that a rule of thumb maximum figure of 10 per cent could be a 'reasonable proportion' when the library is doing the copying.

The Library Association has nevertheless adopted an advisory extent for non-periodical material which is the same as that recommended by the BCC for fair dealing, namely up to one complete chapter or 5 per cent, but the LA goes on to express the view that up to 10 per cent of a short work should be permissible provided that the extract does not amount to more than 20 pages. Although this view was not accepted by the BCC in respect of fair dealing, the LA view still holds, and allows the same limits to be shown for self-service copying as for staffed copying service.

6.12 British Standard Specifications

The British Standards Institution has indicated agreement with up to 10 per cent as a reasonable copied extract from a BSS, whether under fair dealing or library copying. It is recommended that this extent be regarded as applicable also to any other standard specification.

Conditions for copying

6.13 The Act lays down the following conditions governing staffed copying by a nonprofit-based library for research or private study (from SI 1989/1212):

(a) A requester must sign a declaration form (see 6.51)

(b) Requests for substantially the same material are not received by the librarian at substantially the same time.

(c) Only one copy of the extents given above may be made for a requester.

(d) The requester must pay a sum not less than the copying costs, including a contribution to the general expenses of the library.

The word 'substantially' is not defined and is therefore a matter for discretion.

Some libraries or archives which serve the public appear to be unaware of the need to levy Value Added Tax on photocopy charges. However, this is taken as inapplicable to closed communities such as academic staff and students on a given campus – though it does apply between different establishments.

6.14 Multiple copying

The copying conditions reflect the particular care taken by the drafters of CDPA88 and associated Regulations in SI 1989/1212 to close all former loopholes for unauthorised multiple or 'systematic' copying, defined in 5.16 and mentioned also in 8.1.

The use of fair dealing to get a second copy for an enquirer is prohibited by s29(3). (See also 5.6). Multiple copies are specifically prohibited under library copying provisions (s40), but are possible when the copying organisation is licensed, or when a library accedes to a request to copy on behalf of someone wishing to follow one of the 'anything done does not infringe' permissions elsewhere in the Act (Q8).

6.15 Library responsibility

New responsibility is thrown upon libraries, for it is indicated that the librarian must be satisfied that the conditions are followed before making and supplying a copy. However, it is certainly not expected that checks be made through a large file to ensure no duplication of requests, and s37 of the Act allows a librarian or archivist to rely upon a signed copyright declaration (6.13; 6.51) unless there is reason to believe it to be false.

6.16 Unpublished works

As briefly mentioned earlier, any library or archive (profit or nonprofit) may, subject to the same conditions as for published material and nonprofit-based libraries, supply a copy of a part or even the whole of an *unpublished* original work (excluding artistic) in its collection for research or private study by a requester, provided the copyright owner has not prohibited such copying (s43). Photographs could present problems because the same item can be published or unpublished. The suggested solution is to regard them as complete works in themselves and follow the BPLC fair dealing allowance of one copy to an individual for research or private study (5.21). Supply to an individual requester can be via another library as below, but copying unpublished material for the stock of a nonprofit-based library is only permissible under s42 (copying for archival replacement). A declaration form different from that for published material is included in 6.51.

6.17 Declaration forms: filing

As the relevant statute of limitations involves six years, that is the period for which declaration forms must be kept on file, but there is no specified means of filing and no-one appears ever to have been asked to produce a particular form. (See 6.45 in respect of copying other than for research or private study.) Obviously the above conditions cannot be applied by the librarian nor by a requester in cases of self-service copying, which is separately treated in 6.30.

Should a false declaration, after acceptance in good faith by a library as valid under s37, result in an infringement case, only the requester would be to blame. Hence obtaining a declaration even by profit-based libraries in respect of staffed copying service could constitute a form of protection against involvement in litigation.

6.18 Profit-based services

In respect of profit-based services, some remarks have already been made in 6.8 and those should be taken in conjunction with the following comments. It is recommended here, as well as by the Library Association, that as far as copiable extents are concerned profit-based services should simply avoid exceeding any of the extents permitted to nonprofit-based services for research or private study. This view underpins the use of the same 'limits' notice for both staffed copying and self-service.

The publicity afforded to copyright in recent years should have reduced the risk of infringement by individuals in profit-based organisations, at least pro item. Whether obtaining a licence helps to keep the subject in mind or cause a carte blanche attitude is arguable. Industrial, commercial and professional group libraries are well-placed to notice what may occur and to recommend to managements that any regular copying requirement which exceeds fair dealing should be considered for licensing – if the price and other terms are right, and if acceptable rationale can be perceived in the licensing policy adopted (see 8.11). Such library observations would be entirely in line with the spirit of the Act, which puts more responsibility upon librarians, doubtless as the people in charge of most of the available resources.

However, the vast majority of copies made in industry are convenience single copies for research or private study which have never been shown to harm the rights-owners' markets. Moreover, no new periodical subscriptions would be placed if photocopying for that purpose suddenly became impossible. It is regarded as essential that the fair dealing concept should be preserved in any licence taken up – if a licence is sought at all, this should be against the contingency of *non*-fair dealing.

6.19 Although the conditions in 6.13 are not mandatory for profit-based services, and (d) (on charging) in particular can be regarded as irrelevant, it is recommended that at least (a)-(c) be adopted in respect of staffed copying.

Profit-based libraries should not assume, to emphasise a point made earlier (6.7(a); 6.8), that providing a copying service for extra-mural supply could be seen as 'fair' by rights owners, and should seek a 'document supply' licence (8.10) if such a service is contemplated. However, the occasional or isolated extra-mural request might be satisfied, and interlibrary requests as in 6.35-6.38.

6.20 Chart of copiable extents

The recommended copiable extents are shown in Q2 at the beginning of this book, which takes in the extents allowed in rights- owner guidelines other than those of the Music Publishers' Association guidelines (Appendix 1/3) which are commented upon in 6.27 below. A suggested chart for display near photocopying machines appears at the end of this volume.

6.21 Illustrations accompanying a work

Included in nonprofit-based service provisions is permission to copy any illustrations accompanying the work or in the typographical arrangement (ss38; 39), which covers plates, diagrams, and figures in the text which are relevant to the extract being copied. (See also 6.41.) Profit-based libraries who copy will be doing so under fair dealing only. The Act contains nothing to imply that an illustration cannot be extracted for research or private study on its own: hence there is no need to copy the whole item in order to have a copy of an illustration. Nevertheless, an art plate which stands separately from any particular piece of text should preferably be treated as a whole work in itself, for which copying without specific permission should be seen as allowable under fair dealing but not under library copying provisions. Any individual, including any library staff member, can copy on behalf of another under fair dealing, which includes artistic material although that is excluded from library copying, provided only a single copy is provided to an enquirer. It is suggested that library copying permissions should not be taken as excluding all else, when by clear implication their intention is merely to allow unchallengeable but limited copying by nonprofit-based libraries in respect of literary, dramatic or musical material in written or published formats (see also 6.4-6.11, and 6.45).

6.22 Maps

As noted under fair dealing, the Ordnance Survey regards as fair the copying of the following area of an OS or OS-based map: up to 4 copies of an extract not exceeding 625 sq. cm. (roughly A4 size) at scale may be made by an individual. There is apparently no guidance available in respect of non-OS maps, and it is recommended that the OS extent should be followed generally or that permission be requested from the publisher. Similar considerations apply to Experian Goad Limited in respect of their 'Shopping Centre Plans' of which the firm owns copyright jointly with OS.

Although an A4 area is specified by OS only in relation to individuals under fair dealing, any person and any library can copy on behalf of an individual under fair dealing (as remarked in the last paragraph above) hence this should also be regarded as the library extent.

Permission in s47(2) and (3) to copy 'material open to public inspection or on official register' is conditional upon the following annotation in respect of copies from maps. This is taken by the writer to apply to maps displayed in national or local government offices or libraries, such as maps of area development proposals. Putting together the designated phraseology of SI 1989/1099 (maps) and SI 1990/1427 (plans and drawings) which apply very similar conditions, a copy made under s47 from such a map (etc) must be marked as shown on the declaration form concerned cf those in 6.51 below.

It is suggested therefore that any public office (including a Public Records Office) or library required to display such materials should prepare a stock of adhesive labels ready for the versos of any copies made. That which is allowed is: (from s47(1)) '*factual material of any description, by or with the authority of the appropriate person, for a purpose which does not involve the issuing of copies to the public*' (and the latter applies to multiples or re-publication) (from s47(2)) '*for the purpose of enabling the material to be inspected at a more convenient time or place or otherwise facilitating the ... purpose*' (of public inspection) (s47(3) then indicates subjects on which copies can even be issued to the public in respect of certain materials and '*for the purpose of disseminating that information*'.) (See also 7.11 and 7.13.) It is suggested that any library should get a requester to complete a declaration for s47 copying, as in 6.51.

Her Majesty's Stationery Office (Copyright Unit): guidelines

6.23 The main HMSO guidelines appear in letters addressed 'Dear Librarian...' and 'Dear Publisher...'. A digest of the September 1996 Librarian letter appears below. A digest of the main parts of the more detailed and complex February 1997 'Publisher' letters (Crown; and Parliamentary) appears in 6.25 included here because the notes may be taken as covering any organisation wishing to publish or otherwise produce multiple copies beyond the 'Librarian' permissions. The latest form of all HMSO guidance or licensing arrangements may be studied on the Internet (see 5.24). There must be no reproduction for the purposes of advertising, endorsement, potentially libellous statements, unfair or misleading selection of facts, undignified associations. In respect of Parliamentary material, it is pointed out that reproduction must not be for overtly political purposes, nor purport to be published with official authority; and a warning is given that no warranty is provided against actions for libel or defamation, etc..

6.24 'Dear Librarian' digest

These notes apply to any individual as well as a member of staff of a library, archive or information service. In respect of all the categories listed below, anyone may make, without formal permission or charge: **single photocopies** of an entire title or document, subject to

(a) 1 copy only for any individual requester (but including schools and universities etc, where each student may receive his own copy);
(b) 1 copy only for use within any organisation;
(c) no further distribution to other individuals or organisations.

multiple photocopies of an extract or extracts of up to 30% of a whole work, or one complete chapter or equivalent, whichever is the greater, may also be made without permission or charge.

categories covered by these general permissions are –

(i) Parliamentary papers, notably Hansard (Commons and Lords), Bills, House Business Papers, Command Papers, Reports of Select Committees, Bill and SI Lists, Weekly Information Bulletin, Sessiona Infrmation Digest;
(ii) Crown copyright Acts, Statutory Instruments, Statutory Rules and Orders.
(iii) Press releases from official sources.

Other categories of Crown or Parliamentary material, and non-parliamentary publications, are affected by the fair dealing and library copying provisions of CDPA88, and indeed any other statutory permission.

These guidelines are more helpful than the extents noted earlier for nonperiodical material, and care should be taken to study them. Whereas a mandate is held by the Copyright Licensing Agency, the guidelines are more generous for some categories than the CLA extents, suggesting that the latter have become relevant only to non-parliamentary publications or to commercial/industrial multiple copying (noting (b) above). Those published by HMSO are covered by CLA licence terms, but otherwise are treated like any other material – if the need exceeds the fair dealing norms or a licence, permission should be asked from HMSO (alternatively, use a document supply agency; see 8.10 and 6.47 et seq.).

6.25 'Dear Publisher' digests

Guidance in the February 1997 letter, summarised as follows, is given on publishing and other multiple copying needs for (1) Crown material, and (2) Parliamentary material. The terms apply not only to publishers but also to anyone wishing to reproduce the materials.

(1) **Crown material** in the categories below, subject to the conditions stated –

Reproduction of the following in any medium, except the Royal Arms and use for advertising etc (as indicated earlier above), is permitted worldwide in all languages without prior permission and free of charge: Acts, SIs and Statutory Rules and Orders; Press Releases from departments, agencies or other Crown bodies (but not to provide a commercial press releases service) Conditions: Reproduction must be in a value-added context (related compilation, analysis, commentary, annotation, indexing,. etc), including in-house and commercial databases. Source must be stated along with acknowledgment of Crown copyright in the form: *Reproduced with the permission of the Controller of Her Majesty's Stationery Office.* Reproduction must be accurate and in no way misleading as to the intended meaning of the material. Any translation must be undertaken by a competent translator, and the foregoing copyright acknowledgment must be printed both in English and in the language of the translation. Permission is required for posters, maps, or merchandising purposes.

Permitted reproduction covers resetting the text, or scanning the official text, or downloading from Government Internet Web sites, provided no separate other rights are involved (e.g. another publisher's typography, or software of an electronic product). Command Papers and House of Commons Papers: Most are Crown copyright and publishers should apply specifically for permissions.

The 'Crown material' letter also includes details of standard licences for quasi-legislative and National Curriculum material, and indicates that other Crown material not covered by the above permissions or conditions may be subject to specific licensing terms. Some materials may be provided in machine-readable form, subject in many cases to a charge (details on application).

Otherwise, formal applications in writing are required in all cases, and Crown copyrights are reserved (and, it is indicated, will be exercised if necessary).

(2) **Parliamentary material**

Applications must be sent to the Copyright Unit at HMSO in respect of: Lords and Commons Official Reports (Hansard), including

- Official Reports of Commons Standing Committees; Bills of Parliament; Journals of both Houses; the Lords Minute;
- the Commons Order Paper, Votes and Proceedings and other parts of the Vote bundle;
- Select Committee Reports;
- The Commons Public Bills List; Lists relating to the progress of SIs, etc.;
- Lists on the progress of Deregulation Orders; **and**
- all other papers published by The Stationery Office which are Parliamentary copyright, except the following –

Applications in respect of the following must be sent to The Librarian of the House of Commons, c/o The Public Information Office, House of Commons, London SW1A 0AA:

- Weekly Information Bulletin of the House of Commons;
- The Sessional Information Digest;
- House of Commons Library Documents.

Broadcasting is not covered by this guidance, and applications should go to the Supervisor of Parliamentary Broadcasting, Houses of Parliament, London, SW1A 0AA.

EEC publications

6.26 EEC material is covered by the copyright laws of the country of publication, so a large number of items are covered by Luxembourg law. However, the UK Act has been extended to cover all EEC nations and indeed other Berne or UCC signatories (13.10). The Office for Official Publications of the European Communities, 2 rue Mercier, L-2985 Luxembourg should be approached for permission regarding any copying extents beyond research or private study norms, or regarding multiple copies or publishing. Whereas a generous attitude is adopted towards copying from the Official Journal, in the interests of wide dissemination of the information therein, rights must nevertheless be upheld. At such future date as the objective of a 'level playing field' may be more clearly within sight, it would be helpful if a set of guidelines as detailed as those of HMSO could be provided. Readers with CLA licences re copyright will find that publications of governments of other countries named in the licence (see 8.4) are to be regarded as covered by the licence, since they are not in the list of exclusions.

Music

6.27 The Music Publishers' Association Ltd supplies a pamphlet on the copying of printed music entitled *The code of fair practice* (App. 1/3) has been agreed between representative composers, publishers and users, and in fact is the only joint code in existence. Notes indicate that:

(a) MPA Ltd is not associated with the Copyright Licensing Agency or any other collective licensing arrangement (but it now owns the Mechanical Copyright Protection Society, see 12.41)
(b) the code does not apply to all music, and in particular it cannot be applied unless the copyright owner's name is listed in an appendix containing 151 publishers
(c) the code can never be used or applied to imported publications
(d) permissions granted in the code apply equally to organisations as to individuals, and to others acting on behalf of the intending user.

6.28 The MPA code contains 12 'permissions', covering the possible needs of members of the public, students, teachers, orchestras, and so on, and includes among other matters: hired works, band parts, opera chorus extracts, auditions. There is a list of eight 'prohibitions', seven of which are quoted in 5.29 as examples of points to consider when judging 'fairness' in other contexts. Because of its detail, the fact that it is a joint code involving users, and its helpful permissions, plus the present intention of MPA to stay outside collective licensing, this is an important code. Already concise, a full digest would not be appropriate, and those interested should obtain a copy. The more important permissions to the ordinary user are 2 and 3:

> '2. Performance difficulties. A performer who possesses a piece of music and who needs for his personal use a second copy of a page of the work for ease of performance due to a difficult page- turn, may make one copy of the relevant

> part for that purpose ... Copying whole movements or whole works is expressly forbidden... When such a work has been hired, the copy made must be returned with the other hire material after the performance.
>
> 3. Study and research. Bona fide students or teachers, whether they are in an educational establishment or not, may without application to the copyright owner make copies of short excerpts of musical works provided that they are for study only (not performance). Copying whole movements or whole works is expressly forbidden under this permission.'

To comply with the code, it is necessary, when the first page copied excludes a copyright statement, to locate the C notice on the original and inscribe it on to the copy made. Music copyright owners have suffered badly in the past from market damage due to unauthorised copying, and during the period between the 1956 and 1988 Acts there were several notable awards of damages arising from litigation against blatant infringement by education authorities. A standard permission request form, of similar design to that in 6.51 but specifically applicable to music details, appears at the end of the code. Otherwise, where the code does not apply, it may be necessary to rely on other permissions CDPA88, including fair dealing and library copying, treating items like non-periodical material such as reports and pamphlets, but bearing in mind that each piece of music is a complete work in itself.

Microforms

6.29 The copyright situation on microforms has been reviewed already in 2.32, and it is emphasised here that microforms should be treated just like the material represented on them. There is another matter: the British Library has a contract with the US Superintendent of Documents concerning microfiche copies of the AD-numbered series of contractual research reports. Fiche masters are supplied to the BL under contract, from which they replicate microform copies to send out to requesters. The BL sends out microfiche copies in paper sleeves marked with legends prohibiting 'enlargements'. This would be understandable if it seeks to avoid undermining any separate contract between the publisher and a producer of hard copies for sale. In respect of whole documents, this must of course be honoured by organisations which receive the copy fiche for stock, otherwise they should be prepared to buy the hard copy. However, for research or private study purposes, the usual norm of 10 per cent (short book category) should be regarded as applicable to the AD series, whether hard copy or microform. Among US Government publications, the AD series has been regarded as unusual in requiring copyright protection in the UK (see 14.21).

Self-service copying

6.30 Setting aside for the time being the question of 'copying shops', which are in the course of being licensed, self-service copying is regarded by many as presenting serious problems. A manager of whatever kind could theoretically share the blame in the event of infringement by a client on copying equipment housed on the organisation's premises, if no attempt has been made to influence clients, for example by notices and conditions of access. Even nonprofit-based libraries cannot be expected to make self-service copying follow the Act's conditions for copying by library staff, and some means of protection against blame must be applied. Profit-based libraries also must seek to protect their organisations from litigation in the event of infringement by an individual.

6.31 Precautions

Drafts having been exchanged between the British Copyright Council and the Library Association while guidelines were in preparation, the following precautions were agreed as a possible defence for libraries or archives which might otherwise have to share the blame for infringement of copyright on their premises. To quote from the BCC version: '...libraries and other organisations which provide self-service copying equipment on their premises need to take special care. They are advised:

- to display prominently alongside the machines a notice which makes clear to those using them that photocopying is restricted by law and which indicates the nature of the restrictions
- to include similar information in any publicity which explains the services available in the library or organisation
- to include similar information in any user education programmes or other oral explanation of the services available
- to take all reasonable steps to ensure that all staff who are likely to be responsible for the photocopiers, or are likely to be referred to for advice, are instructed about the provisions of the Copyright, Designs and Patents Act 1988 as they apply to photocopying in such circumstances
- to instruct such staff to intervene in order, as far as they can reasonably be expected, to prevent users making infringing copies. (This however is additional to the LA version and is considered to present difficulties.)

If these steps are taken, those responsible for self-operated photocopiers should be able to mount an adequate defence in the event that infringing copies are made.

The last but one of the above precautions is not in the LA version because it is rightly seen as contradictory to the principle of self- service in a context of staff shortages. Nevertheless, the above BCC version should be noted and, should staff happen to pass the equipment and notice infringement taking place, it is advised that they should indeed intervene. Since no management can possibly be sure that a member of staff, or even a visitor, will not infringe, the need for the precautions is clear. No organisation can lightly contemplate the expense of litigation, the effect on public image, or the cost in staff time which would be involved.

6.32 Notices for machines

In order to minimise the danger of confusion and self-service infringement, it is desirable for a notice to show the same limits of copying for fair dealing as those for library copying by a staffed service. The Library Association sells copies of a recommended form of notice for display alongside photocopying machines, and the notice at the end of this volume is an alternative suggestion. Such a notice should be displayed in addition to any concerned with licensing.

Replacement or archival copies

6.33 A copy may be made by a nonprofit-based library or archive of any item in the permanent collection which is wholly or mainly for reference on the premises, or available on loan only to other libraries and archives:

(a) in order to preserve or replace that item in that collection, or
(b) in order to replace in the permanent collection of another nonprofit-based library or archive an item which has been lost, destroyed or damaged, in return for a written statement about such loss, etc., affirming that purchase is not reasonably practicable, and that the copy supplied will only be used for addition to the permanent collection

without infringing copyright in any literary, dramatic, or musical work or a typographical arrangement, including any illustrations accompanying the work, provided it is not reasonably practicable to purchase a copy to fulfill the purpose (s42). The definition of 'reasonably practicable' is left to staff discretion.

Also, when a copy is obtained from another library (of any kind), the requesting library must pay the cost of copying plus a contribution to the general expenses of the library concerned. Although s42 leads off with a reference to *any item* it makes no mention of 'artistic' works, nor of nonprint formats. This means that an extra action is necessary if the item to be preserved is an artistic work or an audiovisual or electronic item: namely, requesting permission from the rights owner.

6.34 Unusually, SI 1989/1212 makes this permission more stringent than the Act itself, adding the above inclusions of:

- wholly or mainly for reference on the premises; and
- in (b) above the requirement for a written statement is added.

6.35 Interlibrary archival copying for stock: nonprofit-based libraries

This is covered by 6.33(b) above. Some interlibrary copying for stock by nonprofit-based libraries of published material is also permitted by the Act (6.38), with less stringent conditions, and the main differences between that and 6.33 in respect of archival copying between nonprofit-based libraries are:

(a) coverage by 6.33 of any kind of copyright work, subject to obtaining permission for anything other than printed matter
(b) whilst 6.38 could allow a nonprofit-based library to end up with an additional copy of any item of printed matter (only), facilitating the preservation of one copy.

Articles of cultural or historical importance

6.36 When an article of cultural or historical importance, such as an artistic work or important document, cannot legally be exported from the UK unless a copy is deposited in a library or archive, a copy may be made for that purpose (s44). This is a general permission without conditions, which applies to any kind of copyright material. Of all the library provisions, this is the only one which by implication embraces artistic material.

Interlibrary copying for research or private study

6.37 The Act does not specify any particular location for a requester, and it is accordingly assumed that a request need not be made personally by a requester on the spot. Someone could visit his local, or any other, library – distance, time and travel costs permitting. It is accordingly advised that any kind of library or archive may respond to an individual request received through another library, despite the advisory limitation of profit-based library copying to in-house needs as far as regular service is concerned. Whatever form of request is received, it must contain a copyright declaration made in advance of copying. This applies to any research or private study copying by any kind of library, including unpublished works as in 6.16. However, both nonprofit and profit-based services should be aware that, as mentioned previously, copying of separate photographs is only possible as stated in 5.21.

Some libraries are uncertain as to where the declarations should be held. The answer is quite simple when it is borne in mind that a declaration serves *only* to cover the action of a copying library, being quite unnecessary for copying by an individual for himself. The declarations should accordingly be filed by the library which does the copying. In the interlibrary context, this means that a requesting library must pass on a duplicate of the form signed on the spot by a requester.

Interlibrary copying for stock

6.38 Some interlibrary copying for stock has already been described for archival purposes in 6.33. Another route applies to the stock of nonprofit-based services but, unlike archival copying under s42, this does not cover copying by a library for its own stock from its own stock (s41). However, it is noted that, although a supplying library can provide only one copy, there is no regulation which prevents a receiving nonprofit-based library which already holds one copy of an item of printed matter from seeking another by this method (16.10). This makes the provision a useful ancillary to 6.33 on archival copying. A letter, *not* a standard declaration, is required from the nonprofit-based service concerned, and the conditions are:

(a) the requesting library must not be supplied with more than one copy of a periodical article or the whole or part of a published nonperiodical item

(b) if the request is for more than one article in a given periodical issue, or for the whole or part of a published nonperiodical item, the request letter must state that the library is a nonprofit-based service and does not know, nor could reasonably ascertain, the name and address of a person entitled to authorise the making of the copy
(c) the requesting library must pay not less than the cost of copying plus a contribution to the general expenses of the copying library.

Although a profit-based service may copy for the stock of a nonprofit-based service, profit-based services are not authorised to receive stock copies in this way. Some librarians have expressed doubts on the applicability of s41 to copying for stock, since those words are not actually stated in CDPA88. This long-standing permission seems never to have been properly applied by nonprofit-based libraries in any case. After answering an enquiry about the s32 limitations on archival copying for stock which SI 1989/1212 had made more restrictive than the Act as passed, the DTI wrote on 8 September 1989: '*Librarians may however copy under the provisions of section 41 ... It does, of course, mean that a library cannot copy from its own collection* (as noted above already)... *a copy can only be made from another library's collection.*' When the above conditions do not apply for any reason, a copy for stock can be obtained from BLDSC using the normal application form but annotating it with an indication that the copy is required for library stock. Whether the donation to stock of a copy made for another permitted purpose might infringe has been discussed in 5.9.

Because the ramifications of the library regulations, as noted in 6.2, have caused confusion for a number of years to many information workers approaching copyright for the first time, Figure 1 contains three simple diagrams illustrating just the permissible supply routes between libraries.

Whole works

6.39 Some 'whole work' capabilities have already been mentioned above: books (s41; see 6.38); anything for archival replacement (s42, see 6.33); unpublished documents (s43; see 6.16 and 6.37; and articles of 'cultural or historical importance' (s44; see 6.36). Caution when copying from 'whole works' is necessary, and implicit in the definition of infringement as involving a substantial part. The BCC's statement on fair dealing includes: poems, short stories and other short literary works must be regarded as whole works in themselves, and not as parts of the volumes in which they appear. In the case of poems and short stories published in such volumes, fair dealing for the purposes of research or private study only will be taken to allow the copying of a short story or poem which does not exceed ten pages in length as in Q2. It is recommended that this should be regarded as applicable whether under fair dealing or library copying provisions of the Act.

Often a poem which is embedded in other text, such as a chapter of a book, could be copied as part of a permitted extract, but discretion should be applied in respect of the extent and nature of the work and whether the whole is really an anthology with critical text interposed. However, the BCC's ten-page allowance should serve most research or private study needs.

6.40 Out of print?

When a work is out of print, the publisher could be asked for permission to copy a proportion greater than Q2 norms, or the whole work. When publishers prove difficult to contact, a nonprofit- based library could be asked to exercise the discretion which it is allowed in deciding what is a 'reasonable proportion', especially since guidelines do not cover this circumstance.

When the publisher or current copyright owner cannot be traced, even copying the whole work could be considered fair dealing if for research or private study. Nonprofit-based library options have already been noted, such as interlibrary supply of a whole book to a nonprofit-based library for stock (6.38).

6.41 Illustrations and slides

As noted in 5.6(d), 'artistic works' in general are included under fair dealing but excluded from nonprofit-based library copying. However, any library can copy artistic works under fair dealing (6.21) for research or private study and some other statutory permissions. And, although nonprofit-based libraries are specifically authorised only to copy from written or printed matter, that clearly includes illustrations accompanying the text or in the typographical arrangement.

Care should be taken with illustrations to be copied for use outside their published context, such as art illustrations or photographs, for they may be whole works in themselves. The BCC has expressed the view that, for instructional purposes which do not involve publication: '*one slide or transparency may...be made of an illustration in a published edition of a work provided that the source is duly acknowledged.*'

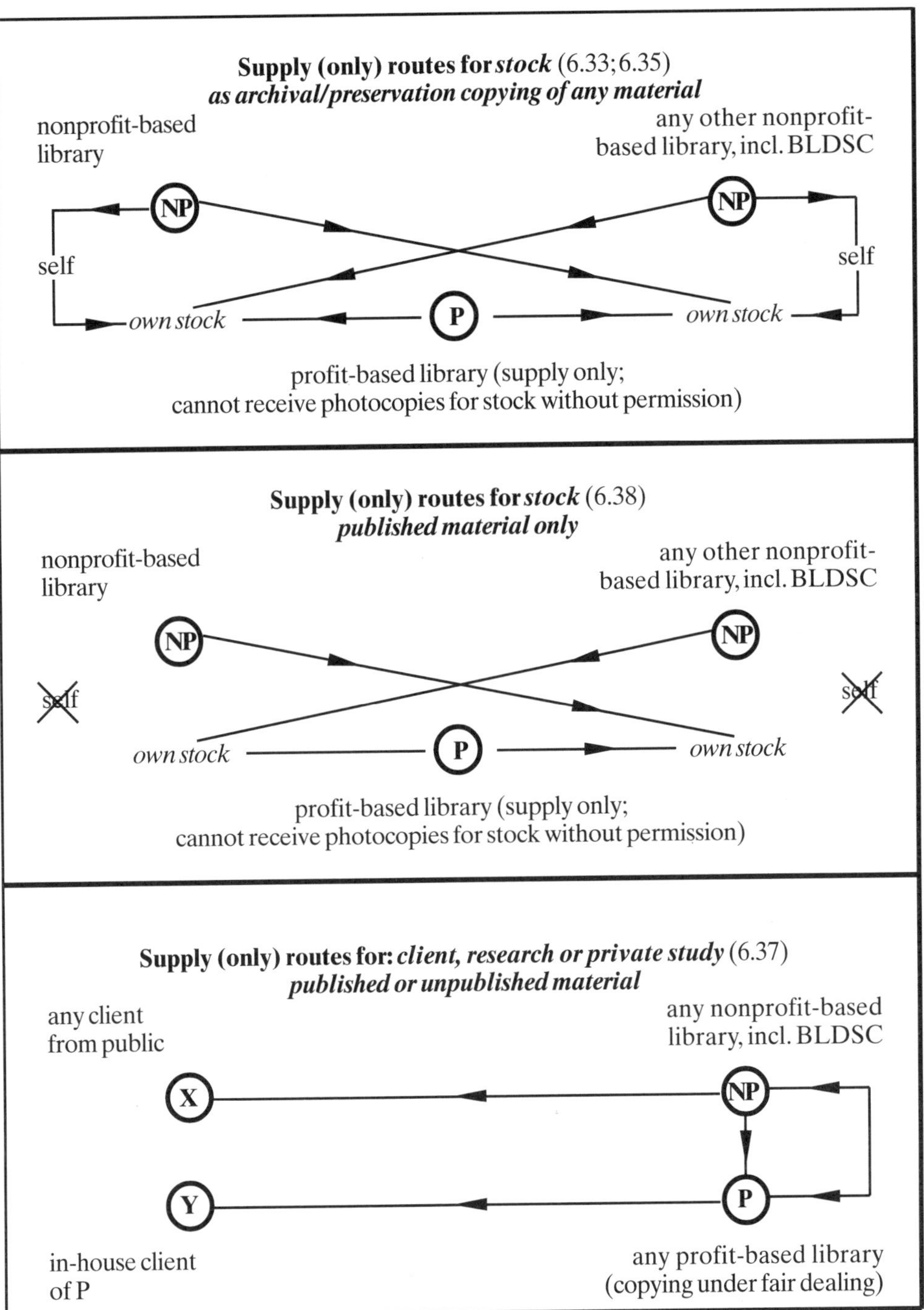

Figure 1: Interlibrary copying

With regard to libraries which are active in slide-making rather than passive collectors, a licence may be required (7.7; 8.29; 8.31).

The British Photographers' Liaison Committee guidelines (App. 1/3) do not agree with the BCC view about slides. The BPLC however would regard it as reasonable for a single copy of a photograph to be 'made by or on behalf of an individual for his private use...' Whilst in general the choice of the word 'private' here is recommended as interpretable as equal to 'research or private study', the notes in 5.12 should be studied.

6.42 Computer programs

Library or archive copying, when carried out under the specific library copying provisions for research or private study, is limited to written or printed matter, as already noted, and this excludes computer programs in electronic form. However, when a program appears in a publication, an extract could be photocopied but not the whole embedded work. Fair dealing for research or private study similarly excludes electronic forms, but computer programs are included in the Act's definition of 'literary work' and remain literary despite physical format, hence fair dealing theoretically applies (5.5). But that would be virtually impossible to achieve as 'fair' in practice from an electronic format, since loading a program is defined in CDPA88 as copying it – that is, all of it. However, a new situation has arisen from EC harmonisation, as noted in 7.15-7.20, and the regulations issued as SI 1992/3233 now closely circumscribe what may be done, including some new permissions. A library or archive could act on behalf of someone in respect of the permissions, as well as apply them for the service's own internal purposes.

6.43 Abstracts

Abstracts of scientific or technical journal articles which accompany the articles (author-abstracts) may be copied to any extent or published, unless a licensing scheme is available (s60; 15.26). Since 'scientific or technical' is a very broad phrase and could be taken to cover even the Social Sciences, just about every situation wherein author-abstracts might be found is covered by this permission, such abstracts being uncommon in the Arts and Humanities. However, though publishers have not ruled out the possibility of a licensing scheme, it is difficult to see how a scheme could apply to any use other than publishing. This permission, though welcomed by producers of current awareness bulletins, including publishers, may create some uncertainty as to whether the abstracts in a published abstracting service are copyright or not, but they are of course copyright as typographical layouts anyway. Accordingly, items in a published abstracting service should all be treated as though they are indeed copyright *and* protected by database right (3.28 et seq.). Another aspect should be borne in mind: that abstracters and precis writers create copyright in their work. However, if a precis is so full as to render consultation of the original work unnecessary, the writer could be accused of infringement (5.22).

Overseas material

6.44 As remarked already (5.34), overseas material should normally be treated in the same way as UK material, unless it is known that an alternative procedure is possible, for example if the source country is known to be non-EEA or a non-signatory to the international conventions (see 13). Those holding licences will need to be aware of the country limitations in the licence, especially in respect of multiple copying. US government publications represent another kind of example (see 14.21).

Further copying by libraries

6.45 There is nothing in CDPA88 to prevent anyone from acting on behalf of another person in respect of the various statutory permissions, with only two exceptions. Many of the permissions would be quite pointless if a library were forbidden to copy for any other purpose than those covered in the 'library copying' provisions for printed matter for research or private study, as already noted in 5.6. Most of the material needing to be copied will be in libraries anyway and much may not be loanable for one reason or another, such as archival preservation. It is emphasised therefore that any persons, including any librarians, should regard themselves as able to act on behalf of someone requiring permitted copying to be done. The only statutory limit on copy numbers is that expressed in s29, where only one copy may be made for someone else for research or private study. This applies to almost all of the Act's permissions in respect of whatever kind of copyright material may be involved. The two exceptions are both in the educational context (see Q5), where the copying concerned must be done by *a person giving or receiving instruction*. A permission which allows *anything* be done may be particularly relevant here (see Q8), such as copying for Parliamentary or judicial proceedings (7.9), or for a *Royal Commission or statutory inquiry* which should include planning submissions (see 7.10), or copying for examination purposes (7.2). It should also be noted that the photocopying limits on the research or private study chart are certainly not intended to apply to other permitted copying.

These other permissions bring in material additional to written or printed matter. It is however advised that a person asking for copying on his behalf for a particular purpose should be asked to make a written and signed request, to be kept on file in case of an approach by rights owners for a suggested 12 years rather than the period of 6 years applied to research or private study declarations. In preparation for requests for planning copies under s46, which are likely to be fairly frequent, libraries should devise and stock standard declaration forms (6.51). All users – from individuals to librarians and archivists – are recommended to see the permissions outline Q3 and summary Q8, plus the photocopying options summary in Q4. Those in academic institutions, and of course teachers and students, should also study the summary on educational permissions in Q5 (plus licensed extents).

Photocopying in excess of guidelines

6.46 This applies to the copying of written or printed matter. When needing extents which exceed the legal permissions and guidelines or advisory limits given in this book, or more than one copy of the same item, or more than one article from the same issue of a periodical, the options when the originals are on the spot are:

(a) seek permission to copy from or via the publisher, using the standard form supplied in 6.51 which has been designed for ease of response. (The 'or via' is because the publisher might refer the enquiry to the author, but even so there is a better chance of the publisher knowing the author's address than the person requiring permission)
(b) if the copy is required by a body which is already licensed by the Copyright Licensing Agency (for whatever purpose) but the licence does not cover the need, contact CLARCS, the CLA Rapid Clearance System (8.13).

If the need is for more than one copy of an item which is within the limits in Q2, but a multiple-copying licence is not held, a user's action must depend on the anticipated frequency of this sort of requirement, and the kind of organisation concerned. The CLA's licensed single-copy limits are the same as its multiple-copying limits, except that non-periodical material is confined to up to 5 per cent or one complete chapter without any leeway in respect of short books as in Q2. An infrequent need is obviously better answered by (a), but a recurrent need in a profit-based library or archive should lead to the weighing of licensing possibilities and costs against staff time. (See also 8.11).

Document supply

6.47 When an item is not held and the required extent or purposes are beyond inter-library loan possibilities, and purchase or permitted downloading from an online service are not viable options, one has long been able to apply to the British Library Document Supply Centre for a 'cleared copy' (8.10). (See also copying for library stock, 6.38.) Many other centres than BLDSC have been licensed to supply photocopies in recent years. This kind of service may in some cases be considered as tantamount to on-demand publishing (3.64). With a plethora of services, their comparison and evaluation becomes ever more important to management decisions (See FIDDO report Appendix 1/3). Document supply centres should now be found covered in listings mentioned in 6.50 below, and most if not all should now involve some degree of 'electronic' activity. Indeed, the first (apparently) use of publisher-provided electronic text for document supply was announced in the April of 1997 (British Library and Elsevier), though all end-use copies will continue to be supplied as hard copies (including fax).

Electronic libraries

6.48 The concept of the 'digital library' was introduced in 3.53. It is suggested that the electronic library concept is broader, including electronic 'housekeeping' for borrowing, reservation, cataloguing, etc systems developed from pioneer work through the 1970s. Such systems, plus an ECMS and a digitized collection, and links to collections and systems elsewhere, form the essential infrastructure for the electronic library. This section outlines the research in progress towards a kind of library capable of digital storage and access in respect of as much material as may be required, both on the spot and remotely, including electronic document delivery via interlibrary loan or from a document supply centre, and the supply a copy to a user in digital form – if desired and if permissible under copyright law or service contract. Much US work is in hand, as already exemplified (3.36). Funding is now globally based, the G7 countries having agreed in 1996 to sponsor electronic library research as part of progress towards the Information Society.

The work begun by De Montfort University in 1991 led to the setting up in 1996 of the University's Institute for Electronic Library Research, having formed cooperative links with other institutions and commercial firms, and EU funding for a range of projects was obtained. In Europe as a whole, the CEC ESPRIT range of research projects includes a number of important work areas. However, the projects financed by the UK as a result of the Follett Report (6.49) probably form the largest and most significant national research effort, necessarily needing rights-owner cooperation. The readiness to co-operate varies, but provided adequate assurance is given of the experimental nature of the proposed usage and promises are made not to re-copy material for other purposes, most publishers are helpful and demonstrate their vested interest in the outcome.

CITED (Appendix 1/8) is an early example of what can be achieved by co-operation between publishers, software experts, and librarians, wherein the British Library was involved as a partner. Other BL research proposals in its *Research and innovation bulletin* (quarterly) show ever-deeper involvement in electronic innovations. Those wishing to monitor electronic library developments will scan the professional press in general, but may find the more fruitful sources to be *The electronic library* (Learned Information (Europe) Limited, Oxford, bi-monthly, 1983 onwards) or *Program: electronic library and inforomation systems* (Aslib, quarterly), together with news items and articles in the long-established *Managing information* (Aslib, monthly).

6.49 Electronic Libraries Programme

The UK's Joint Funding Council (of the Higher Education Funding Councils of England, Wales and Scotland respectively) set up a Libraries Review Group, chaired by Professor Sir Brian Follett, for a government-commissioned study. In response to the Group's report of 1993, the Joint Information Systems Committee (JISC) launched the Follett Implementation Group for Information Technology (FIGIT) Electronic Libraries Programme (eLib). The UK Office of Library Networking (UKOLN) provides an information serrvice on the eLib programme on: *http://www.ukoln.ac.uk/elib* plus a list on e-mail at *lis-elib@mailbase.ac.uk* for discussion of projects. The Higher Education Digitisation Centre mentioned in 3.36 is among those listed.

Up to the time of writing, 61 eLib projects had been set up and a number completed.

With the recently reported commercially-based project for the digitisation by imaging techniques of an ancient Chinese text dating from 858AD in the BL – the *Diamond Sutra* –the 'circle' seems at least joined but expands apace and will never be squared!

The hard copy information package available from the Programme Director at the University of Warwick (e-mail: *cudbw@warwick.ac.uk*) describes and lists the subjects covered as: access to network resources; digitisation; document delivery; electronic journals; electronic short loan collection; images; on-demand publishing; pre-prints and grey literature; quality assurance; supporting studies; and training and awareness. Most of these involve copyright, but the on-demand publishing projects and the new electronic short loan collection projects are said to deal the more directly with copyright issues. However, these two categories overlap considerably in academic libraries requiring better service in respect of short-loan (or 'reserved collection') requests for high-use reading course material. Examples are: the Scottish Collaborative On-demand Publishing Enterprise (SCOPE) at Stirling and Napier universities via the SuperJanet network; and Access to Course Reading via Networks (ACORN). The research team for ACORN is based at Loughborough and works in collaboration with periodicals subscriptions agents (Swets and Zeitlinger). In eLib as a whole, clearance for using copyright materials during the project has not always been easy to obtain, but in ACORN a large percentage of favourable replies has been received from publishers, albeit at widely varying charges. Selected materials are currently being input to the internal network for access by students (Project Acorn web site: *http://acorn.lboro.ac.uk/*). Some image digitisation problems have already been noted in 3.36.

FIGIT and the BL itself are by no means the only sources of research funds for UK venues, which sources notably include the EU as well as the USA, often in collaboration across national boundaries and between publishers and libraries, and the above should be taken as mere specimens of the very considerable work in progress.

The use of publications placed directly on to the Net has been mentioned in 3.49.

6.50 Electronic document delivery

Included in the foregoing are some projects which involve 'electronic document delivery' in the sense of on-line transmission to a user's own system. Such facilities are among those which are the more, and more urgently, desirable to the user, but also those which cause database producers the most hesitation. As might be expected, the reason for producer concern is that on-line receipt would carry 'electrocopying' right through to the user, and could lead to onward or even multiple copying without permission, whether deliberately or not. Until solutions arise, probably from the experiments in progress, users need to note that there is a broader meaning of the phrase, namely the use of electronics as at least one link in the chain but not necessarily the end-result. On-line services containing full text, including electronic journals, already do 'deliver' on-line to the user, but licensed downloading for addition to an in-house database is not at present a general practice.

Another interpretation which many librarians would like is the ability to digitise from stock for an internal database and transmit to a student or other requester for on-line receipt and downloading into a personal system, and this is just what experiments like ACORN, above, are aiming to do. At the University of Surrey, PATRON (Performing Arts Teaching Resources Online) is notable as an eLib project for the on-demand supply of digital copies of multimedia materials to students over networks (*http://www.surrey.ac.uk/library/research/patron.html*).

Systems for the electronic transmission of requests, or delivery by fax of print, or supply on CD-ROM with permission to the user to print within limits, are all regarded as 'electronic document delivery' in its broad sense. These are all important to inter-library loan, of course, and managements need evaluative information on the services available, which seem to grow in number day by day. Some are also important in their ability readily to be 'switched' into on-line delivery when producer consensus is achieved and/or an ECMS becomes generally adopted: for example, UnCover, providing fax copies of articles now but also building up continuously a large full text database by co-operative input from a group of American universities. An example of efforts to assist users to select service options is FIDDO (Focused Investigation of Document Delivery Options). Based on Loughborough University of Technology, this eLib project aims to provide evaluative information on hard copy and electronic document delivery services, in order to aid management decisions on selection and use. The recent FIDDO report (Appendix 1/3) surveys projects as follows: four 'resource-sharing'; six 'network/communication'; seven 'electronic scanning'; and eleven 'electronic document delivery systems'. The report also covers commercial suppliers and services: six 'non-collection based'; seven 'collection based'; and seven 'specialised collection based'. Tables contain concise details for comparison. (Web address for the report is given in App. 1/8). FIDDO may be compared with an American evaluative study for academic librarians by B. B. Higginbotham and S. Bowdoin, reported on along with other material by Elizabeth Finnie in her article *Selection and evaluation of document suppliers* in the *Document delivery special* issue of *Managing Information* (Aslib), vol. 4(3) March 1997, pages 25-26 and 31-32.

Suggested forms

6.51 The following four pages contain suggested forms. The third is included to facilitate service by libraries or archives which have so far confined their copying to research or private study.

- Declaration form for copying for purposes of research or private study, from *published* material (based on SI 1989/1212).
- Ditto, for *un-published* material.
- Declaration form for copying for purposes *other than* research or private study.
- A permission request form, suggested as standard for published material other than sheet music (for which see MPA Code (Appendix 1/3).

DECLARATION

Copying for Research or Private Study from a Published Work by the Staffed Service of a Library or Archive

To the librarian/archivist of (name and address): ....

....

Please supply me with a copy of the following item for research or private study

(delete/complete/abbreviate as necessary)

periodical article – periodical title: ....
author and title of article: ....

....

volume, part and inclusive pagination: ....

or (tick)

part of a book/report, etc: *chapter___ illustration___ map___ table___ other____*
author and title: ....

....

publisher/source organisation: ....
publication year: .... inclusive pagination: ....

I declare that:

(a) I have not been supplied with a copy of the same material by you or any other librarian or archivist;

(b) I will not use the copy except for research or private study and will not supply a copy of it to any other person;

(c) to the best of my knowledge no other person with whom I work or study has made or intends to make, at or about the same time as this request, a request for substantially the same material or substantially the same purpose.

I understand that if this declaration is false in a material particular the copy supplied to me by you will be an infringing copy and that I shall be liable for infringement of copyright as if I had made the copy myself.

Personal signature: .... Date: ....
Name: ....
Address: ....

....

Note for staff: Fair dealing with a map – Ordnance Suryey guideline of A4 size copy should not be exceeded for this purpose without permission. For maps for planning applications, use other form re statutory inquiries.

DECLARATION

Copying for Research or Private Study from Unpublished Material by the Staffed Service of a Library or Archive

To the librarian/archivist of (name and address): ....

....

....

Please supply me with a copy of the following item for research or private study

(delete/complete/abbreviate as necessary)

Description of material

Author, title and part (or whole item) required: ....

....

....

....

Source organisation: ....

Inclusive pagination: ....

I declare that:

(a) I have not been supplied with a copy of the same material by you or any other librarian or archivist;

(b) I will not use the copy except for research or private study and will not supply a copy of it to any other person;

(c) to the best of my knowledge the work had not been published before the document was deposited in your library/archive and the copyright owner had not prohibited copying of the work.

I understand that if this declaration is false in a material particular the copy supplied to me by you will be an infringing copy and that I shall be liable for infringement of copyright as if I had made the copy myself.

Personal signature: .... Date: ....

Name: ....
Address: ....
....
....

DECLARATION

Copying for Purposes other than Research or Private Study by the Staffed Service of a Library or Archive

To the librarian/archivist of (name and address): ....

....

Please supply me with __ copies of the following for the purpose below

(delete/complete/abbreviate as necessary)

description of item and author/title/source/pagination details: ....

....

Purpose of copying *(add yes or no)* –

(1) for **judicial proceedings** which have commenced (copying as permitted by CDPA88s45)? ____

(2) for a **statutory inquiry** as permitted by CDPA88s46 (e.g. planning application)? ____

(3) to **obtain information** (CDPA88s47) from material laid open to public inspection? ____

(4) **other**: ____

Notes for service staff about (3) only:

(a) If the source material is laid open to public inspection or on a statutory register (CDPA88s47) such as local authority area development maps, plans and reports, it may be found that a local planning office is bound by contract with the Ordnance Survey and be unable to allow public libraries to copy from OS-based maps (i.e. those which form part of material laid open for inspection).

(b) **Maps, plans or drawings** copied must be marked as specified under CDPA88: *This copy has been made by or with the authority of [insert name of person required to make the material open to public inspection, e.g. planning officer; or the person maintaining the statutory register concerned] pursuant to section 47 of the Copyright, Designs and Patents Act 1988 ('the Act'). Unless the Act provides a relevant exception to copyright, the copy must not be copied without the prior permission of the copyright owner.*

I declare that the copies required will not be used or recopied for any other purpose, and will not be issued to the public without permission.

Personal signature: .... Date: ....
Name: ....
Address: ....
....
....

PERMISSION REQUEST

(It is suggested that readers make stock of photocopies of this master on to letterhead or use as basis for making a template for fax or e-mail)

To (Publisher): .... Date: ....

Copyright Permissions Department, ...

....

....

....

We should be grateful for permission to make ___ copies of the extract or article referred to below, **or** scan/download (for internal use) into our own database * for the purpose of:

- screen access by, **or** copy supply to, students or selected staff*
- research or private study, but believed in excess of normal extents*
- other* ....

** delete/complete/abbreviate as necessary*

Source – periodical title *or* book author and title: ....

....

Volume: .... Date: .... Pages: ....

Author and title of portion wanted: ....

If you require payment, please indicate this under (2) in the reply portion below – your returned photocopy of this page would then be treatable as a pro-forma invoice.

If at all possible, an early response would be very much appreciated by mail or fax. In case mail is preferred, UK publishers will find a reply-paid envelope enclosed.

Signed: .... Date: ....
Name in block letters: ....
Department: ....
....

Publisher's reply *(on a duplicate of whole page, please)*

1 The above can be supplied immediately as an offprint costing ___ per copy

2 Permission is given for making copies, subject to a cost of ___ per copy

3 Free permission is given to copy as requested

4. Permission cannot be given because: ....

5 Remarks: ....

Signature: .... *Date:*..........................

7. OTHER COPYING PERMISSIONS

General note on database right

Readers are requested to refer to **Q0** before proceeding with study of permissions chapters 5, 6, 7 and 9. Any permissions should be qualified by the details of database right (3.28) if not already specified herein. Absence of mention in a description of a permission must not be taken to imply its relevance to database right.

None of the copyright permissions in this chapter, other than those for public administration (7.9-7.14), is reflected under database right, and any action must relate only to an insubstantial part at least pro tem. However, there is a database right permission relating to 'illustration' for the purposes of teaching or research which, like other database right permissions, does not distinguish between print and nonprint. Although it relates to the extraction or re-utilisation of substantial parts, it is under fair dealing and only constitutes a defence if necessary. Also, commercial purpose is excluded, and the possible relevance to private educational establishments is not yet known. It is not yet known whether a CLA licence can be taken to cover copying from a printed database, but licensees may choose to proceed as though it is unless told otherwise, especially as there is at present no means of detecting which actually qualify for database rights!

Note on scope of this chapter

This chapter is primarily concerned with copyright permissions other than fair dealing or library copying. The remaining permissions in the Act relate to playing, showing or performing, and lending. These are described in chapter 9.

Educational copying

7.1 These notes concern copying alone. The computer program permissions in 7.16 may also be relevant. Other educational permissions are covered in chapters 6 and 9, and all are summarised in Q5 at the beginning of this book. For example, the HMSO permissions in 6.24 include many kinds of document which can be copied freely for non-publishing purposes, and it is made clear that one copy can be made for every student. A database right permission has been referred to under the prefatory general note above.

Manual copying of any original work Copying does not infringe, states s32 of the Act, if done manually by someone giving or receiving instruction, such as using a blackboard or taking notes. Although expressed as a 'permitted act', this is also a restriction because s32 forbids reprographic copying, making either permission or licensing essential for class copies for distribution.

7.2 Examination questions or answers

Anything done for questions or answers with any kind of work, including single or multiple copying, does not infringe copyright, except reprographic copying of music for performance by a candidate (s32(3)). The effect of this on continuous assessment is unclear, but the general availability and necessity of licensing for educational copying makes this question literally academic. However, neither the Act's use of the words 'anything done', any more than a multiple copying licence for classes, can be taken as permitting publication. The publication of a collection of exam questions requires copyright clearance for the inclusion of any extracts larger than the 'quotation' allowances (5.23) from all rights owners concerned. (See also 7.7.)

7.3 Instruction in making films or film soundtracks

Copying sound or video recordings, films, broadcasts or cable programmes does not infringe copyright when done during film or film sound-track preparation during instruction, provided the copying is done by the person giving or receiving instruction (s32(2); see also 9.3).

7.4 'Instruction' cf 'educational establishment'

It should be noted that the above three provisions are all in s32, which is the only educational section which refers only to 'instruction' and not to 'educational establishment', thus broadening the application considerably. An educational establishment is a school or institution of further, higher, or vocational education, however funded, according to clarification of SI 1989/1068 secured from the Department of Education and Science at that time (8.27).

7.5 Multiple copying for classes

Despite the foregoing, reprographic copies of passages from published works may be made by an educational establishment for educational purposes without any infringement, provided

- copying is limited to 1 per cent per quarter from any work
- no licensing scheme is available to authorise the copying (s36).

The aim of this section of the Act was to encourage collective licensing without actual compulsion, which was seen as contrary to the Berne Convention as mentioned elsewhere. This provision has been criticised by some observers as being an absolutely minimal incentive for publishers to join a licensing scheme. That the CLA schemes (8.2) are now available is mainly due to the fact that the licensing movement was already well under way in the education sector when the Act was passed. As yet there appears to be little reduction in the list of excluded publishers from CLA schemes, suggesting that a much larger permission than 1 per cent would have been preferable, despite the rejection of relevant lobbying during the passage of CDPA88. (See also 6.25 re HMSO material.)

7.6 Anthologies

A short passage from a published literary or dramatic work may be published in an anthology without infringement, if advertised and entitled as intended for use in educational establishments for educational purposes. However, the provision goes on to place limitations on inclusion which would cause administrative waste of time to apply in practice: for example, not more than two excerpts from copyright works by the same author in collections published by the same publisher over any period of five years. Some works could be reprints rather than new editions, and out of copyright but not perceptibly so to the uninitiated. Hence it would seem easier to seek permission from relevant publishers for publication of anthologies (s33), especially as some anthologies will probably be databases.

7.7 Slides and transparencies

In 7.1 the prohibition of 'reprographic copying' was noted. As the definition of reprographic process includes a copy which is reduced or enlarged in scale (s178), a slide or transparency can be made and used only within the limits suggested by the BCC guidelines (6.41). A slide could carry copyright both as a photograph and as a copy of a copyright work such as a portrait.The BCC neverthless took the view that one slide or transparency can be made from an illustration for instructional purposes which do not involve publication. The British Photographers Liaison Committee and later DACS (8.29) do not agree with the BCC view. The DACS licence covers *collections*, and would seem irrelevant unless an establishment were to form a collection, whether by gathering in all slides made on the spot or by obtaining copies from elsewhere. Therefore, if obstruction to education were to be avoided, a compromise seemed desirable. Libraries do not normally have any control over the actions of individual teachers, who must have freedom to do their jobs. Accordingly, the following was suggested as a possible qualification which DACS might be prepared to accept as a qualification of the BCC view.

When transparencies are not available commercially or borrowable from a licensed collection, and/or permission-seeking is not feasible, production from published works, by or on behalf of teachers or instructors, might be regarded as reasonable, provided that any resultant slides or transparencies of artistic works:

(a) include sufficient acknowledgement of source, and are subsequently deposited in a licensed collection under the terms of the licence; or
(b) are kept in a personal file until superseded and neither loaned nor further copied.

It is noted that some permissions cover any purpose, such as exam questions or answers (s32(3)), without infringing copyright. An example might be the making by an individual student of overhead transparencies for class showing along with a brief talk, done as part of coursework.

7.8 Off-air recording

The recording of a broadcast or cable programme, or making a copy of such a recording, by an educational establishment for educational purposes is permitted, unless a licensing scheme which covers the desired action is available (s35). Suitable schemes emerged rapidly and rendered this permission unnecessary (8.25). It should be noted that teletext services such as those mentioned in 3.8, are as much subject to educational recording as any other broadcasts or cable programmes.

Public administration

7.9 Parliamentary or judicial proceedings

Anything done for these purposes, or for the purposes of reporting such proceedings, excluding the copying of published reports of the proceedings, does not infringe copyright (s45). The Law Society interprets this provision as allowing 'anything' from the time of issue of a writ, in other words once proceedings have begun. However, the single copies made by or for individuals preparing cases are of course to be allowed as 'research or private study' copies when within norms. This permission also applies to database right.

7.10 Royal Commission or statutory inquiry

Anything done for these purposes, or for the purposes of reporting proceedings held in public, excluding the copying of published reports of the proceedings, does not infringe copyright. 'Royal Commission' includes a Commission appointed for Northern Ireland by the Secretary of State, and 'statutory inquiry' means an inquiry held or investigation conducted in accordance with statutory requirements or powers (s46). This permission also applies to database right. Maps for planning purposes would seem to be included in the permitted copying, but although an Ordnance Survey guidance leaflet has mentioned *statutory inquiry* when mentioning other general permissions such as fair dealing, it was not acknowledged that copying for planning submissions, being required by Town and Country Planning law, could be regarded as permissible without the form of licence which OS offered. However, public libraries in the Map Extract Scheme (8.35) do not appear to have been asked to charge royalties for planning copies requested by individuals.

7.11 Public inspection or official register

Three subsections appear under this heading (s47). What they amount to is that a member of the public can be provided with a copy of material laid open to public inspection as a statutory requirement, or on a statutory register, without infringement of copyright

- to inspect it at a more convenient time and place
- to contribute to fulfilment of the purpose of laying the material open to inspection
- to disseminate information of general scientific, technical, commercial or economic interest;

subject to authorisation by the person made responsible for laying the material open to inspection or maintaining an official register. The venues could be bodies such as a local planning office (maps, plans, rationale for projected road layouts, etc.), the Patent Office (patent specifications), or Companies House (company annual reports).

There is no expressed limitation to written or printed material, and it would seem that any kind of information source could be involved. 'Statutory requirement' means a provision made by or under legislation. 'Statutory register' simply means a register maintained in accordance with a statutory requirement. (Copies made under s47 must be annotated, and a declaration should be obtained from a requestor; see 6.51.) This permission also applies to database right.

7.12 Material communicated to the Crown

When any original work (literary, dramatic, musical or artistic) has been communicated to the Crown in the course of public business – that is, any Crown activity – the Crown may copy the work and issue copies to the public without infringing copyright, unless there is an agreement to the contrary between the Crown and the copyright owner. The Crown is not empowered to take this action when the work has already been published (s48). This permission also applies to database right.

7.13 Public records

Public records which are open to inspection may be copied for anyone without infringement of copyright, subject to authorisation by the officer concerned (s49). The records must be those which are open to public inspection in accordance with the Public Records Act 1958 and equivalents for Scotland and Northern Ireland. However, it is clear from those Acts that any kind of medium can be involved, so there is no limitation to written or printed matter. This permission also applies to database right.

7.14 Actions authorised by statute

Whenever the relevant Act was passed, such actions do not infringe copyright (s50). This permission also applies to database right.

Computer programs

7.15 SI 1992/3233 came into force on 1 January 1993 and arose from EU harmonisation of copyright law (13.12). The SI is entitled: The Copyright (Computer Programs) Regulations 1992, and was made on 16 December 1992. It amends CDPA88 in a number of places, and some comments have already been made in 4.13 and 5.4. The definition of 'literary' in s3 is extended beyond simply 'computer programs' to include preparatory design material for a computer program. Adjustments are made to ss18 and 27 to suit the issue of copies within the EC and their importation to the UK. Some important permissions are given, as follows.

7.16 Permissions concerning computer programs

1. Back-up copies

> [A lawful user does not infringe copyright by making] any backup copy ... which it is necessary for him to have for the purposes of his lawful use (s50A).

So more than one backup copy could be made if circumstances so demand. A person is a 'lawful user' of a computer program if (whether under a licence to do any of the acts restricted by the copyright in the program or otherwise) he has a right to use the program. Agreement terms cannot overrule this permission, thus all relevant contracts are henceforth limited. (See 3.37 for 'lawful user' in database right.)

7.17 2. 'Decompilation' or conversion

'Decompilation' or conversion of a program language from lower to higher level is permitted under a new s50B by a lawful user, subject to specified conditions. Another amendment excepts decompilation from the very general aegis of fair dealing where other – perhaps 'unlawful' – users might otherwise have assumed its inclusion without any conditions. Agreement terms, again, cannot overrule this permission.

Conditions for decompilation:

A lawful user does not infringe copyright by decompilation as defined above when

(a) decompilation is needed to obtain information necessary to create an independent program which can be operated with the program decompiled or with another program ('the permitted objective') and
(b) the information thus obtained is not used otherwise than for the permitted objective, or supplied to any other person who is not relevant to that objective; and
(c) the information is not used to create a program which is substantially similar in its expression to the program decompiled or to do any act restricted by copyright; or
(d) has readily available the necessary information without decompiling.

7.18 **3. Copying or adaptation**, subject to conditions. A lawful user does not infringe copyright by such action when the copy or adaptation (s50C)

(a) is necessary for his lawful use; and
(b) is not prohibited under a contract which regulates the conditions under which his use is 'lawful'; or
(c) may be necessary for the purpose of correcting errors in the program.

These conditions cannot overrule the backup copying and decompilation provisions above.

An 'adaptation', in this context, is defined as an *arrangement* or *altered version* of the program or a translation of it (amendment to s21). The meaning of 'translation' given in s21 is also amended as follows: in relation to a computer program a 'translation' includes a version of the program in which it is converted into or out of a computer language or code or into a different computer language or code (the former words 'otherwise than incidentally in the course of running the program' being now deleted).

7.19 **4. Use of any device or means** to study, observe or test a program in order to understand the ideas and principles which underlie any element of the program. This is effectively an extension by new s296A of the meaning of 2. from s50B.

Agreement terms *cannot overrule* this provision.

7.20 All these permissions not only harmonise with the rest of Europe but also provide the essential flexibility which was lacking in the 1988 Act in respect of computer programs. Education and research should benefit accordingly. Permission 2. could also help the use of programs by educational establishments with hardware and software compatibility problems. The provisions, notably 4., could be seen as amounting to permitted forms of 'research or private study', but without the single copy limitations applicable to the written or printed matter regime. All the permissions should now allow computer science legally to grow and develop via the cross- fertilisation of ideas in similar fashion to other disciplines. Of special value to the user is the rendering void of any contractual attempts to override 1., 2. and 4. This also applies to 3., unless a contract adversely controls the conditions of 'lawful use'. Furthermore, these provisions apply to programs in existence before the SI came into force as well as to new works, except where a contract to the contrary was made before 1 January 1993 – in other words, the regulations cannot invalidate part of a contract made before that date.

7.21 Further computer program possibilities

From enquiries, some users have appeared uncertain that they may consider themselves capable of:

(a) using a program or any part of it for any purpose for which it was produced; or trying out someone else's copy provided it is not reproduced
(b) lending the program to a colleague for use either on the same or similar equipment, provided no re-usable copy is made (this is an interpretation of shrink-wrap limitations on loan as inapplicable to such circumstances)
(c) lending a program free of charge from a non-public library unless contract prevents it (see 12.18) but not to members of public unless licensed (4.35).
(d) photocopying a portion of a program which is published (3.33), for example as part of a book, for research or private study within the usual copying norms
(e) taking any other action which is allowed by the various permissions sections of CDPA88, especially the 'anything done does not infringe' provisions (Q8), including acting on behalf of another person, provided such actions have not been prohibited by contract.

7.22 **'Don'ts'**: even the 'lawful user' of a computer program may not make copies or adaptations otherwise than as a result of the above permissions or a contractual permission, nor may a program be lent from a public library, with or without charging, unless licensed for rental (4.35).

Design copyright permissions

7.23 These are listed in 11.12-11.16, including Crown use permissions.

Copying of artistic works

Facsimile copying is treated in the notes on 'illustrations accompanying text' (6.21). Other copying of artistic works is possible under fair dealing and of course under certain general permissions such as copying for judicial proceedings (7.9). It should be noted that a copy made with statutory or specific permission may contain permitted modifications, adaptations or associated material, etc, and might be regarded, if the variations were significant, as a copyright work in itself similarly to a music arrangement. (See 9.8 on copying of certain works from public display.)

7.24 Advertising sales

Copies of a work can be made and issued to the public in order to advertise the sale of the work (s63).

7.25 Works by same artist

An artist can copy an artistic work, of which he is no longer the copyright owner, to make another artistic work without infringement, provided he does not repeat or imitate the main design of the earlier work (s64).

7.26 Reconstruction of buildings

Anything done does not infringe, whether in respect of artistic copyright in the building itself or in drawings or plans, etc. (s65).

Other statutory copying permissions

7.27 Incidental inclusion

The incidental inclusion of copyright material in an artistic work, sound recording, film (or video) broadcast or cable programme does not infringe (s31). This also applies to the issue to the public of copies of the work which incidentally includes copyright material, or playing, showing, broadcasting or including the work in a cable programme service. (See also 9.17.) Contrived inclusion would of course not be regarded as incidental, especially if an unduly long or emphasised portion of a copyright work were 'incidentally' included.

7.28 Anonymous or pseudonymous literary, dramatic, musical or artistic works

Any action done on assumption of expiry of copyright or death of author does not infringe when:

- authorship cannot be discovered by reasonable and
- it is reasonable to assume that copyright has expired (s57).

Note that, whenever 'and' ties two provisions together, they must both apply. Some transitional provisions relevant to this section of the Act are discussed in 2.44.

7.29 Timeshift recording of broadcasts or cable programmes

This is permitted for private and domestic use (s70). Unless prohibited by service contract, this could also cover the recording of electronic database searches for private and domestic use, but this might be challengeable because of the implication of the 'and' that both conditions must apply, not 'either'. Broadcast general- purpose information services such as Ceefax and Teletext on channels 3 and 4 are clearly included.

7.30 Transfers of copies of works in electronic form

When a work in electronic form has been purchased on terms which allow the purchaser X to copy or adapt the work, anything which the purchaser was allowed to do may be done by a transferee Y, unless the terms of purchase included limits on actions after transfer to another person (s56). The terms which allow X to copy can be expressly stated or implied, or the allowance can be via any legal permission. According to transitional provisions of CDPA88, this is inapplicable to items purchased before 1 August 1989. However, it does apply to subsequent transfer to Z and onwards.

7.31 Any copies made by X become infringing copies unless they are also transferred. But if X has made a replacement copy of an original which has become unusable, this becomes an infringing copy for all purposes after the transfer to Y, and this is taken to mean that the replacement copy can be transferred no further than Y. Bearing in mind that there is no copyright in an electronic form of record in itself (3.12), this provision would have paralleled the implied situation upon the transfer or re-sale of a book or other item of printed matter, or of an audiovisual recording, but for the last two provisos. The applicability of this provision not only to computer programs but also to everything else stored in electronic form will need to be borne in mind, especially as electrocopying develops. The effect on the audiovisual scene may be unfortunate and should be monitored. Some aspects may lead to litigation: for example, the distinction between copies legally transferred and replacement copies could cause confusion. And, after a couple of transfers, could not the communication of terms begin to suffer as much as word of mouth along the proverbial line of soldiers? (That is, unless communicated from computer files since, in the electrocopying scene, the 'troops' are considered infallible.)

7.32 Photographs: television or cable programmes

For private and domestic use a photograph may be made of the screen display of part of a broadcast or cable programme (s71). This would include online electronic database displays.

7.33 Adaptations

Where an action has been permitted in respect of a literary, dramatic or musical work, that action is also permitted in respect of an adaptation (s76).

7.34 Actions on behalf of another, and photocopying beyond guidelines

Attention is drawn to these two topics in 6.45 and 6.46, since they may well apply to anyone as well as to any library, subject to database right considerations.

8. LICENSED COPYING

General note on this chapter

Changes arising from database right (Q0) may not be clearly evident for some time. Meanwhile, 'lawful user' licences will in effect replace the service contracts which have applied until now, but only in respect of electronic databases. As this goes to press, it appears unlikely that the situation for printed matter databases will change as far as availability of licences is concerned, though the terms will no doubt be modified. (A Schedule 2 to SI 1997/3032 covers licensing of database right.)

The focus in this chapter is upon the copying of copyright material under licence to a greater extent or number of copies than the 'research or private study' norms in Q2. Playing or showing works under licence are matters detailed only in chapter 9, and addresses are in 12.31. Licensing organisations are numerous, and only the main ones are described in this chapter. In all licensing, it should be borne in mind that, as terms can be revised at intervals, any specific points made here should be regarded as subject to a check of the licence currently available. Individual licensing or contracts for specific purposes such as regular copying or re-publication of a particular source are outlined in chapter 12 on copyright administration. Chapter 12 also draws together brief notes on current licensing and contracts. The concept of 'point-of-sale' is treated in 12.35.

New schemes thought to warrant special treatment appear at the end of this chapter in greater detail

Licensing is necessary for copying beyond the statutory or guideline extents and/or purposes. Any copying not specifically authorised by a licence or legal permission must be the subject of a request to the publisher concerned. Licensing brings limits – there is no known licence which does not seek to control, often in detail, what a licensee may do, otherwise a *carte blanche* situation is feared by publishers or producing bodies. A form of licence always warrants careful study, and there should be no hesitation in querying doubtful terms. It might be found that the terms are too restrictive for a user's purpose and could cause frequent and time-consuming approaches direct to publishers. If so, a user could consider working without the licence, staying closely within legal allowances, and seeking clearance directly with a rights owner or using document supply agencies for any multiple copies, or copies for other purposes than those in statutory permissions like fair dealing, or for extents beyond the norms.

Education and licensing

8.1 The largest area of licensed photocopying, at least until industry and commerce become widely licensed, is the education sector. This is because it has become recognised that material cited or distributed to a class does not constitute the purpose of 'private study'. The term 'systematic copying' has been used on behalf of the collective licensing movement in order to describe related copying of the same item by individual members of a given group (5.12), and this is reflected in regulations under the Act (SI 1989/1212). Systematic copying must now be considered equivalent to the making of more than one copy of *substantially the same material at substantially the same time and for substantially the same purpose* (s40). Naturally, any licence covering multiples also allows single copies. In any event, the licences should be stated as 'without prejudice' to – that is, do not affect – the fair dealing and library copying provisions of the Act. Desirably, a licence should also be stated as without prejudice to any other statutory permission, but it has to be noted that contracts may override, except when that effect is prohibited by statute.

Comments on educational licensing appear in 8.9.

Copyright Licensing Agency

8.2 CLA began with the education sector but has expanded beyond it. The results of prolonged discussions on industrial licensing are described in 8.11.

8.3 Multiple copying for classes

Schools, colleges and universities are now licensed by the Copyright Licensing Agency. The terms applicable to institutions of higher education will serve to illustrate the coverage, and the term of the licence has been extended to the end of January 1998. Thereafter, a new form of licence may be negotiated, and a small team representing users is studying possibilities on behalf of the CVCP.

Any staff member or any student may copy as follows for any one course of study in one academic year:

- up to 5 per cent or one complete chapter of a book published in countries with whom CLA has links (8.4), which is not in the list of excluded categories (8.5)

- the whole or part of a single article from a periodical issue published in the countries listed below, which is not an excluded category in the list (8.5)
- from a copy of a chapter or an article made for library stock, for example the reserve collection of high-interest items
- although poems, short stories and the like are regarded as whole works in themselves, one item from an anthology of up to 10 pages may be copied; and a poem (etc.) embedded in a book chapter may be included
- illustrations, including maps, diagrams, etc. which form part of an extract as above (otherwise, see 8.5).

Study packs may be provided, as indicated in 8.8.Number of copies of class multiples: not exceeding sufficient copies to provide one to the tutor and each class member concerned.

8.4 Reciprocating countries

Countries which reciprocate with CLA are: Denmark, France, Germany, Iceland, Ireland, The Netherlands, Norway, Spain, Sweden, Switzerland, Australia, Canada, New Zealand, Quebec, South Africa and the USA. These are all fellow-members with the CLA of the International Federation of Reprographic Rights Organisations IFRRO. The list is slowly growing, and its latest state may be ascertained from the CLA notice supplied for display beside photocopying machines, or by to CLA..

8.5 Excluded categories

- works published outside the above countries
- works on the list of excluded works (involving 77 publishers who have excluded some or all of their works from CLA licensing)
- printed music (including words)
- newspapers -- but note inclusion of French and German
- maps, charts or books of tables
- separate photographs, illustrations and diagrams
- bibles, liturgical works, orders of service
- public examination papers
- privately prepared teaching material (such as correspondence courses) restricted to fee paying individuals
- workbooks, workcards or assignment sheet
- industrial house journals
- all unpublished material
- any work containing a notice stating that it is specifically excluded from the CLA licence.

8.6 Indemnity

The licence includes an indemnity against litigation, required by CDPA88 (s136), for those who follow the terms. It must be noted, however, that the terms include a lengthy list of exclusions in small print, double-sided. This list is now in booklet form with a holed corner for display purposes, but it is still unlikely that users will consult it before copying, even if an organisation is willing to add yet another form of notice to the display areas.

8.7 Short courses and conferences

In addition to the above form of licence, CLA added, for short courses or conferences whereof the students or participants are paying fees to an external organiser and therefore are not members of the licensed institution:

- an 'occasional' licence, with a charge per student per week
- alternatively, for example for a regular 'short course centre', a charge per residential place per annum.

8.8 University study packs

During the first three years of the higher education licence ending December 1992 and extended up to April 1993, multiple copying in order to prepare course anthologies has been covered by the terms, provided no publication ensued without permission. From May 1993 onwards, course anthologies – now called 'study packs' – became subject to separate, additional charges via CLARCS (8.13). Up to four packs per course year, each holding up to three extracts, are nevertheless still covered by the main licence. Until then, most university libraries had preferred to stay out of multiple copying for classes, leaving it to the departments. Some libraries have set up a copyright clearance service in respect of items for 'short loan' or 'reserve' collections which exceed the licensed extents, and this can be a time-saving service for the institution as a whole. The treatment of study packs, and of 'reserve or 'short loan' collections, have been major subjects for negotiation between universities and the CLA during several temporary extensions of the 1993 provisions, the last extension being to the end of January 1998. (See also 8.39.)

Other CLA licensing

CLA offers licences other than the above, as follows:

8.9 Multiples for professional sectors

Copying of multiples for particular professional sectors: only two such arrangements have been made so far. One, for example, covers copying for the legal profession by a commercial agency and requires reporting of copying done. (See also 8.14 on membership associations.)

8.10 Document supply agencies: British Library

The first to be licensed was the British Library Document Supply Centre (Boston Spa, Wetherby, West Yorkshire), and a 'cleared- copy' service began in April 1991. A royalty is added to the BLDSC application cost per copy. Users may:

1. ask for multiple copies of a journal article or book chapter
2. request copies of more than one article per periodical issue, or more than one book chapter (though not as a substitute for purchase)
3. re-copy faxed copies for preservation purposes
4. add copies to library stocks
5. circulate copies among staff.

No declaration forms are needed. However, users are asked not to re-copy a copy thus obtained, which is understandable when charges are on a per copy per item basis, though BLDSC copies arriving in a licensed environment should be governed by the licence. (See also 15.12.) Other document supply licences have followed (6.47), though not necessarily on the same terms as the British Library. In 1995/6 CLA launched 'Copywatch', which invites anyone to report illegal copying wherever it may occur.

8.11 Licensing of industry and commerce

An industrial/commercial licence based on sampling became available after several years' discussion between the CBI and CLA. For a fee per professional staff member, a firm is offered a licence to copy up to nine multiples of the standard CLA allowances (one article per journal issue, etc. as in 8.3). Copies are primarily for internal use and must not be sold, though some can go externally to consultants or the like. Copying in excess of licence terms can be referred to CLARCS (8.13). Aternatively, clearance can be negotiated with publishers if special terms are thought jiustifiable, for example in respect of large quantitites of journal articles for marketing purposes. An 'audit' consisting of the listing of periodical titles currently taken must be carried out periodically in order to assist the distribution of funds to rights owners by the CLA.

The fees per professional employee so far mooted may cause concern at such results of several years of discussion. The fees are paid per professional employee per annum, with the higher fees aimed at sectors such as Pharmaceuticals, Oil and Chemicals. Objections arose in respect of: fee levels; levy per professional employee instead of relationship to copiable materials on the spot; and administrative cost, particularly of the audit.

After considerable negotiation on fees and procedures, including the definition of 'professional employee', licensing was adopted by the Pharmaceutical sector in 1995/6 and others are slowly following.

A similar form of licence is on offer to Government departments. The Home Office is now licensed and has negotiated larger extents: up to *two* articles per periodical issue; up to *one* complete case report from published proceedings; and up to *nineteen* copies for committee purposes. This was apparently the first coverage of committee needs in a CLA licence.

8.12 Copyshops

The same extents as those in the educational licence are allowed, with copying fees for all. In respect of jobs of 50 copy pages (one copy of one page) or more, the licensee must account to the CLA for the copying fees and identify the material copied. Jobs of less than 50 copy pages need not be accounted to the CLA, though the licensee must charge the fees set out in a current tariff. There is no mention of fair dealing, but a client could always go to a public library if he only wants a single copy for research or private study within permissible norms. Indemnity is provided for the copyshop, as required by the Act for all schemes.

8.13 Rapid Clearance System

CLARCS, the CLA Rapid Clearance System, is a special computer- based service. It is accessible to licence holders who hold passwords (supplied by post upon request at first intended use), and is of particular value in higher education (see 8.8) and industry. When royalty is chargeable it is quoted according to stored rights-owner wishes; otherwise a standard rate applies. If the fees are acceptable, clearance is confirmed and is subject to retrospective billing.

A system such as CLARCS could be a founding element of a national centre (Appendix 5/2). An obvious addition would be a collaborative committee between users and publishers/producers to study continuously the needs of users and the administration of rights.

8.14 Membership organisations

Two bodies called 'membership organisations' by the CLA have held experimental licences which removed any need for copyright declarations, but the details are not final. In 1996 the CLA reached accord with the London Law Society on a model licensing agreement for the profession, the firm of Denton Hall being the first reported licensee. This development has been followed by similar approaches to the Law Society of England and Wales.

8.15 Electrocopying possibilities

The possibility of CLA involvement in the licensing of electrocopying has been proposed by this author, not necessarily as a collective arrangement but rather as a means of centralised negotiation, coordination and administration of individual contracts with a degree of 'common core'. However, it may be found that CLA may initiate schemes for at least part the rightsholder community. Notes relevant to the licensing of electrocopying, including multimedia, appear in chapter 12.

8.16 The partially-sighted

In December 1996 the CLA announced an extension of the licence agreement between it and the Royal National Institute for the Blind whereby enlarged photocopies up to the whole book or journal may be made for use by partially-sighted students and partially-sighted staff., without additional charge. There are however conditions, such as: relationship to instruction; no copies for Short Loan collections; at least 16-point enlargement; at least one original purchased and available to other students and staff of the licensee; the item copied must not already be in large-print format; blanket licence exclusions do not apply but only enough copies may be made for the purpose of instruction; if CLA requires returns of copying to be made, then all copies made under this arrangement must also be recorded; no electronic storage or transmission is permitted. (See also 15.10.)

Her Majesty's Stationery Office, and Ordnance Survey

8.17 HMSO participates in collective licensing to some degree as a supporter of the CLA, but also makes individual arrangements. The HMSO guidelines have already been digested in 6.24 and 6.25, and include royalty requirements for individual needs.

Ordnance Survey users should seek OS leaflets which give guidance and/ or offer licences. Although a publisher of Crown copyright materials like HMSO, the OS has opted to remain outside collective licensing. Educational establishments other than schools under LEAs are offered licences for multiple copying for classes and for digital mapping. Business or professional use requires a licence also publishing. However, up to 4 copies of an extract of 625 sq sm (roughly A4) are seen as reasonable as fair dealing for research or private study. (Note: 'extract' – a complete map as A4 would require permission.) Local authorities hold copyright licences which permit copying for business and internal use, including multiple copies for classes in schools and colleges which come under the local authority, and for planning activities. However, those planning activities, or car park, etc. maps which involve public distribution or sale may be subject to separate royalty arrangements.

Under a form of local authority licence used for many years, a public library could only supply a copy for planning purposes to a private individual who provided a declaration that he was acting on his own behalf without professional assistance for the purpose of a planning application or in response to a request from the planning authority. If however the local authority joined a separate Map Extract Scheme, public libraries could copy for private *or* professional people for planning purposes. A new form of local authority licence which includes public libraries is on offer, and the factors which may be involved are featured among the examples of 'licensing problems' in 8.30 et seq. Such problems can arise when, as did CDPA88, statute leaves the details of licensing largely to contract.

8.18 Schools

Local authority educational establishments may make class multiples without restriction on size of copies made from OS large scale maps (1:10,000, 1:2500 and 1:1250 scales). However, copies of unamended maps in full colour or monochrome at or near the original scale (facsimile) must not exceed 625 sq. cm. (about A4 size) at the scale of 1:25000 or smaller. This is considerably more generous in respect of copy sizes from larger scales than the higher education licence, though that includes research needs as well as class copying. However, see 8.35 where local authority licensing is discussed.

8.19 Higher education

For higher education, a multiple copying licence covers teaching or lecturing anywhere by the teaching staff of an establishment, and making copies for its classes or 'research staff' (a term perhaps used to avoid impinging upon the area of separate 'business use' licences otherwise available) of parts of maps:

- up to 625 sq. cm. (about A4 size) of scales 1:25000 and less
- up to 1250 sq. cm. (within A3 size) of all larger scales

when taken from OS originals in unmodified form. OS charges a standard annual fee and neither requires records to be kept nor limits the number of copies made, but stipulates that each copy must bear an acknowledgement in a specified form of words (rather lengthy – best added by rubber stamp).

Digital mapping is also covered by the same higher education licence within the same size and scale limitations. The 'unmodified form' phrase was presumably as far as OS felt it could go in a statement, and certainly could not be taken as authorising the multiple copying by anyone of non-OS based maps, and permission should be requested from publishers. It should be noted that higher educational establishments with a licence will automatically extend the OS area allowance of A4 size under fair dealing for individuals, or libraries on their behalf, to A3 size for the larger scales above.

8.20 Other OS licensing

Publishing naturally requires detailed notes on what may be done and the royalties charged, and these should be studied in full at first hand.

An OS 'business use' licence covers the needs of industry, commerce and professional group practices. It should be noted that OS is liable to revise its leaflets annually, and those users with particular interests should ask for the latest versions.

British Standards Institution

8.21 BSI licences multiple copying for teaching or research, thus covering staff and educational classes. Copying must stop short of copying an entire standard including outer covers. In order to cover class needs for complete standards, special discounts for bulk purchase of complete standards are allowed under the licence.

Similarly to OS above, this extends the advisory unlicensed limit of 10 per cent of a standard up to almost a complete standard, a useful feature for staff.

BSI annual charges are on a sliding scale according to the number of copies made, and records therefore need to be kept. Where this is not practicable, an establishment may be allowed to send estimates instead.

Compulsory licensing: broadcast programme information

8.22 Publishers of the 'alternative' radio and television programme magazines which emerged a couple of years ago depend upon s176 and Schedule 17 of the Broadcasting Act 1990, which introduced compulsory licensing for this purpose.

The Magill case is relevant here. An Irish publisher of that name approached the EC in 1988, complaining that three major broadcasting companies (BBC, ITV and RTE) were refusing him a licence to produce a comprehensive weekly publication. The companies already published their own separate weekly listings and licensed others to produce daily and weekend listings. As a result, said Magill, the broadcasters were abusing their dominant position in refusing him a licence. Article 86 of the EC Treaty is intended to control the conduct of companies which have a dominant position in the market. The EC having made an order supporting Magill's complaint and requiring licensing by the broadcasters, the latter appealed to the European Court of Justice (ECJ), which in April 1995 upheld the EC order. Thus, 'the ECJ has confirmed that in certain circumstances the Commission has the power to oblige undertakings to grant licences of intellectual property' (Bristows Cooke and Carpmael Bulletin, April 1995, on which all of the above note on Magill is based). Whether this might provide assistance in respect of the *sui generis* problem with databases which may acquire potentially perpetual protection, even for non-copyright content (see App. 3/5) remains to be seen.

Computer programs in educational establishments

8.23 Since the use of computer software in an educational environment can result in unauthorised copying and adaptation, the rights owners have been concerned for some time, though that concern has not so far resulted in a common policy. Whereas an arrangement for higher education in the form of a code of practice was made with software houses by CHEST, the schools and colleges problem has been under discussion for several years. An offer of a schools collective licence from the Educational Software Publishers Association (ESPA) has still not been made, and theoretically could be raised with the Secretary of State as a request for compulsory licensing (4.44). Whilst it has been suggested in some quarters that the CHEST arrangement could be extended to cover schools and colleges, this is not a licensing scheme as such and in any event does not appear to cover the schools-level educational software concerned. At last, a solution is evolving, however. The British Educational Suppliers Association, of which ESPA forms a part, recently reported that it has been working, often with NCET, to promote licensing by individual software publishers. A BESA survey states that:

> 34% of companies now offer licences for home/school use, 20% offering split site licence arrangements, almost 60% offer network licences, over 50% offer licences for a specific number of users as high as 50 per establishment and 90% offer single site licences *(refer BESA for details, see 12.31).*

Where no suitable arrangement yet exists, schools and colleges can only continue to make available the necessary software and discourage copying or unauthorised adaptation.

8.24 CHEST code of practice

In higher education, the Combined Higher Education Software Team produced a code of practice. Among the requirements is the limitation of programs obtained or copied (under the group arrangements made by CHEST) in respect of use for research towards commercial ends. In recent years, CHEST has begun to include data sets as well as computer programs. The problem of defining 'commercial research', as discussed elsewhere, is arguably a virtual impossibility in respect of fundamental research in general and academe in particular, hence it is suggested that the limitation could only apply to:

(a) the exploitation of a computer program, either obtained at a special price under contract or duplicated with permission, in research clearly and directly concerned with a commercial venture. A purchased product may otherwise, of course, be used by the owner for whatever purpose he wishes, short of infringement or other illegal behaviour

(b) the incorporation of a program into a commercial system, or marketing a program, by an educational establishment or a member thereof, of a computer program developed as a result of adapting part or the whole of a purchased program without rights-owner permission.

In respect of (b), it is of course necessary to notify academic and computer centre staff that no kind of adaptation may be made of any program other than the staff's own works without separate authorisation by the rights owner, since there is probably no secure way to prevent an adaptation, once made, from becoming commercially marketed at some later date.

Off-air recording in education

8.25 Following the encouragement given in the Act, which allowed off- air recording unless a licensing scheme were available (7.8), licences were soon offered by the Educational Recording Agency and the Open University. These now cover virtually everything broadcast that is of educational interest. The ERA contains fewer conditions of use than the OU licence, but nevertheless requires detailed records to be kept of programmes recorded and number of copies made. Each recording must be clearly marked with date, title and the words 'This recording is to be used only for educational purposes' or any other phrase which may be agreed with the ERA.

8.26 The OU arrangement qualifies as a 'scheme' under the Act because the works of more than one author are covered, even though only one broadcaster is involved. The principal rights owners with whom ERA is concerned are noted in 9.36.

The educational licensing of off-air recording has been warmly welcomed throughout the education sector. It has not been easy to organise, owing to the considerable range of kinds of rights owners involved. Until the encouragement of licensing given by CDPA88, only limited recording could be done, licensed via the former firm Guild Sound and Vision of Peterborough. Thus the situation was widely regarded as obstructional to education.

8.27 'Educational establishment'

One difficulty, however, which arose immediately after CDPA88 was the uncertainty of definition of the term 'educational establishment', which appeared from the relevant SI 1989/1068 to mean only establishments under local authority finance and control, plus universities and polytechnics. Thus state financed bodies like nursing colleges, not only needing to record off-air but also wanting the other provisions of the Act in respect of educational establishments, such as 'showing or playing' audiovisual items (9.5), were much concerned – as also, of course, was the private sector of education. However, a ruling was obtained from the Department of Education and Science to the effect that the SI is to be interpreted as including any UK educational establishment, however funded, and this news was distributed by Aslib and the Library Association via information professionals.

8.28 Cable programme services

Returning to the Act itself (s35), the provision which is generally called 'off-air recording' is really a little wider than broadcasting and cable television. It would permit the recording of items in a cable programme service because no licensing scheme is on offer for that action, so that a demonstration of an electronic database could be recorded for repetition – provided of course that this is not overridden by a service contract to the contrary. This has now been confirmed for database right by SI 1997/3032 in respect of a substantial part for illustration purposes in teaching or research, wherever conducted However, commercial purpose is excluded and source must be indicated.

Slides and picture collections: the DACS scheme

8.29 Another problem area long under discussion is the licensing of the 'visual image'. Slides for instruction were mentioned in 6.41, and illustrations in publications are covered by library copying of singles and CLA licensing for multiples.

A difficulty which has grown with the change in photographers' rights – not just as authors but also moral rights – is the need to mark all slides and other separates with source details. This should be done anyway for good housekeeping, as well as search purposes, but practice has apparently varied. For example, if the majority of items in a collection are donated by people who have not recorded any source details, holding to proper storage and retrieval techniques is bound to be in question. There should of course be at least a numerical identifier on each slide or picture, linking with a catalogue or index file.

The Design and Artists Copyright Society (DACS), formed in 1983 as a collecting society (12.31) is one of the licensing bodies associated with ERA (8.26). The DACS range of problems is of course quite wide, taking in paintings, sculptures, photographs, artistic designs, etc., and might give rise to a need for several new kinds of licence in the future. A much-needed DACS scheme was launched in February 1996 to cover 'slide collections', and full details should be studied carefully as with all new schemes. Adjustment in accordance with local circumstances may prove possible to negotiate as with other such licences, and indeed several variants are already mentioned in the explanatory literature available. Prospective licensees may wish to bear in mind the points in 8.31.

Licensing problems: the Copyright Tribunal

8.30 Comments are made in the following sections on various features of licensing schemes or offers, nearly a decade having elapsed since the Act encouraged collective licensing.

The ability of any user to appeal to the CT has apparently not proved of much practical value or reassurance so far. It would seem logical for individual problems to be referred via a professional body, but unfortunately even such an organisation may well see the costs of appeal as prohibitive. Many professional bodies have been in a somewhat impecunious state for years. There would seem therefore to be a risk of imbalance between the potential use of the CT by a commercial publisher and the unexpressed and unresolved needs of a non-publishing user. Two tentative suggestions are:

(a) Reduce CT appeal costs, subsidising legal fees for non-commercial user organisations?
(b) Rights-owner representatives might beware of believing that a prospective licensee accepts terms as fair, when really a non-publishing and/or nonprofit-based user may tacitly feel obliged to accept in fear of litigation for which he cannot afford defence.

Were the CT made easier and cheaper to use, perhaps in the course of time it could act as arbiter on the fairness of any contract terms, not just those concerned with collective licensing. This could be preferable to an expensive lawsuit under the Unfair Contract Terms Act, 1977, but would depend on the interpretation of s135 of CDPA88 as allowing the CT to take other kinds of action than those closely prescribed in other sections. Should it be decided that rights owners were in danger of using contract to making a mockery of statute, perhaps this would be enough incentive to intervene.

As an incidental but significant point, it has been reported that some licensing bodies have demanded a letter from users who refuse a licence. Such an unlicensed user is apparently expected to guarantee no copying. The writer knows of nothing in law on which this practice might be based.

DACS scheme: discussion points

8.31 **1. Single slides**

Clearance is stated as necessary for *'every single slide slide produced'* in an unlicensed establishment and refers to involvement by a *'librarian or member of staff'* in the difficult clearance procedures. The formal nature of a licence has perhaps prevented notice being taken of three facts: (a) the practical needs of individual lecturers to act at short notice; (b) that the entire **non**-involvement of library personnel in such actions is the norm. The DACS does not agree with the British Copyright Council suggestion (6.41) that a single slide for instructional purposes which do not involve publication should be reasonable. In 7.7, suggestions have been made whereby single slides might be treated. However, it might not prove feasible for DACS to include such points in the general or basic form of licence. Accordingly, it is recommended that an educational estabishment could include the 7.7 matters in its staff guidelines or conditions of service, and assure DACS of this in order to avoid measures to include every slide in the licence wherever made in the institution.

2. Statutory permissions

The continued relevance of CDPA88 permissions, such as the inclusion of 'artistic works' in fair dealing copying by anyone or any library, should be made clear, possibly by a phrase: 'the licence applies without prejudice to the permissions in the Copyright, Designs and Patents Act 1988'.

3. Excluded categories

These are film stills, advertisements and trade marks.

4. Collections

It is recommended here that any collections in which the slides are *already* the subject of proper recording , housing and administration **as an entity** should be considered for licensing, along with any relevant new collections which may come into being as a result of (1) above.

UK newspapers

8.32 Newly formed in 1996, The Newspaper Licensing Agency Limited launched its licensing scheme for copying articles from the press. A brochure entitled 'Photocopying newspapers: your guide to the new rules' was provided on copying for 'internal' purposes only – such as press 'cuttings' bulletins produced for staff. (NLA's phrase is 'internal management purposes only'.) The issue of a bulletin extra-murally, or the provision of a commercial cuttings agency, would require separate approach to the NLA. Clearance of individual items (e.g. for external promotion) would need to be sought from the publishers. The scheme requires in-depth consideration of the details.

Whilst the inception of some kind of licensing scheme for newspaper copying may be deemed necessary, the present form of the NLA scheme has so far been regarded by users as requiring careful study. All licences are contracts between parties and the details can usually be discussed in relation to individual requirements. It is of course also possible separately to consult professional bodies, or independent consultants on copyright, or in some circumstances the Copyright Tribunal if agreement should prove difficult.

8.33 NLA scheme: discussion

From a number of features of the brochure on which users might ask NLA for clarification at least until such time as the scheme becomes more widely established, the following are selected:

1. **Statutory permissions.** NLA states that it does recognise the relevance of fair dealing, library copying and other statutory permissions. At present, the wording appears to imply charging for an undefined category of 'ad hoc copying', but this merely describes what the fees will cover, should a licensee choose the one-month sample option wherein all copying is recorded. It is believed that many users would prefer to see what is becoming a customary phrase: 'The scheme applies to copying otherwise than as permitted by the Copyright, Designs and Patents Act 1988'.

2. **Photographs and advertisements** are excluded from the scheme, despite the high proportion of articles accompanied by illustrations. Thus the copying of these could only be covered by copying as per (1). There appears to have been no case in the past of objection by advertisers, however, and perhaps this is due to their appreciation of the wider exposure resulting from copying.

3. **Indemnity** for licensees as required under CDPA88 applies when copying is *as permitted* by the licence. Therefore photographs and advertisements (and other exclusions) would not be covered by the indemnity and only the statutory permissions would apply to those works. Licensees should be prepared for instances wherein copyright owners of photographs, for example, may have to be consulted, but NLA would surely advise in any event.

4. **Other exclusions.** There are six other categories of exclusions: in particular, the prohibition of copying of 'any part' in each of the exclusions reflects no recognition of normal quotation needs.

5. **Coverage.** The scheme began with UK newspapers, but The International Herald Tribune is now included, and others may follow. The CLA continues to cover French and German papers, and enquiries about other overseas materials should be directed to the CLA in any event.) Note that scanning (not mentioned in the brochure) should not be assumed to be permissible, since it is facsimile copying of typographical layout into a computer system. (However, keying in of any news text for the purpose of *reporting current events* under s30(2) would be permissible, even if multiple copies result, subject to sufficient acknowledgement of sources.)

6. Rather than the licence's limitation to 'internal management purposes', licensees might prefer a phrase covering *any in-house purpose.*

(Further study of the fees stated in the brochure has led to further comments, for which see *Managing Information*, expected May 1998 issue.)

8.34 Response to NLA scheme

The response from potential licensees was varied during 1996 and 1997. However, as this goes to press it is understood that the number of licensees will soon top 2,000. Counting organisations which are licensed to cover their subsidiaries, the total number of companies will be over 9,000. Substantial progress has also been made with universities and other user groups, despite some initial misunderstandings.

Ordnance Survey and local authorities

8.35 Under a form of local authority licence used for many years, a public library could only supply a copy for planning purposes to a private individual. If however the local authority joined a separate Map Extract Scheme, copies could be supplied to private *or* professional people for planning purposes. However, the local authority licence included charging for copying, though not specifically related to actual copies, in return for this public library provision, as well as for planning office activities and copying which might occur in schools. The details of payment are included in the form of local authority licence agreed between a local authority and the OS.

The OS leaflet *Copyright 1: internal use by organisations* of January 1994 last referred to the Scheme. It was obvious up to 1996, at least, that the OS acknowledged fair dealing and planning copies to be statutory permissions (s46, submission of plans being required under Town and Country Planning law). The leaflet did not mention that no royalty is due under statutory provisions but that royalties can be required by contract.

The January 1996 and 1997 editions of *Copyright 1*, now bearing the new title *Copying for business use,* also refer to fair dealing but make a significant change. It is stated that fair dealing applies to a map *that you own*, and there appears to be no legal basis for this in CDPA88 – indeed, it would make the provision of fair dealing (with any materials) virtually useless.

The interpretation of the Act followed in this book is that anyone, or any kind of library, may make a single copy from a map as an artistic work under fair dealing *on behalf* of an individual. Similarly, copying may also be done under other statutory permissions, including s46 for planning copies. However, certain map librarians, being uncertain several years ago of the veracity of all that, approached the OS for confirmation. Apparently OS then already had the local authority licence under review. Subsequently at a meeting between OS and representatives of the LA/JCC/WPC and selected libraries, a version of the former Map Extract Scheme was agreed as a free 'library licence' which has since been circulated to chief librarians. The terms were then incorporated into a new form of local authority licence.

The public library 'free licence' includes an OS indication that royalties will not be charged for fair dealing copies (only those being mentioned in this regard). However, using the above erroneous statement (as to ownership being a qualification for fair dealing) as the sole premise, the OS now 'allows' library copying under fair dealing *as an exception,* without increasing the currently 'allowed' copiable area to individuals. The new local authority licence removes the ability of a planning office in an unlicensed authority to make and supply copies from OS maps, all requests to be directed instead to an OS agent or to the public library. There is however no basis in CDPA88 for that restriction, since s46 is taken to apply to anyone copying. No royalty appears to be due under statute, as remarked above already, because the submission of copies is required under Town and Country Planning law. However, a payment to cover copying, whatever its basis, can legally be made part of a contract.

No other benefits from signing the OS 'free licence' are offered to libraries other than confirmation of statutory permissions. Some extra work is required in marking copies under fair dealing and s46 (as well as already required under s47), and securing signed declarations. It is questionable whether the new arrangement can be 'free' in the administrative cost sense. As remarked earlier, royalty-related charges can be imposed under licence, hence such an action by OS would in itself be within the law. However, whether it is legally or ethically appropriate for a member of the public to be made, even unwittingly via community tax, to forego his right to a royalty-free planning copy has apparently never been considered.

Both local authority planning officers and public librarians are recommended to study this situation. The OS has long earned respect at least for trying to give general guidance to users, as well as covering many needs with licensing. Between the 1956 and 1988 Acts, it was probably of special advantage to local authorities to have their needs covered by just one licence for planning, for other internal uses, for school copying, and to clarify public library copying in the face of the ambiguities of the 1956 Act (wherein fair dealing excluded 'artistic' in any event at that time). Certain unfortunate phrases in the OS guidelines were apparently unobserved or never questioned. It is arguable whether, even at that stage, the general local authority licence should have excluded any 'licensing' of libraries, whose uncertainties could have been covered by simple confirmation by guideline of the provisions of CDPA88 in respect of fair dealing and other statutory permissions. Indeed, guideline clarification could have been the response to the uncertainty expressed by map librarians which has led to the 'free licence'. The OS at present uses the licence apparently to achieve copying controls additionally to statute. Is it too late for a renewed approach for separate business and educational licensing, leaving the external-supply copying activities of planning offices and libraries to statute and guidelines?

Be that as it may, it is advised as a general principle that no prospective licensee should readily sign and thus give credence to any unusual interpretation of statute. The prime example is the reference above to fair dealing being possible only to an owner of an item, according to the OS. Such erosion of the fair dealing concept could readily 'leak' to other regimes. The fact that a form of licence is offered does not necessarily mean that one must sign it, especially if there is a risk of obtaining more limitations than benefits.

Sound/video recordings

8.36 Although not at present a UK practice, tape levies are included in the discussion below because of the possibility that they may yet arise here as part of EU harmonisation. It is not surprising, in view of the industries' fear of piracy, especially of sound recordings, that there is no relevant licensing scheme. There is however a draft EC Directive on private copying or 'home taping' which in itself is a symptom of the fear noted. The proposal is a system of levies on blank tapes which would mean an additional 25-30% on the cost of an audio tape and 40% on a video tape. No provision is made in the draft for educational exemptions, but there is a provision concerning people with vision or hearing difficulties. Comments follow.

8.37 Tape levy objections

The allowance proposed by the EC in respect of visually or aurally disadvantaged people goes at least some way towards meeting UK objections to the principle of levies. Strong objections continue to be raised on behalf of the UK, however, on two main bases: a great many tapes may never be used at all for copying recordings, thus the system would be considered manifestly unfair by many purchasers of blank tapes; and as a corollary to the general fear of the industries about piracy mentioned above, a view expressed on behalf of the UK industries is that *carte blanche* might well be assumed by tape purchasers, resulting in widespread damage to retail sales of recordings.

Accordingly, the EC proposal is considered by some observers to be unfair both to users and the industries concerned. Now that rental/lending right exists (4.35 et seq.), the whole basis of the levying proposals may need reconsideration by their exponents. Is home infringement **really** damaging UK sales to a significant extent, especially when compared with overseas piracy? In effect, as with printed matter, market forces make the prices compensatory for overseas piracy to some extent. However, price levels may reduce competitiveness and thereby damage sales to an unknown extent. Infringement must of course be prevented as far as is reasonable and cost-effective. Also, is it fair that purchasers who comply with the law should be penalised by having to pay prices which cover the actions of the offenders, including those abroad?

8.38 Cost to the industry of illegal copying of sound recordings?

Objections by the UK industries to public library 'rental' (as then defined, 4.36) were raised during and after the passage of CDPA88. At that time, very high estimates of annual financial loss believed due mainly to home taping were quoted. Although the tendency, especially among adolescents, to copy their own purchases onwards to friends was noted by BPI members, public library accessibility was regarded as mostly to blame. Whilst greatly sympathising with the industry's sufferings from extensive piracy, it was pointed out on behalf of users that the industry's home taping figures might be considerably over-estimated because:

(a) most users, once convinced of need by evaluation during loan, are believed vastly to prefer purchase of a pristine original complete with packaging and documentation – provided they can afford the price;
(b) those who can afford the price will buy anyway, with or without previous loan;
(c) evaluation during loan by libraries should lead to increased sales, not fewer, via a 'shop-window effect', if the retail price were appropriate;
(d) the value of a cohesive (and, as far as possible, balanced) collection for public access is not borne in mind;
(e) the industrial estimates of very high annual losses due to home copying might be re-examined. Is it possible that bias might have followed from assumptions that optimum pricing had been applied rather than overpricing at the outset followed by dumping surpluses on the market later at a loss and that market research forecasts of user interest linked to affordability were accurate?

The above matters were examined during the discussions, begun in 1987/88 on behalf of the LA/JCC/WPC with the BPI, which led eventually to the conditional acceptance of public library accessibility reported in 4.47 and dubbed a 'free licence'.

Comments on educational licensing

8.39 Although over a decade has elapsed since educational licensing began with schools, it has to be reported that the whole basis of collective licensing still sits nearly as uneasily on the shoulders of some users as it did during the years of controversy about photocopying and licensing. The time-consuming and, it is said, somewhat unreliable sampling basis of payment to rights owners is still in vogue (see Appendix 2). The 'swings and roundabouts' principle applies, of course, but do rights owners regard it as equitable? When an author's name is not recorded, photocopying royalties appear in some cases necessarily to be passed on only via the Publishers Licensing Society and not also the ALCS.

Whether schools should ever have been licensed seems to be just as debatable as the question of fairness to rights owners themselves, since royalties may be unreliably related to particular copyright materials. Licensing only went ahead as a 'Hobson's choice' solution, when local authorities became increasingly fearful of litigation after a Manchester case involving the multiple copying of textbooks by a school. Only a couple of years or so after schools licensing began, it was reported that the PA (a co-founder of CLA) had requested the Booksellers' Association (not a co-founder) to consider allowing a special discount to schools to counter falling textbook sales. The fall was believed due in part to photocopy licensing, and the question 'Was this journey really necessary?' sprang to mind. Educationists had in any event long expressed concern at the risk of feeding pupils a 'diet of photocopies', inevitably to be discarded piecemeal and divorced from desirable context (when copyright's 'paper tiger' may become a pupil's paper aeroplane?). In higher education, as already indicated above, sampling is considered unreliable because interests range very widely and require an enormous range of resources whose actual usage varies between establishments.

It has been recommended in the past that libraries should consider co-ordinating CLARCS requirements, arranging for all requests involving the CLA to be routed through library staff. Currently, projects like Acorn (6.49) are bearing in mind the need to develop electronic files to be shared between institutions, and approach to CLARCS is being replaced by agreements made directly with rights owners. Even so, the need for hard copy sets seems unlikely to disappear. Moreover, it will continue to be desirable for archival or reference copies of the study packs to be held in libraries as well as selling them at cost to students.

However, four matters give cause for concern about the use of CLARCS for study pack preparation:

(a) the cost of study packs permitted via CLARCS, now singled out from the original licence which embraced these needs

(b) uncertainty as to whether CLARCS will reflect the long-standing free – or nominal-cost – permissions from publishers sympathetic to educational aims, or whether a minimum or 'default' charge will always be made
(c) the administrative cost of using CLARCS, including staff time and line charges.
(d) in 1995, Australia's Copyright Agency Ltd and Victoria University of Technology were involved in a test case about photocopied course anthologies. Students were charged only the copying cost, and a key point was whether the institution was making a profit from sales. Since no profit was made, the judge dismissed the case, but an appeal was expected by publishers who may claim this practice to damage textbook publishing.

In respect of (d), this writer has proposed that *all* university licensing of systematic class copying should cease to be based on sampling. Instead, reading lists could be coordinated at a central point and used as the *only* charging and fund-distribution basis. This may be evolving in any case via a number of electronic projects such as Acorn mentioned above. Publishers should welcome this solution, since valuable information could emerge about book and periodical markets and reprinting needs. Academics should also welcome such a central database, which could be updated by individual teachers whenever reading lists were under annual or more frequent revision. Subject to safeguards against undesirable input, students could also have access to the database. Alternatively, might public sector licensing become negotiated with agencies by a government body which would pay collecting agencies such fees as could be afforded from the public purse? Public Lending Right could be seen as a precedent for such an approach. The present administratively wasteful procedure, wherein user groups negotiate on their own behalf, when their budgets are cash-limited anyway, is theoretically open to abuse via continual price-hiking by negotiating with groups one by one, or via victories over user-group representatives who vary in negotiation stamina.

Unlicensed yet legal?

8.40 In the face of a whole range of licensed document supply agencies, the use of CLARCS when material to be copied is actually in a licensee's hands, and electronic databases, professional practices may be well-advised to study the changes of the last few years. For example, the health services of these islands might be better served by avoiding licensing directly and using licensed copying or clearance services instead. The 'selling points' that a licence removes copying problems may be arguably misleading. The constraints of a licence are too limiting for many scientific and technical needs, and the frequency of recourse by a licensee to CLARCS or a copying agency for any need 'over the odds' may well suggest the seeking of an alternative to licence-holding. It is suggested that a simple way to assess the situation experimentally would be: to refer all copying requests beyond accepted norms to a library for a trial period of, say, six months; get that library to use document supply agencies (or permission-seeking direct with publisher if the material is in hand) in respect of *any* need which exceeds fair dealing/library copying norms; and note costs for comparison with licensing costs *plus* use of external services for unlicensed copying needs.

8.41 So much for an experiment – how might busy and highly qualified staff be better served than by leavIng them to apply their own ideas of what a licence or statute allows? The following are some suggestions:

(1) Information service professionals are reasonably well placed to assess what is copyright material and what is not, as well as being able to administer any establishment licensing of special material such as standards, maps, online/offline database subscriptions and their constraints, and Geographical Information Systems (GIS). They can also readily discover the nearest hard copy set when this could help in a particular emergency.

(2) All photocopy acquisition other than obviously permissible copying of material already held should be put into the hands of professional information officers and librarians. It is far from appropriate that medical personnel, for example, such as hard-pressed front-line GPs and hospital consultants, nurses, pathologists, etc should have to bother about whence required copies may come.

(3) Photocopying equipment in all locations would need to be accompanied by notices similar to those in university libraries about research or private study copying norms, but make it clear that self-service copying must be confined to fair dealing with material actually in hand.

(4) Any further needs for copying from hard copy sources should be referred to the appropriate library service by e-mail or fax.

(5) Multiple copy (or downloading) needs arising from on-the-spot use of an electronic database may possibly be met by the system itself, provided librarians have negotiated suitable service contracts for their

area of service to the medical professionals. Some eLib projects for campus network copying should be noted (6.49), for academe may well not be the only environment to attract research funding.

Honesty tempered by discretion?

8.42 As remarked earlier in this book, the successful observance of all copyrights depends on individual honesty. Those who are unaware of offending will continue in ignorance. Those who deliberately intend to offend will regrettably find a way. Moreover, the public at large could perhaps be forgiven for believing that an element of fair dealing should apply to recordings. Unlike the UK, the US 'fair use' concept (5.2) is all-pervasive of materials, though considered less desirable than UK 'fair dealing' on other counts. Whether or not individual users know about and rebel against the UK's omission of fair dealing in audovisual materials, a tendency towards a form of 'discretionary administration' may be observed in personal concepts of 'honesty' and 'legality'. For example, a purchaser of a CD may well think there is no harm in making a tape copy of an extract for his car, since he cannot play both at the same time. No damage to sales can result if no tape version is available of the particular piece(s) desired. When the latter is the case, it would seem unfair to apply a tape levy to compensate for the industy's own failure to offer an appropriate retail item.

8.43 Users who, after years of controversy, bowed perforce to the inevitability of collective licensing in the climate of that time, may be found to have yielded with reservations. However, many appear now to feel that, at least, the principles seem sound even if the fairness of practice may be arguable. That users should pay for substantial permissions is of course beyond question. Also beyond question, surely, is that publishers and producers should not only seek maximum fairness to the rights owners who underpin them, but also avoid schemes which cause extra administrative expense to users or other wastage due solely to licensing itself. Obviously, counter-productive attitudes must be avoided in debate on copyright administration problems, for it is evident that all must work together towards solutions. With regard to licensing as a whole, the search for alternative approaches may only bring an end into sight when an ECMS is in use which contains details of current copyright owners and their works (Appendix 5/2). Meanwhile, users and rights-owners alike should share the need always to remember that, without a balanced system of rights, the whole communication/information structure would break down due to lack of incentive, funding, marketing, and entrepreneurial drive.

9. PUBLIC PLAYING, SHOWING OR PERFORMING; AND LENDING OR RENTAL

General note on database right

Readers are requested to refer to **Q0** before proceeding with study of permissions chapters 5,6,7 and 9. Any permissions should be qualified by the details of database right (3.28) if not already specified herein. Absence of mention in a description of a permission must not be taken to imply its relevance to database right.

Note on scope of this chapter

Firstly, this chapter describes the various copying permissions, and the forms of licensing required when those permissions need to be exceeded. Then, the text deals with the remaining actions which do not infringe copyright under Part I of the Act. Several permissions already described earlier but applicable also in this context are repeated here. Any licensing needs are noted along with the actions. Reference should be made to 12.31 for addresses of the bodies concerned. In 9.6, the remarks on public performance cover anyone and not just the education sector, being included there for convenience.

Rights in performances under Part II of the Act are then outlined, and readers should note that the permissions listed below apply also to recordings of live performances, as summarised by the Act in its Schedule 2.

Fair dealing

The two relevant purposes here are: criticism or review (5.28); and reporting current events (5.31).

9.1 Criticism or review

Any copyright work, or a performance of a work, is covered. Copying aspects have been described in 5.28. However, playing, showing or performing an extract of sufficient extent or significance to affect the market for the material concerned would be unlikely to be judged 'fair' in court, and recompense might be sought. This kind of use is subject to sufficient acknowledgment. In making the choice of context for using an extract, attention should be given to moral rights, especially the right to object to derogatory treatment (10.12).

9.2 News reporting

Any copyright material other than a photograph is covered by this permission, and copying aspects have already been indicated in 5.31. This fair dealing purpose is subject to sufficient acknowledgment, but no acknowledgement need be made when news is reported by means of a sound or video recording, film, broadcast or cable programme. The moral right on derogatory teatment (10.12) does not apply to this permission.

Instruction

9.3 Instruction in making films, etc.

Any nonprint medium, including a recording of a performance, may be copied in the course of instruction in the making of films or sound- tracks, if done by a person giving or receiving instruction. (Already described in the copying context, 7.3.)

9.4 Examinations

Anything may be done for examination purposes for asking questions or making answers, except for reprography of a musical work for performance by a candidate, and the copying context has been noted in 7.2. 'Reprography' as defined by CDPA88 includes electronic means for a work stored electronically, though not for the making of a film, video or sound recording. This rules out not only any facsimile copying but also prevents any electronic means of display of music for performance. Unless teachers and students have permission or purchase copies of the sheet music, therefore, they are reduced to manuscript and/or blackboard for music to be performed by a student, and it is recommended that the views of the Music Publishers Association be sought on this problem.

In respect of material forming part of a printed database (electronic being covered anyway via service contract which now qualifies a 'lawful user'), this permission is not specified as such under the new law. However, a new 'illustration for teaching or research', etc permission applies to both printed and electronic formats and allows 'substantial parts' subject to fair dealing (7, note), as the first use of the fair dealing concept outside CDPA88 s29. Also, the CLA licence has covered copying for this purpose within the extents allowed, though confirmation of inclusion of printed databases is needed.

This helpful permission nevertheless allows the showing, playing or performing of any other kind of copyright work for examination purposes: films, videos, sound recordings, electronic database displays, broadcasts.

An overlap in this context between this permission and the more general permission in 9.5 is noted, but the overlap applies only to 'educational establishments'. The examinations permission and 9.3 apply to any instructional environment.

Education: playing, showing or performing

9.5 This permission embraces performance at an educational establishment of an original literary, dramatic or musical work, or the playing or showing of a sound or video recording or film, broadcast or cable programme, including demonstrating electronic databases or computer programs. When the audience consists of teachers and students, and any other people directly connected with the establishment other than parents, and the purpose is instructional, the performance is not public and does not infringe (s34). Since showing or playing does not constitute extraction or re-utilisation per se (though it might if an extract were dubbed in advance), this would apply also to using a database of sound or video recordings (see 9.4 above; see also 9.36 re lending right and 7 (general note) re databases).

9.6 Performance: licensing

As well as to educational establishments, these notes relate to any public context of use where a permission does not apply. The definition of an educational audience as non-public (end of 9.5) would not apply to an end-of-term showing of a film or video for entertainment purposes, or a performance of a play for which attendance were open to parents and friends. Such actions in respect of any public audience would require specific permission or licence for public performance. For a play, permission is obtainable via the publisher, or for non- professional performances, from an agency from which multiple copies may have been hired for the cast (such as Samuel French, 12.31). The public performance of music, whether live or from sound recordings, including broadcast reception in public areas, is licensed by the Performing Right Society (PRS) on behalf of composers and music publishers. PRS issues site or campus licences for broadcasts and hi-fi etc. in public areas, and bills retrospectively after submission of annual returns from a licence holder. Those planning live concerts should however consult PRS first. An audience is to be regarded as 'public' if it is not 'private and domestic'.

Playing sound recordings in public areas is also licensed by Phonographic Performance Ltd (PPL) on behalf of recording companies – thus an organisation may require both a PRS and a PPL licence for some activities. Broadcasting or cable programme playback of recordings also needs to be licensed by both PPL and PRS. However, in certain kinds of organisation, the playing of sound recordings does not require a PPL licence, though it still needs a PRS licence (see 9.26). A PPL licence is required for using music in any public environment *except* as in 9.26. Video Performance Ltd (same address as PPL), covers music video recordings, such as pop. Some hire services for background music tapes charge royalty in the price by arrangement with PPL, and users should of course check whether they are already covered.

The recording of a performance requires a licence from the Mechanical Copyright Protection Society (owned by the Music Publishers Association Ltd) on behalf of composers and music publishers. Making a recording for broadcasting/cable programme purposes may however be treated as licensed under the Act (ss68 and 69) in certain circumstances (see 9.17-9.18). Re-recording or dubbing from recordings to prepare extracts or compilations, or to use music as background in a video etc recording, requires both PPL and MCPS licences. This is a difficult area, and the above digest should be supplemented by study of 12.41-12.43, and to one or more of the named agencies when in doubt (addresses in 12.31).

9.7 Video recordings

In respect of video recordings produced as 'sell-through' copies and available in shops and supermarkets, labelled 'Licensed for home use only' or the like, the British Videogram Association said in 1988 that it regards a non-public audience in an educational establishment for instructional purposes as 'domestic', as remarked in 4.45. Now named the British Video Association, it confirmed in 1996 that *showing a video outside the normal domestic circle would require the written authority of the copyright holder*, as noted at the beginning of 9.6. However, arising from SI 1996/2967, an author, composer, or film director now has an unwaivable right of 'equitable remuneration' when rental is involved, and this right can only be assigned to a collecting society. Since the BVA is not at present a collecting society, it is not yet clear whether arrangements may be made with various separate bodies representing different groups of people. It is hoped that this new right will not prove an unfortunate complication from the viewpoints of both the industry and public libraries, as well as commercial hire shops where royalties are effectively paid 'up-front' in the purchase price (see 4.47), and it would probably have been preferable for law simplify to stipulate that a contract must include such remuneration. (See also 9.30 et seq.)

9.8 Artistic works

Graphic or photographic representations or images in films can be made of certain artistic works on public display. Such works are named as: buildings and/or models for them; sculptures and '*works of artistic craftsmanship, if permanently situated in a public place or in premises open to the public*' (s62). Representations of these could be shown just as a copy of a book may be shown. Paintings and similar works which are still copyright are excluded from this permission, and art galleries may in any event make their own rules concerning copying on their premises.

Otherwise, artistic works are only copiable under fair dealing, which does not cover group instruction. Artistic works are not mentioned in educational showing or playing or performing permissions in the Act (s34) because there is no right of public performance, showing or playing for such works (s19). A teacher or a student may manually copy any work of art or a representation of it, for display for instructional purposes (s32). However, if someone possessed a photograph of a painting, taken for research or private study, and subsequently showed it to a class, it is doubtful whether the rights owner would object, provided this does not become a regular expedient to overcome the Act's restriction in s32(1)(b).

9.9 Moral rights

These rights were mentioned in 9.1 in respect of criticism or review. Teachers also need to be aware of moral rights. For example, the playing, showing or performing permission could not, of course, be taken as sanctioning derogatory treatment (10.12).

Public administration

9.10 Parliamentary or judicial proceedings

Any action is permitted for these purposes, or for reporting proceedings otherwise than by copying a published report. (Already noted in the copying context, 7.9.) Thus playing or showing an audiovisual recording, for example, could not infringe. The Law Society has defined judicial proceedings as commencing from the time of issue of a writ.

9.11 Royal Commission and statutory inquiry

Any action is permitted for the purposes of proceedings, or for reporting publicly held proceedings otherwise than by copying a published report. Thus nonprint media can be played or shown, or original works performed, for these purposes. Copying aspects have already been noted in 7.10.

9.12 Material open to public inspection

Issue of copies to the public by or with the authority of an 'appropriate person' is permitted (7.11) and this does not exclude nonprint media. This permission is included here because it could apply to the copying and supply of a recording of a live performance.

9.13 Material in public records

The issue of copies with appropriate authority is permitted, provided the records are of kinds required to be laid open to inspection (7.13), but this is a broad area which includes nonprint media.

9.13A Statutory requirement

Any action authorised by statute is permitted, irrespective of when passed (7.14 covers the copying context).

Purposes of sound recordings or films, broadcasts or cable programmes

9.14 Compulsory licensing: unlimited needle-time

Although CDPA88 abolishes a former compulsory licence to copy records sold by retail, a new compulsory licence has been inserted as s135(A-G) of CDPA88 by s175 of the Broadcasting Act 1990, relating to unlimited needle-time.

9.15 Incidental inclusion

The incidental inclusion of copyright material in an artistic work, sound recording, film (or video) broadcast or cable programme does not infringe (7.27). This also applies to the issue to the public of copies of the work which incidentally includes copyright material, or playing, showing, broadcasting or including the work in a cable programme service.

9.16 Use of recordings of spoken words

Such recordings, in writing or otherwise, for reporting current events or inclusion in a broadcast or cable programme service (s58) are permitted subject to the following conditions:

(a) when the record is direct and not taken from a previous one, or from an off-air recording or a cable programme
(b) when the making of the record itself does not infringe copyright, and has not been prohibited by the speaker
(c) when the intended use of the record has not been prohibited in advance of the event of recording by the speaker or copyright owner
(d) when the use carries the authority of a person who is lawfully in possession of the record.

9.17 Incidental recording

A permission relating to the incidental recording of a work or a performance for use in a broadcast or cable programme service (s68) applies when, by means of assignment or licensing, a person is entitled to broadcast or include in a cable programme service:

- a literary, dramatic or musical work, or an adaptation
- an artistic work, or
- a sound recording, film or video recording.

Under the permission, a person may make a sound recording or film, or a copy of those; or make a photograph or film of an artistic work, for broadcast or cable programme service purposes. However, any medium made must not be used for any other purpose and destroyed within 28 days of first use.

9.18 Recording for supervision and control purposes

The British Broadcasting Corporation, the Independent Broadcasting Authority and the Cable Authority are permitted to make such recordings (s69 – amendment by recent Broadcasting Acts is omitted here).

9.19 Reception of a copyright broadcast for immediate re-transmission in a cable programme service

This does not infringe (s73), provided:

- the re-transmission is in accordance with a requirement of the Cable and Broadcasting Act 1984 which requires certain programmes to be included; or
- when the broadcast is made for reception in the area covered by the cable programme service; and
- the broadcast is not a satellite or encrypted transmission.

Both s73 and the related provision s134 concerning referral to the Copyright Tribunal have been amended, and a new s73A has been added, by recent Broadcasting Acts.

Tape levy harmonisation?

9.20 A note is placed here on the EC's perception of a 'private copying' or home taping problem out of convenience rather than relevance to the immediate context, for home taping is certainly not a permission. The notion of a tape levy received much discussion during the passage of the 1988 Act, and both recording companies and user representatives were strongly against it: the former because of the risk of carte blanche assumptions, and the latter because of the fundamental unfairness of payment by the majority of blank tape purchasers for an unlikely use. But certain other EC nations do already have a tape levy, for example Germany, and there is pressure towards a common EC policy, which the UK is resisting. More comments appear in 8.37 et seq.

Archiving

9.21 Export of a work of cultural or historical importance

Making a copy as a condition of export, for deposit in an appropriate library or archive, is permitted (6.36), and this would include a copy of a recording of a live performance.

9.22 Folksongs

A sound recording of a performance of a song may be made for inclusion in an archive maintained by a 'designated body' (s61), provided:

(a) the words are anonymous and unpublished at the time of recording
(b) making the recording does not infringe other copyright (for example, if the performer set the words to some copyright music without permission) and
(c) the performer has not prohibited the recording.

'Designated body' means a nonprofit-based body designated for the purpose by the Secretary of State. SI 1989/1012 designates 12 bodies (App. 2/3.2). An archivist or someone acting on his behalf may supply copies, provided:

- copies are only supplied for research or private study (see declaration from SI 1989/1212 in 6.51); and
- no person is supplied with more than one copy.

9.23 Recording a broadcast or cable programme

Such recording is permitted for archiving by a designated body (s75), and eight bodies are designated by the Secretary of State in SI 1993/74 (listed in App. 2/3.2).

Other purposes

9.24 Anonymous or pseudonymous literary, dramatic, musical or artistic works

Any action done on assumption of expiry of copyright or death of author does not infringe when:

- authorship cannot be discovered by reasonable ; and
- it is reasonable to assume that copyright has expired (already described in the copying context, 7.31; see also 2.39).

9.25 Making subtitled copies of a broadcast or cable programme

For people who are deaf or hard of hearing, or physically or mentally handicapped in other ways (s74) this may be done by a designated body (App. 2/3.2).

9.26 Playing a sound recording by a club, society or other organisation

Sound recordings may be played (s67) as part of the activities of, or for the benefit of, the organisation, provided:

- the organisation is nonprofit-making with mainly charitable aims or otherwise concerned with advancing religion, education or social welfare; and
- any admission charge is applied solely for the purposes of the organisation.

Some have argued that this permits a public sector educational establishment to play recorded music without needing a licence from Phonographic Performance Ltd in respect of the sound recordings even when the audience contains members of the public (9.5). This is however regarded as a dubious assessment of the purpose of s67, which is taken as covering a body such as a medical research charity, or a religious organisation such as SPCK. Even an organisation whose playing of sound recordings is covered by the s67 permission would nevertheless need a licence from the Performing Right Society to cover the public performance rights of composers and music publishers (9.6).

9.27 Free public showing or playing of a broadcast or cable programme

This is permitted, but conditions are specified in which the audience would be treated as having paid for admission, when the permission would be invalid (s72). Residents or inmates would however not be treated as having paid, hence any communal facilities, from old people's homes to hospitals or university common rooms, are not treated as having paid for admission. But, as above, this does not cover performing rights and a licence is needed from the Performing Right Society for non-domestic audiences – that is, groups definable as 'public', including common rooms.

9.28 Performance in public by reading or recitation

The reading or recitation by one person of a reasonable extract from a literary or dramatic work is permitted, subject to acknowledgement (s59). 'Reasonable' is not defined and is therefore a matter for discretion. A sound recording, broadcast or inclusion in a cable programme service of the performance is also permitted, provided the reading or recitation does not form the main material included.

9.29 Transfers of copies of works in electronic form

When a work in electronic form has been purchased on terms which allow the purchaser to copy or adapt the work, anything which the purchaser was allowed to do may be done by a transferee, unless the terms of purchase included limits on actions after transfer to another person (already described earlier in the copying context, where other relevant notes appear, 7.30.).

Rights in performances

9.30 The difference between *performing* (a restricted act in respect of copyright) and *performance* (a restricted act in respect of recording by or with consent of a live performer of his own performance) was noted in 4.22. The rights in live performances or recordings of them are the subject of a separate Part of the Act, namely Part II, with its own statements of qualification for protection and of remedies. The provisions replace the Performers' Protection Acts, 1958 to 1972, which are repealed.

Considerable augmentation and revision of rights has arisen from EC harmonisation, broadly relating to firstly the duration of rights (SI 1995/3297), and secondly to the nature and number of rights (SI 1996/2967). 'Extended' or 'revived' rights in performances are included in SI 1995/3297(30-35). The details of all these changes are outside the scope of this volume, but an outline is made below.

The rights are of two kinds (s180):

(a) a performer's right in respect of exploitation of his performances
(b) rights of a holder of recording rights for a performance.

Both rights subsist for 50 years beyond the end of the calendar year in which the performance occurs. However, if a recording of a performance is released during that period, protection lasts for 50 years beyond the year of release (s191 as amended), resulting in a possible 100 years' protection for music as a sound recording (3.5). It should be noted that video recordings, as moving images, are treated as films under CDPA88 (3.6). Performing and recording rights may be considered peripheral to the needs of some readers, but could be important to any organisation which holds live performances or makes recordings of them, as well as to those who become performers themselves.

A 'performance' means a live performance only by one or more individuals in:

- a dramatic performance (including dance or mime)
- a musical performance
- a reading or recitation of a literary work
- a performance of a variety act or any similar presentation.

- A 'recording' of a performance means a film or sound recording made:
  - directly from the live performance
  - from a broadcast of the live performance or a cable programme including the live performance
  - directly or indirectly from another recording of the performance.

9.31 Performers' rights

These are infringed when, without authorisation, someone makes a recording of, or broadcasts or includes live in a cable programme, the whole or a substantial part of a performance as defined above, other than for 'private and domestic use' – also when such an unauthorised recording is played or shown in public or broadcast, etc. (s183).

The groups: 'property rights' and 'non-property rights' are now set out (SI 1996/ 2967). Some 19 new sections have been inserted into the Act. Non-property rights are:

(a) consent required for making a recording, broadcasting, etc of a live performance (s182);
(b) infringement by use of an illicit recording (i.e. made without consent. s183);
(c) infringement by importing, possessing, dealing, etc with illicit recordings (s184).

These rights are not assignable but may be passed on by bequest. A performer's rights in (a) result in benefit through contracts. Property rights (s191A) arise when recordings of live performances have been made:

i) infringement by making a copy of a recording without consent (s182A);
ii) distribution right – issue of recordings to public without performers' consent (s182B);
iii) rental and lending right (s182C, see 4.35 et seq.), including a right to equitable remuneration. Property rights are assignable, as well as by bequest as *personal or moveable property.*

A live performance represents copying of a work, and the performer must be authorised or licensed by the author, composer, publisher, etc who owns the relevant rights. Similarly, performance of a recording is a copy also, and composers and music publishers are represented for licensing and collecting purposes by the Performing Right Society (9.6 and 12.41-12.43). Formerly, there has been no statutory performer's right in the public performance of a recording, this matter being left to contract between performers and recording companies, because the latter own the copyright in their recordings. The great majority of recording companies have assigned their rights to Phonographic Performance Limited (PPL, see 12.34-12.36). Funds are distributed to member companies. For many years this has resulted, through contracts, in payment either directly to individuals or via a body such as the Musicians' Union. An important change under SI 1996/2967 is the right of performers to equitable remuneration on two counts: public performance or broadcasts etc of a commercially published sound recording (new s182D); and rental right when assigned (new s191G). Neither can be assigned except to a collecting society. (Similar considerations apply to authors/composers in the rental context, see 4.35 et seq.). Thus companies are primarily bound by their contracts with performers, but 'equitable' remuneration for rental must henceforth be provided whether or not included in the contract.

9.32 Recording rights

The rights of a person with an exclusive recording contract are infringed when an unauthorised recording of the whole or a substantial part of a performance is made or put to use involving the public -- playing, showing, broadcast, etc. (s185). Some 13 new sections are now added to the Act concerning performers' property rights, some on licensing. SI 1996/2967 adds a new Schedule 2A of 17 paragraphs to the Act on *Licensing of performers' property rights*. Paragraph 17 makes possible a *licence of right* in certain circumstances, when the Monopolies and Mergers Commission has been involved, the licence being authorised under the Fair Trading Act 1973 (Pt. I of Schedule 8). Provision is made at various points in the SI for action by the Copyright Tribunal.

9.33 Infringement of performers' rights

As may be expected from earlier remarks in other contexts, both primary (ss182; 183; 186; 187) and secondary (ss184; 188) modes of infringement of performers' rights are possible. Secondary infringement of both performer and recording rights can arise from possessing or dealing with an infringing recording, with criminal liability.

The rights are retrospective in that they apply to performances occurring before the Act came into force in 1989.

The Act as amended now contains a number of new sections on infringement proceedings and penalties. Infringement of the 1988 provisions cannot result in respect of actions or arrangements made before the Act came into force, such as a compulsory licence to copy records sold by retail, brought in by the 1956 Act but abolished by CDPA88. However, a case of infringement of earlier law than 1988 could arise. Although all of the Performers' Protection Acts are repealed by CDPA88, they are still relevant to performances before 1988. Rights in performances are independent of copyright or moral rights.

9.34 Remedies for an infringement include a court order for delivery up or seizure of 'illicit recordings'. These include any recording which has been made without authorisation, whether by a performer or a recording rights holder or by statutory permission (such as examination purposes). As in other areas, recordings made with statutory or other context-limited permission become illicit recordings if used for another, unauthorised purpose.

9.35 Permissions or licences re performers' rights

Permissions are extensive, and are identical with those listed in the main portion of this chapter, which is one reason why some of them have been repeated in brief here as well as having been treated in the copying context in chapter 7. Firstly, however, it should be borne in mind that the permissions apply here in the context of live performances and recordings of them. Secondly, in any area like this where a very large number of separate contracts exist between individual performers and their recordists or recording companies, any of the above permissions could be challenged in the event of its being overruled in a contract and done by a party to that contract in breach.

Thirdly, a copy of a recording of a performance acquired before 1 December 1996 is unaffected by any new right in a performance covered by SI 1996/2967.

Licensing of performances

9.36 In 12.41-12.43 there appears comparative information on the various agencies concerned with the licensing of performance, whether live or of recordings. The new law on rental/lending now provides a means for creators of original works and performers to obtain benefits in a manner which might in some circumstances be thought more reliable than individual contracts. It is not clear, and enquiries have brought no reply from certain major bodies, as to whether and to what extent recording companies have contracts which customarily share their royalties already with performers, or indeed with creators of the works. Nor is it readily understood why the collecting bodies cannot cooperate or, if they are doing so already, why they do not say so when asked. When standard tariffs are applied separately by the societies concerned, prospective licensees may rightly or wrongly regard the present procedures in respect of recordings as 'double licensing' of dubbing (MCPS and PPL) and of public performance (PPL and PRS). Another matter for prospective licensees is to ensure that statutory permissions are exempted or else adequately compensated. For example, some agency literature makes no mention of educational or other statutory permissions, and some prospective licensees have been known to make erroneous assumptions about licensing need.

Since the equitable remuneration right can only be assigned to a collecting society, and there is a large range of those 'beneath the surface' of the major bodies in 12.41 et seq., the question of loss through administrative cost of the whole system may need examination. When the EU harmonisation programme tackles the problem of collecting societies, as it is scheduled to do, might authors, performers and users all ask for some rules to be be laid down for all concerned to comprehend?

Lending/rental right permissions

9.37 The Government may make an order, under CDPA88s66 as revised (cf 12.11), regarding the lending to the public of literary, dramatic, musical or artistic works, sound recordings or films. These may be regarded as licensed, subject to payment of reasonable royalty, if no licensing scheme is available. This provision is precautionary, in case of denial of service to the disadvantaged, and would result in a form of compulsory licensing. The user community has *still* failed to take advantage of an earlier version of this provision by applying to the Secretary of State in respect of computer programs (video presenting no problem at present and sound being covered by a LA/JCC/WPC arrangement with the industry via BPI (see 4.47). Computer programs are still included in a revised wordng of s66, but as 'literary works'.

The changes in rights which arise from SI 1996/2967 are presented cohesively in 4.35 et seq., upon which comments apear in Appendix 3. The following should be read in conjunction:

Educational establishments

These may *lend* copies of any kind of work, lending as defined in 4.37. (This is taken to exclude charging for loans to any degree.)

Public libraries and other nonprofit-based libraries/archives

Such services may *lend* copies of books which are covered by the Public Lending Right Act 1979 (see 4.39), though licensing is required for other materials. Those nonprofit-based services which are accessible to public are permitted to charge, provided income does not exceed operating costs, otherwise, service becomes rental and requires licensing.

Note that rental to public requires to be licensed, no matter who does it and how much charged, unless covered by a permission. The nonprofit-based services above are exempted because the definition of 'lending' by such services allows a charge not exceeding the costs of operation of the service to avoid being called 'rental'. In addition, note that any statutory permission which allows *any* action for certain purposes (such as judicial proceedings, 7.9) should also be taken to apply to public lending or rental.

10. MORAL RIGHTS

New Rights

10.1 The author of an original work – literary, dramatic, musical or artistic – or the director of a film has three moral rights, newly introduced as such into the UK by CDPA88. One of the three moral rights ((c) below), although henceforth to be termed a 'moral right', is not entirely new but is based on s43 of the 1956 Act on 'false attribution of authorship'. A fourth right of privacy is accorded to a commissioner of photographs, and this is included along with Moral Rights. A summary of the main points appears as Q9.

Some of the moral rights are overruled by permissions, and these are simply listed in the relevant places in this chapter, being identical with those already described in other contexts. However, the exclusions (10.10, 10.13) should also be noted.

It has been suggested that the Act also provides a fifth moral right, namely that of 'disclosure', for example by unauthorised publication, but this is implicit and to define it separately would take in all the restricted acts, resulting in confusing cross-classification.

10.2 The four rights subsist alongside copyright. As explained earlier, 'artistic' covers films (including videotapes) and photographs. Photographers are now authors of their work, and hence are first owners of copyright unless otherwise agreed by contract, such as a contract of employment or commissioning contract. The rights are:

(a) Right to be identified as author or director of a film (s77) in respect of a work issued to or performed or exhibited in public (or other cognate actions). This 'paternity' right does not exist unless it is asserted as specified (s78), for example in an assignment of copyright. Hence one should assert the right in any event, since such actions may occur in future. Although it is not a legal requirement, publishers should be asked to include a statement on the title page to the effect that the right has been asserted. This right lasts for the duration of copyright, and subsists in favour of the author or director whether or not he is the owner of copyright – in other words, moral rights relate to him irrespective of ownership of copyright.

(b) Right to object to derogatory treatment of a work (s80), lasting for the duration of copyright. Like (a), this right subsists in favour of the author or director whether or not he is the owner of copyright.

(c) Right not to suffer false attribution of a work: this lasts for life plus twenty years only (s84).

(d) Right of a person commissioning copyright photographs or films not to have copies issued to the public, or exhibited or shown in public, or broadcast or included in a cable programme service (s85). This right lasts for the duration of copyright, and subsists in favour of the commissioner whether or not he is the owner of copyright, as with (a).

10.3 Moral rights cannot be assigned. However, (a), (b) and (d) can be willed to someone else, or when there is no such direction in a will the right passes to the person to whom copyright passes, or if neither of these applies the rights can be exercised by personal representatives.

Infringement

10.4 Infringement of the above rights is actionable as a breach of statutory duty owed to the person entitled to the right (s103). Damages may be awarded as well as an injunction against against distribution. In respect of infringement of 10.2(c) after the author's or director's death, the right is actionable by personal representatives, when any damages become part of the estate. A court may grant an injunction against continuance of infringement by the person concerned.

Infringement of 10.2(b) and (c) can also occur from possessing or dealing with an infringing article, as in other cases of secondary infringement (4.27). Some particular dangers of infringement in Internet usage have been outlined in 3.59. Certain of these may readily be predicted by the careful netizen, such as the right to privacy of certain photographs and films (s85) which could become included in multimedia. However, when a netizen behaves correctly and quotes authorship of a quotes source, any paternity right which exists is automatically covered, provided the title etc. details are accurate, of course. The electronic context could bring greater dangers of infringement than print, for example, through the immediacy the keyboard, when slips such as misquotation or misleading links may become all too easy. In following the decision table below re paternity right, one needs to know whether a work is 'commercially published' (see 4.17-4.21), and it should be noted that making a work available in an electronic retrieval system (s175) is 'commercial publication'. Perhaps less readily perceived for any format is a danger for editors who, if the result of their own corrections are not properly representative of the author's work, could well infringe moral rights.

Waivers

10.5 All the above may be waived by an instrument in writing, duly signed (s87). Waivers may relate to a specific work, or works of a specified description, or to works generally, and may relate to existing or future works, and may be conditional or unconditional, and may be expressed to be subject to revocation. Any permission or waiver already given will bind anyone to whom a moral right has passed by will or in association with inheritance of copyright, or to a personal representative who may assume responsibility, as in the previous section.

10.6 It should be noted that 10.2(a) and (b) apply whether or not the author or director is the owner of copyright. In staff conditions of service which state, or by omission leave it to be assumed, that the organisation has first ownership of copyright of works published commercially, some kind of qualification regarding moral rights might seem desirable. However, a general or blanket waiver could not properly be imposed in the conditions of service, because the phrase 'an instrument in writing' in 10.5 above implies action by the author himself. Conditions of service could only, rather questionably, deem waiver to have occurred, which statement might then be expected, along with the other conditions, to become contractual upon acceptance of a post. Staff who expect to be involved in writing to any extent are recommended to question such a statement, should it appear in service conditions or contracts. But general waivers are quite feasible if initiated by the author, whether or not in accordance with conditions of service or contract, as below.

10.7 An organisation which believes it undesirable that these moral rights of individuals should be left in place, when the organisation is first owner of copyright as employer, could seek waivers of 10.2(a) and (b). This might be done by asking staff members involved in authorship of any kind (including photographs) on behalf of the organisation to sign a general waiver of (a) and (b) in respect of all future work done for the organisation. Desirably such a general waiver should be expressed, as implied by s87(3)(b), as open to revocation by separate agreement with the employer in specific cases. Rights 10.2(c) and (d) would seem best left in place.

Decision table to assist comprehension

10.8 The way in which the moral rights apply leads to complex provisions in the Act. Accordingly, a decision table is placed in this chapter with the aim of assisting comprehension of at least the first two moral rights above. Neither the table nor these notes can be as complete as the Act itself and should therefore be used merely as a guide before studying details in the Act, or consulting, where necessary. Notes expanding the above outline now follow on each of the four rights, plus other matters.

Right to be identified as author or director (film)

10.9 As noted in 10.2, this 'paternity' right (s77) only exists when the author or film director has asserted it. The decision table should indicate the circumstances in which this right applies, such as commercial publication, etc.

Joint authors or directors each have the right and a waiver by one does not affect the other.

10.10 Exclusions

The right does not apply to:

- anything done with the copyright owner's authority in respect of works of which the copyright was first vested in the author's or director's employer
- a newspaper or other periodical article, or a collective work of reference
- any work made for the purpose of reporting current events
- a computer program or any computer-generated work
- the design of a typeface

and, unless author or director has previously been identified by published copies

- Crown or Parliamentary copyright
- works in which copyright was originally vested in an international organisation (s168).

10.11 Permissions re paternity right

The Act's permissions overruling this right are (from s79(4)):

- fair dealing by reporting current events by means of a sound recording, film, broadcast or cable programme service (5.22)

		If **YES** go to	If **NO** go to
1.	Is the work a computer program, a computer generated work, or a design of a typeface?	*11*	*2*
2.	Is commercial publication or issue to the public involved?	*3*	*4*
3.	Made by author for newspaper or other periodical, or for a collective work of reference?	*11*	*4*
4.	Made by author to report current events?	*11*	*5*
5.	Did copyright first vest in an employer?	*6*	*7*
6.	Has copyright owner authorised the action?	*11*	*10*
7.	Is the action covered by the Act's permissions?	*11*	*8*
8.	Is the work Crown or Parliamentary copyright?	*10*	*9*
9.	Did copyright first vest in an international organisation?	*10*	*12*
10.	Is author already identified on a copy?	*12*	*11*
11.	NEITHER RIGHT APPLIES		
12.	Must the right be asserted to exist (s78)?	*13*	*14*
13.	PATERNITY RIGHT APPLIES (s77)		
14.	Is action required to avoid comitting an offence, or comply with statutory duty, or for the BBC to avoid broadcast of anything offensive or liable to incite crime or disorder?	–	*15*
15.	DEROGATORY TREATMENT RIGHT APPLIES (s80)		

Rights of paternity (s77) and objection to derogatory treatment (s80) only.

Subject to exceptions and permissions, the rights may cover any copyright work in any action involving the public, including graphic or photographic representations (of buildings or models for them; sculptures or works of artistic craftsmanship).

Figure 2: Decision Table

- incidental inclusion in an artistic work of a sound recording, film, broadcast or cable programme (7.27)
- examination questions (7.2)
- parliamentary and judicial proceedings (7.9)
- Royal Commission or statutory inquiry (7.10)
- use of design documents and models (11.12)
- effect of exploiting designs derived from artistic works (11.13)
- anonymous or pseudonymous works: acts permitted on assumption of expiry of copyright or death of author (7.28).

Right to object to derogatory treatment (s80)

10.12 This right (s80) is also covered by the decision table. Joint authors or joint directors each have the right and a waiver by one does not affect the other.

'Derogatory' means distortion or mutilation or action otherwise prejudicial to the honour or reputation of an author or director. 'Treatment' means any addition or alteration or adaptation other than: a translation of a literary or dramatic work; or an arrangement or transcription of a musical work involving no more than a change of key or register.

10.13 Exclusions

The right does not apply to:

- anything done with the copyright owner's authority in respect of works of which copyright was first vested in the author's or director's employer, unless the author or director was identified at the time of the act concerned or in published copies of the work
- a newspaper or other periodical article, or a collective work of reference
- any work made for the purpose of reporting current events
- a computer program or any computer-generated work

and, unless author or director has previously been identified by published copies

- Crown or Parliamentary copyright
- works in which copyright originally vested in an international organisation (s168).

10.14 Permissions

The following permissions overrule the right and would not infringe (from s81(5) and (6)):

- anonymous or pseudonymous works: acts permitted on assumption of expiry of copyright or death of author (7.28)
- action taken to avoid committing offences (s81(6)(a)
- action to comply with a statutory duty (s81(6)(b)
- for the BBC to avoid broadcasting anything which offends against good taste or decency or which is likely to encourage or incite crime or to lead to disorder or to be offensive to public feeling (s81(6)(c)).

Right of an author or director not to have a work falsely attributed to him

10.15 The decision table is not designed to cover this right (s84). This is partly because of the complexity which would result. It is also confined to a brief mention in this text because it is not a copyright matter (rather the reverse). However, finding one's name taken in vain, so to say, for example through being credited with writing something which could damage a reputation or lower the authority of other work by association, can be as serious as failure to show paternity of an important work.

Joint authors or joint directors each have rights, and a waiver by one does not affect the other. It is however suggested that it would be inappropriate to secure a waiver in respect of this right. Unlike the others, the right lasts for 20 years after death.

Right of a person who commissions copyright photographs or films for private *and* domestic purposes *not* to have copies issued or shown in public, broadcast or included in a cable programme service

10.16 The decision table is not designed to help in respect of this right (s85). Joint commissioners each have the right, and a waiver by one does not affect the other.

Permissions (general)

10.17 Permissions which overrule and do not infringe are:

- incidental inclusion in an artistic work of a sound recording, film, broadcast or cable programme (7.27)
- parliamentary and judicial proceedings (7.9)
- Royal Commission or statutory inquiry (7.10)
- acts done under statutory authority (7.14)
- anonymous or pseudonymous works: acts permitted on assumption of expiry of copyright or death of author (7.28).

Complexity

10.18 In view of complexity and a certain vagueness in one or two places, case law may be needed to clarify some situations. An example is s78(54)(c) which provides that the persons bound by an assertion of the right (to be identified as author, when his right has been asserted by marking the original or a copy, as with a photograph) include anyone into whose hands that original or copy comes, whether or not the identification is still present or visible. No suggestions are made as to how anyone could possibly be bound by an assertion which had ceased to be visible. One can only assume that this provision refers to a situation wherein the assertion was proved to be visible at the time of receipt to a person alleged to be infringing.

Asserting paternity right

10.19 In respect of a literary work (other than a computer program, which is excluded), the assertion can be made in an assignment of copyright – but this does not have to involve publication – or in a separate statement in writing by the author or director which binds anyone to whose attention it is brought. An assertion can also be made by an assignee or licensor of copyright, such as a publisher, on behalf of the author or film director concerned.

It is important to bear in mind that this right exists independently of ownership of copyright. So, even if an employer is first owner of copyright, the author can still have his right asserted, unless his employer has bound him by contract otherwise, for example by conditions of service. An author should study the terms of a licence to publish to ensure that the publisher (or his employer in conditions of service) has not included a waiver clause.

An assertion is liable to be printed on a title page and this is desirable to help protect an author's moral right by informing readers who may need to know. However, as the law does not make assertion compulsory, the non-appearance of an assertion is no guarantee that it does not feature (i) in a licence to the publisher, such licence being unavailable to a reader without special application; or (ii) in a separate letter to the publisher. Accordingly, the recommended procedure, for an author who wishes to assert paternity in the circumstances covered in the decision table, is to ensure that the publisher does indeed include a reasonably prominent note such as that which appears on the back of the title page of this book. On the Internet, a note could appear at the beginning of a work, especially when the work is deemed likely to be vulnerable to infringement (see 10.4). The 'paternity' right will probably become the best known and most frequently encountered of the Moral Rights.

11. DESIGN RIGHT

Duration

11.1 A new design right is provided in CDPA88. It is automatic, like copyright as such, requiring no registration. This unregistered right for 10 to 15 years is one of three ways in which designs are affected by the Act, the other two being:

- copyright in artistic works, for author's life plus 70 years unless a design is exploited commercially, when copyright is reduced to 25 years for the relevant part of the artistic work
- protection under the Registered Designs Act 1949, as amended by CDPA88, including extension of the protection period to 25 years. Henceforth, only designs with aesthetic or 'eye appeal' will be registrable.

Definition

11.2 'Design' is defined (s51(3); s213) to mean the design of any aspect of the shape or configuration (whether internal or external) of the whole or part of an article, other than surface decoration. The various design provisions in the Act overlap in complex ways. Bearing in mind that this topic will be 'fringe' to the interests of many readers, it is not intended to go further here than an outline of the new situation, especially when some detailed studies appear in Appendix 1 and necessarily show the historical bases and controversies leading to current design rights. Other complexities can arise from overlap between design rights as such with patents, domestic and European competition law, trade marks, and 'passing off'.

11.3 Design right appears separately from Copyright in Part III of CDPA88, with amendments to the Registered Designs Act 1949 listed in Part IV. Accordingly, Part III specifies qualification for protection and remedies specific to design right.

Qualification for protection

11.4 To qualify for unregistered design right, a design must be original and not itself a copy or commonplace in the design field in question (s213(4)). However, 'original' is not otherwise defined, and might become tested in court. At present, it would appear that designer B could produce the same design as that of designer A in another context without infringement provided there had been no copying, or claim the right after expiry of designer A's right, provided the design had not by then become regarded as commonplace. A computer-generated design, without human involvement in the course of design, results in a right for the person who has made the arrangements.

11.5 The unregistered design right provides between 10 and 15 years' protection against copying of original designs. The right subsists whether a design is functional or aesthetic, apart from exclusions below, and belongs to the designer unless an employer is first owner, as with copyright. If a design does not result in a marketed product during the first five years after creation, the period of protection is 15 years. However, if a product is marketed within the first five years, the protection period is limited to 10 years. During the second five years when the product has been marketed, or the third five years if not, anyone is entitled as of right to obtain a licence to produce the design, subject to arbitration on terms by the Patent Office if necessary. This provision for a 'licence of right' reduces the exclusive protection to five years only for a marketable design.

Registered designs

11.6 In contrast, the protection period under the Registered Designs Act has been extended to 25 years by CDPA88, provided renewal fees are paid every five years, but coverage is now confined to aesthetic designs. 'Aesthetic' means that a design must have at least some 'eye appeal', which is taken to be the eye of an independent observer or customer and not that of the designer. However, for aesthetic designs, the appeal of registration has been enhanced by the Act's amendments. There is however a serious limitation in respect of artistic works, any copyright in which is curtailed to 25 years after industrial exploitation as a registered design.

Exclusions from unregistered right

11.7 The unregistered right excludes:

- a method or principle of construction
- features of shape or configuration which enable fitting to or matching with another article – the 'must fit' or 'must match' features of a design (s213(3))
- surface decoration.

The 'must fit' principle refers to parts of a design which enable it to fit into or engage with another device or equipment, such as a car exhaust designed to fit on to an exhaust manifold and under a given type of car. The 'must match' principle refers to aspects of the appearance of an article which permit it to form an integral part of another device. Making comparison again with the Registered Designs Act as amended by CDPA88, this now also excludes 'must fit' but retains 'must match'.

Ownership of design right

11.8 The first owner is the designer unless the work has been commissioned or created in the course of the designer's employment, when the commissioner or employer is first owner respectively. (From s215, plus s219 on qualification for protection of commissioned designs.)

Aim of the new right

11.9 The aim of design right was to encourage innovative competition among manufacturers, who are now free to compete, for example in the spare parts field, provided they do not infringe against a registered design. The duration of the unregistered right had to be a compromise. Firstly, it stimulates competition. Secondly, it encourages continual innovative endeavour by all firms to keep abreast of their competition. Modes of primary and secondary infringement are detailed in the Act, along with remedies or penalties.

Records and infringement

11.10 Although having a considerable advantage in being unregistered, a design must nevertheless have been recorded in a design document or an article made to the design, and no unregistered right subsists in a design made before the Act came into force. A 'design document' means any record of a design, whether in the form of a drawing, a written description, a photograph, data stored in a computer or otherwise' (s51(3)). The latter section states that it is not an infringement of any copyright in a design document or model ... other than an artistic work or a typeface to make an article to the design or to copy an article made to the design and this has the effect of transferring protection to design right.

The exception of artistic works is significant, but it may take case law to establish what is meant by 'artistic work' in this context, or even what is meant by 'make an article'. However, there is still copyright in drawings and other records in themselves. Also, there continues to be copyright in an artistic work which might qualify for unregistered design right, but note the above-mentioned curtailment (11.6) of copyright period for an artistic work in the event of industrial exploitation of a design which has been registered.

Key documents and/or electronic files produced at the time of the creation of a design should be dated in the presence of witnesses and securely filed, preferably in at least duplicate and including a set with a bank or solicitor. It may help to consult Stationers' Hall, for it is still possible to register copyright there (The Worshipful Company of Stationers and Newspapermakers, Stationers' Hall Court, London EC4M 7DD) in return for a moderate fee.

Proof of ownership of the unregistered design right could be totally dependent on such care.

Moral rights

11.11 Moral rights apply to artistic works and therefore also to designs.

Permissions

11.12 Copyright in design documents or models

The copyright in design documents or models (11.10), in respect of a design for anything other than an artistic work or a typeface, is not infringed by making an article to the design, or copying such an article, or issuing copies of the article to the public, or including it in a film (or video recording), broadcast or cable programme service. The design documents themselves remain copyright (s51).

11.13 Exploited artistic designs

Artistic designs (excluding films), as effected by or licensed by the copyright owner, are covered by this permission. Where copies have been made by an industrial process and marketed, the work may be copied after 25 years from the end of the calendar year of first marketing for purposes of any kind of articles and anything done in relation to such articles without infringement. Where exploitation is only in part, the provision only applies to the part. The Secretary of State was empowered to define 'industrial process' and exclude any articles of primarily literary or artistic character as he thinks fit (s52). However, the main artistic works are copyright irrespective of artistic quality (s4(1)(a)).

11.14 Artistic works as registered designs

Anything done by an assignee or licensee in the belief that an artistic work has been duly registered under the Registered Designs Act 1949 does not infringe (s53).

11.15 Typefaces as artistic designs

Ordinary use for typing, composition, printing, etc. does not infringe, despite the fact that an article is used which is an infringing copy of the work. The section (s54) however goes on to define secondary infringement in respect of typeface designs and refer to remedies provided by the Act. Another section on this subject (s55) permits the copying, after 25 years from first marketing, of articles specifically designed or adapted for producing material in a typeface which is an artistic design.

11.16 Crown use

There are extensive Crown permissions (ss240-244). Such Crown use covers anything for: defence of the realm; foreign defence purposes; or health service purposes; but is subject to compensation for loss of profit when a design is on the market.

Digest on unregistered design right

11.17

1. Automatic, unregistered protection for an original design other than: a method of construction; or a shape or configuration dictated by what the design must fit or must match, or surface decoration. Hence, no monopoly on production of spare parts.
2. No other discrimination between functional and aesthetic features.
3. Duration for a maximum of 15 years, from recorded date of first design or making, subject to a licence of right by another person to manufacture during the last five years.

4. The unregistered right therefore lasts between 10 and 15 years, with exclusive commercial exploitation for at least five years of that period.
5. Entitlement to royalty from licensed manufacture by someone else (should the need arise) during last five years of right.
6. When a design is made in the course of employment, the employer is first owner unless contracted to the contrary.
7. A computer-generated design right (i.e. generated without human involvement during design) belongs to the person making the arrangements for such generation.
8. A design may have unregistered right, and copyright as an artistic work, in addition to being registered under the Registered Designs Act 1949 as amended, which now protects only designs with aesthetic features (for an extended period of 25 years).
9. An artistic work is copyright for author's life plus 70 years unless exploited commercially by making articles to a design, when protection is reduced to 25 years for relevant features.
10. Making an article to a design drawing or document no longer infringes copyright, but the drawings or documents themselves remain copyright.
11. Any claim would necessitate proof of origination. Hence it is essential that all drawings, computer files, etc. are securely kept and reliably dated and credited. (For example, use the Registry of Copyright at Stationers' Hall – see 12.40).

12. COPYRIGHT ADMINISTRATION

Intellectual property

12.1 Rights exist in order to entitle authors and other originators to economic gain. But of course, gain is unlikely without some means of administering the rights. Copyright administration includes the allowance of actions which would otherwise infringe rights, usually in return for payment. This wide and complex field embraces:

(a) licensing by an individual publisher or producer, such as HMSO and the Ordnance Survey for many years, mostly in respect of re-publishing
(b) collective licensing of individual user organisations by a group of rights owners, such as that effected by the Copyright Licensing Agency Ltd which at present covers the Education sector but is in course of extension to government departments and industry
(c) collective licensing of individual copying agencies, such as the CLA licence held by the British Library, which for several years has been providing a 'cleared copy' photocopying service
(d) notices about copyright, found on items purchased or on associated documentation such as conditions of sale, which may permit more than the law and/or purport to restrict certain actions to a greater extent than the law; or guidelines which give comprehensive aid to the user
(e) service contracts, common to electronic databases, made between individual database producers or host organisations and users
(f) assignment of one or more rights, usually by sale; or bequest of rights (ss.90-93)
(g) remedies for infringement: orders for 'delivery up' of infringing articles or seizure of them; damages and/or imprisonment (ss.96-115).

The administration of rights related to copyright, such as rental and lending rights, is not covered here, though comments have appeared earlier (4.35-4.50).

12.2 Licence

A licence is a form of contract between persons, whether as individuals or as representatives of organisations. Usually renewable at annual intervals, a licence permits certain actions, normally in return for payment. In fact, contracts can vary from the simplest agreement recorded by letter to highly complex arrangements set out in multi-page documents. Any kind of agreement throughout that range must be considered binding on the parties and could result in protestations about 'breach of contract'. Although litigation for breach could be attempted on the basis of even the simplest letter, it appears more usual to have recourse to the courts when a breach of the more formal kind of contract, with signatures duly witnessed, has occurred. Accordingly, the more important agreements are drawn up with legal advice (App. 1/4).

Although it is better for both parties when contract terms are backed up by legislation, this is not a limitation and anyone can stipulate, or agree to, virtually anything – save matters involving public welfare such as criminal behaviour – with only himself or herself to blame if the terms prove unduly restrictive because they were not carefully vetted before exchange of signatures.

The word 'licence' is also used in a more general sense of permission, without any contract being involved other than perhaps a letter. The common phrase in CDPA88: licence of the copyright owner simply means any form of permission whether verbal or written, but care is needed in defining 'copyright owner' when more than one may be involved.

Licences may be required to cover any of the restricted acts (4.10 4.12 et seq.):

(i) copying a work;
(ii) issuing copies to the public (wider than, but inclusive of 'publishing');
(iii) rental or lending of copies of the work to the public;
(iv) performing, showing or playing the work in public;
(v) broadcasting the work or including it in a cable programme service.
(vi) making an adaptation of the work, or doing any of the above in relation to an adaptation.

12.3 Lease

The word 'lease' describes a form of contract which usually involves the temporary acquisition by the lessor of something tangible, ranging from a building or a computer system to a set of technical data sheets. In cases like the latter, a lease can include an associated service such as loose-leaf updating by a visiting assistant during a fixed term between renewals, with the work itself remaining the property of the service provider. However, a lease need not involve tangible things and can refer to access to a service – hence its mention here, since some electronic databases, or suites of computer programs requiring regular updating, may use the word 'lease' in place of the term 'service contract' treated later.

12.4 Individual publisher or producer licensing

The British Standards Institution licenses the production of multiple copies for educational classes (8.21). HMSO and the Ordnance Survey provide guidelines for users as noted in chapter 6 and 8.17. When needs exceed the permissions in guidelines, requests must be made and, when the publisher's typographical layout is to be used as camera-ready copy for re-publication, fees will probably be charged. Licences can result when regular needs are involved, otherwise one-off agreements may suffice. A publisher of microforms may acquire an 'exclusive licence' to produce a microfilm, microfiche or microcard set of official documents of a given type over a given period, thus keeping out the competition. OS licences educational copying from maps, having opted to refrain from joining in collective licensing; and also licences 'business use' and local authorities for such purposes as planning.

12.5 Also, there are many 'one-off' situations wherein the need to make an individual approach involves other material than printed matter, for example when a videotape is to be played to a public audience – unless it is a music video, for which a collecting agency exists (12.31). Whether a cinematographic film can be shown to a public audience should be clear from conditions of sale before purchase or hire, the latter being the more frequent choice because of the considerable purchase price of films.

12.6 Apart from music videos, film and video producers administer their own rights. They have suffered considerably from piracy, particularly from the illegal replication of videos, and their concerns were a major spur towards the introduction of the phrase 'criminal liability' into UK law in 1988. An organisation co-ordinates action against pirates – the Federation Against Copyright Theft (FACT), based in Isleworth, Middlesex. The latter body should not be confused with FAST, the Federation Against Software Theft, the London-based organisation which takes action against piracy in computer programs. Otherwise, computer software houses administer their own rights, although there is an Educational Software Producers' Association which has been in discussion with the National Council for Educational Technology for several years towards an educational licensing scheme (8.23).

12.7 Some kinds of intellectual property, such as designs, require individual treatment almost by definition. However, apart from specific information professional bodies and legal advisers, a designer could be assisted by the London-based Chartered Society of Designers, which links designers producing work for industry or commerce. A user is free to make a direct approach irrespective of the existence of licensing administered by a collecting agency, and may well do so if it is believed that more favourable terms might result, for example when charities or medical purposes are involved.

Collective licensing of individual user organisations

12.8 Rather than include an outline of the licensing controversy in the main text, it appears in chapter 15. Also, some licensing problems are described in 8.30 et seq. The first task here is broadly to describe the provisions of CDPA88 on 12.1(b) above.

As remarked elsewhere, the Act sought to encourage collective licensing without actually making it compulsory and thus – according to one interpretation – contravening the Berne Convention. However, this in no way rules out other forms of licensing or contract.

12.9 Licensing schemes

'Licensing scheme' is the Act's term for a collective licensing arrangement operated by a 'licensing body'. That body must either own or expect to own copyright or be an agent for owners, and must offer licences covering the works of more than one author. This does not mean more than one publisher, so schemes can be small or large: for example, the Open University off-air recording licence offered separately from the general licence available from the Educational Recording Agency (8.26).

12.10 Certified schemes

How is collective licensing encouraged? By following one of the Whitford recommendations (App. 1/7), namely that some provisions should state that reprographic reproduction will not infringe unless a 'licensing scheme' is available. This is only applied in six cases for which a scheme may be certified by the Secretary of State (s143):

- recording of broadcasts and cable programmes by educational establishments (s35) – certified ERA and OU schemes available
- copying abstracts of scientific or technical articles (s60) – scheme appears unlikely at present but beware definition of 'database' which might now be claimed to include a periodical issue (3.28);

- lending of literary, dramatic, musical or artistic works, sound recordings and films to the public (s66 as revised by SI 1996/2967(Reg. 11) – note that 'lending' is defined in the SI as done only through an establishment which is accessible to the public. Schemes may be needed for musical scores, or any materials not in book form as per PLR coverage, i.e. computer programs in electronic form, maps, sound/video recordings, or offline databases such as CD-ROMs (see 4.35 et seq.);
- making sub-titled copies of broadcasts or cable programmes for the deaf or otherwise handicapped (s74 specifies a designated body, now in use; no licensing scheme;
- licensing by the *performer* of reproduction right and distribution right in respect of films or sound recordings (new Schedule 2A to CDPA88, in SI 1996/2967 Reg.22); and
- reprographic copying of published works in educational establishments (s141) – covered by CLA licence but not certified.

The process of 'certification' does not imply government approval, but only that the Secretary of State is satisfied that the intended licensees, works covered, and charges to be made are clear. In the area of educational off-air recording, with so many rights owners involved, it appears probable that this encouragement was helpful. For many years, the attitudes of some rights owners in this field had been regarded as unjustifiably obstructive by educationists, but the real reasons of course were associated with the number and diversity of rights owners concerned with a given item.

12.11 Intervention by Secretary of State

Special encouragement to generate a satisfactory scheme is afforded by provisions (ss137-141) which would enable the Secretary of State to intervene in respect of educational schemes, even to the extent of providing a statutory licence if his recommendations are not followed by rights owners.

12.12 Implied indemnity

The Act specifies that an 'implied indemnity' exists in every licensing scheme for reprographic copying of published written, graphic or printed material (s136). The indemnity protects a licensee from liability for infringement when the terms of a licence have been followed: for example, a user copies an item not excluded by the licence, but a copyright owner decides to sue. The indemnity exists whether or not it is written into the terms of a licensing scheme, but it is of course clearer for licensees if it is included, such as in the CLA educational scheme.

12.13 Copyright Tribunal

A Tribunal was set up under the Act (ss145-152), and became available when the Act came into force, being formed by extending the coverage of the existing Performing Right Tribunal. Efforts to obtain representation of information and library professional bodies were unsuccessful, and members of the Tribunal, consisting of not more than eleven people, are lawyers or civil servants. Rules of operation soon appeared and the current form is SI 1992/467.

The details of matters capable of reference to the Tribunal (ss117-134) do not limit its general obligation to have regard to all relevant considerations (s135). The matters detailed include: disputes over the terms of a proposed or existing scheme, which may accordingly be varied by the Tribunal; complaints by prospective licensees of unreasonable refusal of a licence; and licensee applications for a ruling that a licence unreasonably due to expire should continue. So far, users appear to have made little use of the Tribunal. Perhaps this at least in part because some people believe that high costs would be unavoidable (see 8.30). It is recommended that, where the Act gives some backing, an applicant should endeavour to present his own case rather than involve legal assistance. The cost of application itself should not be seen as significant. Nevertheless, the CT should normally be used as a 'long stop' rather than as a first point of reference, for it is better to try negotiation first.

Collective licensing of user groups

12.14 The Copyright Licensing Agency (CLA) offers licences to user groups in both the public and the private sector for reprography in excess of fair dealing and library copying permissions. Beginning in the mid-80s with schools and colleges under local education authority control, licensing was soon extended to universities and virtually all educational establishments are now involved. The first form of an industrial licensing scheme was announced in April 1993, and a number of firms have become licensed (8.11). (See also notes on CLA in 12.31.)

The user community has questioned from time to time the logic of sampling as a basis for licensing fees and the distribution of income to rights owners. In schools, sampling as a rough guide to what is copied has been accepted as 'Hobson's choice' at a time when teachers were not expected to record their copying. In universities, where the activities and people and resources vary so much from one establishment to another, it is doubted whether sampling can be sufficiently relevant. Thus it could be unfair to rights owners and users alike. Academic and industrial authors, as well as essayists, novelists, poets and dramatists, should become aware of the somewhat uncertain basis of royalty collection in relation to what is actually copied beyond legal permissions. There is no evidence that anyone has ever spared the time to check through sampling results to ensure that no material which is 'out of copyright' is included in the total assessment, and indeed it would be administratively very costly. It is not surprising that some users observe the various snags (limits, excluded categories, etc.) and cynically conclude that the result is just a method of 'buying an indemnity'. Nevertheless, until such time as an electronic system could take over administration and hold specific records (3.55), collective licensing by such methods will doubtless continue.

Collective licensing of copying agencies

12.15 On the basis that only nonprofit-based libraries or archives are legally authorised to provide what is in effect a public copying service, the CLA is licensing commercial photocopying or 'copying shops' and requiring a standard royalty on every copy made from copyright material. The CLA also licenses copying or 'document supply' agencies of which the number grows steadily (see 6.47 et seq.). One specialised copying agency serves the legal profession with multiple copies, not least because the Law Society agreed a definition of the 'judicial proceedings' permission with the CLA (7.9)

The British Library has also become licensed by the CLA in order to provide 'cleared copies' for any purpose short of publication, levying a standard royalty per item per copy, but this arrangement does not affect photocopy requests for single copies, within norms of extent, for research or private study. The licence covers the supply of more than one copy of a book chapter or a periodical article, and more than one article from the same periodical issue as long as the whole issue is not thus copied.

Any other library interested in being able to act on a similar basis should apply to the CLA. The above notes repeat the essentials from chapter 8.

Notices about copyright

12.16 Augmenting the © notice at the beginning of a book, an addition or modification may be found. Sometimes a variation aims to save office time on simple clearance enquiries, such as adding after 'publisher' the words '*except for the quotation of brief passages of criticism*' From Copyright, by E.W. Ploman and L.C. Hamilton. Routledge and Kegan Paul, 1980.) Others aim to emphasise the electronic scene, for example:

> All rights reserved. No part of this publication may be reproduced, stored in a retrieval system, or transmitted in any form or by any means, electronic, mechanical, photocopying or otherwise without the prior permission of the publisher. (From Security and crime prevention in libraries, edited by M. Chaney and A. F. MacDougall. Ashgate, 1992.)

Another example similar to the latter adds 'electrostatic', 'magnetic tape' and 'recording' to the 'any means' list, and requires publisher permission to be in writing, which any user ought to prefer and securely file in any event. A special difficulty for publishers, of course, is to make the wording applicable in any country targeted as a market.

Publishers and producers will need to devise a form of notice for printed databases. Otherwise, fellow rights owners and users alike will be unable to determine readily whether a handbook or directory (etc) is entitled to database right (3.31).

12.17 BCC notice

Doubtless realising that such notices are certain either to cause confusion and enquiry or else to be ignored by those in the know in respect of legal permissions, the British Copyright Council photocopying guidelines (App. 1/3) introduce a much more acceptable statement.

> Except as otherwise permitted under the Copyright Designs and Patents Act, 1988, this publication may only be reproduced, stored or transmitted in any form or by any means, with the prior permission in writing of the publisher or, in the case of a reprographic reproduction, in accordance with the terms of a licence issued by The Copyright Licensing Agency. Enquiries concerning reproduction outside those terms should be sent to the British Copyright Council ... (address).

If other publishers take up this form of notice, perhaps users will see the end of unfounded restrictions in respect of books. One example other than copyright, mentioned because it has caused some irritation in libraries for years unless simply ignored, is the blunt statement found in some paperbacks to the effect that binding in hard covers is 'not permitted'.

12.18 Restrictive notices

Phrases printed on items, or issued in association with them at the time of purchase, have never been established to be 'contractual', but have latterly been believed capable of judgement as 'implied contracts' when known by a purchaser to be the custom for a particular producer or publisher to print a particular phrase on his products. Some forms of copyright notice are welcomed by users, such as special permissions declared on some journals about educational copying requirements. Although it may seem to rights owners somewhat churlish to welcome those permissions whilst quibbling about restrictions, it is suggested that the more commonly found phrases on printed matter which purport to restrict user actions in contradiction of statutory provisions are unlikely to gain much sympathy in court. (However, it is recognised that sympathy and logical judgement are not necessarily related.) An attempt to get a section into the 1988 Act which would have prevented a contract from restricting permission to any greater extent than statute failed because it was seen as contrary to Berne. Nevertheless, this principle has not hindered the EC from preventing contractual interference with provisions on computer software (7.15-7.20).

There is of course no objection to the helpful reminders which may appear on legal permissions, and certainly not to the even more helpful statements which sometimes give wider permission than statute. It is now becoming fairly widely accepted that restrictive phrases such as those on shrink-wrap may not be contractual unless seen (and/or signed) before purchase, with the opportunity for a purchaser to return an item for refund if unable to comply.

A possible defence in the event of a claim of infringement based on a restrictive phrase, which could only be made at all on grounds that the phrase were contractual, might be founded on the Unfair Contract Terms Act, 1977. Such a defence does not appear to have been tested in this context. However, there has been a case on computer software wherein, on appeal in 1996, it was held that, in contracts for programming, 'the law imposed an implied term that computer software must be fit for the purpose for which it was supplied' (D. Eilon, in *Campbell Hooper Legal update*, August 1996 supplement).

12.19 Contractual?

Otherwise that the above, case law would be needed to establish whether a restrictive phrase printed on an item could be regarded as contractual. Such a conclusion might be conceivable in narrower or more specialised markets than that for books. An example is the exhortation on computer program shrink-wrap or the like to refrain from any lending, which is surely not intended to prevent a user from lending a program (7.21) to a colleague with similar computer equipment and needs – providing no further electronic storage, or a re-usable copy, ensues. Beyond that circumstance, however, it is recommended that this type of restrictive notice should be followed.

12.20 It has been suggested that, when the user market can be assumed to be aware that the appearance of the notice is customary, knowledge of its details in advance of purchase may also be assumed, making it contractual. Conditions of sale which are only discoverable upon receipt of an item would seem less likely to be considered contractual in court. If conditions of sale are indeed made known in advance but without signature requirement and without being spotted by a purchaser, it is recommended that the conditions be regarded as contractual, whilst being ready to negotiate for better terms before purchase in future if there are difficulties in complying – and it is always better to do that through a professional body, especially one with sizeable market significance. A possible safety measure is to include a standard phrase on order forms, to the effect that 'this order is only placed on the understanding that the item(s) can be used without further permission for purposes of ... (library stock; or research; etc.)'. However, it must now be remembered that there could now be other reasons for paying attention to a notice about lending: namely, the new public rental and lending rights (4.35 et seq.).

Lastly on this matter, statutory provisions per se do not require publisher notices on items to back them up, and should of course be followed when any non-contractual notices appear.

Assignment of rights

12.21 Contracts between an author and publisher for the assignment of the right to produce copies in book form are mostly in wording adopted by the publisher as standard, after legal advice (App. 1/4). Contracts for audiovisual and electronic media can bring in other rights owners such as photographers and computer programmers. Some authors may prefer to assign all their rights in a work to a publisher, whilst others who foresee alternative future needs for parts of their work may wish to reserve appropriate rights. Novelists commonly employ a literary agent to negotiate a contract with a publisher, and have bodies like the Society of Authors and the Writers Guild from which to seek advice. Academic or industrial authors may turn first to a locally available librarian or to their own professional associations, though another possibility is registration with the Authors' Licensing and Collecting Society (12.31) in case royalties may be forthcoming for photocopying.

12.22 For periodical articles, contracts are rare, for usually it is taken as implied that a contract exists when an author supplies copy for publication and frequently there is no payment for the author. A very simple form of contract for journal articles is suggested below. Some publishers endeavour to have total rights assigned to them, in order to cover the electronic copyright scene in future. The form suggests rights which should desirably be retained, and such contents could be insisted upon by an author. The ALCS has published a pamphlet advising authors re electronic rights (App. 1/4).

Below is a suggested concise form of agreement on periodical articles for publication.

Databases: service contracts

12.23 This section focuses firstly upon electronic databases and the contracts for service between a user and either a host organisation or a database producer. Service contracts specify what uses may be made of a database without seeking special permission. The contracts govern the actions of subscribers, since they override statute. However, if a contract is unclear on downloading, permission may be assumed at least for the purposes of summarising a search and printing out.

Among the difficulties suffered by users in respect of contracts are:

(a) variation in terms and conditions for the various databases
(b) prohibition of service to third parties which, for information professionals, in theory means all their clients, in-house or extra-mural.

Needless to say, (b) is largely ignored for in-house clients, but there is widespread uncertainty as to what to do about external users, especially

SUGGESTED CONCISE AGREEMENT ON PERIODICAL ARTICLES FOR PUBLICATION

1. (Article): ....
2. Submitted for publication in (Journal): ....
3. Copyright in the above article is hereby transferred subject to the following reservations, if any, to (Publisher): ....

4. The author(s) reserve(s) the following rights:
   - (i) All proprietary rights other than copyright (such as designs and patents).
   - (ii) Right to re-use all or parts of the above paper in other works.
   - (iii) Reproduction for personal use of up to ___ copies, subject to marking them with a copyright notice and excluding sale.
   - (iv) Pre-publication distribution to colleagues of a limited number of copies in the form submitted for publication, excluding sale.
   - (v) Right to permit or refuse the re-publication or translation of the article by third parties, this right being shared with the publisher.
   - (vi) Rental/lending right.

5. The publisher shall initially pay a single fee of ___ for transfer of copyright as above.
6. In addition to a fee, if any, a royalty shall be separately agreed in the event of the use of the full text in an electronic database.

Delete and initial (4) or (5) and/or (6) if inapplicable.

Signed: .... Name: .... Date: ....

as sole or first author, on behalf of the following co-authors if any, who have been informed: ....

Signed: .... Name: .... Date: ....

on behalf of publisher: ....

Suggested concise form of agreement on periodical articles for publication.

when they are charged on no more than a cost-recovery basis, the greater portion of charge being for professional search expertise. Clarification has long been sought from rights owners with discouraging lack of response due to their own uncertainties, but at last there are signs of progress towards standard contractual terms (see EBLIDA work in App. 4/3).

Secondly, before the UK's compliance (I January 1998) with the EC Directive on databases (3.28), there was no statute which would prevent a user from supplying any enquirer with re-keyed author-title details of sources relevant to an enquiry, provided they did not amount to a substantial segment of the diskette as a compilation, and provided they do not include copyright abstracts. Now, any extraction or re-utilisation of parts of databases, whether electronic or printed, must be subject to permitted actions of 'lawful users' or to additional licensing. Fair dealing for research for 'commercial purposes' is not permitted for databases, whether printed or electronic. It is really up to users to examine CD-ROM introductory frames and accompanying documentation and object to any unreasonable claims, bearing in mind that there is no copyright in an electronic format in itself. User needs for compulsory sale of records, especially of non-copyright content, are considered in Appendix . Thirdly, 'lawful user' is considered this author to warrant closer definition than that relevant to computer programs (7.16) or that now given in respect of databases: *any person who (whether under a licence to do any of the acts restricted by database right in the database or otherwise) has a right to use the database.*

12.24 The problem of variation in service contract terms has caused much confusion to users in recent years, and will continue to do so until publishers arrive at the consensus which is essential for an ECMS and progress towards the Superhighway (3.65; App. 1/8). Considerable discussion is occurring, and progress is at last being made towards standard agreements (see ECUP work, App. 4/3).

In 1996, The Joint Information Systems Committee and the Publishers Association agreed to set up five joint working parties: standard licensing agreements; clearance mechanisms; fair dealing in the electronic context; provision of and access to networks; and retention of electronic materials. By April 1997 the working party on fair dealing had reported, containing *Guidelines for electronic fair dealing.* In June 1997 a *Model licence for digitisation/electronic use,* drafted by Ingrid Winterenitz, was issued for consultation by a Working Party of the PA and the universities' Committee on Electronic Information.

12.25 Breach of contract

When a contract is clearly against any downloading at all, breach of contract could of course be claimed if downloading becomes apparent to the copyright owner, and might conceivably result in litigation for damages. Unless deliberate infringement of copyright under CDPA88 for profit were involved, breach of contract is more likely to cause suspension of service. Where deliberate infringement does occur for profit, infringement litigation could bring punitive damages – that is, damages which do not have to be confined to the extent of any financial loss to the rights owner. Therefore contracts should be carefully studied before signing, and stringent terms questioned if they are not backed up by statute, or where statutory permissions may have been overridden by the contract terms. If possible, an adjustment to a contract should be arranged, to say something like 'these terms and conditions of use are without prejudice to any relevant statutory permissions', which users are advised always to be reluctant to sign away. Some specific licensing problems have been discussed in 8.30 et seq.

12.26 The service provider is responsible, like a broadcasting company, for compensating any author of content. Thus, if unqualified permission is given in a service contract for an amount and purpose of downloading, it should be assumed that clearance from authors of original material is not also needed.

A host system will have a contract to share the rights of a database producer, but that is entirely between them and should not affect the user except in relation to cost, and then 'invisibly'. For obscure reasons, database producers in general have seemed reticent about the Act's principal protection for them in respect of downloading: namely, a form of service copyright for 50 years from first inclusion of a particular item (3.18).

12.27 Database right

However, the new 'database right' (3.28 et seq.) should provide more than adequate protection against extraction of content from a whole range of compilations, not just electronic databases. Up to a late draft stage of the EC Directive on the legal protection of databases, certain provisions were welcomed by users. For example, it was specified that licensing of the commercial use of extracted data must be provided on 'fair and reasonable terms'. This was greeted by some users as comparable with the helpful control of contract evinced by a Directive in respect of computer programs (7.15-7.20). However, that provision, among others favoured by users, was omitted from the final Directive passed in March 1996, although certain curbs on the overriding of permissions by contract were included. In implementation, the UK has passed SI 1997/3032, in which the EU's *sui generis* right becomes 'database right' (3.28).

12.28 Contractual aims

Many contracts do state clearly what downloading is considered reasonable. Others are much less clear, indeed unduly restrictive, sometimes with an attempt to create rights which thankfully do not have any basis in law, such as a 'right to control the use of information' which has been mooted as an aim of some publishers. Instead of such attempts which are doomed to failure, it is suggested that online database producers should simply license the rights they hold in law – like other rights owners in respect of printed matter. A possible copyright statement suggested for online database contracts is suggested below.

12.29 Multimedia contracts

Multimedia contracts could become subject to excessive variation in terms, thus causing confusion, unless a centre is set up with a coordinating function. The situation is complicated by the need to cover works in any medium from any country. This may be exemplified by the several kinds of 'model contract' emanating from the French PA (translated in *IPA Bulletin* vol. 11(2) and (3), 1995). Judging by a draft form of contract proposed by the French PA agreement on a common form could prove difficult. The suggested draft required each author's assignment of all reproduction rights in any format (including electronic), in any language, translation right, royalty collection right, third party licensing right, performance rights, all languages and countries, by any distribution method. One provision would make it possible for a producing body to have changes made by a third party, making that a co-author, if the original author should refuse to make the changes, remuneration then being shared. Also, the producing body would have the right to modify and adapt for harmonisation purposes. It is arguable whether a solution could really arise from even more all-embracing assignment of rights to publishers and producers, instead of pursuing user-access system-based remedies which are probably only feasible with a form of ECMS.

A study by T. Hoeren (App. 1/8.1) published in 1995 by the EC reviews and weighs pros and cons of various direct or collective licensing methods. A section on 'technical devices' covers *copyright information systems; copy-*

SUGGESTED STATEMENT ON COPYRIGHT FOR INCLUSION IN A SERVICE CONTRACT

Note: The following is a simple form of notice about copyright for inclusion in a service contract which sets out to license the rights held by a database producer in respect of an online service. It was volunteered as a draft for consideration by a producer who intended a 10 per cent surcharge for users other than nonprofit-based libraries or information services. Contracts should always be drawn up by legal experts, of course. With progress now being made towards standardised forms of licence (see App.4), the following should be seen as merely a checklist of conditions which users might wish to ensure are represented in some way or another in an electrocopying licence.

Copyright and licensed rights

(1) The online databases to which access is hereby licensed by the Data Provider are protected by copyright, both as compilations and as services, in addition to any rights which may exist in the actual items of content. Thus, unless specific permission is sought, downloading may only occur as provided by these terms and conditions.

(2) The Licensee may print out one copy for an end-user and one for a file or search log, and also electronically store retrieved information to assist the collation of search results, subject to the limitations of (7) below, provided this record is deleted as soon as the search is complete and no other copies are made.

(3) A Licensee who wishes to supply information from a database to an external or extra-mural end-user other than an employee or colleague is defined as a Broker, irrespective of whether the organisation is nonprofit-based. Brokers must register as such with the Data Provider and may be required to pay a surcharge percentage. Nonprofit-based Brokers such as those in public and academic libraries, registered charities and charitable trusts, shall not be subject to a surcharge for brokerage.

(4) The Licensee may not publish, re-sell, input to a database, or otherwise further distribute the retrieved information except as agreed, for example in respect of Brokers.

(5) Brokers may supply sufficient information to answer a specific enquiry, but should take care to avoid supplying a broad category of information from a database without considering the danger of infringing copyright in the database as a compilation.

(6) Any charge made by a Broker to an end-user for professional search expertise and time must include and show separately the database service name and cost without mark-up (online service plus telecommunication charges).

(7) The Licensee must ensure:
   (a) that end-users, whether in-house or external, accept that information is only supplied to them on the understanding that it will not be further distributed or re-input to a database without permission;
   (b) that print-out bears name of source database and date of search.

Suggested copyright statement for online database contracts right clearance systems; and Electronic Copyright Management systems. A possible solution is given as *a single, world-wide organisation* for electronic copyright management. Hoeren attempts *to take a visionary look how licensing may look like in the 21st century*, wherein a user can download from an international database without specific permission. (This could provide a form of electronic 'browsing', as sought by the LA/JCC/WPC and ECUP.) However, for permanent storage, the user *asks the database for licensing conditions* and, if then licensed, is debited accordingly. Any further use is prevented digitally via special encryption devices. Some requisite developments are indicated, including suggestions for further EU harmonisation of copyright law.

Remedies for infringement

12.30 It has already been recommended (4.30) that remedies for infringement of copyright in Part I of the Act, such as a court order for 'delivery up' or seizure of infringing copies, should be studied directly (ss96-115) or made the subject of consultation, and nothing further need be said here except to note that other Parts (designs; performance) have their own provisions as to remedies.

Collecting agencies and related organisations

12.31 The following are examples of organisations which are directly involved in copyright administration. (See also 12.37-12.39 for other organisations of interest.)

Authors' Licensing and Collecting Society (ALCS)
14-18 High Holborn, London EC1N 2LE.

Apart from collective licensing interests exercised through CLA, ALCS covers cable re-transmission and overseas lending right. Member organisations of the ALCS include The Society of Authors (SoA) and the Writers' Guild of Great Britain (WGoGB). British Copyright Council, 29-33 Berners Street, London W1P 4AA, with over thirty member organisations, including a number of professional bodies.

British Educational Suppliers Association (BESA)
20 Beaufort Court, Admirals Way, London E14 9XL.

Includes ESPA (below). Has encouraged licensing of the use of computer programs in schools. Offers free advice and information on issues appertaining to IT in education (*http./www/besa.org*).

British Phonographic Industry Ltd (BPI)
25 Savile Row, London W1X 1AA.

Covers interests in the UK of the British record industry. Not a licensing agency – see 12.41-12.43 for comparative treatment of licensing agencies for music. However, BPI has been instrumental in arranging for public library rental/lending of sound recordings via a 'free licence' subject to acquisition restrictions (4.35).

British Standards Institution (BSI)
Linford Wood, Milton Keynes, MK14 6LE.

(Copyright Manager, BSI, 389 Chiswick High Road, London W4 4AL)

Licences educational copying.

British Video Association (BVA)
167 Great Portland Street, London WIN 5FD.

Formerly British Videogram Association. Not a licensing agency, but has indicated the preference of the industry to avoid collective licensing of public rental/lending. Although it is believed probable that the preference will continue despite new rights having been accorded to individual authors and performers (4.35 et seq.), this is not yet certain.

CCN Goad (formerly Goad) *see* Experian Goad

Christian Copyright Licensing International,
Christian Copyright Licensing Ltd.
26 Gildredge Road, Eastbourne, East Sussex BN21 4SA.

Produces concise notes on copyright and the CCL licence for churches, covering the reproduction of hymns and songs for assemblies, etc. (Note: these are excluded from the CLA licence for schools.)

Combined Higher Education Software Team (CHEST)
University of Bath, Claverton Down Bath BA2 7AY.

Negotiates standard forms of contract for the use of computer software and (more recently) data sets in higher education. Now includes colleges.

Copyright Licensing Agency
90 Tottenham Court Road, London W1P 9HE.

Member of the International Federation of Reproduction Rights Organisations (IFRRO) which links some twenty nations. At present covers multiple or otherwise excessive photocopying for educational, industrial and professional purposes, on a collective or near-blanket basis, by means of licensing schemes. Also runs the CLA Rapid Clearance System for users who first obtain a password. CLARCS is an electronic database which stores data on rights-owner royalty wishes re royalty levels, authorises copying of specific items and charges if necessary. Accessible on the Web to discover charges (*http://www.cla.co.uk*) but usable for clearance only if a CLA licence is held. Has started *Copywatch* with the slogan *Help stop illegal copying* and invites reports via a hotline on suspected infringement.

From the user viewpoint, CLA is the most important collecting agency, albeit developed during times of controversy. Formed in 1982 following the work of several committees, beginning with the Wolfenden Committee after the Whitford Report of 1977. Incorporated in 1983 as a non-profit making company limited by guarantee. Member organisations responsible for its establishment are the Publishers Licensing Society (PLS) and the Authors' Licensing and Collecting Society (ALCS).

Design and Artists' Copyright Society (DACS)
Parchment House, 13 Northburgh Street, London EC1V 0AH.

Artistic works in any medium are licensed by DACS, which is the collecting society for visual artists within the UK. DACS states that it has agreements with similar societies in almost every country in the world, and is in collaboration with the British Photographers' Liaison Committee (9-10 Domingo Steet, London EC1 0TA) in respect of photographs, slides and other transparencies, and picture collections. A 'slide collections' licence was launched in 1996.

Educational Recording Agency (ERA)
New Premier House, 150 Southampton Row, London, WC1B 5AL.
http://www.era.org.uk

Licenses educational establishments for the off-air recording of broadcast and cable programmes for instructional purposes. Licensees must be definable as 'educational establishments' (8.27). See 12.41-12.43 for comparison of music rights groups.

Educational Software Publishers Association (ESPA),
in British Educational Suppliers Association, 20 Beaufort Court, London E14 9XL

Arranges licences for school use of educational computer software.

Experian Goad Ltd.
formerly Charles Goad, Salisbury Square, Old Hatfield, Herts., AL9 5BJ.

Licensed by OS to produce maps of shopping centres and other forms of town plan, also as a specialised service. An agent for OS, supplies other maps, multimedia, globes, etc.

Goad, Charles, Limited, see *Experian Goad*.

Her Majesty's Stationery Office (HMSO)
Copyright Section, St. Crispins, Duke Street, Norwich NR3 1PD
or Crown Copyright Unit, St.Clements House, 2-16 Colegate, Norwich NR3 1BQ.

Individual licensing, or granting of permission, for any purpose other than advertisement, which is barred. (Guidelines in Appendix 2 are digested in chapter 6.)

International Federation of Phonographic Industries
54 Regent Street, London W1R 5PJ

Concerned with certain sound recordings, mostly foreign items not on the UK market. Licenses public performance, broadcasting and cable distribution rights for such works.

Mechanical Copyright Protection Society (MCPS)
Elgar House, 41 Streatham High Road, London SW16 1ER.

The Non-retail Department (which is of principal interest to many users other than recording companies) is now at Copyright House, 29/33 Berners Street, London W1P 4AA. Owned by MPA. Membership includes composers, authors and music publishers. Licenses the recording of music, for example by sound recording companies. Also licenses the re-recording of music, in the UK and overseas, for example of background music dubbed from a recording on to a videotape, or re-recording for broadcasting (see 12.41-12.43).

Music Publishers Association Ltd (MPA)
3rd Floor, Strandgate, 18-20 York, Buildings, London WC2N 8JU

Not a licensing agency, but owns MCPS – see App. 1/3, also 12.41-12.43 below.

Newspaper Licensing Agency Limited (NLA)
17 Lyons Crescent, Tonbridge, Kent TN9 1EX

Licenses copying from UK newspapers for internal purposes (i.e. not commercial press cuttings services, which should separately approach NLA).

Open University Worldwide
The Berrill Building, Walton Hall, Milton Keynes MK7 6AA.

Does not participate in the ERA scheme. OU's own licence is: 'Licensed off air recording scheme' and four licence types cover: schools, primary or secondary; further and higher education; non-educational companies and other organisations; and qualifying establishments in the Irish Republic.

Ordnance Survey (OS)
Copyright Branch, Romsey Road, Maybush, Southampton SO9 4DH.

Licences educational copying up to a specified area of an OS or OS-based map. Issues 4 leaflets which may be subject to annual revision, covering 'business use' (the general one), 'publishing', 'digital map data', and 'commercial publishing'. (See also Experian Goad.)

Performing Right Society (PRS)
29-33 Berners Street, London W1P 4AA.

Acting on behalf of composers and music publishers, British and foreign, licenses public performances and broadcasting. A performance is 'public' whether it is live or mechanically reproduced, and whether that reproduction is effected from a recording held on the spot or via radio or television. For uses of dramatico-musical works, such as amateur opera, enquirers are passed on to the music publisher or other relevant rights holder. (See 12.41-12.43, and note that both PPL and PRS may be involved in a given user requirement.)

Phonographic Performance Ltd (PPL)
1 Upper James Street, London W1R 3HG.

On behalf of record companies, licenses dubbing, public performance, broadcasting and cable distribution of sound recordings. Users wanting a licence in respect of foreign and certain other recordings may be referred to the International Federation of Phonographic Industries, 54 Regent Street, London W1R 5PJ. PPL acts on behalf of recording companies, who in turn compensate performers, etc. according to contract. (See 12.41-12.43.)

Publishers Licensing Society (PLS)
5 Dryden Street, Covent Garden, London WC2E 9NW.

Acts on behalf of members in respect of collective licensing through the CLA. PLS was formed by the Publishers Association (PA), Periodical Publishers Association (PPA), and the Association of Learned and Professional Society Publishers (ALPSP).

Samuel French Limited
52 Fitzroy Street, Fitzrovia, London W1P 6JR.

Licenses amateur public performances of plays (with Warner Chappell Ltd, which see). Professional performances of plays and dramatico-musical works such as ballet and opera must be the subject of negotiation with the copyright owners (see PRS).

Video Performance Ltd (VPL)
address as PPL.

Concerned with music videos. Licences public performance, broadcasting and cable distribution. Warner Chappell Ltd, 129 Park Street, London W1Y 3FA. Licences amateur performance of plays (with Samuel French Limited).

Compulsory licensing

12.32 Although CDPA88 abolishes the compulsory licensing of the copying of retail recordings provided by previous law, the Act itself contains sections which aim to encourage rights owners to set up collective licensing schemes otherwise users are to regard usage as licensed. Also, provisions which circumscribe the ability of contract to override statute have begun to enter the scene, for example in respect of computer programs (7.16-7.19) and more recently on databases (3.37). However, the publishers and producers refused to allow any compulsory licensing at all to feature in the Directive on extraction from databases, the very area wherein users could most benefit. Other Acts have inserted a degree of compulsory licensing into CDPA88, such as the Broadcasting Act 1990 (see 9.14; see also 13.5).

12.33 Compulsory licensing and Berne

But for Berne and the strong resistance of publishers, it would seem that compulsory licensing could have been introduced, resulting in much briefer and less ambiguous law. Compulsory licensing was one of the failed efforts of the user lobby in the run-up to 1988, Government having taken the view that it would be contrary to Berne, which it was on the verge of ratifying at long last (although the UK was already a signatory). The literal provision is Article 9(2) of Berne, which only allows signatory nations to reproduce literary and artistic works in certain cases, subject to conditions.

12.34 An EC report comments on Berne 9(2) as follows:

> Any member country of the Union which wishes to introduce compulsory licensing therefore has to fulfil three conditions:
>
> (a) the reproduction can only be 'in certain special cases'
> (b) it shall not conflict with 'the normal exploitation of the work'; and
> (c) it shall not unreasonably prejudice 'the legitimate interests of the author'.

The report goes on to suggest interpretations of these conditions, and studies the extent to which CDPA88 effects some compulsory licensing by making a permission if a collective licence is not available. A point not considered in the report is whether Berne may be even more out of date than many already believe. Its origin in authorship protection appears to have been eroded in favour of publisher interests over the years. Should not the fact that compulsory licensing can actually benefit authors by broadening uses and markets be borne in mind? Publishers might not gain as much of the total control that their more militant members appear to seek, but there might be less danger of undermining foundations in authorship.

Point of sale licensing

12.35 This phrase was coined to describe any method of indicating, on or in association with an item to be purchased, by what means and at what cost it could be copied, at least in part – or, if such detail could not be given, to whom a permission request could be made for rapid response. During lobbying in 1987, a proposal made to Government was that anything which did not bear such details should be regarded as being in the public domain for non-publishing purposes. The same would have applied if a permission request brought no response for a given period, had the proposal been accepted as viable. As with a number of other proposals, this was seen as compulsory licensing and rejected.

12.36 Percentage mark-up

This author has many times recommended a simple, straightforward point of sale licensing method for industrial, commercial and professional subscribers to periodicals. A percentage mark-up on journal subscriptions of, say, 10 per cent should cover the contingency of nonfair copying of up to 10 copies of an article. Gordon and Breach, when they introduced such a method over a decade ago, were attacked by some subscribers who could not see the future possibilities if a few procedural adjustments were made. This fact should not deter any periodical publisher from considering this method. An excuse given by a pro-collective licensing publisher was that there were worries about 'risk of assumption of carte blanche'. How can this possibly be any worse than collective licensing? The percentage could be levied directly by those journal publishers who so wished, at levels they wished – leaving market forces to operate, and leaving each publisher in control of his own rights, which some have expressed a preference for anyway. There would be closer relationship to what was actually copied, and minimal administrative wastage for all concerned.

It is not clear whether periodical publishers in general were made aware of this proposal, nor whether they were offered a suggested alternative: namely, perhaps the collection by CLA of a percentage of annual spend on journals from each firm. However, the CLA business licence is now available and, despite some problems, it appears to be the best option currently on offer to a business which wishes to guard against the contingency of excessive copying by staff, even though the fees are payable whether copying is actually done or not, with one proviso. The proviso relates to whether attempts might be made to increase fee levels as a result of the new discrimination against fair dealing for commercial purposes in respect of databases (5.6).

Advice

12.37 As a general principle, especially when guidelines are available but are insufficiently clear to a user (see App. 1/3), a professional person should first approach his or her relevant professional body, unless a short cut or individual consultant is already known. This helps to ensure co- ordinated responses to new developments on behalf of users, and without co-ordination much confusion could ensue. In the legal profession, Copyright and other areas of intellectual property law, is a special subject, but there are many firms which could help: The Law Society maintains lists of members in all areas of law. The main rights-owner representative bodies have already been listed in 12.31, and they should all be regarded as potentially helpful, especially in their own fields and licensing arrangements, though naturally some may be less impartial than others. Some associations and societies of interest may be found in a CLA pamphlet: *Copyright concerns: a pocket directory of organisations involved in the administration of copyright and rights in performances*, October 1992, which drew in turn upon a British Copyright Council publication by Denis de Freitas: *The law of copyright and rights in performances*, 1989. The following are examples.

12.38 Associations of authors and performers (not licensing bodies)

Association of Photographers
9-10, Domingo Street, London EC1Y 0TA.

Formerly the Association of Fashion, Advertising and Editorial Photographers. Represents UK professional photographers and aims to improve their rights and standards.

Association of Learned and Professional Society Publishers
(last address c/o Professor Donovan, 48 Kelsey Lane, Beckenham, Kent BR3).

Has about 100 members and, along with the PA and PPA, underpins the PLS.

Association of Professional Composers
34 Hanway Street, London W1P 9DE.

Represents the collective interests of British composers.

British Academy of Songwriters, Composers and Authors,
34 Hanway Street, London W1P 9DE.

Represents British songwriters and composers of light music.

British Actors' Equity Association (Equity)
8 Harley Street, London W1N 2AB.

Represents actors and other performers, whether in theatre or broadcasting.

British Computer Society
13 Mansfield Street, London W1M 0BP.

Has over 30,000 computer professionals as members. Aims to improve standards and protect members' interests.

British Institute of Professional Photographers
Fox-Talbot House, Amwell End, Ware, Herts. SG12 9HN.

Concerned with protecting the interests of some 4,000 members.

British Photographers Liaison Committee
9-10 Domingo Street, London EC1 0TA (as the Association of Photographers)

BPLC has produced guidelines as *The ABC of photographic copyright* (App.1/4).

Broadcasting, Entertainment's, Cinematograph and Theatre Union
111 Wardour Street, London W1V 4AY.

A trade union for the various groups of workers involved, with some 20,000 members.

Chartered Society of Designers
29 Bedford Square, London WC1B 3EG.

Represents designers who work for industry and commerce, whether they are independent in private practice or salaried.

Composers' Guild of Great Britain
34 Hanway Street, London W1P 9DE.

Protects the interests of UK music composers.

Institute of Journalists
2 Dock Offices, Surrey Quays, Lower Road, London SE16 2XL.

Represents journalists in all fields and public relations workers, plus other professionals in related occupations. Both a chartered professional body and a trade union.

The Law Society of England and Wales
Records Department, Ipsley Court, Berrington Close, Redditch B98 0TD

The Law Society maintains lists of members in all areas of law and can advise you of the names and details of copyright law practitioners within your locality.

Musicians' Union
60-62 Clapham Road, London SW9 0JJ.

A trade union with about 42,000 members who each perform, compose, arrange or copy music.

National Union of Journalists
Acorn House, 314 Gray's Inn Road, London WC1X 8DP.

Has over 32,000 members concerned with printed media and broadcasting.

Periodical Publishers Association
Imperial House, 15-19 Kingsway, London, WC2B 6UN

With the PA, underpins the PLS which, along with the ALCS, underpins the CLA.

Publishers Association
1 Kingsway, London WC2B 6XF.

Includes some 600 publishers and, along with the ALPSP and the PPA, underpins the Publishers Licensing Society which in turn underpins the CLA.

Royal Photographic Society
RPS National Centre of Photography, The Octagon, Milsom Street, Bath BA1 1DN.

Organises educational activities, including exhibitions. Keeps an important collection of books on photography, prints and equipment.

Society of Authors
84 Drayton Gardens, London SW10 9SB.

Trade union promoting the interests of literary and dramatic authors in all media. Has various specialist groups, for example, on scientific, technology, and medical writers.

Writers' Guild of Great Britain
430 Edgware Road, London W2 1EH.

Trade union, covering the interests of writers in the theatre, films, broadcasting and publishing.

12.39 Information and library professional bodies

Aslib, The Association for Information Management
Staple Hall, Stone House Court, London EC3A 7PB
http://www.aslib.co.uk

Aslib's members include the Copyright Licensing Agency, and links are also maintained with consultants. Aslib is interested in a fair balance between the rights of copyright owners to benefit and the needs of users to access materials.

British Library Document Supply Centre (BLDSC)
Boston Spa, Wetherby, West Yorkshire.

Has an important copyright department headed by Graham Cornish. Provides photocopies as fair dealing or cleared copies under CLA licence.

European Bureau of Library, Information and Documentation Associations (EBLIDA)
P.O. Box 43300, 2504 A H The Hague, The Netherlands.

Described as an *independent non-governmental umbrella organisation*, aimed at promoting interests of member organisations with the European Commission, European Parliament, Committee of Regions and the Council of Ministers. EBLIDA offers its members: a voice in Europe; helpdesk for copyright questions (ECUP+); consultation and advice; the latest news on European Developments; and active involvement in Working Groups and Advisory Boards. (ECUP: European Copyright User Platform.)

ECUP is a focal point for copyright campaigning at European level. The Internet site *http://www.kaapeli.fi/eblida/ecup-list* contains reports, articles, links to other projects, etc. (See also App. 4).

European Council of Information Associations (ECIA)
(address through national secretariats: in the UK via Aslib).

Links national information associations in 7 EU countries. From its pamphlet:

> ECIA... acts as the voice of the unified opinion and collective expertise of the key European information and documentation associations to major governmental and non-governmental bodies. The Council promotes the exchange of views between the 11,000 members of the associations and their 34,000 contacts across the countries of the E...U..., and encourages the development of a pan-European approach ... to the needs of the information society.

Institute of Information Scientists (IIS)
44-45 Museum Street, London WC1A 1LY

The IIS is a member of the JCC Working Party on Copyright and also lobbies on behalf of its members on all aspects of copying relevant to the work of information scientists in the UK and the EU. (May soon merge with The Library Association.)

Joint Information Services Comittee (JISC)
Higher Education Funding Council, Northavon House, Coldharbour Lane, Bristol BS16 1QD

Now involved in work towards electronic licensing solutions (App. 4/6).

Library Association (LA)
7 Ridgmount Street, London WC1E 7AE

Includes the Secretariat of the Joint Consultative Committee Working Party on Copyright (JCC/WPC). The Working Party co-ordinates all the major information, library and archive professional bodies of the UK, including Aslib, in respect of monitoring developments, negotiating on forms of licensing, responding to CEC draft Directives, lobbying on new legislation, etc.

Library and Information Commission
British Library, 2, Sheraton Street, London W1V 4BH (see App. 4/6).

Society of Archivists
c/o T. Padfield, Public Record Office, Ruskin Avenue, Richmond, London TW9 4DU.

12.40 Other examples

Educational Copyright Users' Forum
National Council for Educational Technology, 3 Devonshire Street, London W1N 2BA

Provides a forum for exchange of experience and advice on copyright problems.

Federation Against Copyright Theft (FACT)
7 Victory Business Centre, Worton Road, Isleworth, Middlesex, TW7 6ER.

Collects evidence of infringement of films and other works, and initiates proceedings.

Federation Against Software Theft (FAST)
2 Lake End Court, Taplow, Maidenhead, Berks., SL6 0JQ.

Collects evidence and brings cases in respect of piracy or other infringement of the rights in computer programs.

Patent Office: Copyright Directorate
25 Southampton Buildings, Chancery Lane, London WC2A 1AY.

Apart from patents, trade marks and designs, the Patent Office is involved in drafting of any new copyright law and regulations (such as Statutory Instruments), and co-ordinating UK responses to European draft Directives on copyright. Also the address of the Copyright Tribunal.

Producers' Alliance for Cinema and Television
Gordon House, 10 Greycoat Place, London SW1P 1PH.

Represents the interests of UK producers of film and television programmes.

Registry of Copyright at Stationers' Hall
The Registrar, Stationers' Hall, Ave Maria Lane, London EC4M 7DD.

It has been possible since the establishment of the Registry in 1924 to make entries to prove the existence of books, scripts, maps, music and designs, etc. at a given time in case of infringement.

Music: comparison of rights-owner representative groups

12.41 Confusion having been observed as to the relative licensing (etc.) functions of various organisations for the use of music, the following is a comparative presentation. These notes are necessarily concise, for the scene is quite complex as already indicated (9.6). Only the main organisations and licensing needs are covered here. A user requiring a licence should consult the relevant agency or agencies for full details in relation to specific problems. Permissions, such as playing or showing to a non-public audience in an educational establishment for instructional purposes (9.26), are not repeated at this point. These organisations have already been listed above; for addresses, see 12.31.

Mechanical Copyright Protection Society (MCPS, owned by MPA)

Acts for composers and other authors (arrangers, songwriters, librettists,) and publishers. Note that publishers have rights in the printed format, but may also have acquired all other rights, including electrocopying). MCPS is said to:

> represent the great majority of music copyright owners in the UK and (by agreement with other societies) most of the world. It grants licences for making recordings of its members' musical works and collects and distributes the royalities due. It deals with a whole variety of music users such as record and video companies, audio visual companies and broadcasters.

For some purposes, approach to an individual recording company is an alternative to asking MCPS.

- *Making a recording of a live performance*
- *Re-recording or dubbing, including compilations* (see also PPL)
- *Both the above include purposes of broadcast/inclusion in a cable program service* (unless affected by 9.17-9.18)

Performing Right Society (PRS)

Represents same rights owners as MCPS.

- *Performing written or printed music in public*
  Playing recordings in public (plus PPL)
- *Broadcasting music (live or recorded) or including it in a cable programme service* (see PPL re recorded)

Phonographic Performance Limited (PPL)

Represents over 1700 record companies, covering some 95% of all commercially released recordings. Also covers pop music videos via Video

Performance Limited, a closely related agency. Separate approach to an individual recording company is, unlike MCPS, not a viable option because PPL indicates that almost all UK companies have mandated control.

- *Re-recording or dubbing, including compilations* (plus MCPS) this includes purposes of broadcast/cable programme service unless affected by 9.17-9.18
- *Playing recordings/dubbings in public* (plus PRS)
  Broadcasting a recording or including in a cable programme service (plus PRS)

Notes

(a) such PPL literature as has been studied shows no reference to the Act's educational permission for playback (9.5 re s34);
(b) but no payment should be expected from educational establishments for playback in the conditions indicated in the Act.)

British Phonographic Industry Limited (BPI)

Not a licensing agency. Member record companies are mostly represented by PPL above. BPI is mentioned here because of its agreement with public libraries re acquisition of sound recordings for loan (the 'free licence' in 4.47).

Music Publishers Association (MPA)

Not a licensing agency. Member publishers are not currently involved in collective licensing.

- *Copying written or printed music:* apply direct to publisher, preferably using application form as per the MPA's *Code of fair practice* (App. 1/3).

Educational Recording Agency (ERA)

Represents Authors' Licensing and Collecting Society (ALCS); BBC Enterprises Limited; Channel Four Television Corporation; The Design and Artists' Copyright Society Limited; The Independent Television Corporation, The Mechanical Copyright Protection Society Limited; Sianel Pedwar Cymru; The Musicians' Union; British Actors' Equity Association, The Incorporated Society of Musicians' Unions; The British Phonographic Industry Limited and Open University Worldwide (OUW).

- *Both ERA and OUW licences cover recording and use by educational establishments of broadcast or cable programmes for educational purposes.*

12.42 Examples of licensing needs for music

1. The making of an orchestral set having been permitted by the publisher (e.g. using MPA application form), performance in public requires a PRS licence. A recording of the performance may be made under MCPS licence (but see 9.17-9.18). Playing that recording in public, or broadcasting it, or using it in a cable programme service, requires a PRS licence. If the recording has been made by a commercial record company, playing it in public (or broadcasting, etc.) also requires a PPL licence.
2. A compilation of extracts from recordings is required for educational purposes. Licences for dubbing from commercially released recordings are required from **both** MCPS and PPL. If playback is not to be in an educational establishment (s34 permission), or if the purpose is other than educational (apart from 9.26, q.v.), both PPL and PRS licences are needed for public performance.
3. If a compilation of sound extracts is required for entertainment purposes (perhaps as background in lifts or restaurants, or common rooms), it is simpler to:
   (a) hire items from a firm which has been licensed by PPL to dub for such purposes, the royalty being subsumed by the hire charge; or
   (b) specify particular requirements to such a firm, rather than seek licences from MCPS and PPL on one's own account which might not be available.

Neither approach would remove the need for coverage also by PRS licence, usually a blanket one for a particular site in respect of public playback, or radio/TV in public areas, etc.

12.43 Comments on music and other performance licensing

Attempts to obtain clarification of some details have been unsuccessful due to pressure of work in the larger organisations. The above is the information available as an expansion of 9.6. MCPS, PRS and PPL have a wide range of licences and therefore problems with which to deal. Prospective licensees should make enquiries directly in respect of specific needs. From PPL statements, although its control on behalf of the recording industry is some 95% in respect of dubbing and public performance, but only the recording companies are represented. It is not known in what manner royalties may be shared at least by performers according to their contracts.

As indicated in 4.35 et seq., the new law on rental/lending now provides a means for creators of original works and performers to obtain benefits in a manner which might in some circumstances be thought more reliable than individual contracts. It is not clear, and enquiries have brought no reply, as to whether and to what extent recording companies customarily share their royalties already with performers, or indeed with creators of the works. Nor do users find it easy to understand why the collecting bodies cannot cooperate or, if they are doing so already, why they do not say so when asked. It is surely undesirable that, partly because standard tariffs are applied separately by the societies concerned, prospective licensees should be confused and be left to assume the present procedures in respect of recordings to be 'double licensing' of dubbing (MCPS and PPL) and of public performance (PPL and PRS). Another matter for prospective licensees is to ensure that statutory permissions are exempted or else adequately compensated. For example, some agency literature makes no mention of educational or other statutory permissions, and some prospective licensees could make erroneous assumptions about licensing need.

Since the equitable remuneration right can only be assigned to a collecting society, and there is a large range of those 'beneath the surface' of the major bodies in 12.31, the question of loss through administrative cost of the whole system may need examination. When the EU harmonisation programme tackles the problem of collecting societies, as it is scheduled to do, might authors, performers and users all ask for some clear rules for all concerned?

Changes in law

12.44 However, changes in UK law in compliance with EU harmonisation Directives may take more time than the period allowed (normally two years). When that period is exceeded a Directive becomes applicable in whatever respect it may be relevant to the adjustment of national laws. Accordingly, until the UK makes new law by means of SIs, consultation usually occurs between the Patent Office, publishers, and user groups. All concerned should be ready to comment on any consultative documents and/or draft SIs which may surface. Until the harmonisation programme can be regarded as more or less complete, CDPA88 will be undergoing revision from time to time. This should be borne in mind when consulting legal handbooks which may not relate to the latest state of the Act. The loose-leaf *Aslib guide to copyright* contains the Act with updating as necessary in respect of all those provisions which are regarded as of interest to the expected readership.

Droit de suite: artists

12.45 These comments follow on from 4.52 in anticipation of forthcoming discussion among those concerned. At first sight the principle of allowing a share of later sale proceeds to artists seems sound enough. Is it not fair for an artist or his beneficiaries to gain from an increase in the value of his work? However, there are practical reasons for doubt. Firstly, a work of art may appreciate in value owing to shifts in fashion which may have little to do with quality of work, and there is no way of forecasting or compensating for this. After all, why could the theory not apply in reverse? Would it not be just as 'fair' for an artist who is judged to have lost popularity and income to be provided with compensation, and if so by whom? The consequent judgments needed of quality and popularity, and of value over time, surely defy any attempt at public control or market administration which might be thought fair to all concerned, and indeed could expend more money in bureaucracy than sums actually paid to artists.

The draft Directive envisages a form of percentage levy on resale price. Owing to differences in trade procedures, it has been suggested that the levy could shift the emphasis of art dealings to New York. Ultimately, dealers in the already-thriving American art market would surely gain but, taking all aspects into account, just who in Europe would gain in real terms and in the long run? Why the apparent focus on struggling artists? What about struggling novelists, etc. etc.?

For example, should a writer's descendants get benefit from resale of a volume which has become rare? Just where would it all end? Surely, changes in art profitability should be seen as no more than changes in fortune? The Whitford Committee (App. 1/7) found the right to be neither equitable, logical nor practicable, and this view is currently shared by many information/library professionals as well as many in the Art world. Therefore it is suggested that the UK should only countenance the creation of *droit de suite* if it became absolutely essential for 'single market' reasons which could demonstrably benefit UK artists and the art trade.

Author representation

12.46 From the start, licensing champions claimed author participation, but they meant essayists, novelists and poets and perhaps a few writers of school texts – in other words, the members of the Society of Authors and the Writers' Guild. The need for greater representation of the vast number of academic and industrial authors was publicised on behalf of users, and the CBI and AUT (Association of University Teachers) were asked to do something but without result. Recruitment efforts by the Authors' Licensing and Collecting Society (ALCS, 12.31) followed, apparently with a degree of success but numbers have not been publicised.

12.47 It seems highly desirable that as much author representation as possible should be sought to achieve balance. The vast majority of academic and industrial authors publish in order to disseminate their work – and want easy access to the work of others. Researchers have complained increasingly in recent years about the annual cutbacks in library subscriptions due to prices which spiral beyond inflation rates. Militant publishers have blamed library cutbacks on photocopying, apparently ignoring the possibility that their own pricing policies might be a major cause. Others have pointed to overseas piracy – that is, in two-thirds of the periodicals market. Some publishers must surely be aware that, since prices are set according to the actual market expectations, they are compensated for all copying anywhere. However, it is obvious that copying which causes repercussions between markets must be separately compensated in order to avoid distortion of prices and help to flatten the spiral of price increases, and involvement of academic and industrial authors could have helped in recent years. At least, the novelists, poets, etc. should be reassured now, for surely the only copying (other than re-publication) likely to occur from their particular work is done in Education, covered by CLA licensing. It is suggested, therefore, that a concerted effort be made by the CBI and professional bodies to inform academic and industrial authors of the situation and the need for involvement when necessary.

Tracing copyright holders

12.48 In the course of time, funds permitting, help of another kind may become available to scholars and librarians working with archives and manuscripts. WATCH (Writers And Their Copyright Holders) is a joint US/UK project to build up a database on the Internet of copyright holders of works in the Humanities. The Copyright Office in Washington and the ALCS in London hold files mainly of published works of living authors. The US base is the Harry Ransom Humanities Research Center of the University of Texas, and the UK centre is the University of Reading. Funding is from charitable trusts (see *Writers and their copyright holders: the WATCH Project*, by D.

Sutton, Managing Information, vol.4(2) April 1995, p36-37 (Aslib); and/or e-mail: *D.C.Sutton@reading.ac.uk*). This is laborious, time-consuming work and accordingly expensive. Certainly such information about an author or subsequent assignee may be badly needed by other authors. However, whether this project can survive on the existing funding basis or must receive more help, or indeed whether eventually it may be better incorporated in the future ECMS, are matters for conjecture.

Of course, it is not just workers with archives and manuscripts who continually suffer. There must be a very considerable number of expensive manhours wasted in seeking clearance by all involved with identifying rights owners in any kind of copyright material. In photocopying, a partial solution has arisen from the setting up of CLARCS. The latter does not involve registration of copyright, which Berne's 'automatic' stipulation makes unnecessary, though only in the legal sense. It is understandable that the Convention should so protect authors, whoever and wherever, but some departures from its restrictions could benefit authors more substantially if Article 9(2) were interpreted more flexibly (13.5; 13.7; App. 5/1).

Future administration

12.49 Surely a project such as WATCH should not be dependent on charity? Why not a statute to place the onus on all copyright holders to key in the details of their publications and changes of ownership to a central point? Computers make possible a central registration system affecting economic entitlement as well as forming a valuable record and a control point for the addition of identifiers and any encryption required. The incentive for recording ownership status could be the absence of entitlement to any economic benefit, nor indeed any kudos or acknowledgement, unless details were fed into the system. In such circumstances, publishers and database producers could find it advantageous to fund such a centre, which could form the necessary nucleus of an ECMS (App. 5).

12.50 Increasing EC harmonisation of copyright law and variety of media are making it more and more difficult to attempt concise and clear explanations or advice. The new climate should not be allowed to prevent users from pressing for the retention of fair dealing and other existing present forms of statutory permission, certainly where hard copy is involved. Outside such permissions, usage of CLARCS by CLA licensees has gone some way towards reducing previous user objections to the recording of photocopying actions which – along with publisher mistrust of users to follow guidelines unbacked by licence – led to educational licensing. The fact that source details must necessarily be recorded *somewhere* in any event was apparently overlooked by the objectors, and teachers were perhaps unfairly maligned in being thought incapable of following a standard procedure of copyright clearance. A future scenario (App. 5) might supersede licensing with consultation of an ECMS for every occasion of electrocopying where legality/permission is otherwise unclear, with charging when applicable being simplified by stored data on rights-owner preferences for standard needs as in CLARCS. Thus copyright might eventually be administered as far as possible by the machines which created not only advantages but also complexities.

13. INTERNATIONAL COPYRIGHT

What is 'international copyright?'

13.1 Some enquirers wonder why the Act contains nothing about international copyright: 'What can we copy of American publications?' is a typical question. The title of this chapter is a phrase customarily used to describe the subject. It does not mean that there is a kind of copyright called 'international' which subsists in a work or can be claimed, although -- as should be clear later -- that is the effect in terms of minimum protection for a given work. The subject would really be better decribed as 'international agreements on copyright'. Complexity arises because of the various revisions of an agreement and the variant levels of acceptance of the revised details by the states originally concerned. The situation was further complicated for some years as a result of bilateral agreements between some states, but these now play little part.

The battle for ever bigger profits through complete control of markets by publishers and producers rages not only within a nation but also internationally, with interactive effects between the two frontiers. As this goes to press, even the most 'laid back' information professional might be pardoned for concluding that user needs for flexibility are in danger – and that almost every action will require licensing before too long, unless the 'front line' is held firmly.

Berne Convention

13.2 In 1886 in Berne, the first and still pre-eminent agreement was signed: 'Convention for the protection of literary and artistic works', which became known as the Berne Convention and began the Berne Union of signatory states. Berne is concerned with the exclusive rights of authors, based on three principles:

(a) mutual protection – among Berne Union members, each state must protect the works of others to the same level as in their own countries, provided the term accorded is not longer than that for its own works (see 13.10).
(b) minimum standards for duration and scope of rights – author's life plus 50 years or, for anonymous works, 50 years after making available to the public (see note below)
(c) automatic protection, with no registration.

NB: A degree of recriprocity applies to (b) – see 14.21 for an example.

13.3 Since 1886 there have been several revisions of Berne, increasing the scope of protection, the latest being Paris 1971 which covers exclusive rights of:

- reproduction and translation
- public performance of dramatic or musical works
- recording of musical works
- broadcasting
- cine films
- adaptations
- moral rights.

13.4 Some signatories to Berne did not ratify immediately. The UK, the second largest exporter of copyright materials, was among these and, although adhering to Berne in the interim, delayed ratifying until after the Copyright, Designs and Patents Act 1988 was passed. After its own Copyright Act, 1976, the USA – the world's largest exporter of copyright materials – did not join the Berne Union until March 1989. The Berne Convention set up the International Bureau, to be financed partly from fees for services but primarily from subscriptions by member states.

13.5 Berne protection

After its minimum protection levels, perhaps the most significant part of Berne is Article 9(2). Under this, national legislatures may authorise the reproduction of copyright works in 'certain special cases, provided that such reproduction does not conflict with a normal exploitation of the work and does not unreasonably prejudice the legitimate interests of the author'. The word 'and' is emphasised here to show that the two conditions must both be satisfied. Article 9(2) has been widely interpreted as ruling out compulsory licensing because, it is believed by those who adopt the interpretation, a copyright owner must have the right to control the exploitation of his own work. It was this interpretation which thwarted attempts during lobbying towards the passage of the UK's CDPA88 to bring in some 'rights of access' to material already made available to the public: for example, to have a fixed term unrelated to lifetime for photocopying for non-publishing purposes; to put every journal issue without a copying fee printed on it into the public domain; and to impose compulsory licensing for copying beyond fair dealing for non-publishing purposes when rights owners were unreasonably obstructing access.

World Intellectual Property Organisation

13.6 In 1967 the Berne Bureau became the World Intellectual Property Organisation. WIPO is not concerned only with copyright, but administers most international agreements on intellectual property. WIPO's International Bureau arranges all conventions and may also contain an 'International register of trademarks, industrial designs and designations of origin', although in late 1997 doubts about expense and timescale were still arising. However, at that time some proposals for the coverage also of Internet domain names were discussed. In 1994 the WIPO Arbitration Center: International Center for the Resolution of Intellectual Property Disputes announced its services. A conference was held in Geneva, January 1995, on *Rules for institutional arbitration and mediation.*

13.7 From 1990 onwards, WIPO has produced drafts of a 'possible protocol' to Berne working towards protection in the Information Society. There is risk of reinstatement of the discrimination against 'commercial research' as fair dealing which the UK Bill contained until its removal in the autumn of 1987. Also, the new copyright treaty would effectively mean that any library could only copy if licensed.

Other drafts have appeared since 1990 (see Section 9 of *Aslib guide to copyright*). Had the first draft protocol introduced a concept of compulsory licensing of reproduction for non-publishing purposes for example, the draft could have been welcomed by users. A favourable interpretation of Berne Article 9.2 (13.5 above) is arguably possible if the licensing were made subject to reasonable royalties, since rights owners could gain much that inaction, or piecemeal contractual confusion across the spectrum of works, could otherwise prevent. The UK itself has already gone very close to, if not literally into, compulsory licensing with the 1988 Act's provision for compulsory licensing when rights owners do not act appropriately in certain circumstances.

An International Publishers Association 'position paper' was adopted at a Barcelona meeting in April 1996 (App. 4/8). That meeting was followed by in December 1996 by an international WIPO conference in December 1996 in Geneva about a treaty for possible changes to Berne (see ECUPWeb site – *http://www/kaapeli.fi/eblida/ecup* – the link to use is 'other reports'). The proposals immediately became controversial, for publishers' rights would be much stronger without balancing that with user privileges and would end fair dealing and library privileges in the new digital enviroment. Two new rights are proposed – (i) browsing right, concerning the viewing of screened material without permission; and (ii) communication right (or transmission right) to prohibit tranmission by any telecommunication method otherwise than by permission. There is also a proposal for new legal protection for electronic copyright management systems (ECMS, see 3.55). The *Library Association Record*, vol. 99(2), February 1997 p.66 reported that lobbying at Geneva resulted in a number of governments being '*persuaded to put forward IFLA's viewpoints ... The treaties now confirm that limitations and exceptions currently permitted can continue into the future.* (IFLA views are to a large extent reflected in an ECUP document, see App. 4/3.) However, when in late August 1997 the UK's draft SI in compliance with the EU's Directive on legal protection of databases (3.28) was sent out for consultation on a very short timescale with proposed commencement of 1 January 1998, it was evident that no account had been taken of the Geneva result on greater flexibility.

It is not feasible in a text of this kind to chronicle all significant developments, and only examples have been given here to illustrate the trend towards even greater control by publishers and database producers and loss of flexibility for the user community.

Universal Copyright Convention

13.8 In 1952, a UNESCO conference in Geneva sought to replace the worst complexities between the Berne Union countries and the Americas with a unified approach. The Universal Copyright Convention was the result, and represented a compromise between Berne and the various conventions originated by or between the countries of North and South America. The main features of UCC are:

(a) works of a given country must carry a copyright notice to secure protection in other UCC countries
(b) no formalities other than (a)
(c) foreign works must be treated as though they are national works (known as the 'national treatment' principle)
(d) a minimum term of protection of life plus 25 years (not 50 as Berne)
(e) the author's translation rights may be subjected to compulsory licensing.

It should be noted that (c) can be advantageous when an author lives in a country with poorer protection than that in another UCC country. Furthermore, Article IV allows nationals of non-signatory countries to have protection for a work, provided they publish it for the first time in a Convention country.

13.9 The UCC requires each published work to bear a specified form of notice, showing the copyright owner at the time of publication: © by Jack James, 1993 or © 1993 by Jack James. The mandatory C in a circle is an internationally recognised symbol. The second alternative can help when more than one name needs to be stated. The © notice has long been used to replace the need for a UK work, for example, to be registered under the USA system in order to be protected there and in other non-Berne states. Now that the USA is in Berne and has automatic copyright, some say the C notice could be replaced with a simple 'all rights reserved' notice. But this would seem undesirable unless the UCC itself becomes revised, because the C notice can be useful as an indication at least of the start of publisher copyright, as well as the body to contact if wanting copyright permission or first purchase of rights, and is also widely accepted as a reminder of the subsistence of copyright in a work. However, a © notice in itself may well be of no help in determining authorship, or duration of rights other than a publisher's, or other matters included in a publishing agreement. Sound recordings need a near-equivalent, the P symbol and notice, under the Rome Convention 1961. Nearly all countries interested in copyright materials are members of Berne or UCC, plus other conventions.

Extension of UK law to other countries

13.10 From time to time UK copyright law is extended to other countries, in the sense that their works receive the same or similar protection here as UK works, subject to specific exceptions and – in the case of the 1988 Act – transitional provisions. For example, Statutory Instrument 1993/942 specifies exceptions and then lists various countries enjoying protection under CDPA88, as reproduced below (13.17). Readers should note the wording which heads the lists appended to this chapter, for example: 'The countries ... either are parties to ... Berne ... and/or ... Universal Copyright Convention ... or otherwise give adequate protection under their law', because which agreement may apply, particularly Berne or the UCC, is not specified against each country.

It is important to note that the EEA term of protection does not apply to non-EEA states. Hence the new longer 70-year duration can only apply to a Berne/UCC country when it is also an EEA state, or if it is found that such country itself has a term of 70 years pma (see 13.2(a)). Otherwise, duration is that of the non-EEA state concerned, provided it does not exceed the EEA period. Countries which are not signatory to Berne or the UCC may not be entitled to protection unless there are other agreements involved. Specialist help should always be sought for international issues.

Other conventions

13.11 The important agreements are listed in Appendix 1/5. Those not mentioned above concern neighbouring rights: Rome 1961 (performing, phonograms, broadcasting organisations); Geneva 1971 (phonogram producers); Brussels 1974 (programmes via satellite); and two European agreements – Brussels 1958 (programme exchange via television films) and Strasbourg 1960 (television broadcasts).

Commission of the European Communities: harmonisation

13.12 Having in 1988 produced a Green Paper as a consultative document, the CEC went ahead with the following programme of Directives:

(1) computer software, which became a Directive early in 1993 and has resulted in SI 1993/3233 to modify UK law (7.15-7.20)
(2) rental right, lending and certain neighbouring rights (done – see 4.35 re SI 1996/2967)
(3) legal protection of databases against unfair extraction of data for commercial purposes (Directive done and UK's SI draft, see 3.28)
(4) harmonisation of the term of protection for copyright and certain neighbouring rights (done – see 2.2 re SI 1995/3297)
(5) co-ordination of certain rules concerning copyright and neighbouring rights applicable to satellite and cable broadcasting (done – SI 1996/2967)
(6) home copying of sound and audiovisual recordings (under discussion, see 8.37)
(7) reproduction right – the responses to a CEC questionnaire on reprography and relevant permissions, several years ago, had resulted in postponement, but 'reproduction right' is now expected to encompass this (see below).
(8) consultation on a *droit de suite* (artists' resale right, see 4.52) has so far brought some objections, especially from the UK.
(9) communication to the public right (see below).

13.13 Further CEC harmonisation effort

The CEC's *Follow-up to the Green Paper on copyright and related rights in the information society* of November 1996 considered the case for a 'Communication to the public right', to embrace on-demand transmissions (3.14). It is reported that:

> where the transmission of a protected work over the net involves reproductions, the reproduction right should ensure adequate protection. Both Member States and interested parties are, however, agreed that such protection would not be sufficient as the transmission of a work in a network environment 'on-demand' will not necessarily imply acts of reproduction. In order to allow for interactive transborder services to be provided throughout the Single Market, it is considered necessary that rightholders should have available to them an additional right which enables them to adequately control 'on-demand' transmissions of their works or other subject matter.

However the UK, at least, already regards public availability from electronic databases as 'commercial publication' (s175).

13.14 Preparation of EC Directives

Proposals are generated by CEC officials in Brussels, discussed with national representatives, sent out as drafts for comment to selected organisations (usually with tight deadlines), reviewed at hearings for invited representatives of national organisations, and then submitted to Council for adoption as Directives. The general reaction of the UK user community is a preference for seeing, as far as possible, the translation (in both senses) of the UK's CDPA88 into the European scene, since many believe that this Act has a fair balance between the interests of rights owners and users. However, some EC Directives have shown limitation of contractual capability which is helpful to users, whilst not damaging rights despite Berne 9(2), and there could be some safeguards against restrictive trade practices (14.7). Some of the harmonisation effects might accordingly be regarded as desirable by users, as well as rights owners seeking a 'level playing field' for the single European market begun in 1993.

The CEC's *Follow-up to the Green Paper on copyright and related rights in the information society* of November 1996 (App. 1/8.2) considered the case for a 'Communication to the public right', to embrace on-demand transmissions. However the UK, at least, already regards public availability from electronic databases as 'commercial publication' (s175).

The publication of a detailed consultancy study was announced at the October 1996 Frankfurt Book Fair. The study was carried out at the behest of CEC DGXIII (Directorate General XIII: Telecommunications, Information and Exploitation of Research; see report entitled *Europe's Multimedia Challenge* in App. 1/8.1). After notes on 10 'Theses' on fundamental aspects, the Executive Summary sets out 10 'Perspectives' on Information Society developments to be expected by the year 2000. Then follow 10

'Recommendations' for action by publishers. Notes on essential points in the legislation of member states are appended. It is suggested that the whole report should be seen not only by publishers and information professionals but also communications system experts (for example, *Thesis 3: the next mass market transmission technology for online EP use emerging after modems is digital broadcasting rather than on-demand multimedia infrastructure*).

In a digest document of November 1996, the CEC focused upon four new rights as '*priorities for legislative action*'. The proposals, which are associated with increased WIPO activity, became embodied in a draft Directive issued in December 1997 and sent for comment to working groups:

- reproduction right, including the *harmonisation of the limitations/exceptions*, which could endanger existing UK fair dealing and library copying privileges;
- communication to the public right, including the *making available to members of the public individual access to works and other protected matter*, to protect digital 'on-demand' transmission services;
- distribution or 'issue to the public' right, including the confinement of the principle of exhaustion of rights to goods only (e.g. publications) and not to the provision of services (e.g. on-line);
- anti-copying system right, to provide protection against circumvention, etc.

A number of points in the draft proposal may give rise to controversy and cause a longer period of gestation for the final Directive and resultant state laws than the very short one to two years to implementation required by the CEC. (The draft was received for comment in the second week of February 1998 with a request for comments to the Patent Office, preferably in time for its first CEC-level discussion, due in that week.)

Other matters in plan for harmonisation are: broadcasting right; law enforcing rights; moral rights; and the 'collective management of copyright and neighbouring rights and collecting societies'. A problem of standardisation is also envisaged, because the CEC is concerned that technical standardisation aims may be hindered by the intellectual property rights of the standards-making bodies.

13.15 At all stages towards Directives, it would seem essential for the UK user community to be aware of the dangers of losing some of the features of UK law which are at present seen as necessarily fair and flexible for research and private study and other purposes, without any qualification of the word 'research' to exclude commercial ends. Directives require member states to bring in specified legislation within a given timescale, usually two years. In some cases, abrogation or opting out of a particular provision is permitted, though obviously this has to be rare in an endeavour to provide trade equalities. When a member state already provides suitable law, no action need be taken. For example, the UK already has public rental right and public lending right, and the changes in 4.35 are not as extensive as they might have been in respect of 13.12(2) as far as can be foreseen at present. (However, quite extensive enough, in a most complex SI!) Some proposals, like database protection against extraction (3.28), have needed considerable discussion and long gestation.

General recommendation

13.16 None of the CEC drafts currently under discussion are listed in the bibliography or detailed elsewhere in this volume, firstly on grounds that they are not by any means in a final form, and secondly that they do not apply unless positively added to the law of member states. Here in the UK, no Directive can have any effect unless a Statutory Instrument has been passed by Parliament containing the required adjustments to UK law. Thus it would seem appropriate at this point to stress the advice which applies to any member of any state, not just the UK: follow national law, as modified by contract or licence, irrespective of the country of origin of any copyright item under consideration, unless it is known that the country concerned does not adhere to either Berne or the UCC.

An action may infringe in one country but be quite legal in another. Data transmission across national boundaries has stimulated some discussion, but the problems should be capable of coverage within contracts (though commonality of contractual provisions is highly desirable, as in other contexts).

Confusion of long standing has existed among users who think they must comprehend the law of individual states to determine behaviour in respect of foreign material. Such laws apply only to nationals of those states, and need not be studied by UK users except by companies or authors intending to publish there.

Extract from SI 1993/942, Copyright (Application to Other Countries) Order 1993 as amended by SI 1995/2987; reproduced by courtesy of HMSO

13.17 *NB. Double asterisk precedes additions since 1993*

SCHEDULE 1 Article 2(1) and (2):
COUNTRIES ENJOYING PROTECTION
IN RESPECT OF ALL WORKS EXCEPT
BROADCASTS AND CABLE PROGRAMMES

The countries specified in this Schedule either are parties to the Berne Copyright Convention and/or the Universal Copyright Convention and/or the Agreement Establishing the World Trade Organisation (including the Agreement on Trade-Related Aspects of Intellectual Property Rights); or otherwise give adequate protection under their law.

Albania
Algeria (28th August 1973)
Andorra (27th September 1957)
** Antigua and Barbuda
Argentina
Australia (including Norfolk Island)
Austria
Bahamas
** Bahrain
Bangladesh
Barbados
** Belarus (25th December 1991)
Belgium
Belize
Benin
Bolivia
** Bosnia-Herzegovina
** Botswana
Brazil
** Brunei Darussalam
Bulgaria
Burkina Faso
** Burundi
Cameroon
Canada
Central African Republic
Chad
Chile
China
Colombia
Congo
Costa Rica
Côte d'Ivoire
Croatia
Cuba
Cyprus, Republic of
Czech Republic
Denmark (including Greenland and the Faeroe Islands)
** Djibouti
** Dominica
** Dominican Republic
Ecuador
Egypt

	El Salvador		Lesotho
**	Estonia		Liberia
	Fiji		Libya
	Finland		Liechtenstein
	France (including all Overseas Departments and Territories)	**	Lithuania
			Luxembourg
	Gabon	**	Macau
	Gambia	**	Macedonia
**	Georgia		Madagascar
	Germany		Malawi
	Ghana		Malaysia
	Greece	**	Maldives
	Guatemala		Mali
	Guinea, Republic of		Malta
	Guinea-Bissau		Mauritania
	Haiti (27th September 1957)		Mauritius
	Holy See		Mexico
	Honduras	**	Moldova
	Hungary		Monaco
	Iceland		Morocco
	India	**	Mozambique
**	Indonesia	**	Myanmar
	Ireland, Republic of	**	Namibia
	Israel		Netherlands (including Aruba and the Netherlands Antilles)
	Italy		
**	Jamaica		New Zealand
	Japan		Nicaragua
	Kampuchea (27th September 1957)		Niger
**	Kazakhstan (25th December 1991)		Nigeria
	Kenya		Norway
	Korea, Republic of		Pakistan
**	Kuwait		Panama (17th October 1962)
	Laos (27th September 1957)		Paraguay
**	Latvia		Peru
	Lebanon		Philippines

	Poland			Sweden	
	Portugal			Switzerland	
	Romania			Taiwan, territory of	(10th July 1985)
**	Russian Federation		**	Tajikistan	(25th December 1991)
	Rwanda		**	Tanzania	
**	Saint Kitts and Nevis			Thailand	
**	Saint Lucia			Togo	
	Saint Vincent and the Grenadines			Trinidad and Tobago	
**	Saudi Arabia	(13th July 1994)		Tunisia	
	Senegal			Turkey	
**	Sierra Leone			Uganda	(20th July 1964)
	Singapore		**	Ukraine	
**	Slovak Republic			United States of America (including Puerto Rico and all territories and possessions)	
	Slovenia			Uruguay	
	South Africa			Venezuela	
	Soviet Union	(27th May 1973)		Yugoslavia	
	Spain			Zaire	
	Sri Lanka			Zambia	
	Suriname			Zimbabwe	
**	Swaziland				

(The SIs also contain:

Schedule 2: Countries enjoying full protection for sound recordings;
Schedule 3: Countries enjoying protection in respect of broadcasts.)

14. 'OUT OF COPYRIGHT?'

14.1 What would it have been like to live and write in Bali with intellectual property treated as community property? A topical, as well as tropical paradise, perhaps? But we of the industrialised world know ourselves well enough to understand that such an arrangement would not work for people driven by economic and kudos incentives.

Look what happens, though, when a copyright period ends in respect of a popular book or play. The air of relief and fresh stimulus to produce adaptations or imitations without having to ask permission is almost tangible. Kenneth Grahame's *Wind in the Willows* was a particular favourite in childhood for many of us. When that copyright ended at the close of 1982, there was a sudden surge of new children's books and dramatisations which must have been prepared as the great day approached. Since then William Horwood has successfully imitated Grahame's style in several sequels.

As indicated in 2.2, a EU Directive has increased the duration of copyright to life plus 70 years. The UK has amended the law to increase its post mortem 50 years accordingly, despite the feelings of many users of coyright materials (including authors) who feel such a duration to be unnecessary and even outrageous. Under the new provisions, because Grahame's works were still in copyright in another European state on 1 July 1995, those works now have *revived* copyright to make up the 70 EU total, resulting in them coming back into copyright for 20 years from January 1996 to the end of 2016. Publishers – and related industries such as producers of ornaments and art prints, if their contracts allow – should benefit very considerably, and in any event copies made before the end of 1995 can continue to be sold. Many other famous names are involved, examples being Claude Monet, Kipling and Elgar.

Then there is *extended* copyright, applicable to works which were still in UK copyright at the end of 1995. The estate of A. A. Milne (who died in 1956) as holder of rights in *Winnie the Pooh* and other Milne works will now enjoy those rights for a further period of 20 years beyond 2006. So, until imitators enter the scene in due course, the original 'Poohsticks' will float safely onwards until the end of 2026, well into the new millenium – when a lot more water will have flowed under the bridge. (This may be worth comparing with the SI 1996/2967 reference (near foot of p25) to copyright (like anything or anyone else in fact) being *due to expire by effluxion of time*!)

The consequences of the EU's action are examined in *Textual monopolies: literary copyright and the public domain*, edited by P. Parrinder and W. Chernaik, (London, King's College, 1997. The EU's 'harmonisation' must be duly appreciated by publishers who welcome parity with Germany, which already had a post mortem period of 70 years. However, Europe is now out of line with the largest exporter of copyright materials, namely the USA, and the multimedia situation is likely to be even more complex. Obviously, not only is 'out of copyright' by no means synonymous with 'out of mind', it may also not be quite final. This chapter considers topics similar to, even sometimes mistaken as copyright and, in the case of 14.19, the question of material which may be copyright-free.

Perpetual rights

14.2 New perpetual right

During the copyright period, the author and publisher, and/or anyone to whom the rights are assigned, can benefit. Usually any benefit is quite minimal from non-fiction, unless the item becomes a course- book or is a get-rich-quick character assassination of some unfortunate public figure (though how much is non-fiction?). In a realm of purer fiction, a work which earned well was Sir James Barrie's *Peter Pan*. Many will know something of the way in which the famous Great Ormond Street Hospital for Sick Children has been helped over the years by royalties in all rights to Peter Pan since they were bequeathed to the Hospital by Sir James. For some works like this, as with Shakespeare, there is no end to the appeal and probably no end to the adaptations, plays, films and so on. With this in mind, CDPA88 makes special provision for royalties to continue to be required and paid to the Hospital for public performances, publication, broadcasting, etc., of *Peter Pan*, including 'any adaptation' in the future, despite the expiry of copyright at the end of 1987 (s.301). This new perpetual right, similar to those granted to some ten academic institutions by the Copyright Act 1775, may not be assigned in any way and would cease if that were attempted.

Royal prerogative and university privileges

14.3 Royal prerogative, and its delegation to others by means of letters patent in the 17th century and never revoked, can be a source of uncertainties. Letters patent were granted by the Crown to the Queen's Printer, and to Oxford and Cambridge universities in respect of the Authorised Version of the Bible and the Book of Common Prayer. Then there was the Copyright Act 1775, which permitted ten institutions, including Oxford and Cambridge universities, to exercise perpetual rights in respect of any copyrights given to them in the past or future, provided they did not re-assign in which case the rights would cease.

Only slight treatment of such fringe interests is considered necessary here, but this outline should be supplemented firstly by referring to the notes on the Bible (15.46); secondly by the facts that:

(i) royal prerogative is continued by the 1988 Act (s171), though little or no difficulty is anticipated as a result;
(ii) the university privileges under the Copyright Act 1775, rarely used in any event and never in modern times, will at last cease under the 1988 Act's transitional provisions, but are allowed to continue for a further 50 years until 2039, now assumed to be 2059 in view of harmonisation (see also 7.28 on assumptions re expiry of copyright);

and thirdly by consulting the various extensive legal works in the Bibliography when this topic is of special interest.

Common law

Two examples are given here, as follows.

14.4 Breach of confidence

When information imparted in confidence is made known to others, an action for breach of confidence could result in an award of damages. If national security or other matters of public interest were involved, there could be a criminal action. A form of protection akin to copyright can thus exist in ideas, despite the earlier observations about copyright itself where ideas are concerned (1.12). For example, if a designer discussed his plans in confidence in advance of marketing a design to someone who then stole his ideas and beat him to the market, a case could be brought.

14.5 Passing off

This is frequently confused with copyright. Although usually regarded as a deceptive practice which is applicable only to goods, it can have a bearing on the titles of copyright works which are otherwise unprotected because they are items of fact. For example, the publishers of a certain magazine were unlikely to be wasting their market research budget last year when their researchers canvassed views of passers-by about closely similar journal titles. Some such cases have been successful in the past, but only where the courts decided there was a danger of confusion, since that is never regarded as necessarily consequent on a similar title.

Now that moral rights have been added to UK law (10), the risk of infringing these must be borne in mind as well as copyright per se. The use of a famous author's name for one's own work could offend not only on moral right grounds (false attribution, 10.2(c)) but might also lead to accusations of 'passing off' under common law. One should accordingly avoid using forms of name, or name-plus-title combinations, which could cause confusion to the public. With regard to book titles per se, infringement might be claimed in respect of a long or otherwise uncommon title, especially of a well-known work such as a bestseller. However, use of the same title should not necessarily be ruled out: for example, a new book title 'Little women', though in danger of confusion if it were children's literature, should be safe enough as a scientific study of child development through adolescence! In any event, confusion would depend on context: listing in a title-only catalogue might be taken by some people to refer to the famous work by Louisa May Alcott. But this happens to be an example of a claim which could never succeed now, because, although the 1869 classic is immortal, the author regrettably was not.

However, it would seem that similar book titles would have to show closely similar names of author and/or publisher to be in danger of causing confusion to the extent of damaging a market. A problem for those contemplating a legal action is that, according to Lord Diplock in 1979 (the Advocaat case, *Warnink etc. v. J. Townend and Sons (Hull) Ltd*), five elements must all be present to amount to a valid claim:

(1) a misrepresentation
(2) made by a trader in the course of trade
(3) to prospective customers of his or ultimate consumers of goods or services supplied by him
(4) which is calculated to injure the business or goodwill of another trader (in the sense that this is a reasonably foreseeable consequence), and
(5) which causes actual damage to a business or goodwill of the trader by whom the action is brought or, in a quia timet action (brought in fear of possible damage), will probably do so.

Contracts

14.6 Contracts can override any statute other than the criminal code or other areas of the law where the public interest is involved. A publisher or producer can put every purchaser under contract, such as users of online electronic databases. Then, unless the contract is a collective licence and complaint can be made to the Copyright Tribunal, there is little to save the user from over-stringent terms other than competition on the one hand and the Unfair Contract Terms Act 1977 on the other.

Restrictive trade practices

14.7 Copyright tends to be used from time to time as a means of achieving restrictive trade practice (see also 3.28). For example, a directory publisher, A, is preparing a new edition, and finds that, since his previous edition, another publisher B, has produced some lists which update his own. Accordingly, since such data items are matters of fact, he keys the new data into his own database to update his own files. But B then sues A for infringement of his compilation, and this becomes a battle between two publishers for a particular directory market. In such a case, when the extent copied is not specifically prohibited and the judgement required is really a definition of 'substantial part' in the particular circumstances, who should get the benefit of the doubt? A court should desirably consider whether A had asked B for permission to include the required names and addresses in his own work and, if so, whether permission had been unreasonably withheld or offered at a prohibitive fee by B in order to block A from publishing successfully. This illustrates why 'substantial part' is one the terms left undefined in the Act.

Statutory provisions other than copyright

14.8 Public lending right

Introduced by the Public Lending Right Act 1979, this has been described earlier in this volume (4.48; 4.49) in the same context as rental right, because the two rights go together in a draft EC Directive. Since the UK already has lending and rental rights, however, no changes to UK law are expected to arise from the impending Directive.

14.9 Legal deposit

Many think that copyright is dependent on the deposit of copies of books in certain libraries by the publisher, but this has not been the case since the Copyright Act 1842. 'Books' has been defined to cover any part or section of a book, a pamphlet, printed sheet, printed music, tables, maps, plans or charts, and periodicals. Section 15 of the Copyright Act 1911 contains the latest provisions on legal deposit, apart from the change of 'British Museum' to 'British Library' by the British Library Act 1972. That section was among several left unrepealed by the 1956 Act. In the 1988 Act, although the preamble which begins 'An Act to restate the law of copyright...' conveys the impression that all previous copyright laws are repealed, this is not entirely the case. And although the 1956 Act is repealed in toto, the 1911 Act does not appear at all in the list of repeals in Schedule 8. Despite much discussion on legal deposit in recent years, no actual new legislation has yet been framed (14.13 below).

14.10 Copyright libraries

The British Library must be supplied with a copy automatically. Five other copyright libraries, as they used to be known, can claim copies from a publisher within one month of publication. A claim for a first issue of a periodical is interpreted as covering all future issues. The five are: Bodleian Library, Oxford; University Library, Cambridge; National Library of Scotland; Trinity College Dublin; and National Library of Wales (with exceptions).

14.11 Whitford recommendations on legal deposit

The Whitford Committee made a number of recommendations concerning legal deposit, for example (Appendix 2/1.3 s833):

(a) leasing the financial burden to publishers by fiscal concession should be considered
(b) the question of microform publications should be considered
(c) revised provisions for deposit should be the subject of legislation separate from copyright law
(d) national archives of films and published audiovisual recordings should be established, subject to further investigation of desirability and feasibility.

The last has been under consideration for some years, with the Office of Arts and Libraries being approached from time to time by library professionals and publishers. The former are anxious, as ever, to ensure completeness of collections despite continuing budgetary restrictions; whilst the latter are in strong opposition to the existing deposit of books and journals, let alone any extension to audiovisual works and microform.

14.12 Archiving of data

There have been a number of suggestions from professionals about the need for some form of archiving for valuable research data in an electronic database which becomes defunct, but more action and a co-ordinated policy are needed. Whether data sets can be found a home, for example by the ESRC Data Archive (Essex University), must surely depend not only on communication but also on relevance, physical form, currency and costs.

14.13 Nonprint media deposit in general

Following 'ground-swell' discussion among information professionals for a number of years, a 1990 British Library report included in a prefatory note:

> There are no regulations covering legal deposit of non-book materials, such as film, videotape, recorded sound, computer programs, or text stored on magnetic or optical-electronic media, although non-statutory arrangements exist for some materials. This Briefing discusses the nature and purposes of legal deposit and considers the possibility of the extension of legal deposit to electronically published materials, including the issues of definition, selection, acquisition, storage and access.

At an autumn 1995 BL invited seminar, a possible solution for the UK was proposed involving the assignment of control to the BL, associated with a range of specialist archives. Relevant years are noted here to indicate the extent of interest. In 1996, the BL envisaged four classes of media: (a) microforms; (b) handheld electronic (such as CD-ROM); (c) sound and video recordings; and (d) databases published online. Athough immediate extension of legislation was suggested, it was considered that (d) could be left pro tem until more stability has been achieved in electronic publication.

A Government consultation paper of February 1997 led to much discussion. The whole problem is of course international, as evidenced, for example, by study of the work of the International Association of Sound Archives (IASA). The preservation of electronic and audiovisual publications will probably involve the most problems. In the electronic regime, possibly the first problem would be to preserve unchanged; find a 'foster-parent' and get updated; or 'ditch' – perhaps after COM (Computer Output on Microfilm) preparation and indexing of broad coverage.

It is evident that information professionals will not be content to rely too much on the voluntary deposit arrangements which have arisen for certain media, unless those arrangements are strengthened by legislation. The LA Multimedia Group sees CD-ROMs and multimedia as secondary sources at present, which use primary materials that are the more vulnerable, such as sound, film/video and print. Other Group responses were: need for as broad a definition of 'publication' as possible; the naming of exclusions rather than prescribing particular formats to be deposited; the need for laboratory facilities for both preservation and change of format for access purposes; requirement for decisions on copyright issues of access especially electronic online; treatment of omissions from BL proposals such as slides, computer games, photographs and broadcasts; and study of remote access through networks.

Computer games and other 'light' material may not be seen as equally vital to the preservation of the nation's cultural heritage as others, but it could be argued that they do form part of the whole and – like popular novels as at present – should not be overlooked.

14.14 In contrast, Norway already has new legal deposit legislation which came into force in 1990 to cover all publicly available media of recorded knowledge. This is 'enabling law', since the details are left to the professionals. The problems in respect of electronic media are difficult but solutions are not impossible. It would seem that the UK urgently needs similar enabling legislation without any connection with copyright law, and this action would be in accordance with the Whitford Report as already mentioned (14.11).

14.15 Personal data protection

Lastly there is the question: To what extent if any do the provisions on personal data protection affect copyright? In general, they do not, but could indeed affect non-copyright bibliographical data. The Data Protection Act 1984 caused much concern at first because its excessively close mesh, perhaps for trial and error reasons, failed to exempt bibliographic or other data which are already a matter of public record. The nearest was the second of three 'unconditional exemptions': personal data which the user is required by law to make public – which could be said to apply in conjunction with legal deposit. The matter was soon cleared up by the Data Protection Registrar in respect of the UK. However, the EC is on the verge of introducing a Directive on Data Protection which does not exempt bibliographical data, although member states may make their own exemptions of these and certain other kinds of data. It has been proposed on behalf of the UK that an appropriate exemption should appear in the Directive at the outset in order to avoid confusion and uncertainty to information services.

Clearance or permission-seeking

14.16 It is just as important to know how to discover whether an item is still copyright as to understand the law itself. Of course, any action for any purpose, including re-publication, can be taken when an item is out of copyright. There are several points to bear in mind when seeking clearance or permission in cases where copyright currency is uncertain:

(a) When copyright duration involves a lifetime, it can be extremely difficult to discover whether a work is still copyright, or otherwise how to obtain copyright clearance for a given action, unless an author is well known. Otherwise, birth and death dates in some catalogues (such as British Library) may help.

(b) After the 'event' from which a period of copyright dates, the years stated are complete calendar years beyond the end of the year in which the event occurs, such as the death of an author. So 70 years after an author's death can mean just 70 years or very nearly 71 years after death.

(c) A reprint of a 'published edition' of printed matter, or a re-issue or re-release of a sound or video recording or film, only starts a new period of copyright in respect of any new material.

(d) For recordings, the event of release date is not always clear.

(e) Broadcasts and cable programmes have copyright which dates from the year of first inclusion of a particular item, resulting in highly complex copyright status at a given point in time. This status is further complicated, of course, by the considerable number of rights owners in the background, for example of a broadcast.

(f) It is even more difficult to ascertain the current owner of rights, which may have been assigned or re-assigned several times. Enquiries, or permissions requests, should always go in the first instance to the publisher or producing company but, if as sometimes happens the enquirer is referred to an author without an address being provided, a search can be long and hard and is only undertaken when such a search could be worthwhile – that is, could lead to considerable profit from re-publication or re-release.

14.17 Hence verification of copyright state is not to be undertaken lightly for many works and, if there is any helpful information printed on an item, reliance tends to be placed on that. Otherwise, the general rule 'when in doubt, consult' applies here as well as in many other situations in copyright. In (a) above, the absence of a date of death is of course scarcely a positive piece of information, and may make a determined enquirer track down an author's place of work, or professional body membership, or author's registration with the Authors' Licensing and Collecting Agency. A costly advertisement may even be needed. There is increasing difficulty when overseas addresses are involved. Small wonder that such copyright clearance searches are only attempted in special cases, such as a need to adapt or reprint the whole of an important work from a publishing house which is no longer in business. A book by Crabb (App. 1/3) looks at copyright from the clearance viewpoint.

14.18 When requiring permission to photocopy an extent greater than the fair dealing or library copying norms, the form given in 6.51 can be used as standard. It has been designed for ease of response by busy publishers, allowing them to annotate and then photocopy the whole form for return to the requester.

Public domain

14.19 A few words about material which may be in the public domain, as copyright-free items are styled, seem desirable here. After a perhaps wistful reference to Bali at the beginning, this chapter mentioned a famous work in which the copyright had expired and was then revived. But what of material which has never been copyright? In the UK (and EC) every work is automatically copyright. Consequently the Act makes no mention of the concept of 'public domain', leaving it to be realised that all copyright-expired material is in the public domain, along with a fact or idea extracted in isolation from its context. But it is possible to find material which, whilst it really has copyright, is described by its originators as 'copyright- free'. A particular example is the copyright-free music which some groups of performers provide, wherein a group has waived its own performing right in respect of music in which the copyright has expired. This can be useful when requiring background music without having to pay royalties for re-use of recorded music to the Mechanical Copyright Protection Society Ltd (12.31), for example for an educational videotape or tape-slide presentation.

Following a EC Directive, a new 'publication right' has been added to CDPA88 which applies to publishing archival material for the first time: that is, when it is copyright-free and has not been previously 'issued to the public' (defined more widely than in other contexts (see 4.52)).

14.20 UK and other EEC states

Although UK government publications are indeed copyright, the generous allowances by HMSO (6.23) effectively bring some documents quite close to being in the public domain. EEC documentation is covered by the copyright laws of the country of publication, so a large number are covered by Luxembourg law (see 6.26 for notes on copying and the address for permissions).

14.21 USA and reciprocity

The Berne Convention leaves it to each member state to determine protection for official texts of a legislative, administrative and legal nature (Article 2(4)). The United States government has no copyright in its own publications, and they are mostly in the public domain from the outset. The US government can however hold rights acquired from others, such as the contractors who originate the AD- numbered series of reports available from the Superintendent of Documents in Washington (see 6.29). Adherence to the main provisions of the Berne Convention (13.2) would cause UK users to accord 50 years' protection – the protection which is already afforded to the AD series in the UK – to US government material which is in the public domain in the USA. However, Article 7(8) of Berne requires that, unless national law indicates otherwise, the duration of protection shall not exceed the term fixed in the country of origin of the work, thus establishing a form of reciprocity. Therefore, a copyright duration of nil for any overseas material theoretically puts it in the public domain in the UK also, unless there is UK law to the contrary. This would not apply in reverse, for the USA is required under Berne to protect UK government publications for the 50-year minimum applicable to anonymous works, though users across the Atlantic would probably feel it reasonable to follow the HMSO guidelines.

Continuing the theory, when it is observed that a particular kind of overseas material habitually does not bear a © notice, a check could be made to discover, firstly, whether the country had acceded to Berne or UCC and, if so, whether the material was in the public domain in the source country. If the material does bear a © notice, a check could determine whether the source country had acceded to Berne or the Universal Copyright Convention or both. (There are certain differences: for example, the UCC minimum protection period is half that of Berne.) The works of states outside these conventions normally enjoy no protection abroad. Why 'normally'? Because other factors can apply, such as bilateral treaties between particular states which require reciprocal protection of copyright material.

In practice, before treating recent overseas material as being in the public domain in the UK, it is recommended that a user should ensure that the legal situation has not changed. Although unlikely, US law is conceivably subject to change, perhaps as part of legislative adjustments arising from relatively recent accession to Berne in 1987. The full international situation can therefore be quite complex. There may be instances where users can arrange to keep the ramifications under review and know how far they can go with the works of a particular nation. Otherwise, many users may well find it far simpler in practice to treat all overseas material like that of the UK, at least for ordinary day to day requirements.

Other material

14.22 Other documents such as research reports, whether from research establishments or firms or academe, are certainly copyright, even when the originators omit © notices, and any copying must be within the usual permissions. Those users who have recurrent need for copying from a series of reports or a particular periodical, especially when they obtain a full set on subscription or mailing list, may gain from asking the source whether any general permissions might apply in their case, for example, making more than one copy of an extract for strictly internal purposes.

15. PROBLEMS

This chapter consists of responses to a selection of common questions, plus a few less common ones to illustrate or further expand points made in earlier chapters. Some answers may illustrate the old adage that 'circumstances alter cases' and the complexities which lie just below the surface of almost every question. Where the problems arose through consultancy, they have been modified so as to make identification of the enquirer impossible.

NB. The new database right (3.28) must be borne in mind when reading the following, since it may modify answers.

Amateur operatic or dramatic societies

15.1 *A colleague who is a member of a local operatic society told me of some enquiries which he made recently. The aim was to stage some excerpts from a late nineteenth century opera, but PRS put him in touch with the music publisher who holds rights despite the music itself having been out of copyright for some years. The royalty asked by the publishers would have put the society in debt, for it was to be taken as a significant percentage of gross with no thought for the society's costs. Unfortunately, it had only occurred to them fairly late that performing right permission might still be required despite their belief that they had chosen something safely out of copyright. Despite the society's charitable status, the fee could not be reduced and performance had to be called off at great loss and trouble to members. Why should this sort of thing happen?*

Dramatico-musical works have what are known as 'grand rights'. This term is applied to the rights when a work is accompanied by action. PRS is sometimes able to help concerning excerpts, but not with complete works, for which application to the copyright owner is necessary. Upon examining this case, it appeared that the only rights still in existence were held by the music publisher, to whom the enquirer was passed on by PRS. At least, PRS was able to confirm that the publisher's acquired rights in the translated libretto were still current even though the published music had long been in the public domain. PRS applies standard fees to materials under their control, but the publishers in this instance were entitled to charge absolutely anything they wished.

Had the society made enquiries sufficiently far in advance, a translation which was out of copyright could have been selected for performance and no royalties would have been due at all for live performance. In this case, it was too late for the society to switch, having already been in rehearsal for several months. Incidentally, when approach has to be direct to a rights owner like this, it should not be forgotten that other obligations may arise. For example, if the performance were to use purchased recordings, either instead of a live orchestra or just for certain scenes, or use copyright recordings in any other way for the event, both PRS and PPL should be consulted. The Music Publishers' Association produces an excellent eight-page pamphlet on *The performance of dramatico-musical works*, which should be acquired by all who believe they might have future need – but only for *guidance*, because like many copyright topics this can become a real 'can of worms'. It is not only circumstances and purposes of use that can make a case highly complex, but also past changes in the law which may still apply because of copyright duration. As a general point, people have not always found time to update pamphlets like this, or the original compiler has retired, etc., so one must always bear in mind the question of currency of detail. This applies particularly to EU harmonisation developments.

Audiovisual materials: lending to retirement homes

15.2 *Can a public library lend audiovisual materials to a local retirement or nursing home? We note that sound recordings can be played without infringement in the recordings in such an establishment, but what about films and videos – can we lend them to homes for showing to groups?*

Cinematographic films – only with public showing permission, which may be given on the container or accompanying documentation when hiring, or through enquiry to the hiring agency, or by contacting the film company.

Videos – beware of new lending and performers' rights (4.35) – the BVA has not so far indicated any departure from its policy of allowing public libraries to carry on lending videos and regarding such loans as being for 'domestic' use, but it is not yet known whether the new performers' rights may be used to change that situation in some way. Meanwhile, therefore, loans to individual persons should be OK for use privately or within small groups of residents. The LA/JLC/WPC is monitoring developments in case modifications in practice may be needed, after a couple of years' 'settling time' in the new rights, perhaps.

Similar caution should apply to sound recordings, despite the permission to which you refer (relating to a nonprofit-making body with certain main objects, including social welfare, which should apply in this case). This is partly because of the possible new performers' rights situation. Mainly, though, note that the relevant permissions cover copyright in a recording but make no mention of the original works contained (9.26; 9.27), so PRS licensing may apply on behalf of composers and music publishers (consult the MPA, see 12.31). Loan to individuals may well continue to be covered by the BPI's public library arangement (4.47). A general word of advice to retirement home managements might be given concerning PRS licensing for playing recordings, broadcasts, etc in public rooms (see 9.6 and 12.41-12.43). Incidentally, another (broadcast/cable programme) permission may well apply to retirement homes but, although mention is also made of sound recordings or films, note that the permission only relates to those when they are included in a broadcast/cable programme, so – again – PRS licensing is needed for playback of sound recordings in public rooms.

Audiovisual recordings made during instruction

15.3 *We have a 'media' series of courses. In film-making instruction, for example, it would be helpful for a student to be able to make his or her own extract from a film – is this OK?*

See 7.3, which effectively notes that such copying from any audiovisual medium is permitted to *a person giving or receiving instruction.* So, the teacher or the student can copy during, or in preparation for, instruction in film or film-sound-track making. If the copying is for examination purposes, the student would be doubly covered (7.2).

Author-abstracts

15.4 *We want to copy all author-abstracts but find that, in several of the more important and expensive foreign journals which we take, the publisher prints a prefatory notice which forbids any copying at all, not just copying of the typographical layout. Also, at the beginning of every article, each author-abstract, as well as the article itself, is a prominent publisher's © notice.*

The publishers clearly hold copyright in the typographical layout of an author-abstract, whilst the author has copyright in the content. General notices are of course phrased so as to apply to the world market. In any event, it is possible that the publishers believe, because they have acquired all rights in an article from the author, that they can forbid copying of the content of an author-abstract. There is nothing to support this view in UK law, which provides a statutory permission regarding the content only (see

15.27). At present (i.e. no licensing scheme as yet), you are permitted to key in the content of an author-abstract but not photocopy or scan in the typographical layout. This applies to journals received from anywhere, since it is UK law which governs.

The Bible and publishing

15.5 *We are considering the production of an adaptation for children of the New Testament, and thought it would be preferable to go right back to the Authorised Version of 1611 to avoid copyright problems, but have recently heard that there may be other rights involved which date back several centuries. What is the situation?*

The situation is not very straightforward, and drove the Whitford Committee to comment in the Report of 1977 (App. 1/7 s653) that the exact extent and scope of the existing rights, both in terms of letters patent and privilege, might warrant further enquiry. This author's own contribution to that 'further enquiry' is essentially as follows.

15.6 Exclusive rights

There are three kinds of exclusive right which might conceivably apply to the Bible in the UK:

(1) perpetual rights, applicable only to the Authorised Version of 1611 (the King James Version) and the 1662 *Book of Common Prayer*, granted by royal letters patent to Oxford and Cambridge Universities and the Queen's Printer;
(2) copyright, applicable to any modern translation; owned by the translators or their commissioners and any chosen publisher. For example, for the *New English Bible* (1962 and 1971) the Bible Societies arranged with CUP and OUP jointly to publish, and assigned the copyright to them;
(3) Oxford and Cambridge additionally hold royal letters patent which cover more than just the Bible itself, including the right to publish without consent of a copyright owner.

15.7 Conclusions

Each category was researched and the full results can be spared little space here, but the main points follow.

Whilst it would seem unfortunate that CDPA88 did not take advantage of the opportunity to bring perpetual royal printing prerogatives to an end (the Act preserves them as rights and privileges under other enactments or the common law (s171)), perpetual rights affect only the 1611 Authorised Version. Translations covered by copyright have the usual duration of rights: the *New English Bible* above, for example, having no named or personal author, has copyright vested in OUP and CUP for 70 years beyond publication year.

Any person who, despite the existence of superior modern translations, wishes for some reason to adapt directly from the 1611 AV, should consult CUP (on behalf of OUP also, in this regard). Otherwise, CDPA88 should be taken to apply to copyright Bibles. Likewise, other religious books such as the Koran are covered by CDPA88. A new commentary or concordance or adaptation (with permission) with its own personal author would carry copyright for author's life plus 70 years, and other points may apply (see 2.2).

Those with special interest may wish to note a publication supplied by CUP: *The Cambridge Bible Handbook* (1994).

Bible: photocopying

15.8 *What about copying from the Bible?*

In respect of extensive copying, see 5.29 plus the guidance on quotation extents in 5.23. It is recommended that, whether perpetual rights (the 1611 AV) or actual copyright is involved, any user should feel entitled to copy at least to the extent advised for 'research or private study' purposes in Q2. Multiple or extensive copying from a copy of the AV of 1611 would require permission from whichever printer under letters patent were involved – in England and Wales, CUP as above.

Multiple or extensive copying from a copyright version would require permission via the publisher in the usual way. The churches have their own guidelines (for example, Appendix 1/3 Church of England).

Book covers, record sleeves, etc

15.9 *Can we copy book covers when, as so often happens, they get torn or stained? Similarly, can we copy record sleeves, CD cases and bibliographical (author/title/contents) data, and indeed any material accompanying an item such as biographical snippets?*

All such material is copyright to some degree. Even a portion which bears only author/title data may well have artistic copyright in an illustration, and in the typographical layout, though not in the mere non-copyright facts that make up bibliographical data. Author/title facts could be re-typed, of course. Producers are unlikely to object in principle to a photocopy of a whole page, but they could well complain of any degradation effect on illlustrations, general appearance, etc. if you copied a cover. Taking sound recordings as an example, the 'shop-window effect' recognised by BPI as support for the principle of giving public sector libraries a free licence to lend, might be considered reduced. Libraries are not permitted to copy for their own loan stocks. Non-profit-based libraries such as public libraries are permitted to make one replacement or archival copy of any reference item for reference stock (see 6.33), but this is only provided purchase is not *reasonably practicable*, so this cannot help you with a loan collection even though purchase just for the covers could hardly be seen as 'reasonably practicable'. A suggestion is offered: try writing to the producer whose works are found to be the more frequently damaged, for blanket permission to replicate a damaged cover or sleeve and any accompanying information. Report any successes when writing to other companies with similar requests.

Braille

15.10 *A blind student here is keen to read the full reading list issued to sighted students, but many of the items are not available in Braille. He asks whether they can be copied for the purpose of sending off for Braille translation at his expense.*

The latter is likely to be exorbitant, surely. Are there problems in listening to the audio output from the library's Kurzweil reading machine? If there is a problem regarding Kurzweil recognition of particular typefaces, there is other equipment on campus which could help, such as a scanner with character recognition capability and any character set output. Furthermore, what about asking the National Library for the Blind, Stockport, for the latest position on automatic Braille translation? This has been technically feasible for longer than the genesis of the Kurzweil machine. It has been obvious for about a quarter of a century that, as soon as all publishers were using computers, from simple word-processing up to photo-typesetting, discs should be made available when the item is not to go on to CD-ROM anyway. The National Library for the Blind could lend such discs for VDU representation in the largest possible font, and/or use them for automatic Braille translation, or a Braille display panel for touch seems feasible. Perhaps the scene will clear when publishers decide what to do about the licensing of electrocopying.

However, to answer the question:

(a) any kind of translation is an adaptation requiring rights-owner permission, so contact publishers in the first instance if a Braille translation is to be produced;
(b) copying which produces a temporary copy, whether for Kurzweil reader use or Braille translation, would be most unlikely to offend if the copy were destroyed later.

Charges for photocopying

15.11 *A medical nonprofit-based library has asked a question as follows. 'We copy for doctors and feel we cannot stop a consultant, having urgently received a copy, from departing in a hurry without being bothered with a request for payment. We have therefore adopted a method of simply clocking up the amounts involved for different departments. Is this acceptable?'*

It is suggested that charge records should be kept and accountants notifed annually of departmental debits to be credited to the library budget. The Act does not specify how charges should be made, only that they be made, and to the implied benefit of the copying library's budget for purchase of originals. Another library states: 'We do a lot of interlibrary copying and do not charge because of the administrative costs of transferring small sums to and fro.' It is suggested that charge records should be kept on a debit and credit basis, with a periodic exchange of cash differences between the libraries.

Class copies outside a licensed campus

15.12 *Our public library is visited by local university students, who sometimes ask for copies which fall into the category of multiple or systematic copying for classes. We are refusing staffed service in accordance with the law, but what about self-service? We have suspected that some self-service machine users may be copying the same item. The students belong to licensed institutions and if they copied on their own campus there would be no difficulty. Should we ignore them?*

15.13 You are not recommended to ignore them, of course! There are at least four alternative answers here:

(1) The notices beside your machines should indicate that only a single copy is permissible under fair dealing. That – and not library copying provisions – constitutes the main legal permission applicable to self-service. If the staff happen to notice a lack of compliance, a warning of refusal of access could be issued, but no library can afford supervisory staff for self-service machines.

(2) Outside the environment where they are students and known to be so, and indeed they are licensed for copying needs, it is conceivable that the taking of one copy each by a group of students, one by one, could be seen as fair dealing. This argument would not hold up in an unlicensed university's defence against litigation, but might be viable for you, because you do not normally know, nor are you obliged to discover, every reader's background or reason for using self-service equipment, and must perforce rely upon your fair dealing notices beside machines for every self-service machine user whether a student or not. This however does not mean condoning actions when you do know, as per (1).

(3) When students are known to want systematic or multiple copying, stipulate either that they must bring copyright permission, or else allow the making of only a single research or private study copy. That copy could be taken into the licensed environment for clearance via CLARCS, paying for one CLARCS copying permission and making the required multiples under the licence.

(4) A student could be told to note the requirement and make a request to his or her own library. If not in that library's stock, the nonprofit-based library privilege of obtaining a copy for stock from any other library could be used. Thus the institution concerned could acquire a photocopy for stock which, like other material legally acquired for stock and not subject to contractual restrictions, would be covered for multiple copying by the institution's licence. The same would apply to a single cleared copy obtained from the BL. The choice of policy has to be yours. Even if you refused access to copying machines, you could apply (4) and thus avoid being entirely unhelpful.

15.14 This problem arose soon after the school licence came into force when pupils visiting public libraries wanted copying of material for school projects. Attempts have been made, during the several years since licensing became adopted in the education sector, to persuade those concerned to accept that anyone belonging to a licensed establishment could copy a class reference wherever he or she happens to go, within the extents permitted as fair dealing at his or her particular location. A possible reason for rights-owner reluctance is the lack of inclusion of such copied material in periodic sampling of a particular institution's copying. But, during a sampling period, it could be required either that copying be restricted to campus, or that students should report extra-mural copying. However, considering the relatively tiny proportions of the whole copying total which are involved, even the latter would seem an unnecessary piece of pedantry. If the CLA gathered reading lists (8.39) instead of using sampling, there should be no difficulty like this. The problem certainly needs resolving for, apart from the obstruction presented to education, this sort of situation can damage honesty among users of copyright materials as well as proper respect for copyright in general.

Clippings/topic files

The following sections draw together many questions which have been raised about the legality of keeping files of photocopies, or clippings files which contain some photocopies as well. There are several levels.

15.15 Clippings

Clippings in the true sense, culled from purchased or donated originals, can of course be collected by anyone. But can odd backs of pages be copied when two desired items are adjacent, or can a second copy of an item be made for another file? Any objection from a publisher would depend on the frequency of recourse to this procedure as far as their own materials were concerned, and on the size of items copied, hence objections would seem unlikely unless there is a concentration of interest on a narrow range of publications. When that is liable to occur frequently, it is normal practice to buy second subscriptions to selected titles or arrange for staff with personal copies to donate them after use. Otherwise, a second copy of a large article, especially one in an expensive journal, could be the subject of a request to the publisher or, if the organisation is licensed, a call to CLARCS (8.13). Those with a document supply licence should ensure this internal need is included. (See also 15.18 on news bulletins.)

15.16 Topic files

This refers to files of photocopies. It would be administratively punitive to order every single item even if available from publishers, yet it is essential for a library to provide so useful a service and make maximum use of expensive subscriptions. One interpretation of the Act, on archival or replacement copies (6.33), might allow the compilation of topic files, containing photocopies of originals which are kept wholly or mainly for reference on the spot, by nonprofit-based libraries if it is not reasonably practicable to purchase copies of the items concerned. The basis would be the preservation of the originals from damage. There could however be objections unless the files were themselves kept for reference only and the originals were only accessible, if at all, on a restricted basis from an archive store.

Just when is it not reasonably practicable to purchase a copy? Firstly, some might maintain that this applies when an original journal issue, for example, has gone out of print, which is a very rapid occurrence, especially with some American publishers. Secondly, if the setting up of arrangements to monitor every addition to a topic file and get permission, or purchase odd separates, would be punitively expensive in staff time as well as cost per item, purchase might well not be reasonably practicable. This could lead to less money to buy originals, whilst being of scant benefit (or even an embarrassment, depending on the cost of the publisher's accounting system per transaction) to the publisher concerned. Nevertheless, as with clippings files, those with a document supply licence should ensure that internal needs are also covered.

However, nonprofit-based libraries have another important mechanism for supplying photocopies for stock to each other. This is independent of what a given library already holds or whether the stock is for reference or loan. (See 6.38.)

15.17 Unless a file of deposited items is held on behalf of a specific research group and kept only for the members of the group, a profit-based library has no legal basis on which to compile a file of photocopies, unless permission has been received for copying for stock (see 15.59). Hence it should be ensured that library needs are included in any licence affecting the organisation in future. Meanwhile, since the activity is very important to an information service, the staff could decide to continue until the licensing scene becomes clearer, or – especially if they think the organisation as a whole may not decide to become licensed – write to each publisher whose journals are regularly taken for a form of blanket permission, since this would seem the only suitable option other than licensing.

15.18 Clippings: news bulletins

The last suggestion above is one alternative for organisations producing photocopies from newspapers and distributing copies externally. Commercial news clippings services operate on the basis of arrangements with individual publishers to supply photocopies of extracts. It may seem unlikely that many individual publishers would worry much about bulletins distributed only to selected internal staff, for often this is an alerting and source-co-ordinating procedure rather than the sole means of discovering that a particular item is in the news, for many personal copies may be around in any event. However, there is now a licensing scheme (see NLA, 8.32-8.34) which should be studied in respect of *any* news bulletin using clippings. Nonprofit-based libraries might argue in justification of their internal bulletin for their own staff that circulation of originals would cause too much wear and tear on copies due to be filed and later bound for reference (6.33). In short, discretion is required in deciding policy. Rights owners like to be asked, though preferably not for every separate tiny item! And UK newspapers are excluded from Copyright Licensing Agency coverage, although French, German and Spanish newspapers are covered.

Committee papers

15.19 *As chairman of a busy committee, I frequently feel that we sail rather close to the wind in respect of copyright. What should we do when a report needs study in committee?*

This problem affects rights owners just as much as other users of copyright materials. The legal permission of fair dealing for 'criticism or review' is of little help, for it would be undesirable to exceed the small extents regarded by rights owners as reasonable for quotation (5.29). The Government was asked to include a special provision in CDPA88 about copying followed by later destruction, but without success. Of course this is not an area of need which justifies the provision of a specific licence, though all who become licensed for other purposes should naturally ensure they are covered for such administrative purposes as well. The CLA may well add this need to their educational and industrial licences. Otherwise, some general comments are offered below, but only as opinions, for this is virtually 'uncharted territory' in spite of the need for clarity:

1) **Free copies.** When an item is a discussion paper or unpublished report of any kind, issued without a price and on limited distribution, you might choose to make the needed multiple copies if there are no security restrictions involved, subject to the last comment in (2).
2) **Publications on sale.** When publications are in print and priced, multiple copies should not be made of any *extract* beyond 'criticism or review' extents without permission or coverage by a licence. So if they are of UK origin, fax or e-mail publishers for permission.

If permission is not forthcoming, or if a publication is from overseas, or if the need is for *entire* copies and not just extracts, purchase a copy for each committee member if obtainable in time. After all, the cost probably pales into insignificance compared with other committee expenses.

If any work is out of print or otherwise unavailable within the required timescale, or the publisher cannot be contacted, or you do not have a licence and therefore cannot use CLARCS (8.13), you will need to decide whether to make the necessary number of copies. you might choose to overstamp the first page of each copy with:

For committee use only

and ensure collection and destruction of copies when the relevant study is complete.

3) **Nonprint material** (films, videos, sound recordings, off-air recordings, etc.). Once a copy has been legally obtained or made, these present only the question of whether the group viewing of a loaned or purchased copy by a properly constituted committee for reasonable purposes (i.e. not frivolous, or derogatory from a moral rights viewpoint) can be considered 'public showing' when behind closed doors. Any showing which is not educational or *private and domestic* should be treated as 'public', but a committee cannot be said to be domestic and the word 'and' is important. However, if *criticism or review* is the purpose, performance is permissible (s30). In any event, it is believed unlikely that producers of nonprint, other than broadcast or cable programme media, would complain, but it would be common courtesy, especially if the findings of the committee could be of interest to the producers, to provide them with a copy of any resultant report. If the purpose is *judicial proceedings*, anything is permitted other than the limitations in 7.9.

4) **General.** It has to be pointed out, especially in respect of the more expensive or otherwise hard-to-get items, that there seems to be an unfortunate tendency to photocopy as the easiest option. When proper preparation time is allowed, a better option may be to sit down and produce a short write-up or digest of the more important aspects, and hand round one or two purchased or loaned originals for further reference during meetings. The amount of photocopying done is probably very much less in quantity, but parallels in principle, the convenience copying syndrome whereby many photocopies of journal articles never get attention beyond filing for possible future reading which does not occur. Would not a digest get more committee attention anyway?

Computer programs accompanying books, etc

15.20 *I know that computer programs are 'literary' by definition and that, when a program appears in textual form within a book's main text or even as an appendix, it should be seen as part of the book or other literary item concerned and could be lent. But what happens when the program is in electronic form, perhaps in an envelope inside the back cover?*

The implication so far has been that the author and publisher intended even that format to be considered part of the book, unless some restriction appears which could be contractual. Now, with the advent of more extensive rental/lending rights (4.35 et seq.), the situation has been seen to need confirmation for public libraries, though academic libraries can lend anything. Already, some encouraging response from the software industry is reaching the LA/JCC/WPC (12.39). Otherwise, advice of long standing, that you would be entitled to money back if restrictions were only discovered after purchase and you didn't like them, may not apply to statutory restrictions on public lending. Whereas it *ought* to be the case that a book with nonprint accompaniment should be treatable just as a book, if you wish to be more certain of your ground in lending discs – or any accompanying item for a book, or indeed a mixed media kit – you could include on your order forms a bold-face statement such as *This order is placed on the understanding that copyright owners claim is no statutory or contractual limit on lending the material by libraries*. Existing stocks as at end November 1996 are unaffected by the new rights.

Contents pages of journals

15.21 *Can this library make photocopies of contents pages?*

The permitted extent from an issue of a periodical is one article, defined as 'any item'. The contents page or pages for one issue is believed to constitute one item. The permitted purposes of copying exclude library needs for circulation or display of contents of newly arrived periodical issues, let alone multiple copying of this kind. The author-title details of each journal article are not copyright, but a publisher has its own copyright for 25 years in the typographical layout of a page. So the answer is 'Not legally!' Therefore what you may decide to do depends on the weighing of probabilities. There are three main kinds or levels of the queried practice, as follows.

15.22 (1) *Is it harming rights owners in any way to display or circulate one copy of a contents page? (In the case of display, this might be for a closed clientele or for visitors to a public library.)*

Answer: 'Probably not'. No rights owner has ever complained – indeed, many would question whether such a transgression was worth litigation, unless someone wanted to establish a point by means of a test case.

15.23 (2) *Would it harm anyone if a library produced multiple copies of contents pages to send to selected staff in-house or in the immediate locality, instead of circulating copies of issues?*

Here, the uncertainty grows. Although, again, no complaint has emerged from publishers, some might maintain that this practice reduces wear and tear on an original, and therefore reduces the possible demand for additional copies for circulation purposes. So the answer has to be 'Some publishers may feel their market to be sufficiently damaged to complain'.

15.24 (3) *Would it cause concern to rights owners if copies of contents pages were exchanged between libraries or offices in various localities, in lieu of producing a current awareness bulletin?*

Answer: 'Probably' – increasing to 'very probably' if the copiers were profit-based libraries whose organisations were thereby less motivated to obtain a photocopying licence; and to 'certainly!' if those profit-based libraries were offering a back-up photocopying service as well (see *Current awareness bulletins*). Another aspect creeps in at this point, for the established current contents services operate by virtue of arrangements with all the individual publishers of the journals they cover. It would cut right across such arrangements if publishers tolerated the external supply of copies. Naturally, it could be argued that only a small selection of titles is covered by contents-listing services and that the above procedure would be a useful endeavour, but this is of course no defence, only an excuse. It goes without saying, then, that if you published your own current contents service without permission by photo-reducing contents pages, and did not desist immediately if so requested by publishers, retribution might follow.

15.25 Recommendation re contents pages

Thus a library which wants to make copies, especially multiple copies, of contents pages without permission must weigh the odds, as dubious a procedure in this context as it always is at a racecourse. There appear to be only two sure ways to win. The first is to write to each publisher whose journals are taken and ask them for permission – if you chose to do that, you could ask them at the same time about their views on clippings/topic files (see that problem, below). The second is to re-key, since the information itself is factual (subject to provisos concerning databases). A profit-based library in an organisation which seeks licensing should ensure that its own needs are licensed as well as those of the rest of the organisation.

Current awareness bulletins

15.26 *We subscribe to around 300 journal titles in a specialised field. Can we publish current awareness bulletins of selected articles for others interested in this field?*

Author-title-source details of articles, like those of any copyright material, are not copyright in themselves. Anyone, whether a library or not, can provide a current awareness service containing such data, without any worries provided the data are keyed in again and not photocopied (see *Contents pages*, above). This is a well-known and important in-house form of information service. But other questions arise which need answers here, even though you have not asked them:

15.27 *Can abstracts be included?*

If they are author-abstracts, published along with articles, 'Yes, at present, if you key them in'. This is a legal permission (6.43) unless a licensing scheme is available (and none has appeared as yet), but the permission does not embrace typographical layout. If the abstracts are from a published abstracting service, there is certainly copyright in the typographical layout and photocopying must not be carried out for this purpose. There will also be copyright in the abstracts themselves if the abstracting service has not simply used author-abstracts, and you cannot know which is which. It is also very probable that there will be database right in the service used as source. However, you could produce your own 'abstract of an abstract', or devise your own short 'descriptive abstract' based on the information gleaned about the main purpose, size and target readership, etc. of an article from its abstract, provided you acknowledge the source. (One acknowledgement per bulletin per abstracting service so used would of course suffice, usually in a note at the end.) Of course, there is nothing to prevent you from producing your own abstract anew, with your own copyright in it.

A related enquiry is as follows:

We want to copy all author-abstracts but find that, in several of the more important and expensive foreign journals which we take, the publisher prints a prefatory notice which forbids any copying at all, not just copying of the typographical layout. Also, at the beginning of every article, each author-abstract, as well as the article itself, is accompanied by a prominent publisher's © notice.

The publishers clearly hold copyright in the typographical layout of an author-abstract. General notices are of course phrased so as to apply to the world market. In any event, it is possible that the publishers believe, because they have acquired all rights in an article from the author, that they can forbid copying of the content of an author-abstract. There is nothing to support this view in UK law, which provides a statutory permission regarding the content only (see 6.43). At present (i..e. no licensing scheme as yet), you are permitted to key in the content of an author-abstract but not photocopy or scan in the typographical layout. This applies to journals received from anywhere, since it is UK law which governs.

15.28 *Can a photocopying service be provided as back-up?*

This is not only the point at which libraries have to be separated from non-libraries, but also the juncture at which to separate profit- based libraries from nonprofit-based. Only nonprofit-based libraries are legally authorised to provide a copying service to the public – that is, as compared with ad hoc or isolated instances of requests for copying under fair dealing on behalf of someone, or as compared with in-house service by a profit-based library, also under fair dealing.

15.29 Recommendations on back-up copying

(a) Profit-based libraries which want to provide a back-up copying service should seek a 'document supply' licence from the CLA, or clear individual items via CLARCS (8.13) if their organisation has a standard CLA licence already.

(b) A nonprofit-based library which wishes to provide a back-up copying service beyond its normal area of service commitment (the commitment for which the whole service is run), is recommended either to act as per (a) or to consult on details. In any event, declarations must be signed before copying and the other conditions of permitted library copying apply (6.13).

(c) If a nonprofit-based library wishes to be able regularly to exceed the copying norms, it should act as per (a) and seek a document supply licence from CLA. If occasions of excess need are sporadic, one could either use BLDSC's cleared copy service (8.10) or another licensed agency, or ask publisher permission.

(d) Organisations or independent information workers which are not libraries but wish to provide a back-up copying service to current awareness, or to an abstracting service, should seek a document supply licence from the CLA.

See also notes on news bulletins in 15.18.

Declaration forms

15.30 *One particularly common question is: 'Can we send forms out along with copies for them to be returned duly signed?'.*

The British Library, because the vast majority of its photocopies are supplied remotely, has been able by agreement to transfer responsibility for obtaining and keeping a declaration to the recipient library, via its regulations relating to document supply. As most libraries have an internal interlibrary request form which in any event contains a declaration, this procedure saves administrative costs for the BL whilst causing no particular problem for recipients.

All other libraries or archives which copy are governed by regulations which specify two kinds of declaration by a person wanting a copy for research or private study, one for published material and the other for unpublished (6.51). The forms not only bind the enquirer but also protect the library or archive which copies. They must be signed before copying, otherwise control could not be exercised when necessary and the copying organisation's responsibility would therefore play no part. (See also 15.39 on electronic signatures.)

15.31 Filing

Many people ask 'Do we really have to file the forms indefinitely?'

The relevant statute of limitation for documents such as copyright declarations for research or private sudy copying is six years, so forms have to be kept for that period as a minimum. However, the Act does not specify any means of storage, and there is no record of anyone having been asked to produce particular forms. Accordingly, the simplest possible storage method would appear to be parcelling into chronological blocks, with a note to destroy at a given future date. When copies are made under other statutory permissions, such as maps for planning, or judicial enquiries, etc., a modified declaration (see 6.51) should be obtained from a requestor, and this should be filed for at least twelve years. Librarians should understand that the purpose of a declaration is to protect them against infringement accusations, hence the forms are important and should always be stored by the library which actually copies (except the BL, 15.30 above). But self-service copying does not require declarations (15.33).

15.32 Items covered: more than one?

Some ask whether more than one item can be covered by a single declaration.

The wording of a declaration (6.51) clearly implies its use for only one item, since deletion of inapplicable wording is specifically indicated. However, in principle it should be possible to adapt the wording, which is not insisted upon as 'set in concrete'. The actual regulation in SI 1989/1212 requires the declaration to be substantially in accordance with the form provided. There would seem to be nothing against modifying it to cover more than one item, making the faxing of declarations much more feasible in cost terms (see 15.39). Should any request be impossible to fulfil at the time, it could easily be deleted, of course. But a declaration should certainly *not* be made open-ended to allow details to be filled in after copying – it must relate to the copying requested and be received by the copying staff before copying.

15.33 Self-service copying also?

Others enquirers are unclear as to whether forms are needed for self-service copying.

The forms apply *only* to situations where control of the copying is exercised by library or archive staff. Users of self-service equipment are required to follow notices beside machines, as reinforced by access regulations (6.31).

Document supply from abroad

15.34 *We receive copies of journal articles from document supply services in countries X, Y and Z. We accept e-mail requests for users of our own nonprofit-based library service for copies, and get declaration forms signed when they receive copies from us. Moreover, what about electronic supply from overseas and transmission through a network to our users? By what nation's laws are we bound, the UK's or those of the supplying countries concerned? And, of course, we need to know whether those laws permit our actions.*

Your actions are governed by UK law. It is assumed that you are re-copying document copies supplied by licensed agencies abroad, but what is to be said applies also to UK document supply agencies. Note however, that a number of agencies, including BL and UnCover, prohibit further copying of a document supplied, although as remarked elsewhere (for example, in connection with BL's 'cleared copy' service), it would seem in order to allow fair dealing singles when copies have been acquired legitimately for stock. However, if you have signed a contract of some form with the supplier, it must be honoured until revised, but you should have ensured that it did not seek to exclude statutory permissions. If you hold a CLA licence, for example for educational copying, you may find that it allows copying, whether single or multiple, from *any* material held, including photocopies legally acquired for stock – but recipients can only be members (including students) of a licensed establishment.

As a nonprofit-based library service, there is nothing in the Act to prevent you from supplying hard copies for research or private study in response to requests, provided no contractual limitations about re-copying have been passed on by the agency concerned. But declarations must be signed before copying is done. Faxed forms, returned signed, will suffice. Fax could also be used to send a hard copy of an article, when copying is permissible, provided no more than a single copy results – such as keeping a copy or set of copies for faxing to someone else – a copy made just for that purpose should be destroyed after faxing. (But see 15.45 re a file copy as record of the action.) You must not assume a parallel here with electronic transmission through a computer or network because, while fax is seen merely as a channel of communication (15.44), scanning or re-keying into a database is electrocopying and provides the recipient with multiple copying capability, and destruction of the original after such use is of no help whatsoever.

There is no permission at present regarding your proposed networking of any material supplied electronically. Nor should you offer such a service in reverse unless appropriately licensed, whether by re-keying or downloading. Developing a database of reading list material is presumably one of your aims, and you should note that this is precisely what some eLib projects are researching, but only with rights-owner permissions during the research period. Any similar venture of yours should only be attempted after obtaining permission via publishers/database producers.

Drawing

15.35 *As a graphic artist, I produced a drawing of a toad for a friend who was writing a report on the environment, and provided a photographic negative of it – yes, it was a green toad ... Later I found that the illustration had been reproduced in a book by the head of the organisation at which my friend worked. There was no acknowledgement, and moreover the quality of the drawing had been degraded by the printer. My friend had not been approached regarding permission to use the drawing. What should I do?*

As a senior member of the organisation, the book author probably assumed that he had use of anything which had appeared in reports, the copyright in which belonged to the organisation. It was wrong of him not to check regarding illustrations, and there are grounds for complaint there – also for the degrading of the resultant printed illustration which, had it been credited, might not have enhanced the artist's reputation (see moral rights re derogatory treatment, 10.12). For now, a letter of complaint is indicated – though it will probably bring no more than an apology. For the future, it is recommended that no work be sent out without a name on it and an assertion of paternity right if commercial publication may occur (10.9; 10.19).

Electoral registers

15.36 *Many enquirers are uncertain of the position regarding the copying of electoral registers, commonly referred to as voters' lists.*

The details are in Statutory Instrument 1986/1081 which sets out various actions for the registration officer. The most relevant action relates to deposit of an inspection copy in a suitable place, usually implying a public library. Other actions include the sale of parts of a register by the local registration officer. Enquirers usually want to know to what extent the register may be copied, whether for personal purposes or the preparation of commercial mailing lists. The copyright of the register is vested in the local authority concerned, and any copying is governed by the usual permissions, and their relevant norms of extent. What, however, is a 'reasonable proportion' of a register for a library to supply to an enquirer for research or private study? It is recommended here that copying should normally be limited to the extent needed to answer an enquiry about such matters as missing relatives or friends. Otherwise, the registration officer is authorised by the above SI to supply copies of parts of the register at the rate of £2 per thousand names. His ability to prepare name and address labels automatically is strictly limited to selected authorised people. Anyone who wishes to input data from a purchased part of a register to a database should consult the local registration officer – and, since the intention may be to augment the file with protected personal data as well as just names and addresses, check with the Data Protection Registrar (see 15.37).

Electrocopying: directory

15.37 *Can we electronically scan in, or at least manually key in, a large portion of this directory in order to use it for distribution of circulars to prospective clients?*

Note that under the UK's SI in compliance with the EU Databases Directive (3.28), any directory of EU origin which has sophisticated selection and arrangement and has involved the maker in substantial investment could qualify for database right, whether it is print or nonprint. You can extract and key in selected factual data, which is after all non-copyright in itself, provided the amount extracted is insubstantial. You may be in danger of infringing copright in the compilation as a whole if too much is taken, as well as database right. You should certainly not scan in without permission – this is included in the definition of 'electrocopying', which in this case involves constructive multiple copying of a typographical layout, since your intended input to a database could have many future uses. If you decide to put personal names and addresses into your own electronic file, and add other personal information to each entry, you should check the position regarding registration with the Data Protection Registrar (Springfield House, Water Lane, Wilmslow, Cheshire SK9 5AX, tel. 01625 53577).

15.38 It is suggested that you should get in touch with the publishers, telling them why you want the information and the approximate quantity. Their response can be obtained in writing by letter, or by use of the standard permission form (6.51) duly modified, or by fax, and any permissions should be filed indefinitely. Their answer may well depend on what kind of clients you have. If they are prospective students on short courses, for example, few publishers would cause any hindrance to your work. If they were junk mail recipients, the publishers may want some compensation for any scanning for input, bearing in mind that the selling of mailing lists has become big business. Rights owners like to be asked, though desirably not for every tiny instance of photocopying, of course, which many prefer to leave to fair dealing or the CLA. They are usually most understanding and helpful, particularly in respect of medical, educational, charity or social welfare needs.

Electronic signatures

15.39 *Are electronic signatures acceptable for interlibrary loan applications or photocopy declarations?*

There has been much discussion on this point, for it would of course be much easier in the electronic environment. It simply is not secure enough, therefore scarcely in accord with the copyright declaration for personal signature (6.51). Allowance of use in some form or another (but certainly not PIN as some have proposed) *must* occur when an ECMS is in use. However, a specific change in the law would be needed, says the Patent Office.

Examination questions: publication

15.40 *The Act permits multiple copying for examination purposes, implying specific exams, but what if we want to publish collections of questions for general sale?*

Provided the typographical arrangement or printed page is not reproduced, quotations of small extent with due acknowledgement in exam questions could be regarded as covered by fair dealing for criticism or review. However, when the amount of material included is more than just a quoted paragraph, or when diagrams or printed pages need reproduction, permission to publish must be sought by contacting each individual publisher involved.

Examination room copies

15.41 *We have learned that using material for multiple copies of exam papers is acceptable, but what if we wish to place copies of complete journal articles or book extracts, etc. on exam desks for use by candidates?*

The permission (7.2) allows *anything* to be done for setting questions or producing answers, *the only exception* being that music for *performance* by candidates cannot be copied without permission. But you could demonstrate a computer program, or play recorded music or moving image (etc) to the group if required, even if you are not an 'educational establishment'. If you have a CLA licence, you are covered anyway for hard copy within the licensed extents. If wishing to go beyond licensed extents, or if no licence is held, ensure the collection of copies after the exam, and destruction when no similar use is intended in the immediate future – otherwise, clear via CLARCS before retention by candidates.

A similar enquiry was made about a student sitting an open exam who was told that he could take up to x cm thickness (!) of documents into the exam. room with him. For that purpose he wished to make copies of two chapters, not just the licensed one, from a book which he had purchased. There is nothing in the permission (7.2) to limit it to action by the teacher. Such a student may accordingly assume permisson to make copies of two chapters (or indeed more). Those made from a source other than the book which he has bought should be either: (a) destroyed if in excess of licensed extents and total numbers for the establishment, or beyond the licence's exclusions; or (b) handed to the teacher for appropriate action, such as keeping for other students if within the licence.

A database right permission covers 'illustration for the purpose of teaching or research', excluding commercial research, but confirmation is needed as to whether this would include examination purposes (anthologies, e.g., might be affected). Meanwhile, it is advised to proceed on that assumption.

External subscribers or users

15.42 *What happens re copyright if a nonprofit-based library wants to have external subscribers?*

A profit-based library is less likely to raise the question but, if it did, the answer is the same for both. There is no reason why external users should not be allowed access to whatever facilities or services the library cares to offer, subject to the following precautions:

(a) access conditions or regulations should warn about copyright and draw attention to the notices which should always be found beside photocopying machines;
(b) if the organisation is licensed for copying, it should be made clear to external users that they must not follow the copying notice (orange) relevant to CLA licensing, but the separate notice concerning research or private study copying (see end of volume);
(c) if a staffed copying service needs to supply an extract from a database (see 3.28), this could only be made under fair dealing, but not for research for a commercial purpose. Otherwise, extraction or re-utilisation of an extract from a database could only involve an 'insubstantial part' (evaluated qualitatively and/or qualitatively).

It is advisable to have all users sign a declaration on a registration card to the effect that they will abide by the access conditions which the card contains.

15.43 Database use for external enquirers

When an online database producer is obviously under the impression that 'profit' is actually occurring in an 'information intermediary' situation, how do we proceed?

Fair dealing now applies to databases (5.6) provided a commercial purpose is not involved. Note that copying for a commercial purpose could now infringe if a substantial part is extracted or re-utilised (3.28), but a producer's notice or service contract should make this clear anyway. Otherwise, it is suggested that the producer be told the real situation, that:

(a) charges made are for search expertise and the bare cost of an online search without mark-up;
(b) the search could easily include many sources, hard copy or electronic;
(c) the lion's share of the charge is for the search expertise of the staff plus a contribution to the running expenses of the library. (See 6.3 for a definition of 'profit' in this context.)

Many producers do realise that most of their business comes through equipment held by libraries and information services. However, when online search brokerage is done by an individual who does not have other resources to hand, but only seeks to profit by selling a service from a particular range of electronic databases, the situation is different. It is then not surprising, albeit ethically uncertain, that some producers want to share any potential profit by charging a mark-up.

If a service contract limits work for third parties without making it clear that any library client can be served (since all clients could be termed third parties whether internal or external), the contract should be queried with the producer or host before acceptance. Difficulties should be notified to the appropriate professional body, or to the LA/JCC/WPC (12.39), or to a consultant.

For offline or portable databases which are subject to an updating service, wherein a service contract may forbid use for third parties, this prohibition should be interpreted as enquirers who do not attend on the spot, or else be queried with the producer.

Fax: use for supply of copies, etc?

15.44 This gives rise to a number of questions. Fax is a method of making 'facsimile copies', and these feature in the Act's definition of 'reprographic process', and reprography is at first sight a 'restricted act'. But the definition further states that the term includes copying by electronic means, but limits this to instances where the work to be copied is held in electronic form. As it happens, fax itself is excluded from the definition of 'reprographic process'. However, in a test case it seems likely that fax would be seen simply as a method of facsimile copying and therefore *included* in the definition, leaving the rider about electronic forms to apply solely to copying via fax from database to database. A library or archive is unlikely to have such problems with a single copy of permitted extent and purpose, because the Act does not specify any particular method of making 'a copy', which could be by manuscript, xerography, full photography or microphotography, or any other way of transferring the content and/or image of an original to a copy. And individuals copy mostly under fair dealing anyway.

Making a copy of an extract of a permitted extent is acceptable for the purpose of using it in a fax machine, provided only one copy is actually kept, namely that in the hands of the requester. The copyright declaration form signed by a requester (or, in the case of a nonprofit-based library urgently wanting copy for stock, a letter of request (6.38)) has to be faxed, duly signed, to the copying library before the copying is done. The form must be capable of assessment by staff for validity, otherwise the declaration could be seen as giving no protection, either to rights owners or to the copying library.

15.45 File copies of faxes?

A frequent question arises: 'Is there any way in which we can keep the copy used for faxing as a file copy?'.

The strict answer is that this would be illegal when only a research or private study copy for an individual has been permitted, because the file copy would become an infringing copy, capable of repeated use to create further infringing copies. However, if the copy used for faxing were defaced, for example, by overstamping to forbid use other than filing with enquiry records, this might constitute a defence in the most unlikely event of a publisher basing an infringement case on a single file copy kept for the sole purpose of removing the need for re-location of an item in the library's stock which might have been loaned or damaged or lost since faxing. Such re-location would be necessary in cases of follow-up enquiries about, for example, citations in the item copied.

It would be entirely a matter for the copying library to decide whether the likelihood of such follow-up enquiries would be sufficient to justify the trouble of arranging to overstamp the file copies and keep them in one place, thus taking reasonable precautions against misuse.

A factor in favour of the publishers, if one did bother to bring a test case, would be the availability of alternatives – for example, obtaining a copy for stock from another library if the organisation is nonprofit-based, instead of keeping illegal file copies. However, a possible response to that by the defence could be the consequent delay to an enquiry. But publishers themselves use fax and understand these problems, hence this question might be an unnecessary source of concern. These considerations suggest the conclusion: if you must keep the copies, strike through at least the top page of each, and put it in a box which is emptied at intervals into the w.p.b. – otherwise, put them directly into the bin!

However, an academic library with a CLA licence would have no problem keeping a file copy, even for re-copying for the institution's own staff and students, because such a use is embraced by the higher education licence within the maximum allowed. A profit-based library should either: (a) ensure that it is covered by the parent organisation's photocopying licence for situations of this kind, including the keeping of clippings or special topic files of photocopies for reference, and other desirable library activities, or (b) obtain a cleared copy for its files from the British Library's licensed service, or get permission from a publisher, or through CLARCS when its parent body becomes licensed.

Framed?

15.46 *My daughter, dispirited by the employment situation, decided to set up her own business, framing and selling posters and art prints. When visiting a supplier of prints recently to negotiate bulk rates of purchase, she was refused purchase and told: 'You can't do that! We ourselves have an outlet for framing and selling prints and we have the copyright on that work!' Is my daughter breaking the law?*

Anyone can set up a business to do what your daughter is doing, without reference to the seller of the prints or posters which are framed. The supplier concerned appears to know little of the law, or else was attempting to apply a little discouragement of competition, though this would amount to his own form of 'restrictive trade practice'. There is normally no 'copyright' in picture frames, and in respect of moral rights it is unlikely that your daughter would frame a picture in such a manner as to conceal an artist's name or cause 'derogatory treatment' of his work. Only if your daughter were copying some frames of a distinctive design which were currently protected under Registered Design Right (or by a patent for special parts designed for ease of assembly), might the supplier have any cause for complaint. Unfortunately, this advice cannot help to persuade him to allow cheap bulk rates for his prints and posters!

Hypertext Markup Language (HTML)

15.47 *Is a page in HTML copyright? That is, not just the contents, but the format itself? I have seen some pages labelled 'copyright', but know of nothing to support that claim in the law. Some have even claimed that HTML text is a computer-generated work which is original and hence copyright.*

Without a test case, should anyone think it worth the enormous cost of bringing it to court, there are perhaps more questions than answers. Views are offered:

(a) The original computer program containing HTML codes and controlling their insertion is copyright as a literary work, likewise the several elements of a hierarchy of programs from high-level to compiler to machine code. (The machine code produced by a compiler automatically has also been said to be a computer-generated work.)

(b) If a page formatted through HTML format is really an original computer-generated copyright work, then every application of every computer program used for printed layout could arguably be claimed as copyright also. If credence be given to that, might chaos follow?

(c) However, if someone were able to separate out and copy the HTML software itself, this could infringe the programmer's rights.

(d) The textual content of a page, with or without HTML, could be copyright both in itself and as part of a compilation (and could become subject to *sui generis* right as well, see 3.28).

(e) Codes used in HTML which are peculiar to the program could be held to be copyright when they form part of the whole program but not individually.

(f) Were the HTML software to produce an unpredictable and *original* result in terms of perceivable record (not manipulation capability, which is not a copyright concept; nor codes which are not displayed) rather than one which could be achieved manually, then it might be possible to argue that such a result is an original work. However, if there were indeed originality, surely it would be due to the human input which created the original layout? That layout could be manually tagged and keyed, or a document produced with the desired layout could be scanned, software such as HTML Assistant then being used to interpret the wordprocessor positional codes and produce HTML codes.

(g) Conclusions: This is computer manipulation, not generation, using copyright software. Even if it be established in future that there is such a thing as copyright in page layout, it is difficult to see how HTML results could be seen as original. However, a court may have to decide!

Implied licence and the Web

15.48 *We are told that, in some circumstances, for example when a situation is clearly comparable with one which is known to be covered by permission, one can assume 'implied licence'. Then there is the email 'free for all' where many Netizens have passed on messages in various ways, although automatically copyright. If a document has been put on to the Internet, is there an implied licence to download?*

This would clearly be 'electrocopying' (see 3.45) and no such licence should be assumed. Deciding what requires permission and what does not is likely to remain difficult, especially with news items, but care should be taken. Acknowledgement of source should always be made, whatever is done. Copyright does not need to be 'claimed' in a notice, though it is desirable that anyone contributing material of worth should include some kind of copyright notice (see 3.49) for the sake of clarity and to aid assessment of copyright currency. This is an electrocopying situation, and there should be no assumption of implied licence. However, one could use agreed procedures within groups making regular contact. Note that fair dealing for research or private study (but not for commercial purposes) now applies to database right, under which there is no distinction between print and electronic databases.

Lectures: recordings

15.49 *Some lecturers in our department have begun to produce tape cassettes of their lectures, sometimes also transcripts, which they deposit in the departmental library for students to borrow. The aim is to reduce the risk of timetable clashes. Undoubtedly, students are copying tapes and/or transcripts. Three questions arise:*

- *(a) Who is the copyright owner, the lecturer or the establishment?*
- *(b) Does either the lecturer or the establishment give tacit permission for student copying by virtue of making recordings and transcripts available in this way?*
- *(c) Should we develop a policy on this matter?*

Any organisation is entitled to first ownership of copyright in work by employees under 'contract of employment' (see 4.2). All your staff will be under such contract, whether as reinforced by conditions of service known before appointment and made contractual by signing to accept an offer of a post, or simply by signing acceptance when the offer letter has made clear the necessity of abiding by official regulations and conditions of service. Most establishments have conditions of service which allow staff complete freedom in respect of literary work for publication and enjoy any economic benefits of authorship. Increasingly, some are realising that they need a 'catch-all' for work by staff and students alike (see 4.56) to permit intervention, if necessary, in respect of audiovisual materials and computer programs commercially sold, etc. produced by using establishment equipment with the help of colleagues. It is advised that conditions of service referring to lecture material should make clear that, whilst publication of literary material is entirely up to the author, the establishment may wish to use lecture notes and related materials in other contexts, especially when incorporating research results. Staff should also be warned not to include copyright material of others without permission (e.g. by educational licence).

Tacit permission, you ask? Pardon the levity, but this reminds me of the cartoon of a tutor making an all-too-rare personal appearance at a classroom door to check on playback of his tape. Instead of rows of students listening to his cassette being played back, there are rows of little tape recorders. Seriously, when materials are placed in a library without any special conditions of access, the students may be pardoned for assuming that they may be copied, so tacit permission may be assumed. But lecturers should take care that their copyright is reserved in the event of a future wish to publish. Accordingly, it might be a good idea to have a general label on all relevant items with something like:

> © *by ___, 1998 of Department ___. This cassette/these notes contain copyright material and may only be copied by students and other members of the establishment on condition that copies are for research or private study and should not be distributed externally without asking the author or departmental head.*

Perhaps the above is a sufficient answer, inter alia, to question (c) about policy. But the communication problems of any large educational establishment may undermine your efforts. Firstly, it may take up to a year or so just to get regulations made or altered via the levels of staff-student committees or staff working parties on conditions of service. Then, after a further year or less, few will recall the development of a policy at all! This reinforces the desirability of using a label on all items as proposed above, in this case as a 'fail-safe' attempt.

Letters

15.50 News publication

Several years ago, a letter written by a member of the Royal Family got front-page coverage in respect of a fairly delicate situation. It transpired subsequently that pemission to publish had neither been asked nor received. Wasn't this infringement of copyright? If so, why didn't they sue?

On the basis of these details, infringement would probably have occurred in respect of other people, not only the Royal Family. In terms of everyday diplomacy, however, it is often better to assume a low profile on delicate matters to avoid exacerbating the situation. Goodness knows what the Royal Family has suffered in recent years, but these remarks would apply to anyone at all. Worse, though, is the reluctance – indeed, often inability – of the average person in this position to afford to sue, bearing in mind the enormous costs of legal proceedings and the risk of losing the case. One hopes, of course, that professional integrity will deter journalists from taking advantage.

15.51 Other publication

I am compiling an account of a court case involving a bank robber who is at present under a very long sentence. Despite what he said in court, he has written a series of letters addressed personally to a cousin of his. It would help my book considerably, I think, if I could reproduce selectively any parts which might throw further light on his descent into crime and his general honesty and character, including his statements at the trial, wheren I was a witness for the prosecution. The cousin has given all the letters to me for the purposes of my book. My questions are:

(i) can I extract as I see fit?

(ii) whilst I realise that his reputation could not be further damaged, that of the cousin might possibly be affected. Do I need permission from the author of the letters as well as that already given by the cousin?

The situation which you outline is almost entirely beyond my area of interest and experience. All I can do *directly* is state:

1) Copyright in letters belongs to the writer, unless transferred to someone else. The act of sending a letter to a relative as addressee does not constitute any transference of rights, actual or implied. Hence publication requires permission of the right holder except in certain circumstances which I do not think would apply to you in this instance. For example, statutory permission to use any material for judicial proceedings applies (by Law Society agreement) to proceedings in progress rather than a closed case.

2) An author has a moral right to '*object to derogatory treatment of a work* (CDPA88, s80), where 'treatment' means '*any addition to, or deletion from or alteration to or adaptation of the work ... the treat-*

ment of a work is derogatory if it amounts to distortion or mutilation of the work or is otherwise prejudicial to the honour or reputation of the author …'.

On other aspects, and entirely without prejudice to properly qualified legal advice, I offer the following as points which occurred to me whilst reading your letter:

(a) Surely, any new light on the trial should be discussed in detail with experts and/or police?
(b) When someone writes to a close relative, believing it to be in confidence, might his words differ somewhat from something written or said in defence?
(c) The utility of 'proxy' permission from a relative may be questionable.
(d) You say you realize that, while his reputation cannot be further damaged, that of his cousin could. There are two points here: (i) I doubt if a court could be guaranteed to agree in respect of possible defamation of the author; and (ii) his cousin may have had no clear idea of your intentions. For example, he might have thought publication would excuse the bank robber's behaviour in some way; thus the law of confidence might be invoked.

Those are my reasons for suggesting that you should seek expert legal advice unless acting with written permission from the author before extraction of content and publication in your own context. The Law Society of England and Wales could refer you to an appropriate expert. (Law Society address: Records Department, Ipsley Court, Berrington Close, Redditch B98 0TD).

Mixed media

15.52 *Otherwise known as 'media packs', these are found mainly in the education and training field. A text portion may be accompanied by a sound tape and/or a computer program diskette, or a videotape, or more expensively a CD-ROM disc. If I make copies of my packs available externally, how much protection is given by copyright?*

Each medium carries its own copyright. Firstly, it reflects copyright in the content. Secondly there is copyright in each physical medium, except CD-ROM which only reflects rights in the content. When a CD-ROM is updatable at intervals, many producers use contracts to limit use for third parties by which they should be taken to mean enquirers other than the normal catchment area or other local clientele. Thus you may wish to protect a CD-ROM via conditions of sale at least, if it is desired to limit its use to the purchaser's own use only. In respect of the copyright in the content of the separate media, vested in the authors for 70 years beyond the year of death, presumably the right to publish in a multimedia pack will have been assigned to the questioner.

The enquiry must also be concerned with whether a pack is a 'compilation', defined as a literary work, and an opinion is offered as follows. 'Literary' includes any work which is written, spoken or sung. Therefore, each medium which contains text or spoken literary material, is at least partially literary. Computer programs are 'literary' regardless of physical format. Tables are also literary. On that basis, all the media in a multimedia pack should qualify to some degree as literary works, and there would seem reason to regard the whole pack as a 'compilation'. Irrespective of the works contained in the separate media, the copyright in the compilation is vested in the compiler for 70 years beyond the year of his or her death. However, should no personal name of a compiler appear on the pack, it would be assumed to be anonymous and carry copyright for no more than 70 years beyond the year of publication. Under the new database right (3.28) it should be noted that many compilations will be definable as databases whether in print or electronic format, and that a copyright permission under CDPA88 may be overridden by database right when anything more than an 'insubstantial part' is involved.

Online services

15.53 *We have been reminded by one of the online services that their service contract does not include 'third party' supply – yet this is a library with no other purpose than to assist what they call a 'third party'. How do we stand?*

Firstly, it is suggested that you ask service providers to regard your users as effectively 'joint second parties' with you! Secondly, this sort of comment is not unusual and has been known to occur when an online database producer has the impression that 'profit' is ocurring in an intermediary service. Thirdly, it is recommended that they be told that the service is primarily for in-house use, but may be used at times for extra-mural enquiries –

but any charges made are for search expertise, plus the bare cost of an online search without mark-up (plus other points listed in 15.43).

See 6.3 for a definition of 'profit' in this context.

Many producers do realise that most of their business comes through equipment held by libraries and information services. But this does not stop some others from trying to create novel forms of right by contract, with resultant confusion among the user community. When online search brokerage is done by an individual who does not have other resources to hand, but only seeks to profit by selling a service from a particular range of electronic databases, the situation is different and it is perhaps not surprising, albeit ethically uncertain, that some producers want to share any potential profit by charging a mark-up.

Page layout copyright?

15.54 These notes follow on from the last problem above. Some people have claimed that a CD display and printout is copyright as a typographical layout, despite the fact that there is no copyright in the electronic record. The argument is apparently based on the fact that the formating software is copyright, therefore... etc. This could take one into the definition of 'published edition' and how to decide what that constitutes in an electronic context. It would also beg the question as to whether there really is such a thing as 'page layout' copyright as well as that in typographical arrangement. Those who wish to claim page layout copyright might first consider the Act's omission of showing/performing right in respect of artistic works. A publisher's copyright in the typographical layout of a published edition may be regarded in effect as an exception, brought about by the 1956 Act. Users who deny page layout copyright in a printout will no doubt continue to point to the fact that the printer concerned is subject to local control. Further EC harmonisation may deal with this matter before long, and may be expected to rule that there is no difference between a printed work and one in electronic format, hence that publisher's right applies. Nevertheless, should contractual terms apply, we must always remember that 'Contract rules, OK?'.

Performance of recordings

15.55 *Our audiovisual collection has just about enough space for a hi-fi listening booth. How do we stand in respect of copyright if we install one?*

You must of course be referring to a public library, since the sound recording industry is unlikely to license any other organisation to lend to the public. For a booth, the UK's fair dealing for 'research or private study' would be unlikely to apply because that excludes sound recordings and films. Some might think that fair dealing for 'criticism or review', with its wider coverage, could apply (9.1), but: (a) both words imply the written or published nature of resultant 'criticism or review', which is unlikely to be the predominant aim in your case; and (b) the extent played back might be sufficient to make recording companies believe that their market was being damaged, so an expensive defence might need to be mounted if infringment were alleged.

The right concerned relates to playing, performing or showing in public. If the booth were not adequately sound-proofed, you would very probably be performing a recording in public when the library were open. However, with a small sound-proofed booth with room for only one or two persons, would you be performing a recording in public? Public performance does not on the face of it imply performance by or for one individual, or even a small group, in an environment which might be circumscribed in some way so as to be capable of being claimed as 'domestic'. But a succession of individuals might be judged to add up to 'public', especially if playback were allowed to be sufficiently extensive as to make a purchase less likely. Control by way of a time-switch is feasible, but what interval should apply, if the notion were acceptable at all to rights owners? Should you decide to proceed with the idea, it is suggested that PPL and PRS be consulted and/or legal advice be sought.

Rights owners would need to weigh the show-room or on-approval function which could *increase* sales against the risk of *losing* sales through sampling of large segments, or of happening upon a displeasing passage which could be unrepresentative of the whole. Sound recordings are lent by public libraries under the BPI free licence (4.47), and that action is suggested as being less hazardous than providing a listening booth. Even if licensed, such a booth could lead to disturbance for other users and even queueing by those listeners who just wanted a 'quick fix' of pop!

Performances: videotaping

15.56 *Our local dramatic society duly obtained clearance for the public performance of a play. The town newspaper's critic raved about the quality of the production, especially the acting and the scenery. But we find that an amateur camcorder owner had videotaped our efforts in sound and vision. Now, a further education programme producer wants to broadcast large segments of the videotape as examples of what can be done with limited local facilities and amateur though enthusiastic actors. What is the copyright situation?*

The camcorder owner had no permission or licence from you, in respect of each performer's own copyright in the live performance, to make a recording. It is of course the society's decision as to whether even to allow the camcorder to retain the recording illegally made, or whether to insist on its erasure. Best to view it before deciding, to assess its quality and whether it does justice to the society in terms of moral rights. At least, the camcorder owner could be told that he requires the society's agreement to enter into a broadcasting contract – or indeed any public showing or any further commercial use of the recording – in which agreement the society may wish to claim the greater share of any benefit.

Permission-seeking

15.57 *When we ask publishers for permission, the response is sometimes by 'phone? Is this appropriate?*

Whilst duly appreciative of the desire of a publisher to be of help by responding by 'phone, you are advised to beware of relying on unwritten permissions no matter from whence they come. Whether you do so or not will depend on the nature of your request and your intended purpose. Generally, though, you should send, by mail or fax, a request in a form such as that suggested in this book (6.51), which aims to make written response as easy as possible. And permissions (to publish) should be filed indefinitely. You may suffer occasions when, through urgency and inability to trace a copyright owner, a decision must be made whether to go ahead or not. In such cases, you may decide to go ahead, but make due apology and recompense (if necessary), should your action bring reaction from an owner! If publishing, prefatory notes, as recommended for collections of photographs (15.64) on work done to trace owners unsuccessfully, are advised – and naturally your files should be permanent in that respect.

Photocopies

15.58 Copies of photocopies

It is commonly said that it is illegal to photocopy a photocopy. Is this always the case?

This is one of many situations in copyright which require care and the consideration of specific circumstances, underlining the need for every organisation using copyright media to any significant extent to have a senior staff member who is knowledgeable about copyright. As a general rule, note that when a copy is made legally, you should always record the source but do not need to act as though the copy is still integral with its original context, such as a compilation or database (but source details should be given). Some extracts, however, may be claimed to be complete works, such as periodical articles taken out of their 'issue' context, and new database right (3.28) would in any event apply to a compilation which is a database with substantial investment in its making.

15.59 Stock copies

Any library or archive which receives a photocopy from elsewhere with permission for addition to its library stock is fully entitled to regard it as just like any purchased original. There is in fact no obvious reason why the library's staffed copying service, or anyone else, should not make a single copy of such a photocopy for research or private study, desirably within recommended copiable norms, since fair dealing could apply to a whole work. If copied by self-service and therefore under fair dealing, which has no specific legal limits other than single copying, there is of course the possibility of a publisher challenge on the grounds of unfairness. A challenge might arise, should a case be thought worth bringing at all:

(a) if any library were in the habit of making a copy from its own stock for its own stock without permission, otherwise than by a nonprofit-based service as archival or replacement copying as permitted (6.33) or

(b) if the service were profit-based and hardline publishers attempted to win their claim that a periodical article is a complete work in itself as far as a profit-based service is concerned, and therefore that only the re-copying of 5 per cent of the whole article would be regarded as 'fair' (5.14).

Any organisation might be accused of infringement if its library had a policy of collecting photocopies which were originally made for research or private study in order to add them to stock. Any such practice should cease as soon as the organisation concerned obtains a licence for other purposes which can also embrace this sort of need, in similar manner to the licensed coverage of academic 'short loan' or 'reserve' collections of extracts (see also 15.67).

Provisos:

(1) Care should be taken about the licensed maximum of multiple copies. In a university, it would be allowable to re-copy a stock photocopy of the licensed extent, provided the total number of copies made did not exceed the relevant student class numbers. In the CLA's industrial licence, firms may not exceed 9 licensed copies (plus a tenth fair dealing copy) of any item. As most batches of 9 are likely to be made at the same time, this means avoiding making further photocopies of the licensed copies, though it is difficult to see how this could apply in practice.

(2) The BLDSC cleared copy service prohibits the making of a copy from that supplied. This is despite its having been described as cleared, and capable of addition to library stock, thus creating an anomalous situation. Whilst in general any stock copy may be treated just like an original as stated above, any contractual limitation such as this must be upheld, especially as the BLDSC charge and royalty element is per copy per item. Again, however, it is difficult to see how fair dealing copies could be prevented. And a BLDSC copy which arrives in a licensed environment should be governed by the licence as in (1), and the licensor should be asked by anyone in doubt.

15.60 Infringing copies

Some parts of 15.59 need to be balanced by considering the purpose for which permission is given to make a copy in the first place. CDPA88 makes it clearly illegal, for example, to re-copy a copy made for use in judicial proceedings for any purpose unconnected with those proceedings. The Act's s27 specifies certain permissions under which copies may be made, but indicates that a copy becomes an infringing copy if made under permission for one of the named purposes and used for another. (See 15.59 about donation of research or private study copies to libraries.) However, researcher A can show a photocopy to researcher B even though he or she has promised not to supply a copy of it to any other person. This must remain as part of the flexible nature of collaborative research. But, if B then makes his or her own copy as self-service, that will be done under fair dealing where a declaration is not required. And, as B's purpose is as much research or private study as A's, why worry? In any event, there could be nothing against a research team sharing a common filing system which would include photocopies made for research or private study if the file is not accessible to researchers outside the team.

15.61 Photocopy licensing

Some profit-based bodies have asked 'What if a publisher tells us to contact the CLA because it is handling all requests? And then, upon approaching CLA, what if we are told that our only option is to take out a full licence, or else pay an exorbitant amount for permission to copy?'

Firstly, in assessing what amount may be 'exorbitant', you should regard as a theoretical maximum the purchase price of an original, minus the cost of copying and of any downgrading compared with the original (such as no colour), provided the original is still in print. If the item is out of print, one would expect a much lower price if the material is accessible anyway in libraries.

Secondly, however, it is not at all clear why you should apparently think a responsible agency capable of stooping to a policy of telling you that a full licence is your only option, even if your need is occasional, or of creating an exorbitant price deliberately in order to encourage your compliance. Treating the question as purely hypothetical, therefore, my answer is that, should any agency appear to take such an action, first get confirmation directly from the chief executive. Then, if confirmed, report the matter to your professional body for appropriate action, such as appeal to the Copyright Tribunal, or weighing of the position in respect of the law on restrictive trade practices. In other words, in the most unlikely event of need, there would be redress. Meanwhile, you would still need to copy, and Q4 should indicate your options if remaining unlicensed.

15.62 Photocopying: self-service

If I notice someone copying disc sleeves, CD or tape leaflets, and the like, what should I do? Are we more vulnerable than usual now that we have a colour copier?

The purpose might be to give a friend details of content, or to copy some biographical notes on a composer for research or private study, or to replace an original sleeve (etc) that you have bought but which your small son has ruined with some kind of goo, and there should be no problems there. However, should the purpose be to make up an outer covering, with supporting information, for an illegal copy of a sound recording, your equipment would be used for infringement and (if you are aware of this) you might share blame. See 6.30-6.32 for precautions in respect of self-service copying machines, from which it should be clear that (a) the responsibility is that of the person copying; (b) you certainly cannot monitor everything a person does or there would be no point whatsoever in having self-service equipment; (c) but that if you happen accidentally to spot something unusual an enquiry might be made – though with care and *tact*, of course.

15.63 Photocopying notices

Why do some libraries have at least two notices beside machines? Is either going to be read at all?

Whilst it is agreed that the more notices are displayed the less attention will be given to them, there are good reasons:

(a) licensing schemes require the display of notices specific to their terms, such as the orange notice of the CLA. This is quite long and detailed, necessarily – but unfortunately so from the point of view of consultation. The associated list of exclusions, in small print and double-sided, is usually unsuitable for display but should be kept readily available to answer any enquiries;

(b) visitors to the organisation will not be covered by a licence anyway and need a separate coverage of copying for research or private study, under fair dealing for any self-service copying done;

(c) for a staffed copying service, the staff need a reminder of such single copying norms, even if it is local policy for a library to stay out of the copying of class multiples, as is the case in most universities.

In order to keep matters as simple as possible – always a relative statement – the recommended research or private study notice (end of this volume) holds to the same extents for both (b) and (c). As to whether any notice is read at all, even if it were found that no-one reads a notice, this would not remove additional reasons to (c) for displaying it: in support of the law and guidelines and against unbridled copying; as a precaution against the organisation being blamed for infringement during self-service (which needs as clear and as prominent a notice as possible at each copying point); as a check for people unaware of licensed copying; and as something to point to (and possibly base refusal of further library access on) if happening to observe a transgression when near the photocopying machines.

Photographs, anonymous: publication

15.64 *We have a collection of photographs of 19th and early 20th century views of this town. The collection was bequeathed to this library (local public branch) some years ago, and we have been asked for loan along with permission to publish. We have always assumed that the donation was accompanied by ownership rights, but have traced no supporting documentation on file. There is also no trace of a photographer, or even of the person who made the donation, who might have owned the rights. How do we stand?*

You appear to have nothing at all to go on. If a last try with any local, or county, or national photographic society, or local history group, or individual local historian, brings no evidence of copyright ownership, it is suggested that you might go ahead. This is not an uncommon problem, and there can occur such instances when, for information or general cultural reasons, an anonymous work should be published, but all reasonable efforts to trace an author or current copyright owner have failed. Not only have photographs a somewhat chequered UK history, but foreign photos can also bring problems for which there is no space here. The first step of course is to consider whether copyright might in any event have expired (7.28), but bearing in mind that extended or revived copyright may apply (2.2).

15.65 If it were a book under discussion, a deceased author with unexpired copyright might be traced, but it might still be impossible to ascertain the current owner of rights – for example, if the author had died without willing his or her rights to someone else and it is not possible to trace any heirs with whom to check. In your case of the anonymous photographs, copyright would not necessarily have belonged to the photographer under the law at the time concerned. However, in view of the period concerned, an assumption of expiry of copyright would seem reasonable.

Photographs could cause difficulties because a librarian or archivist (2.43), when receiving a donated collection of photographs, cannot know how many other copies may have been made from the negatives and located elsewhere – and perhaps even be in course of publication in some other context elsewhere. It is suggested therefore that, in this and similar cases, it would be a precaution to include in the publication a prefatory note on whatever efforts have been made to ascertain copyright ownership and authorship. (See also publication right, 4.51.)

Photographs on exhibition

15.66 *Now that photographers have copyright just like any other author, how do I proceed when I want to exhibit photographs?*

There is no right of 'showing or performing' for artistic works, so actually exhibiting is no problem. But care should be taken to accord credit. CDPA88 s78(3) specifies ways of asserting paternity right (10.19) in respect of artistic works on public exhibition. Other moral rights should also be borne in mind. And no replication should occur without permission, except a single slide for instructional purposes or a single research or private study copy.

Short loan/reserve collections

15.67 (1) *Can students photocopy a photocopy in Short Loan?*

If made legally or under CLA licence for library stock, the answer is 'yes – provided the copying is within the totals covered for the class and subject concerned'. However, that point would not apply if the copying need were unrelated to class copying purposes, and should be seen as fair dealing.

(2) *How many copies can we make for Short Loan?*

The following view is expressed without prejudice to decisions which may arise from CVCP negotiations with the CLA on this matter. As understood at present, the CLA licence allows copying for internal needs of any material held which is not excluded, up to the total relevant to the subject/classes concerned. Logically, therefore, the only limit on numbers is the latter, for a large number of copies could theoretically be placed in the collection instead of providing students with them. This would reduce the totals per item in the establishment as a whole, thus rights owners should prefer this procedure rather than have a large number of copies held individually.

(3) *Staff sometimes donate materials which include many research or private study copies. Can we add them to stock?*

The copyright declaration does not bind requestors not to pass on copies, but rights owners might be pardoned for thinking that a regular policy of accepting such items could lead to abuse through getting staff to copy and thus overcome the prohibition against a library copying for its own stock, so a regular policy of acceptance should not apply. Discretionary acceptance might apply when: (a) the item could be expected to be obtained from another library for stock in any case; (b) addition could usefully augment short loan holdings, being covered by CLA licensing and in line with reading lists, and thereby reduce further copying for that purpose. But, if all goes well, and the rights owners allow electronic storage and network supply (for example, Project Acorn, 6.49) all three questions above will become redundant!

Slide to video?

15.68 *Can we video a slide set, for example to convert a tape/slide presentation into a video?*

If the rights are all yours, or if the illustrations concerned are out of copyright, yes of course you can. Otherwise, permission is required from rights owners.

Slides for sale?

15.69 *When, as a public library, we make a slide for an enquirer, can we make copies for sale?*

If you have a DACS licence, study it and consult DACS with any queries. If not, there are six points to be made here.

(a) The norm of one transparency for instructional purposes, which appears on the suggested chart for photocopying machines (end of this volume) means just that: one copy.
(b) The purpose would include 'self-instruction', i.e. research or private study.
(c) Although that was approved by the BCC, the DACS has recently claimed that BCC has withdrawn its statement, but there appears to be no official word from BCC as yet. The DACS has been insistent that even ad hoc needs for single slides should be embraced by its licence, which is a practical impossiblity in academe for which a compromise proposal was made in 7.7. Whether or not you have an organised slide collection, you may wish to follow that. However, if you *do* have an organised collection and seek a licence, it might result in a clearer

position for all concerned if you negotiate for the inclusion of that compromise proposal in the licence arrangement.

(d) Note particularly that the preference should be to obtain commercially available slides when that is at all possible, bearing in mind however the problems of finding what is available and whether it is quite suitable for the purpose, also the time-frame involved.

(e) Having said all that, take care not to 'sell' or hire slides, apart from making a charge for one copy for local use on a similar basis to that for photocopied pages, unless you have obtained permission from the copyright owner. That person will be the artist or photographer or illustrator even if the item appears in a book, but the first enquiry should go via the publisher. DACS should be consulted when in difficulty.

(f) However, if permission has been obtained, copyright vests in the photographer who has made a slide, or your library if he or she is employed by you as a photographer and is covered by 'contract of employment' (4.2). In such a case, you can make and sell copies.

Sponsored research

15.70 *A researcher supported by a joint project with another organisation has produced a training video for operating theatre nurses on a particular medical procedure, and it could be used worldwide. A chemical company has offered to mass-produce up to 1,000 copies for free distribution to training colleges and hospital units, and urgently needs the master copy before commissioning a recording company. The other research organisation approves, but is this OK from this establishment's viewpoint?*

Has anyone checked the research contract with the sponsoring organisation, for such a body usually claims copyright in any result of the research? A possible compromise while the latter is checked, to meet an urgent need for the master, would be to send it off with a covering letter saying this is supplied on the understanding that no copies will be made beyond 1,000 or marketed commercially until a suitable form of contract has been drawn up between the parties. Note also that Government department material is no longer Crown copyright in itself, in view of the deliberate omission from CDPA88 of a former phrase relating to Crown copyright (4.7), so a Government department or establishment should be seen as entitled to speak for itself on permission for inclusion of official data in a publication when it is not labelled Crown copyright or affected by transitional provisions on this point.

Study packs

15.71 *The present CLA licence covers study packs. Are there any guidelines of their use for 'distance learning' purposes?*

If the students are yours (your institution receives payment for them and has registered them) the answer is simply 'yes'. There do not appear to be any separate guidelines on use for distance learning. If the students are *not* yours, then (a) those in other academic institutions could be supplied with a list of copies required for them to request from their own libraries; or (b) – provided you have a CLA licence – you could use CLARCS in respect of all copying, not just that which exceeds CLA terms per se. When ECMS control becomes possible, the acquisition of sources for distance learning should be greatly simplified, of course, and some eLib research projects are relevant to this sort of application.

Taped interviews

15.72 *When an interview is taped, who holds rights in the recording?*

Logically, the person recording or the organisation by which he or she is employed under contract to do this work (such as the BBC, or even the Police) should hold rights in the recording, provided it was made with the interviewee's permission. Any 'performer' has the right to give or withhold consent to the making of a recording. This could be held to include 'implied' permission when an interviewee is told in advance that taping will occur, or is talking in circumstances wherein the need for recording is commonly known (such as in a broadcast studio).

Trade catalogues

15.73 *We have an enormous collection of free noncopyright catalogues containing important technical information, and we are running out of storage space. Some sets are in multiple. We must store the essential data portions, but want to access the contents more easily than handling hard copy. Is it OK to scan in large segments of noncopyright material into our own database?*

It is thought necessary here to go beyond copyright alone and enter the realm of product information service also. Unfortunately for you, the catalogues are not really 'noncopyright'. There is the manufacturer's right as author of a compilation, plus copyright in the typographical layout. Even if the latter were the only problem, you would need nevertheless permission anyway for scanning that, because it would be electrocopying (3.45). Also, a catalogue may now be claimed to be a database (3.28 et seq.). Generally, then, you cannot assume that any trade catalogue may be copied freely. An exception would be a catalogue which contained a notice giving permission to copy any of the contents by any method. The misconception that product information brochures are public domain items, as well as usually gratis, possibly arises in part from the BL's refusal to accept legal deposit copies as part of their general entitlement to receive copies of all new copyright material, because of the quantities involved. (This is unfortunate, since otherwise a national product information system could have arisen in BL with reliably comprehensive coverage.)

What *can* you do, then? Well, you could extract factual data and tabulate it comparatively, perhaps, and these noncopyright facts could be keyed into your database (if they amount to an 'insubstantial part' in the event of database right). Or you could put your multiple sets to good use by dismantling them and grouping the information of value into hard copy topic files. If you still want to scan material in, it is suggested that you should ask every firm involved for permission. Should you go to the trouble of being selective, it would seem a pity not to act in collaboration with other interested organisations and, if that were the case, permission would probably be readily given. Note that commercially based product information systems operate under agreement with the firms involved, otherwise they could not microfilm catalogues or put them into electronic databases. This brings in the remaining option, namely, to contact such a company and ask it to provide you with a custom service (again, better shared with others interested) if their existing systems do not meet the need. After all, the manufacturers concerned may have given *exclusive* copying licences to product information companies.

Trade names and trade marks

15.74 *Are company names and trade names or marks, etc copyright?*

The short answer overall is 'They *might* be so claimed in some circumstances, if other claims failed'. Choosing a name too similar to another, or any other kind of confusion or false impressions, must be avoided for other reasons than copyright (including 14.5). Although these topics are really outside the scope of this volume, enquiries have been frequent enough to suggest a need for brief guidance here. These notes are however intended merely as pointers towards sources of expert and authoritative advice.

A UK-based company should be registered with Companies House (CH), and there are legal matters (including criminal offences) which are even more sensitive than any copyright considerations which might apply. Pamphlets in a 1997 CH series are available free of charge on enquiry to the CH's Cardiff offices, and should help newcomers to this topic. Examples are:

New companies (CHN 1)

Choosing a company name: notes for guidance (CHN 2)
The use of some words or names within a company name may be a criminal offence, and a whole range of legislation is quoted. The main aim is to avoid misleading or confusing the public, such as by misrepresenting a firm's pre-eminence or skills in a particular professional area such as medicine or dentistry.

Sensitive words and expressions (CHN 3)

Change of company name (CHN 4)
The Registrar may require change of company name, for example, if CHN 3 is relevant or if someone objects.

It may also be necessary to consult the Office of Fair Trading and/or the Trade Marks Registry, but CH should be consulted at the outset for general guidance.

15.75 Trade marks registration

The Registrar does not cross-check with the Trade Marks Registry (at the Patent Office), which should be separately searched for clashes, for example with an intended choice of name. The Patent Office provides a free pamphlet: *Registered trade marks – basic facts*, Patent Office, 1997. A Trade Marks Registry and Advisory Service is available, and a search can be made of the UK Register of Trade Marks. Whilst a quite small firm working in a restricted locality or subject area may wish to avoid the expense of registration, it should be noted that such registration protects against risk of infringement of another's registered mark or logo and consequent litigation.

Logos and icons

15.76 *Can I copy someone else's logo or icon and alter it a bit so that it is a new artistic work for me to use myself?*

A logo or other graphic design is an artistic work, as well as a trade mark in some contexts. Artistic copyright might be claimable by the rights owner if his logo were used by a company which had not registered the mark. In the event of risk to a complainant of damage to business, however, 'passing off' might well be the first choice for action (14.5). There are therefore dangers in what might be called 'graphical paraphrase' similar to those in textual paraphrase or plagiarism, and probably the key would be whether you had taken simply an idea for a *kind* of icon/logo or used the image itself to form your own. However, another danger is the risk of causing confusion through wrongful attribution being assumed by users of your work, and this – quite apart from possible 'passing off' accusations – could involve moral rights and damage your own 'image' no matter what!

Translation

15.77 *There is a frequent need for translations in my organisation. Are they legal?*

Translations are 'adaptations', the making of which is a restricted act (4.24). Thus permission should be sought via the publisher when publication of the translation itself is intended.

When a copy is required only for research or private study, however, note that fair dealing for that purpose includes 'literary' works as well as printed matter or published editions, but naturally embraces any manual copying, and does not limit any copying to a particular language. Hence such translations should be regarded as fair dealing. But it would be a courtesy to notify publishers, and any co-operative translations index which may be in vogue, to reduce the risk of duplication of expensive effort.

Trust hospital

15.78 *This hospital has assumed trust status. Does this mean that, since we aim to make a profit, we are 'established or conducted for profit?'*

It is suggested that this is not the case, firstly because one is told that trust hospitals are primarily funded by the NHS, hence any profit-based work is merely in the cost-recovery category, and secondly because mere cost-recovery should not be regarded as 'profit' unless practised as part of the activities of a commercial firm (6.3).

Videotape loans

15.79 *Can an educational establishment charge for loans of videos to students?*

See 4.35 et seq. 'Lending' by an educational establishment is specifically exempted from the new lending right. Since the definition of 'lending' involves an organisation being accessible to the public, which could be difficult to claim in respect of an educational establishment, the exemption appears to be unnecessary on the face of it. Bearing in mind that the drafting of SI 1996/2967 lacks clarity in other respects also, it is suggested that this exemption be taken merely as confirmation that the drafters thought your establishment is 'accessible to public' in a comparable sense to public libraries and the like, which would not necessarily prove it so in fact. It is recommended that you should beware of concluding that your action would be OK as long as receipts do not *go beyond what is necessary to cover the operating costs*, because that proviso only applies to an establishment which clearly *is* accessible to the public. Should you lend extra-murally to the public (if it is correct to assume that 'public' means people other than your students and staff, including parents), your action would become 'rental' if *any* charge at all were made, and permission would therefore be required to run such a service. Otherwise, there would seem to be nothing in the new law to prevent you from charging your own students and staff for loans of videos other than those made off-air, when those people are not definable as the 'public'. (Any use of tapes made off-air under ERA licence must be governed by the terms of that licence.)

Why a licence?

15.80 *This is a busy, medium-sized firm, and we have no time to fiddle about with licences which have lots of exclusions and detailed terms to follow, and cost too much anyway. We do not have a library. Can I manage without a licence?*

Many ask this sort of question. The answer depends on how much copying you do. If you only need the odd journal article or extract from a standard, you may find that fair dealing covers your needs. But under the new database right, a periodical may be considered a 'database' in printed format (see 3.28), and extraction or re-utilisation of a substantial part from a database would infringe if for a commercial purpose. However, one article from an issue would seem unlikely to be judged a substantial part of an issue containing, say, ten articles.

Copies of articles or extracts from material you do not hold, or cannot copy because they exceed fair dealing norms, can be obtained from the British Library, either as interlibrary loans via your nearest public library branch, or through the BLDSC cleared-copy or any other document supply agency (6.47 et seq.).

However, if you copy extensively and cannot see your way to reduce that, collective licensing via CLA could be the solution if the price is right. The options are summarised in Q6. Reducing the amount of copying which takes place can be done, and so can keeping within the 'research or private study' norms in Q2. The general tendency for most people is to make a copy of something they have come across, to read when time allows or to add to a private collection of useful material for future use. For many this is almost a reflex action, and in effect takes the place of reading, since much material merely sits in filing cabinets or desk drawers. You could train your staff appropriately to reduce the risk of needless and indeed wasteful copying. Whatever you do, the precautions about self-service copying in 6.31 should be adopted in full. And, if you have space for another notice near the photocopier, a slogan like 'Is your copying really necessary?' might help! However, note that all this may well change when database right (3.28) gets fully under way and perhaps becomes accompanied by new EU limits on reprography.

APPENDIX 1 – BIBLIOGRAPHY

The prime purpose of this bibliography is to list works of relevance to CDPA88 and beyond, with special reference to the UK. A number of the items listed are given as references in the text, but the reverse does not necessarily apply. Specific references in the main text are only repeated below when there is particular reason.

This Appendix contains:

1/1 Intellectual property in general
The majority of UK legal texts since 1988

1/2 Copyright and related rights, UK
Manuals and handbooks on copyright law.

1/3 Guidance for users

1/4 Guidance for rights owners

1/5 International copyright
Examples.

1/6 Design right (unregistered)
Main books.

and, chronologically arranged,

1/7 Background
Selected earlier works

1/8 Steps towards the Superhighway
Examples:
1/8.1 Multimedia
1/8.2 Information Society

Although certain works are repeated under more than one heading, readers should bear in mind that the topic of an item under a specific heading may well be treated to a useful extent in a broader work under a general heading. Most of the works in 1/1-1/4 are UK based, but several US works have been included when thought to be of possible interest. Some overseas materials are included in 1/5-1/8.

In consulting any of the items listed, readers should be prepared for differences of opinion, since copyright is by no means an 'exact science'. Where prices are available, they are relevant only to the UK, or Europe in general, unless otherwise indicated.

Currency can be roughly estimated from publication dates, compared with EC Directive dates (see App.2): for example, pre-1992 items will not contain any EC changes affecting UK law, whereas 1997 items may have been late enough in the year to take in the new database right.

No attempt has been made to compensate for the lack of specific books on certain areas, such as moral rights, by selecting articles (for which consult abstracting services) or commenting on cases (for which see various larger works, for example the *Aslib guide to copyright*).

1/1 Intellectual property in general

Bainbridge, D. I. *Cases and materials in intellectual property law*. Pitman, 1995. 0 273 60719 7

Bainbridge, D. I. *Intellectual property*. 3rd ed. Pitman, 1996. 0 273 622279 X. £27.99.

Black, T. *Practical guide to intellectual property*. Butterworths, 1989. 0 406 10140 X. £28.50.

Blakeney, M. *Trade-related aspects of intellectual property rights*. Sweet & Maxwell, 1996. 0 421 5360 6

Booy, A. and Horton, A. eds. *Sweet & Maxwell's EC intellectual property materials*. Sweet & Maxwell, 1994. 0 421 51200 8

Cabinet Office. *Intellectual property in the public sector research base*. HMSO, 1992. 0 11 430071 2. £10.50.

Coleman, A. *Intellectual property law*. Longman, 1994. 0 85121 847 4

Cornish, W. R. *Cases and materials on intellectual property*. 2nd ed. Sweet & Maxwell, 1996. 0 421 53530

Cornish, W. R. *Intellectual property: patents, copyright, trade marks and allied rights*. 3rd ed. Sweet & Maxwell, 1996. 0 421 53510 5. £48.

Cornish, W. R. *Materials on intellectual property*, ESC, 1990. 0 906214 67 X

Cotter, S. *International intellectual property law: European jurisidictions*. Wiley, 1995. 0 471 94086 0. £75.

Denton Hall. *Practical intellectual property*. Professional Publishing Ltd, 1992 onwards. Looseleaf. 0 852 58909 3. £95.00.

Department of National Heritage. *Legal deposit of publications: a consultative paper*, February 1997.

Edenborough, M. *Intellectual property law*. Cavendish, 1995. £17.95. 1 87424 147 3

Flint, M. F. and others. *Intellectual property: the new law*. Butterworths, 1989. 0 406 50307 9. £18.95.

Gare, S. *Statutes on intellectual property*. Blackstone Press, 1992. 1 85431 186 7. £14.50.

Goldstein, P., Kitch, E. W., and Perlman, H. S. *Selected statutes on international agreements on unfair competition, trademark, copyright and patent*. Foundation Press, 1997. 1 56662 492 4

Halstead, R. R. *Managing intellectual property*. ICSA, 1993. £30. 0 902197 64 9

Halstead, R. R. *Protecting intellectual property: understanding and using trade marks, patents, designs and copyright in business*. 2nd ed. ICSA Publishing, 1996. 1 872 86093 1

Holyoak, J. H. and Torremans, P. *Intellectual property law*. Butterworths, 1995. 0 406 05245 X

Holmes, N. and Venables, D. *Researching the legal web*. Butterworths, 1997. 0 406 89771 9. £45.

Intellectual property litigation yearbook. (occasional, last edition 1996), supplement to *Managing Intellectual Property* magazine (Euromoney Publications, ISSN 0960 5002, 10 issues per year, US$440)

Irish, V. *Intellectual property rights for engineers: the legal protection of innovation*. Institution of Electrical Engineers, 1994. 0 85296 850 7

Jacob, R. *A guidebook to intellectual property: patents, trade marks, copyright and designs*. 4th ed. Sweet & Maxwell, 1993. 0 421 48730 5

Jussawala, M. *Economics of intellectual property in a world without frontiers*. Greenwood Press, 1992. (Contributions in Economics and Economic History Series, no. 131.) 0 313 27620 X. £35.95.

Lloyd, I. *Information technology law*. 2nd ed. Butterworths, 1996. 0 4506 89515 5. £24.95.

Marett, P. *Intellectual property law*. Sweet & Maxwell, 1996. 0 421 55420 7

Metaxas-Maranghidis, G., ed. *Intellectual property laws of Europe*. Wiley, 1995. 0 471 95212 5

Miller, C. and Pearson, H. *Commercial exploitation of intellectual property*. Blackstone Press, 1990. 1 85431 044 5. £21.95.

Nathanson, N. *The laws of the Internet*. Butterworths, 1995. £85. 0 406 00249 5

Nichols, S. J. 'Legal information' *Managing Information* (Aslib), **3***(2)*, March 1996, pp. 27-30. (A concise guide, including databases.)

Oppenheim, C. *The legal and regulatory environment for electronic information*. 2nd ed. Infonortics, 1995. 1 873699 23 9. £45.

Organisation for Economic Cooperation and Development. *Competitition policy and intellectual property rights*. HMSO, 1989. 92 64132422. £11.00.

Patfield, F. *Intellectual property in international trade*. Leicester University Press, 1993. 0 7185 1325 8. £45.

Pearson, H. E. and Miller, C. G. *Commercial exploitation of intellectual property*. Blackstone, 1990. 1 85431 044 5

Phillips, J. ed. *Butterworth's intellectual property handbook*. 3rd ed. Butterworth, 1997. 0 406 89527 9. £65.

Phillips, J. and Firth, A. *An introduction to intellectual property law*. 3rd ed. Butterworths, 1995. 0 406 04515 1. £21.95.

Wadlow, C. *The law of passing off*. 2nd ed. Sweet & Maxwell, 1995. 0 421 50170 7. £112.

Yelpaala, K., Worley, D. R., and Campbell, D., eds. *Licensing agents: patents, know-how, trade secrets and software: conference papers*. Kluwer, 1988. 90 654 4314 2

1/2 Copyright and related rights: UK

Aslib guide to copyright. J. Phillips, managing editor; R. A. Wall and C. Oppenheim, eds. Aslib, 1994– (looseleaf) £124 per annum. 0 85142 311 6

Bainbridge, D. *Software copyright law*. 3rd ed. Butterworths, 1997. 0 406 89421 3. £40

Chesterman, J. and Lipman, A. *The electronic pirates: DIY crime of the century*. Routledge, 1988. 0 415 00738 0. £25

Copinger, W. A. and Skone James, E. P. *Copyright*. 13th ed. Sweet & Maxwell, 1991. 0 421 39200 2. £170

Cornish, W. R. *Intellectual property: patents, copyright, trade marks and allied rights*. 3rd ed. Sweet & Maxwell, 1996. 0 421 53510 5. £48

Davenport, A. N. *United Kingdom copyright: a brief history*. K. Mason, 1990. 0 85937 359 2. £49.95.

Dworkin, G. and Taylor, R. D. *The Copyright, Designs and Patents Act, 1988: the law of copyright and related rights*. Blackstone Press, 1989. 1 85431 023 2. £18.95.

Feather, J. *Publishing, piracy and politics: an historical study of copyright in Britain*. Mansell, 1994. 0 7201 2135 3. £50.

Freegard, M. and Black, J. *The decisions of the UK Performing Right and Copyright Tribunal*. Butterworth, 1997. 0 406 89549 X. £85.

Freitas, D. de. *The law of copyright and rights in performances*. British Copyright Council, 1990. 0 901737 05 4. £4.95.

Frith, S. *Music and copyright*. Edinburgh University Press, 1994. 0 7486 0481 2. £29.50.

Gendreau, Y. *Retransmission right: copyright and the rediffusion of works by cable*. ESC, 1990. 0 906214 65 3. £26

Groves, P. *Copyright and designs law: a question of balance*. Graham and Trotman, 1991. 1 85333 364 6. £91.95

Gurnsey, J. *Copyright Theft*. Aslib Gower, 1995. 0 566 07631 4. £28.50.

Henry, M. *Current copyright law*. Butterworths, 1998. 0 406 89620 8. £45.

International Federation of Reproduction Rights Organisations. *Report of the IFRRO Working Group on Electrocopying*. Chairman: Charles Clark. IFRRO, 1989

Laddie, H., Prescott, P. and Vitoria, M. *The modern law of copyright and designs*. 2nd ed. 2 vols. Butterworths, 1995. 0 406 61697 3 (set). £250.

Laing, A. R. and Fosbrook, D. *The Creative person's guide to copyright*. Butterworth-Heinemann, 1991. 0 7505 0146 9. £14.95.

Lehrmann, M. and Topper, C. F., eds. *A handbook of European software law*. Clarendon Press, 1993. 0 19 825754 6. £150.

McFarlane, G. *Practical introduction to copyright*. 2nd ed. Waterlow, 1989. 0 08 033074 6. £29.95.

MacQueen, H. L. *Copyright, competition and industrial design*. 2nd ed. Edinburgh University Press, 1995. 0 7486 0733 1. £9.95.

Marett, P. *Information law and practice*. Gower, 1991. 0566 054027

Merkin, R.M. and Black, J. *Copyright and designs law*. 2 vols. Looseleaf. Longman, 1993. 0 85121 797 4. £195.

Phillips, J., Durie, R. and Karet, I. *Whale on copyright*. 5th ed. Sweet & Maxwell, 1997. (Intellectual Property Guides.) 0 421 59380 6. £38.

Prime, T. *The law of copyright*. Tolley Publishing Company Limited (UK) and Fourmat Publications, 1992. 1 85190 180 9. £30.

Reed, C., ed. *Computer law*. 2nd ed. Blackstone, 1993. 0 85431 227 8. £18.95.

Rose, M. *Authors and owners: the invention of copyright*. Harvard University Press, 1993. 0 674 05308 7. £21.50.

Shaw, L. *The practical guide to patents, trademarks, copyright, designs*. Bilgrey Samson (Birmingham), 1996- (looseleaf). 0 950 85592 8. £26.95.

Sherman, B. and Strowell, A., eds. *Of authors and origins: essays on copyright law*. Oxford University Press, 1994. 0 19 825792 9. £35.

Sterling, A. *Intellectual property right in sound recordings, film and video*. Sweet & Maxwell, 1992. 0 42 1 45470 9. £130.

Sterling, A. *Intellectual property and market freedom*. Sweet & Maxwell, 1997. 0 421 61510 9. £30.

Stone, P. *Copyright law in the United Kingdom and the European Community*. Athlone Press, 1990. 0 485 70004 2. £45.00

Thorn, E. A. *A question of copyright: covering the 1988 Act*. 2nd ed. Jay Books, 1989. £1.50. 1 870404 05 X

Thorn, E. A., ed. *Understanding copyright: a practical guide*. Jay Books, 1989. £6.50. 1 870404 03 3

Trade and Industry, Department of. *Copyright protection for foreign sound recordings*. HMSO, 1989. 0 11 515208 3. £8.95.

Wall, R. A. *Copyright made easier*. 2nd ed. Aslib, The Association for Information Management, 1998. £32 (£26 to members). 0 85142 393 0

Young, D. *Passing off: the law and practice relating to the imitation of goods, businesses and professions*. 3rd ed. Longman, 1994. 0 7520 0033 0

1/3 Guidance for users

These introductions to or interpretations of the law are addressed particularly to user needs or guidelines by professional bodies or rights-owners or their representatives.

Library Association pamphlets

These pamphlets have been vetted by the British Copyright Council and the Copyright Licensing Agency.

Copyright in public libraries. 3rd ed. 1996

Copyright in industrial and commercial libraries. 3rd ed. 1996

Copyright in further and higher education libraries. 3rd ed. 1996

Copyright in school libraries. 3rd ed. 1996

Copyright in health libraries. 2nd ed. 1996

Copyright in voluntary sector libraries. 2nd ed. 1996

These were addressed to particular library groups, and there is considerable overlap in consequence. The first on public libraries is the most comprehensive of them all. One copy of the pamphlet relevant to a library type is at present sent free to each library which is a LA member. Similarly to the Aslib notice for display beside photocopiers, the LA offers copies of its own form of notice for sale. One of the LA guides could be used as a concise overview for a given library type, though this book should be found to update and expand on the above pamphlets, including the notes of advice on problems.

Other guidance for users

In addition to this bibliography, further user guidelines may be available on enquiry to specialist publishing groups, societies or professional bodies. Guidance can of course also be obtained from rights-owner statements on licensing, although it is recommended that key points be cross-checked with independent sources. Where such statements have been published or fairly generally distributed, they are included below.

Aslib guide to copyright. J. Phillips, managing editor; R. A. Wall and C. Oppenheim, eds. Aslib, 1994– (looseleaf) £124 per annum. 0 85142 311 6

Christian Copyright International (CCI). *Copyright: serving schools in worship*. 1994 (leaflet).

Church of England, Central Board of Finance. *Liturgical texts for local use: guidelines and copyright information*. Church of England, 1988

Confederation of British Industry and Copyright Licensing Agency. *Coping with copyright. CBI and CLA*, 1993. £10. (Report on the results of the several years of discussion which led to industrial licensing.)

Clark, C. *Photocopying from books and journals: a guide for all users of copyright literary works*. British Copyright Council, 1990. £2.50. 0 901737 06 2. (This completely supersedes the withdrawn *Photocopying and the law* (of 1965 and 1970), and *Reprographic copying of books and journals* (1985). It should also be assumed to supersede the more liberal *Photocopying from periodicals: a code of fair practice* by the Periodical Publishers Association Limited (1980) which, though never officially withdrawn, is no longer distributed by the PPA. A revision of the BCC guide may appear in 1998 in consequence of the new database right law.)

Copyright Licensing Agency Ltd. (Various pamphlets include:)

CLA (general introduction)

The Copyright Licensing Agency: what it is, what it does, how it works

Fair dealing and library privilege: copying for research and private study

Copyright concerns: a pocket directory of organisations involved in the administration of copyright and rights in performances. 1992

Actual licences are regarded as between the parties and hence unpublished in detail.

Cornish, G. P. *Copyright: interpreting the law for libraries, archives and information services*. 2nd ed. Library Association Publishing, 1997. 1 85604 168 9. £19.95.

Crabb, G. *Copyright clearance: a practical guide*. 3rd ed. National Council for Educational Technology, 1990. 0 86184 191 3. £8.95.

Crabb, G. *Copyright in education handbook*. National Council for Educational Technology. 1992. Video cassette, booklet and wall chart. 1 85379 193 8. £24.99.

Delemore, C. *Copyright explained*. RIBA Publications, 1994. 1 85946 000 3.

Design and Artists' Copyright Society Ltd (DACS). *Slide collection licensing scheme: an introduction*. 1994

Educational Recording Agency Limited. *Off-air recording for educational establishments*. 1993, (plus annual tariff statements).

European Copyright User Platform. *ECUP position on user rights in publications digitised by the library*; (and) *ECUP position on user rights in electronic publications provided by the publisher*, EBLIDA/ECUP, Brussels, 1996. (Position papers, see App. 4)

EUSIDIC. *Codes of practice and guidelines: information brokers*. EUSIDIC, 1989.

FIDDO Research Team (A. Morris et al.). *Overview of EDD research and services: FIDDO report to eLib*. Loughborough University, Department of Information and Library Studies, March 1996. (EDD: electronic document delivery; FIDDO: Focused Investigation of Document Delivery Options; see 6.50, *http://dils2.lboro.ac.uk/fiddo/fiddo.html*)

Flint, M. F. *A user's guide to copyright*. 4th ed. Butterworths, 1997. 0 406 04608 5. £40.

Her Majesty's Stationery Office. *Dear librarian: photocopying Crown and Parliamentary copyright publications*. HMSO, 1996.

Her Majesty's Stationery Office. *Dear publisher: reproduction of Crown and Parliamentary copyright material*. HMSO, 1997.

Her Majesty's Stationery Office. *Duration of copyright in Crown copyright photographs*. September 1996.

Jensen, M. B. *Does your project have a copyright problem? A decision-making guide for librarians*. McFarland & Co., 1996. 0 78640282 2

Mechanical Copyright Protection Society Limited. Various publications include the following: *Sound and vision: MCPS guide for the use of music.*

Nelson, N. M. and Nissley, M. *CD-ROM licensing and copyright issues for libraries*. Meckler Ltd., 1990. 0 88736 701 1. £19.50.

Music Publishers' Association Ltd. *The code of fair practice agreed between composers, publishers and users of printed music*. Rev. ed. MPA, 1992.

Open University Educational Enterprises Ltd. *Licensed off-air recording scheme*. 1994.

Ordnance Survey, Copyright Branch. *Copyright: reproduction of Ordnance Survey mapping for educational purposes*. Leaflets (subject to annual revision): *Copyright 1: copying for business use*; *Copyright 2: publishing*; *Copyright 3: digital map data*.

Penn, C. 'Photocopying Crown and Parliamentary copyright publications.' *Library Association Record* **92**(*2*) 1990, pp.117-118.

Performing Right Society. *Performing rights handbook*, 1994. (Contains considerable guidance on copyright, including permissions, and concise flowcharts on licensing procedures and needs.) Other PRS publications include leaflets as follows: *General copyright notes*; *Useful publications on copyright and the music industry.*

Phonographic Performance Limited (PPL). *Information sheet.*

Post, J. B. and Foster, M. R. *Copyright: a handbook for archivists*. Society of Archivists, 1992. 0 902886 43 6. £10.

Pratt Green Trust, compiler. *The churches' copyright directory*. Stainer & Bell Ltd, 1992.

Robbie, G. and Wretham, J. *Copyright: a brief guide for Government departments.* HMSO, 1992.

TLTP Copyright Working Group. *Copyright guidelines for the Teaching and Learning Technology Programme*. TLTP, Bristol, 1994. 32 pages. (TLTP is jointly funded by the four higher education funding bodies: HEFCE, SHEFC, HEFCW and DENI.)

Wall, R. A. *Copyright made easier*. 2nd ed. Aslib, The Association for Information Management, 1998. £32 (£26 to members). 0 85142 393 0

1/4 Guidance for rights owners

NB: In addition to the following, other rights-owner guidelines may be available on enquiry to legal practices specialising in intellectual property and to specialist publishing groups, societies or professional bodies.

Arnold, R. *Performing rights and recording rights: UK law under the Performers' Protection Acts 1958-72 and the Copyright Designs and Patents Act 1988*. ESC, 1990. 0 906214 60 2

Authors' Licensing and Collecting Society pamphlets:

- ALCS (general description)
- Miscellaneous rights collectively administered
- Educational recording
- Cable retransmission
- German public lending right
- Authors in the electronic age

Barber, H. L. *How to protect your rights worldwide.* McGraw-Hill, £14.95. 0 07 005104 6

Bate, S., Bridge, R. M. and Lane, S. *Video law*. 2nd ed. Longman, 1992. 0 85121 682 X. £75.

British Photographers' Liaison Committee. *The ABC of photographic copyright*, BPLC, 1994. (Booklet.) 0 9514671 1 5 (Revised and expanded edition of *The photographers' guide to the 1988 Copyright Act*, BPLC, 1989).

British Printing Industries Federation. *Printers' guide to copyright*. BPIF, 1994. 0 85168 195 6.

British Standards Institution. *Code of practice for legal admissibility of information stored on electronic document management systems*, BSI/DISC, 1996 (PD 0008).

Carr, H. and Arnold, R. *Computer software: legal protection in the United Kingdom*. 2nd ed. Sweet & Maxwell, 1992. 0 421 44380 4.

Cavendish, J.M. and Pool, K., eds. *Cassell handbook of copyright in British publishing practice*. 3rd ed. Cassell, 1993. 0 304 32635 6. £30.

CITED Consortium. *Copyright in transmitted electronic documents: CITED final report*. IFLA/COPYRIGHT (at British Library) and EURITIS (France), September 1994. (ESPRIT II, Project 5469.) 0 7123 2115 2.

Clark, C., ed. *Publishing agreements: a book of precedents*. 5th ed. Butterworths, 1996. 0 406 00932 6. £50.

Copyrights and trademarks for media professionals, Focal Press (USA) (Broadcasting and Cable Series), 1997. 0 240 80276 4. £16.99.

Design and Artists' Copyright Society. *DACS international membership* (pamphlet), also a pamphlet inviting membership.

Donaldson, M. C. *Clearance and copyright: everything the independent filmmaker needs to know*. Silman-James Press (USA), 1997. 1 879505 30 4. £20.99.

European Commission, Consulting Trust. *Strategic study on new opportunities for publishers in the information services market*. January 1997. Available on *http://www2.echo.lu/impact/projects/studies/en/electrpub.html*

Garrett, J. R. and Alen, J. S. *Towards a copyright management system for digital libraries*. Copyright Clearance Center (USA), 1991.

Grover, D. *The protection of computer software: its technology and application*. Cambridge University Press, 1992. 0 521 42462 3. £19.95.

Halstead, R. R. *Protecting intellectual property: understanding and using trade marks, patents, designs and copyright in business*. 2nd ed. ICSA Publishing, 1996. 1 872 860931

Henry, M. *Publishing and multimedia law: a practical guide.* Butterworths, 1994. 0 406 03768 X. £85.

Howard, C. *Journalists and copyright.* National Union of Journalists, 1994. 0 514578 1 0

Jones, H. *Publishing law.* Routledge, 1996. 0 415 15110 4. £60.

Mechanical-Copyright Protection Society. Various pamphlets on membership agreements for different purposes, commission rates, etc.

Muller, P. *The music business – a legal perspective.* Quorum Books, 1994. 0 89930 702 7.

Norman, S. *Digital property: currency of the twenty-first century.* McGraw-Hill, 1997. $22.95.

Owen, L. *Selling rights.* 2nd ed. (Blueprint series.) Routledge, 1994. 0 415 13664 4. £30.

Performing Rights Society. *Performing rights handbook*, 1994. (Contains considerable guidance on copyright, including permissions, and concise flowcharts on licensing procedures and needs.) Other PRS publications include leaflets as follows: *General copyright notes*; *Useful publications on copyright and the music industry.*

Robertson, R. *Legal protection of computer software.* Longman, 1990. 0 85121 684 6. £35.

Saunders, D. *Authorship and copyright.* Routledge, 1992. £40.00. 0 415 04158 9

St. Aubyn, J. 'Notes on learned journal copyright'. *Learned Publishing* **3**(*4*) 1990, pp.203-212

Shaw, H . C. *Copyright law for writers: how to protect yourself and your creative work.* How To Books, 1996. 1 85703 416 3. £8.99.

Sopido. *Piracy and counterfeiting.* Kluwer Law and Taxation Publishers, 1997. 90 411 0947

Vickers, P. and Martyn, J. *The impact of electronic publishing on library services and resources in the UK: report of the British Library Working Party on Electronic Publishing.* British Library, 1994. 0 7123 3293 6. £25.

Wayner, P. *Digital copyright protection: techniques to ward off electronic copyright abuse.* Academic Press Inc. (Australia), 1997. 0 12 788771 7. £39.95.

1/5 International copyright

Beier, F-K., Schricker, G. and Fikentscher, W. *German industrial property, copyright and antitrust laws: legal texts with introduction.* 3rd ed. VCH Verlagsgesellschaft, 1996. 3 527 28730 2. £50.

Beier, F-K. and Schricker, G., eds. *From GATT to TRIPS – the agreement on trade-related aspects of intellectual property rights*. VCH Verlagsgesellschaft, 1996.

Commission of the European Communities: Commission staff. *Copyright and information limits to the protection of literary and pseudo-literary works*. Office for Official Publications of the European Communities, 1992 (via Saur). 92 826 3666 6. ECU 27.

Cook, T. and White, A. *EC copyright law*. Chancery Law Publications (now part of John Wiley Professional Division), 1995. £50. 0 471 952 80 X.

Davies, G. and Hung, M. E. *Music and video pirate copying: an international survey of the problem and the law*. Sweet & Maxwell, 1993. 0 421 48450 0.

Department of Trade and Industry, Information Society Initiative. *Development of the Information Society: an international analysis*, 1996. 0 11 515424 8. £24.95. Available on *htttp://www.isi.gov.uk*

Department of Trade and Industry, Information Society Initiative. *Moving into the Information Society – an international benchmarking study.* 1997.

European Commission, Consulting Trust. *Strategic study on new opportunities for publishers in the information services market*. January 1997. Available on *http://www2.echo.lu/impact/projects/studies/en/electrpub.html*

Flint, M. F. *The new copyright treaties: seminar on 17 April 1997*, chairman Gerald Dworking. Intellectual Property Institute, 1997. 1 874001 529.

Goldstein, P., Kitch, E. W., and Perlman, H. S. *Selected statutes and international agreements on unfair competition, trademark, copyright and patent* 1996. Foundation Press Inc., 1996. 1 56662 399 5.

Gotzen, F. *Copyright and the European Community: the Green Paper on copyright and the challenge of new technology*. Story-Scientia. 90 6439 606 X. BEF 1,000.

Hugenholtz, P. B. and Visser, D. J. G. *Copyright problems of electronic document delivery: a comparative analysis of the exceptions and limitations within the copyright laws of all EU and EFTA states*. Institute for Information Law (Amsterdam). European Commission, DG XIII, Luxembourg, 1995 (EUR-10656-EN). iii, 69 pages. 92-826-9565-4. (See also associated works noted in 1/8 below.)

Jussawala, M. *Economics of intellectual property in a world without frontiers*. Greenwood Press, 1992. (Contributions in Economics and Economic History Series, no. 131.) 0 313 27620 X. £35.95.

Levine, A. (Editors: W. Schipper and B. Unruh). *Global copyright issues in the secondary information industry*. National Federation of Abstracting and Information Services (USA), 1990 (NFAIS Report Series, No.4). 0 942308 28 X. $100.

Murphy, J. D. *Plunder and preservation: cultural property law and practice in the People's Republic of China*. Oxford University Press (Pakistan), 1995. 0 19 586874 9. £30.

Nakayama, N., Chairperson of the Multimedia Committee. *A proposal of the new rule on intellectual property for multimedia*. Institute of Intellectual Property, Japan, 1994. (Paper given at an international symposium: Exposure '94. Surveys Japanese copyright law in relation to international needs and discusses some issues.)

Nimmer, M. B. and Geller, P. E. *International copyright law and practice*. Matthew Bender and Company Incorporated, 1988-1994 (loose-leaf). 0 8205 1399 7. $360.

Nordemann, W., Vinck, K. and Hertin, P. W. *International copyright and neighbouring rights law: commentary with special emphasis on the European Community*. English version by G. Meyer, based on the translation by R. Livingston. Weinheim, VCH Verlagsgesellschaft mbH, 1990. 3 527 26188 5. £84.

Organisation for Economic Cooperation and Development. *Competitition policy and intellectual property rights*. HMSO, 1989. 92 64132422. £11.00.

Patfield, F. *Intellectual property in international trade*. Leicester University Press, 1993. 0 7185 1325 8. £45.

Porter, V., ed. *Beyond the Berne Convention: copyright, broadcasting and the single European market*. Libbey, 1991. 0 86196 267 2. £15.00.

Porter, V. *Copyright and information: limits to the protection of literary and pseudo-literary works in the member states of the European Community, a report prepared for the Commission of the European Communities (DG IV)*. Luxembourg, Office for Official Publications of the European Communities, 1992. vii, 242p. 9 28263666 6. £19.95.

Schultz, J. S. and Windsor, S. *International intellectual property protection for computer software: a research guide and annotated bibliography*. Fred B. Rothman and Company, 1994. (American Association of Law Libraries Publications Series, vol. 46.) 0 8377 9294 0.

Stewart, S. M. and Sandison, H. *International copyright and neighbouring rights*. 2nd ed. 2 vols. Butterworth. 0 406 66221 5. £210. Vol. 1 only: 1989, 0 406 66222 3, £160. Vol. 2 only: 1993, 0 406 03158 4, £50.

Stone, P. *Copyright law in the United Kingdom and the European Community*. Athlone Press, 1990. 0 485 70004 2. £45.00.

Trade and Industry, Department of. *Copyright protection for foreign sound recordings*. HMSO, 1989. 0 11 515208 3. £8.95.

UNESCO staff and WIPO staff. *Copyright laws and treaties of the world with new twenty-sixth supplement*. BNA Books, 1992. 0 87179 689 9. $695. (Covers laws, orders and regulations of over 150 countries, together with international conventions. Foreign text is provided in English translation.)

International Conventions

Berne Convention for the protection of literary and artistic works (Paris Act, 1971). (Latest of a number of revisions since the first version of 1886.)

Universal copyright convention, Geneva, 1952 (Paris revision, 1971)

International convention for the protection of performers, producers of phonograms and broadcasting organisations, Rome, 1961

Convention for the protection of producers of phonograms against unauthorised duplication of their phonograms, Geneva, 1971

Convention relating to the distribution of programme-carrying signals transmitted by satellite, Brussels, 1974

European agreement concerning programme exchange by means of television films, Brussels, 1958

European agreement on the protection of television broadcasts, Strasbourg, 1960 (amended 1965)

NB: The above conventions are drawn together in the work by Stewart and Sandison above, and other comprehensive works. The main documents also appear in: Copyright Licensing Agency Ltd. *The four international copyright and related conventions: Berne, UCC, Rome and Geneva*. CLA, 1992.

1/6 Design right

(See also sections of other works listed above.)

Fellner, C. *Industrial design law*. Sweet & Maxwell, 1995. 0 421 45190 4. £58.

Franzosi, M. *European design protection: commentary to Directive and Regulation proposals*. Kluwer Law International, 1996. 90 411 0112 8. £112.50.

Johnston, D. *Design protection: a practical guide to the law on plagiarism for manufacturers and designers*. 4th ed. Gower, 1995. 0 566 07553 9.

MacQueen, H. L. *Copyright, competition and industrial design*. 2nd ed. Edinburgh University Press, 1995. 0 7486 0733 1. £9.95.

Merkin, R.M. and Black, J. *Copyright and designs law*. 2 vols. Looseleaf. Longman, 1993. 0 85121 797 4. £195.

Tootal, C. *Law of industrial design: registered designs, copyright and design right*. CCH Editions, 1990. 0 86325 223 0. £79.

1/7 Background material

The following examples reflect the controversy which preceded the CDPA88, listed in chronological order.

Copyright and designs law. Report of the committee to consider the law on copyright and designs. Chairman: the Honourable Mr Justice Whitford. HMSO, March 1977 (The Whitford Report, CMND 6732). 0 10 167320 5. £11.20. (The report recommended, among other things, a statutory framework for licensing. After objections from the user communities, the Government decided against following many of its recommendations, as shown by subsequent Green and White Papers of 1981 and 1986 respectively.)

'Photocopying rights and wrongs: a librarian's view'. R. A. Wall. *Aslib Proceedings*, **34***(2)*, 1982, pp.113-127. (Includes proposal for a national clearance service.)

'The case for research as fair dealing'. R. A. Wall. *Aslib Information*, **16***(9)*, 1988, pp 206-7: and *Library Association Record*, **90***(8)*, 1988, p 438 (Based on briefings to the House of Lords in October 1987, on behalf of the Joint Consultative Committee Working Party on Copyright, the CBI, and others, about the intended discrimination against 'commercial research'.)

Copyright licensing. J. Shuter, ed. MCB Publishing, 1988. (Library Management Series.) £33.95. 0 86176 353 X. This booklet represents publisher, author and librarian views. Because much of the material is still current as far as issues are concerned, the contents are listed here as follows:

- Collective administration of literary works: principles and practice: the British experience. Charles Clark and Colin Hadley. (9pp.)
- Statistical survey methods. Ronald A. Pluck. (8pp.)
- The collective administration of literary and dramatic rights – Authors' Licensing and Collecting Society (ALCS). Janet Hurrell. (3pp.)
- The effect of copyright on libraries: one assessment. Barry Woodward. (8pp.)
- Copyright licensing and librarians. Raymond A. Wall. (10pp.)
- Copyright licensing – the international scene. Janet Shuter. (9pp.)

1/8 Steps towards the superhighway

The examples below are in chronological order.

1/8.1 Multimedia

An assessment of long-term solutions in the context of copyright and electronic delivery services and multimedia products. T. Hoeren. European Commission, Directorate-General XIII E-1, Telecommunications, Information Market and Exploitation of Research, 1995 (EUR 16069 EN). 92 827 0275 8. (In the series noted in A1/6.)

Study of institutional issues regarding multimedia: a report on discussions by the Working Group of the Subcommittee on Multimedia of the Copyright Council, Agency for Cultural Affairs, Japan, February 1995. 66 pages. (Translation by Copyright Research and Information Center.)

The politics of multimedia: gobal challenges — national issues, conference, PITCOM (Parliamentary Information Technology Committee), 1995. Comments in *Managing Information,* vol. 2(6), 1995, p24-25.

Copyright in multimedia: summit meeting to negotiate a new copyright dynamic between creators, producers and users in the emerging digital era. Aslib, The Association for Information Management in collaboration with the Department of Trade and Industry, London, 18-19 July 1995.

Multimedia Industry Advisory Group report, Department of Trade and Industry, December 1995.

Europe's multimedia challenge: strategic developments for the European publishing industry towards the year 2000, by Andersen Consulting for EC/DGXIII, Luxembourg, 1996. (Cover title begins "Electronic publishing ...".) Executive summary: x, 46 pages, illus. (This study, made in the context of INFO 2000, focuses on online publishing and the explosion of Internet-based services which use the World Wide Web. The main report is available in hard copy or on CD-ROM for £60 (£80 for the two documents). Can be obtained via Aslib.)

Practical guide to copyright for multimedia producers, produced by the AIDAA (International Audiovisual Authors Association) on behalf of the European Commission Directorate-General XIII (sic). (Researcher: Gilles Vercken.) Luxembourg, European Commission Directorate-General XII: Science, Research and Development, 1996 (EUR 16128 EN, ISSN 1018-5593). 226p, figs., tabs., paperback A4. 92-827-8285-4. ECU 21.50 excl. VAT in Luxembourg; £19.50 from HMSO Books. (Contains a timely overview of the relevant law. Of incidental use is its list of association addresses, especially those involved in collective licensing in member states for different media. Also contains a list of the current statutes on copyright of member states.)

1/8.2 Information Society

Europe and the global information society: recommendations to the European Council. Commission of the European Commmunities, Brussels, 1994, (known as the Bangemann report and believed to be one of the prime movers in Europe).

Aspects of copyright and related rights in the information infrastructure *"Superhighways",* EC conference, Brussels, 7-8 July 1994.

Copyright in transmitted electronic documents: CITED final Report, by the CITED Consortium. IFLA/COPYRIGHT (at British Library) and EURITIS (France), September 1994. (ESPRIT II, Project 5469.) 0 7123 2115 2

Creating the Superhighways of the future: developing broadband communication in the UK. Department of Trade and Industry. HMSO (Cm.2734), 1994. 0 10 127342 8. £6.75. G7 conference on the Information Society, Brussels, 25-26 February 1995. (Aims and themes are concisely stated in *International Publishers Bulletin,* vol. 11, issue 2, 1995, p1.)

Information technologies programme: building the information society: 4th famework programme of research and technological development (1994-98). Luxembourg, Office for Official Publications of the European Communities, 1995. (Cover title: Science, research and development: General information: ESPRIT.) 92 827 6789 2. £6.

Copyright and related rights in the Information Society (Green Paper), Commission of the European Communities (CEC), Brussels, July 1995 (COM(95) 382 final). 90 pages. (Comments appear in *Managing Information*, vol. 2(12), 1995, p26-27 and 30-31.)

Copyright problems of electronic document delivery: a comparative analysis of the exemptions and limitations within the copyright laws of all EU and EFTA states. P. Bernt Hugenholtz and Dirk J. G. Visser (Institute for Information Law, University of Amsterdam), European Commission, DG XIII, Luxembourg, 1995 (EUR-10656-EN). iii, 69 pages. 92 826 9565 4. This was the first published of a four-part study on *Copyright on electronic delivery systems and multimedia products*. Others are:

> *An investigation of current practice with contractual arrangements and copyright clearing services,* by Charles Clark (EUR-16067-EN).
>
> *An analysis of the impact of harmonized legislation with regard to copyright on multimedia, by Michel Vivant* (EUR-16068-EN).
>
> *An assessment of long-term solutions in the context of copyright and electronic delivery services and multimedia products,* by Thomas Hoeren (EUR-16069-EN).

Information Superhighway: applications in society, House of Lords Science and Technology Committee, December 1995 (as a "call for evidence" or consultative document).

The future of copyright in a digital environment: proceedings of the Royal Academy Colloquium organised by the Royal Netherlands Academy of Sciences (KNAW) and the Institute for Information Law. P. B. Hugenholtz, ed. 1996. 90 411 0267 1.

Follow-up to the Green Paper on copyright and related rights in the Information Society, CEC, Brussels, November 1996. 30 pages. Digested in: *Communication on copyright and related rights in the Information Society,* CEC, Brussels, November 1996. EC Spokesman's Service, IP/96/1042.

Development of the Information Society: an international analysis. Department of Trade and Industry, Information Society Initiative, 1996. Available on *http://www.isi.gov.uk*

The use of digitised copyright works in libraries. International Publishers Copyright Council on behalf of: International Publishers Association, and International Association of Scientific, Technical and Medical Publishers. November 1996. (Also issued simultaneously by the Federation of European Publishers. See App. 4).

Fifth report from the House of Lords Science and Technology Committee (Session 1995-96). (HL Paper 77) HMSO, 1996.

Information Society: agenda for action in the UK. Select Committee on Science and Technology. Report. The Lord Phillips of Ellesmere (chairman of Subcommittee 1). HL Papers 1995-96, 77. 0 10 407796 4. £14. First Select Committee report to appear on the Web: *http://www.hmsoinfo.gov.uk/hmso/document/inforsoc.htm.*

Also the subject of the tenth IIS/ISI Lecture at Brunei Gallery, September 1996, by The Lord Phillips of Ellesmere. (On the work of The House of Lords Select Committee on Science and Technology). *Journal of Information Science*, **23***(1)*, 1997, pp.1-8.

Principles for copyright Directives. Ad Hoc Alliance for a Digital Future. Brussels, 1997 (see App. 4).

Moving into the Information Society – an international benchmarking study. Department of Trade and Industry, Information Society Initiative. 1997 .

eLib information service, on *http://www.ukoln.ac.uk/elib* plus a list on e-mail at *lis-elib@mailbase.ac.uk* for discussion of projects (see also hard copy information package available from the Programme Director at the University of Warwick, *cudbw@warwick.ac.uk*; details in 6.49).

New library; the people's network. Library and Information Commission, 1997. (Said to be *a milestone in the development of the public library service, linking it into the National Grid for Learning and the development of an information community that is genuinely global and local in its membership.* As noted in Appendix 4, this report is on the Web and therefore openly accessible at: *http://www.ukoln.ac.uk/services/lic/newlibrary/* and a discussion list is provided at this site.)

APPENDIX 2 – LEGISLATION

A2/1 Background to current state of the law

The main law provided by CDPA88 having emerged during a period of controversy between publishers and users, an historical outline follows.

A2/1.1 Xerography

This equipment for high-quality reprography was developed during the 1950s and its use spread, whilst ever-better machines were designed, until by the 1960s it had become a major help to the whole information world – including publishers, as well as users needing research or private study copying from library materials.

A2/1.2 Serials pricing

The periodicals price increases, observable from post-Second World War onwards, were triggered by global inflationary trends. When numbers of individual subscribers began to fall off, some of the large publishing companies blamed libraries, in the belief that they were providing each other with photocopies instead of buying originals. However, as the publishers also believed that individuals who had formerly subscribed were reading their issues in libraries instead of buying, at least one of the complaints was obviously arguable. It is not known whether any STM publisher ever considered reducing its subscription prices to regain individual subscribers. It seemed reasonable to some US publishers to respond to what they saw as the threat of photocopying. The method chosen was to charge differential subscriptions for libraries because they are seen as 'multiple-use' situations subject to photocopying, and the practice soon spread, both within the US and to the UK. Regrettably, subscription rises soon converted the inflationary trigger into an annually boosted spiral system. Publishers naturally competed for the best profits, raising prices to what they thought the market could stand, which was unfortunately not always appropriate for industry, and never for academic, libraries. As prices went up:

(a) Individual subscriptions for 'serious' journals fell even further to a negligible figure, leaving the multiple-use charge as a new 'standard', and libraries were blamed again for loss of subscribers.
(b) Libraries were forced into annual cancellation of the more expensive or less-used titles (where use was assessable at all), due to tight budgets with quite inadequate inflationary allowances. This time-consuming process spread extensively across the working year for departmental users as well as libraries, and led to much internecine strife!

(c) Then, publishers who observed the cuts would further increase prices to seek a comparable level of profit as formerly, hence the description 'spiral' above. This became a dog-eat-dog situation in which the titles of less focal departmental concern – the interdisciplinary or 'fringe' but nonetheless important journals – were in danger of being trampled or swallowed by core journals. Also, the efficacy of education and of research inevitably suffered.
(d) Publisher concern grew at the extent of overseas piracy, accompanied by frustration at their inability to do much about this highly damaging effect on some two-thirds of the market. The concern was and still is shared by information professionals, since the user community suffers through price levels which have to compensate for piracy in order for periodicals to remain viable.

There are some users who believe that, in a global sense, market forces ensure that all photocopying, even piracy, is compensated for – however undesirable it is that the majority of users should share the burden of increased prices. Librarians increasingly look to electronic systems which enable use as required, which in theory at least should be cheaper overall than subscribing to everything of mainstream interest. This does nothing to improve the lot of the fringe or interdisciplinary journals, however. Nor does it provide the on-the-spot serendipity effect of browsing across a range of journals and deriving the research boost which can result. Nor does it allow build-up of hard copy reference sets for research unconstrained by computer time.

A2/1.3 Whitford

The work for this Report under the chairmanship of Lord Justice Whitford was undertaken as a result of publisher pressure for licensing of photocopying. The recommendations of the Whitford Report in 1977 (App. 1/7 s 927) sought to encourage collective or 'blanket' licensing. This was defined by Whitford as licensing which would involve a:

> group of copyright owners foregoing their rights to take individual action... Instead of individual authors and publishers being responsible for collecting their own royalties, remuneration at a standard rate is collected by a central collecting agency or society which undertakes the task of distribution of the revenue... (App. 1/7 s274)

To facilitate this distribution in an attempt at an equitable manner some sort of return of usage or sampling was considered inevitable. From the user's point of view the essence of a blanket licence is that it should cover all the works he or she wants to copy. For a single annual fee, went the theory, he or she would get permission to use any or all of the works in the licensor's repertoire. However, a blanket licence does not yet exist, but CLA's comes as close as its mandates allow (8.2).

A small nucleus of strongly commercial publishers, plus some poets, essayists or novelists who imagined their work to be subject to photocopying, began pressure towards licensing after the Whitford Report. Academic, industrial and professional group authors – along with students, the principal user group – were and still are more interested in kudos and career advancement, together with flexibility of access to the work of other authors. Publishers had expected new law to enforce the setting up of a licensing system. This was not done by the Government because they saw it as a form of 'compulsory licensing', hence disallowed under the Berne Convention according to their interpretation. Instead, the Government pointed out in a 1981 Green Paper that collective licensing was possible within the present legal framework, in other words, by contract.

A2/1.4 Reactions to Whitford by user representatives

Information and library service professionals and learned societies sprang to the defence of user interests and declared the Report biased. Apart from the administrative costs and complexities of collective licensing, few could see any way of achieving fair distribution of revenue on a basis of sampling, or of keeping administrative costs down, and held that the concept was therefore flawed at the outset. Others could not see how blanket licensing could be achieved, and their worries have been borne out by later developments, since it has not been achieved. There was particular concern because licensing would affect the media most copied, namely periodicals. The multiple-use approach to publishers' subscription levels meant payment by libraries whether or not copying occurred, and whether or not it was covered by statutory permissions. The purchase of 'packages' of articles in the form of periodical issues results in a 'dross factor', for relatively few of the contents are really relevant or worthwhile to a given user organisation. Hence, goes the argument, why not be able to make fuller use, without further cost, of those which *are* of value? In response to the presumed militancy of publishers wanting licensing, bitterness grew among user representatives who felt that, if rights owners do not want their products to be used, they should simply not publish.

A2/1.5 Resistance to licensing

During the whole decade up to CDPA88, the pro-licensing group was resisted on behalf of users. The Copyright Licensing Agency Ltd was set up (8.2; 12.31) as the central collecting agency in respect of reprography, at least. The licensing lobby was unpopular with users for targeting initially the Education sector, well known to be increasingly short of book funds anyway. Moreover, educationists feared encouraging what they called a 'diet of photocopies' in schools – a fear which later events, with claims of a fourfold increase in educational copying, may have shown to be well-founded. The licensing lobby was also particularly unpopular for attempting to override fair dealing and library copying by the licence terms, for this would have pre-empted and influenced the new legislation which was then being drafted. Fortunately, the Government declared its intention of preserving fair dealing and library copying, though not of allowing loopholes for multiple copying to continue.

A concern for users is that licensing terms can vary with the user group, which appears unfair if the relevant literature prices do not vary between interested groups. Another concern is the apparent unlikelihood now of achieving real blanket licensing which covers all the needs of a user group. Then there is the question of policy variation, for any of the various collecting agencies may sometimes be driven by 'hardline' mandaters to press for maximum returns regardless of administrative costs to, and economic states of, the user groups. At other times, agencies might be able to make fairer the more extreme demands of some rights owners. The general feeling persisted that there were strongly commercial publishers who did not realise, or were not concerned, that any licensing fees inevitably affect library budgets for originals, particularly in a continuing cash-limited situation. However, a 'Hobson's choice' view later prevailed.

A2/2 The 1988 Act

It was against this background that the Government took the unprecedented step of issuing a draft copyright (etc) Bill to interested groups in 1987, and this assisted both 'sides' in the dispute. Lobbying on behalf of users during the passage of the Bill persuaded the Government to remove an initially intended discrimination against 'commercial research' in fair dealing, and there were a number of smaller but significant achievements on behalf of users. With careful drafting, the Act aimed at greater clarity and less ambiguity than hitherto experienced with the 1956 Act, which was in any event out of date as soon as passed. Since 1988 various Statutory Instruments have supplemented the legislation. More recently, EC harmonisation of copyright law has brought about some sweeping changes, as noted in Appendix 3 and elsewhere in this volume.

A2/2.1 Main features of CDPA88

- Fair dealing is confirmed from earlier law, and effectively clarified to show that anyone or any library can act on behalf of someone in this respect provided no more than one research or private study copy is made for the requestor. No discrimination is made against research for commercial purposes. For the first time, 'artistic' works are included under fair dealing, thus completing the list of kinds of original work. Physical formats other than written or printed matter, namely, sound recordings and films, remain conspicuously absent from the research or private study permission.
- Library copying is also confirmed for 'prescribed' libraries/archives, limits being specified in respect of certain kinds of work, and fair dealing cannot be used to circumvent the limits, for example on number of copies of extracts from those works. Fair dealing can however be used for copying kinds of original work which do not appear under library copying provisions. Loopholes for multiple copying are closed throughout the Act.

  Computer programs are literary works regardless of format. A rental right is however established for audovisual materials and computer programs in electronic format. Videotape is included in the definition of 'film'.
- A new category 'Parliamentary copyright' now accompanies Crown copyright.
- Non-interactive electronic databases which are publicly accessible via a telecommunications system carry a form of service right for the database producer, similar to that in broadcasts; in addition to any copyright in content. The word 'database' does not appear anywhere in the Act, but 'electronic retrieval systems' are defined as publications. Compilations and tables are included in the definition of 'literary works'.
- Licensing is encouraged on a voluntary basis by making certain procedures royalty-free unless a licence becomes available. A Copyright Tribunal is formed out of the Performing Right Tribunal, authorised in respect of collective licensing matters.

- The Act left points of detail on voluntary licensing to be sorted out with rights-owner representatives in order to devise suitable licensing. Much progress was made despite a slow start (only to be slowed again recently, this time by new rights of authors and performers in respect of lending/rental). It is important always to channel enquiries on the progress of negotiations through professional bodies. Unilateral approaches, other than simple permission requests, can cause confusion and have adverse effects.
- A photographer is now an author and first owner of works, unless an employee in the course of employment, when the employer is first owner unless otherwise agreed. Moral rights appear for the first time in UK law: 'paternity right' (author or director); 'derogatory treatment'; false attribution; privacy for a commissioner of photographs taken for private and domestic purposes. Moral rights cannot be assigned but can be waived.
- 'Criminal liability' is mentioned for the first time in this context, although it was possible formerly to be sent to prison for certain infringements of former legislation. Some 20 sections cover 'remedies for infringement', and damages need not be limited to an estimate of economic loss by a rights owner but can be made punitive.
- Appended to the Act are: Schedule 1 covering 'transitional provisions and savings'; and Schedule 7 containing 'consequential amendments'. It is via the latter that public libraries were made liable in respect of rental royalties even if no charge is made for loans (now altered by new lending/rental right SI 1996/2967).

The Act has been amended in various ways since 1988, mainly by secondary legislation in SIs but also to some extent by legislation on other matters, such as the Broadcasting Acts. The changes in CDPA88 which may most affect the anticipated readership of this volume have been included in the main text, reflecting the following SIs. The detailed provisions themselves (Act plus selected SIs in full) can be found in an updateable reference work such as the looseleaf *Aslib guide to copyright* (1994 onwards). Comments appear in Appendix 3 on certain aspects of changes wrought by EC harmonisation.

A2/3 Selected SIs since 1988

A2/3.1 Designated bodies Orders

- SI 1989/1012 Copyright (Recordings of Folksongs for Archives) (Designated Bodies) Order 1989;
- SI 1989/1013 Copyright (Sub-titling of Broadcasts and Cable Programmes) (Designated Bodies) Order 1989

  NB: the section of the Act (s74) under which this Order made applies not only to deaf and hard of hearing but also to those who are 'physically or mentally handicapped in other ways', and the provision is not limited to subtitling but can include copies 'otherwise modified for their special needs'. It is surprising that an Order has apparently not been sought on behalf of the blind.

- SI 1993/74 Copyright (Recordings for Archives of Designated Class of Broadcasts and Cable Programmes) (Designated Bodies) Order 1993

A2/3.2 Designated bodies by purpose and relevant SI

Broadcasts and cable programmes (re s75; SI 1993/74):

British Film Institute
British Library
British Medical Association
British Music Information Centre
Imperial War Museum
Music Performance Research Centre
National Library of Wales
Scottish Film Council

Folksongs archives (re s61; SI 1989/1012):

Archive of Traditional Welsh Music, University College of North Wales
Centre for English Cultural Tradition and Language
Charles Parker Archive Trust (1982)
European Centre for Traditional and Regional Cultures
Folklore Society
Institute of Folklore Studies in Britain and Canada
National Museum of Wales, Welsh Folk Museum
National Sound Archive, British Library
North West Sound Archive
Sound Archives, British Broadcasting Corporation
Ulster Folk and Transport Museum
Vaughan Williams Memorial Library, English Folk Dance and Song Society

Subtitling (re s74; SI 1989/1013)

National Subtitling Library for Deaf People.

A2/3.3 Libraries/archives

- SI 1989/1212 Copyright (Librarians and Archivists) (Copying of Copyright Material) Regulations 1989
- SI 1989/1098 Copyright (Material Open to Public Inspection) (International Organisations) Order 1989
- SI 1989/1099 Copyright (Material Open to Public Inspection) (Marking of Copies of Maps) Order 1989
- SI 1990/1427 Copyright (Material Open to Public Inspection) (Marking of Copies of Plans and Drawings) Order 1990

A2/3.4 Educational establishments

- SI 1989/1067 Copyright (Application of Provisions Relating to Educational Establishments to Teachers) (No.2) Order 1989
- SI 1989/1068 Copyright (Educational Establishments) (No.2) Order 1989

A2/3.5 Licensing

- SI 1989/1129 Copyright Tribunal Rules 1989, as amended
- SI 1990/879 Copyright (Certification of Licensing Scheme for Educational Recording of Broadcasts and Cable Programmes) (Educational Recording Agency Limited) Order *(as amended 1992/211; 1993/193; 1994/247; 1996/191)*
- SI 1990/2008 Copyright (Certification of Licensing Scheme for Educational Recording of Broadcasts) (Open University Educational Enterprises Limited) Order 1990 *(as amended 1993/2755; 1996/190)*

The CLA scheme was already in existence in 1988, so was not submitted for certification.

A2/3.6 EC harmonisation

The following have wrought the more significant amendments to CDPA88. It should be noted that they are not always entirely represented by the amended state of the Act, and reference may be needed to an SI itself – especially in respect of transitional provisions which may supplement rather than amend Schedule 1 to the Act.

- SI 1992/3233 Copyright (Computer Programs) Regulations 1992

- SI 1995/3297 The Duration of Copyright and Rights in Performances Regulations 1995
- SI 1996/2967 The Copyright and Related Rights Regulations 1996 *(includes rental or lending to the public)*
- SI 1997/3032 The Copyright and Rights in Databases Regulations 1997

A2/4 CDPA88: extent of amendment

In addition to many additions or amendments to the Act itself at subsection level, and to the need to take various Regulations in SIs in conjunction, the following new sections have been added to the Act. These are included in order to help readers identify section titles, the section numbers of which they may find referenced in this and other guides, and perceive the context when they have only a 1988 copy to hand. Of course, further reference may well be necessary to the full Act as amended up to date in several reference works (such as the looseleaf *Aslib guide to copyright*, App. 1). The new sections are listed below.

Part I, Copyright

Chapter I, Subsistence, ownership and duration of copyright

Descriptions of work and related provisions

Databases	3A.
Sound recordings	5A.
Films	5B.
Safeguards in case of certain satellite broadcasts	6A.

Duration of copyright

Duration of copyright in sound recordings	13A.
Duration of copyright in films	13B.
Meaning of country of origin	15A.

Chapter II, Rights of copyright owner

Infringement by rental or lending of work to the public	18A.

Chapter III, Acts permitted in relation to copyright works

Education

Lending of copies by educational establishments	36A.

Libraries and archives
Lending of copies by libraries or archives 40A.

Computer programs: lawful users
Back up copies 50A.
Decompilation 50B.
Other acts permitted to lawful users 50C.

Databases: lawful users
Acts permitted to lawful users of databases 50D.

Miscellaneous: lending of works and playing of sound recordings
Lending to public of copies of certain works 66.

Miscellaneous: films and sound recordings

Films: acts permitted as assumptions as to expiry of copyright, &c 66A.

Chapter V, Dealings with rights in copyright works

Copyright
Presumption of transfer of rental right in case of film production agreement 93A.

Rental right
Right to equitable remuneration when rental right transferred 93B.
Equitable remuneration: reference of amount to Tribunal 93C.

Chapter VII, Copyright licensing

References and applications with respect to licensing schemes
Licensing schemes to which following sections apply 117.

References and applications with respect to licensing bodies
Licences to which following sections apply 124.

Factors to be taken into account in certain classes of case
(omitted as outside the scope of this text) 135A-H.

Compulsory collective administration of certain rights
Collective exercise of certain rights in relation to cable re-transmission 144A.

APPENDIX 3 - EC HARMONISATION

Comments on changes in UK law from 1993-1997

In Appendix 2/3.5 the UK SIs which implement the relevant EC Directives are listed.

This Appendix comments selectively on certain of the effects of the EC harmonisation programme of copyright and related rights

A3/1 Computer programs (SI 1992/3233, in force from 1 January 1993)

Welcomed by many people for:

(a) its confirmation of treatment of computer programs as literary works;
(b) establishment of a 'lawful user' concept with rights of use, the first reference to user 'rights' in UK copyright law;
(c) statement of those rights or permissions, making them incapable of being overridden by contract (i.e. a contract other than a lawful user licence);
(d) a right to make back-up copies is particularly helpful to users, also the allowance of decompilation (or 'reverse engineering') to create an independent program, this being excluded from fair dealing because it is now a right of a lawful user. Some other copying or adaptation by a lawful user is also allowed.

Those who hoped that 'shrink-wrap' restrictions would be generally discredited were disappointed, however, but neither was shrink-wrap use confirmed as contractually viable.

This SI creates retrospective legislation, covering programs made before commencement of the SI as well as later, except for cases of contract entered into before 1 January 1993.

A3/2 Duration of copyright and rights in performances (SI 1995/3297, in force from 1 January 1996)

Whilst the confirmation of some aspects of UK law was appreciated, the main provisions were received with mixed feelings by the user community. To provide a further 20 years of protection to an author, when 50 was seen as having been proved not only adequate but optimal in the UK for many years, is not welcomed. It will be even more difficult than hitherto to ascertain whether an item is still copyright. The transitional provision situation is more complex than before, especially as a result of the concepts of 'revived' or 'renewed' copyright. Authors form the principal group within the user community as far as 'serious' material is concerned, and there is no evidence that they will gain significantly but instead will face longer restrictions on use of other work. However, the descendants of a best-selling novelist, and of course virtually all publishers, should gain very considerably.

Those concerned with transitional provisions will need to use the SI alongside the Act as amended to date, because those provisions do not amend Schedule 1 of CDPA88 but are additive. It is believed that the various changes have been discussed in the main text as fully as necessary in a book of this nature.

A3/3 Satellite broadcasts and cable re-transmission; distribution right; rental and lending right; publication right; performers' rights (SI 1996/2967, in force from 1 December 1996)

The basis was the new right of an author or a performer either to permit or prohibit the lending or rental of his or her works to the public. The SI's provisions cause complexities, particularly for public libraries, which must now seek licences to lend materials other than books covered already by Public Lending Right. Authors and performers of non-book material are entitled to 'equitable remuneration' for lending or performance, and the ramifications will require a period of adjustment.

Copyright Tribunal jurisdiction is extended to cover the new rights, and CDPA licensing provisions are modified. A new 'publication right' is established alongside copyright, whereby a person publishing a previously unpublished work – currently in the public domain – will have the right for 25 years beyond publication year. Authorship of sound recordings and films is clarified, also some transitional provisions on photographs. A new and detailed Schedule 2A on licensing performers' property rights is added to CDPA88.

The SI includes transitional provisions and savings which do not amend but are separate from Schedule 1 of CDPA88, thus the SI must be available for use alongside the latest state of the Act.

A3/4 Rental and lending, summary of comments, leading on from 4.35 et al. Some comments may be regarded as issues for discussion

(1) 'Lending' means making available for use, on terms that it will or may be returned, otherwise than for direct or indirect economic or com-

mercial advantage, through an establishment which is open to the public. If payment does not go beyond operating costs, there is no such advantage.

(2) Educational establishments are permitted to *lend* any kind of material without licence, but see (8) below. Nor is lending by such establishments affected by performers rights, as per end of (4).

(3) Only rental and lending 'to the public' are affected. Provision of 'on-the-spot' reference in respect of any materials is exempt. Under new s40A to CDPA88, the lending of 'a book' by a public library does not infringe copyright of 'a work of any description', if the book is covered by Public Lending Right. However, 'work' is defined under new s18A as 'a literary, dramatic or musical work', and this omits 'artistic' and accordingly is taken to exclude books of maps, or 'atlases'. In this permission, the absence of mention of physical formats other than books (4.39) – audiovisual materials, CD-ROMs, etc. – means that they cannot be loaned, even free of any charge, except under licence. 'Public libraries', in the PLR context, are defined as libraries under local authority control. On behalf of these libraries, the LA/JCC/WPC is in discussion with rights owner representatives concerning licences to lend materials other than books.

(4) Nonprofit-based libraries/archives other than public libraries are similarly permitted to lend books but should seek licences for other materials (the SI Reg. 11(2) may have drafting errors). It is presumed that the PLR sampling of public library loans is taken as adequate compensation to rights owners for public lending of books. However, lending of anything by any nonprofit-based library or archive is unaffected by performers' rights in recordings of live performances (new para.6A of Schedule 2 to CDPA88).

(5) Lending between establishments which are accessible to the public is exempt.

(6) Authors or performers are in a position to prohibit public lending in their contracts with producing companies, but in theory may nevertheless allow loans whilst requiring recompense via licensing for rental. However, such prohibition would seem unlikely unless they wished to force public lending of their works to be made 'rental' in order to have the chance of more income through sharing a profit-based situation. Books subject to PLR are preserved from this risk by statutory permissions, but any other works would not be so preserved. The price of copies to libraries should of course be no higher than that to commercial outlets,

otherwise the rights owners could lose the 'shop-window' effect of relevant library services and they would very probably cease.

(7) If authors, individual producing companies and performers do *not* prohibit public lending (i.e. non-profit by definition), an industrial association would have no statutory basis for the imposition of licensing of a lending service as a condition of supply of copies. This consideration might not stop an industrial association, or an agency on its behalf, from exercising its freedom to offer a licence. This could conceivably arise if some advantage of control might ensue for the body concerned: for example, as in the present BPI 'free licence' (4.43) which limits the number of copies acquired. However, potential licensees should be reluctant to agree unless the contract brought advantages not otherwise readily attainable, such as discounts or other inducements compared with retail purchase, and/or freedom from any liability related to individual loan events.

(8) 'Rental' is the making of loans for direct or indirect economic or commercial advantage, i.e. profit and not mere recovery of operating costs. *There are no permissions relating to rental.* 'Rental right' means the right of a copyright owner to authorise or prohibit the rental of copies of the work.

(9) Lending becomes 'rental' when (8) applies, even in a public library. For establishments which are *not* accessible to the public, loans become rental when any charge at all is made (4.40).

(10) Authors have an unwaivable right to *equitable remuneration* for *rental* to the public of sound recordings and films, when rental right is transferred.

(11) Performers are entitled to equitable remuneration for performances which use fixations (sound recordings or films) of their live performances for performance in public. Such remuneration rights cannot be assigned except to a collecting society. Thus if there is no such assignment there will be no such remuneration, since authors and performers can hardly collect it themselves. What is 'equitable' is to be determined by agreement, aided by the Copyright Tribunal, which may not rule out a single payment in lieu of individual payment per event, which would seem to be the preferred procedure (see (13)- (16) below).

(12) Rental right can be (and usually will logically be) transferred to a producing company by an author of an original work, or a performer. As current holder of rental right, the producing company then becomes liable to pay equitable remuneration via a collecting society to

those authors and/or performers who have not only transferred rental right to the producers but also mandated a collecting society and thus qualified for that remuneration. Although in respect of rental there is no mention in the SI of a single payment alternative to rental royalty per event, the CT will have power so to rule if it sees fit when its arbitration is sought.

(13) The general application of the principle of a single payments system (9-10 above), as practised in the video industry (4.47) as part of the purchase price, would of course be preferred by services, not least for administrative reasons.

(14) It is suggested that, if cost-effective arrangements for rental are to be achieved, much will depend on the relevant industrial associations. These would need to encourage individual producing companies to provide, and authors/performers to accept, equitable remuneration as a single payment, payable via the relevant collecting society. Similarly, the producing companies who hold transferred rental/lending right may become persuaded to accept a single payment to cover their entitlement to royalties. Otherwise, the expenses of setting up and running arrangements for gathering and collating rental/lending data *per event* could of course be quite disproportionate. This could not only negate benefits to rights holders but also place an intolerable administrative burden on public services which are perpetually short of staff and funds.

(15) Assessment of past events suggests that neither the sound nor video industrial bodies (BPI and BVA) seem anxious to go to the expense of running collecting societies for these purposes, while actions in respect of cinematograph films are controlled by the individual distributors and this is expected to continue. However, difficulties and variations may arise from the freedom of action and decision now open to authors and performers who naturally seek optimum income.

Example, as this book goes to press, the Spoken Word Publishers Association has responded to LA enquiries by giving notice of its intention to seek equitable remuneration for public rental, on behalf of performers and authors.

(16) It is suggested, though, that the logic of the single payment method rests in part on the need repetitively to replace purchased copies because they soon wear out in the public loan situation. This should generate additional royalties via sales for authors and performers as well as their equitable remuneration for rental/lending.

(17) Uncertainty is expected to prevail for an unknown period, but the video hire industry is believed to be lucrative for the producing companies, who may wish to leave it as undisturbed as possible. Thus, suitably stable arrangements might be the first to appear there, with the possibility that others may follow and result in a clearer picture overall.

(18) Public libraries have already stated, in respect of sound recordings, their concern at their inability to continue providing loans of recordings if new administrative costs were to arise, such as for the collection of royalties, or if differential purchase prices were applied compared with the commercial hire market with the effect of *excluding* such materials from public services.

(19) Market forces, since public libraries form a healthy proportion of the market affected, may remove the risk of a 'doomsday scenario' in which materials became available only through personal purchase or through commercial hire services of widely varying quality and coverage. Otherwise the latter procedure could in theory destroy the whole concept of cohesive, representative, unbiased, publicly owned collections and information services based on them. It could also allow standards of quality of available works to fall to the common cultural denominator so obvious from commercial video hire shelves.

(20) Finally, this author had hoped that these EC changes might be effected entirely via PLR, but the Government had no plans to expand PLR. There were perhaps doubts about the possibility of 'compulsory licensing' accusations in respect of proposals made concerning payment by the producing companies in accordance with loans, in order to allow for higher payment levels and variations in the AV regime.

A3/5 Copyright and rights in databases (SI 1997/3032, in force from 1 January 1998)

This is probably one of the more important changes in copyright law made for many decades, and is believed to justify extra space for comments here in supplementation of 3.28 et seq.

This section refers to selected Regulations on the legal protection of databases. Some of the comments or questions below were sent on behalf of Aslib to the Patent Office in response to the consultative draft received in autumn 1997.

The SI consists of Parts I to IV, a Schedule 1 on *Exceptions to database right for public administration,* and a Schedule 2 on *Licensing of database right.*

After Part I as introduction, Part II is on the *Amendment of the Copyright, Designs and Patents Act 1988* (CDPA88) in respect of copyright only, subject to certain of the savings and transitional provisions in Part IV. From Part III on *Database right* to the end of the document, no attempt is made to modify CDPA88 and one concludes that the SI will be used for some time as a stand-alone piece of legislation in respect of database right. This marks the beginning of a difficult period for information and library services, and for individual users dependent on their own devices, for adjustment may take several years and not be over before the next EC Directives and resultant SIs appear! It will be necessary for information professionals to monitor developments and note new additions to looseleaf services such as the *Aslib guide to copyright.* The two main subjects are:

(1) copyright in a database, arising from existing coverage of 'compilations' in CDPA88; and
(2) database right, the UK's term for the EC Directive's *sui generis* right, to be implemented alongside copyright.

Notably, the SI contains some retrospective legislation affecting existing databases. Where copyright permissions are not repeated under database right, the latter applies and extraction or re-utilisation may only involve insubstantial parts.

A3/5.1 Part II of SI, amending CDPA88 re copyright in a database

Regs. 5 and 6: definitions

Existing s3(1)(a) of CDPA88 is amended to show, as a literary work, 'a table or compilation other than a database'. It being assumed, apparently, that any 'preparatory design material' for *any* database will also be 'literary', this is added to s3(1)(c) as a literary work also.

Then, a new s3A for the Act defines a database as reported in 3.29. However, a new s3A(2) goes on to state that:

> a literary work consisting of a database is original if, and only if, by reason of the selection or arrangement of the contents of the database, the database constitutes the author's own intellectual creation.

This appears to say that such a database only qualifies for *copyright* if it is original (etc).

Comments

The wording of new s3A(2) leads to questions:

(1) What about a non-literary database (e.g. images, music or multimedia) which is appropriately arranged, etc? (The answer obtained on checking was that digitisation, whether of text or images or sound, is regarded as 'writing' and hence covered by s3A, which is still arguably unclear.)
(2) New s3(1)(a) establishes by implication the existence of a compilation *other than a database*. New s3A(2) relates to a database which qualifies for copyright if it is original, etc (although it does not need to be original for database right). Therefore a 'literary-only' *compilation* which is not a database, because it does not satisfy that definition, could nevertheless continue to have copyright vested in the compiler, thus continuing the 'sweat of brow' possibility, despite the Directive ruling copyright to be inapplicable in respect of a sweat of brow database. (Anomaly: a compiler who simply 'lumps' material together gets protection under copyright for life plus 70 years; whereas a compiler who takes care with selection and arrangement gets only 15 years (initially) under database right!)
(3) Can one conclude in respect of a printed compilation that, when copyright is not indicated in a © notice as being vested in the author, the compilation carries only the publisher's right in the printed page, and that it is not a 'database'?
(4) If (3) is correct, it is assumed that any contents which are non-copyright because they are factual can be re-keyed without any limitation on extraction except a reasonable proportion of the whole compilation, which has been the situation prior to the SI anyway. And from an electronic compilation which also does not satisfy the 'database' definition, would the same liberty apply to downloading unless that is limited by contract?
(5) The *maker* of the database is first owner of copyright, thus providing some new clarity concerning compilers as 'authors' in this context (but subject to the usual 'employer' (s11) and 'joint author' (s10) considerations).
(6) Is it not worse that 'database' can now be applied to a great many written or printed or electronic works? And just how do users distinguish between a database and an 'ordinary' compilation? Much of the new law appears to have been drafted to provide bases for litigation between database producers, without thought for confusion to users.

The draft EC Directive started out to cover only noncopyright material and only electronic databases, but was expanded successively to cover both copyright and noncopyright, and both written/printed and electronic format. Discussion ran for four year until passage of the Directive in March 1996, requiring implementation two years later. Successive negotiators do not appear to have 'thought through' the effects of applying decisions made at the outset to the expanded version.

A3/5.2 Reg. 28 Duration of copyright in databases

A database created on or before 27 March 1996 which is in copyright on 31 December 1997 will continue to be copyright for up to 70 years beyond the author's death year. When there is no personal author, duration will continue up to 70 years beyond creation year if unpublished or 70 years beyond publication year. Otherwise, duration of protection is that stated under 'database right' below.

Comments

(1) It is noted that the traditional UK copyright duration in a compilation which is *not* a database (that is, made by 'sweat of brow' but not much intellectual effort) will be inapplicable to new works from 1 January 1998. New printed compilations, including sweat of brow (as noted under A3/4.1(2) above) after the end of 1997, which are not databases would carry traditional duration up to 70 years beyond author's death year; plus publishers' right in the typographical arrangement for 25 years beyond publication year. It is noted that new compilations in electronic format (only) which do not satisfy the definition of database will nevertheless carry traditional copyright at compilation level, because there is no distinction between electronic and print formats in the new law (just treated as kinds of 'writing'). Hence, incidentally, an electronic edition is a published edition just like text, but still subject to doubt re typographical arrangement. All this may be difficult for many users to comprehend, especially as it could lead to some anomalies.

(2) Determining what is or is not protected will be as difficult as it is in other contexts, requiring study of dates of publication on printed matter and author details. Desirably, dates of publication and nature of authorship should be made clear in respect of electronic databases.

Reg. 8 Permission under copyright: research or private study

Fair dealing with a database for the purposes of research or private study does not infringe any copyright in the database provided that the source is indicated.

However, it is made clear by a new s29(5) that copying from a database for a commercial purpose is not fair dealing (without defining 'commercial purpose').

Comments

How 'commercial purpose' could be properly defined is not at all clear – it is just as vague as 'commercial research' was in the Copyright, etc Bill in the autumn of 1987, before it was removed in response to lobbying. In the EC, lobbying is not feasible, although several Patent Office meetings were held to gather views of both publishers and users, though the latter were always outnumbered. The result in such circumstances must inevitably be a bias in favour of those national negotiators who are present at meetings in Brussels and their relative strengths and knowledge, not to say stamina.

Reg. 9 and Reg. 19 Lawful users

> A lawful user of a database which has been made available to the public in any manner shall be entitled to extract or re-utilise insubstantial parts of the contents of the database for any purpose. (Reg. 19 from SI 1997/3032)

This affects database right, and not also copyright in the compilation nor the items within it. Contracts cannot override this provision. However, since he is only a 'lawful user' when under licence or otherwise having permission, this should be expected to include the normal expectations, whether stated or not, of any purchaser of goods or services.

New ss50D and 296B will prevent a lawful user's right from being overridden by other contracts.

Comments

(1) It is of course to be expected that a lawful user is able to use a database for commercial purposes if his permission/licence so allows. This is taken also to apply to a library which is a 'lawful user'. In short, a 'lawful user' of a database is a subscriber or a licensee. That is, no user whether an individual or a library/archive, may become a lawful user except by some kind of 'licence'.

(2) In the latter, to what extent purchase might be regarded as 'licence' is not at all clear. Whether all information/library services may need to become licensed in respect of *any* database, thus taking in printed databases as well as electronic, cannot be foreseen at present. Much will depend on whether rights owner representative bodies are prepared to consider present copying norms (such as one article per periodical issue) to be 'insubstantial parts' and publish guidelines to that

effect. Although understandable for electronic databases with copyright contents, it would be quite intolerable if some form of licensing affected every compilation which qualifies as a database with two kinds of copyright (compilation level; any rights in items of content) in addition to database right to restrict extraction or re-utilisation of contents whether they are copyright or not. Such compilations which may be seen as databases include many well selected/arranged and original directories, dictionaries, encyclopedias, handbooks, as well as many electronic databases with noncopyright contents.

(3) However, Reg. 16 (see A5/3 below) defines 'infringement' of database right as ocurring only in respect of the whole or a substantial part (comparably with copyright law). Hence, *anyone* and not just lawful users may extract/re-utilise insubstantial parts for any purpose, including commercial. A possible difference is slightly firmer ground in Reg. 19 in the event of 'substantial' versus 'insubstantial' assessments.

A3/5.3 Part III of SI, on database right

Reg. 13 Definition of the right

This 'property right' subsists in a database 'if there has been substantial investment in obtaining, verifying or presenting the contents of the database', subject to *qualification as EEA national* (etc). It is affirmed that whether the contents are copyright is immaterial. Database right is vested in the 'maker – he who takes the initiative ... and assumes the risk of investing' ... etc.

Comments

It should be noted that the user has no means of judging whether a maker's investment has been 'substantial', this being so much a matter of opinion. For example, an information professional might find the work easier and cheaper, being so much in line with training skills. Accordingly, a maker can virtually claim anything he or she likes, and users should beware accordingly unless they are able and willing to afford an expensive defence. (The costs of appeal to the Copyright Tribunal could be thought to make that course generally flawed for the average organisation, as well as obviously so for an individual.)

Reg. 16 Infringement of database right

This occurs when a person *extracts or re-utilises* all or a substantial part of the contents. Note that *'the repeated and systematic extraction or re-utilisation of insubstantial parts ... may amount to ... a substantial part of those contents.'*

'Extraction' is the transfer, whether permanent or temporary, *'of contents to another medium by any means or in any form.'*

'Re-utilisation' is defined as *'making those contents available to the public by any means.'*

'Substantial', *'in relation to any investment, extraction or re-utilisation, means substantial in terms of quantity or quality or a combination of both.'* (See remarks on periodicals, A3/5.6(5).)

Comments

As might be expected, no guidance is given to the user as to whether – or indeed how – he should count the times he or any number of colleagues takes insubstantial parts (also judged qualitatively as well as quantitatively) and, if so, to what reasonable norm he and/or his colleagues should work!

Reg. 17 Duration of database right

The right lasts for 15 years beyond the calendar year of its completion, that is, from creation. However, under Reg. 29 a database completed on or after 1 January 1983 which is still in copyright on 1 January 1998 will begin a term of 15 years on that date, thus enjoying up to almost twice the norm of database right duration.

When made available to the public within 15 years of completion, a new period of 15 years begins after the end of the year of publication or availability. Moreover:

> 'Any substantial change to the contents ... including a substantial change resulting from the accumulation of successive additions, deletions or alterations, which would result in the database being considered to be a substantial new investment shall qualify the database' for a new period of 15 years.

Hence an updated service such as a bibliographic database or looseleaf handbook could enjoy indefinite protection. Thus there is potential monopoly in noncopyright data!

Comments

(1) In the Directive itself, Recital 45 states

> Whereas the right to prevent unauthorized extraction and/or re-utilization does not in any way constitute an extension of copyright protection to mere facts or data.

Despite Recital 45, the Directive accords potentially perpetual *sui generis* right to every single item of non-copyright data in a regularly updated database whether paper or electronic, such as bibliographical details, hard scientific data, etc., as well as having stipulated coverage by copyright of a whole or a substantial part of a collection as a compilation. A proposal was made during Patent Office discussions of the Draft Directive that 'time-stamping', necessary anyway for system reasons to show last revision could be used as the basis of copyright duration in an item if made displayable. That proposal did not succeed, but C-Dilla's (Reed Information Information Services) 'time-expiry' encryption system may be of interest in this context.

(2) As elsewhere, this brings in matters of opinion, and again a user is virtually at the mercy of the 'maker' (!). It is difficult to see how any amount of case law could help – even if users can wait for that – any more than case law could help with fair dealing copying extents when applied generally, since each case has its own peculiarities. However, in respect of licensing, case law based on the SI's Schedule 2(15) *could* establish an important principle (like the Magill case) for bodies such as publishers who can afford the litigation and the delay.

(3) As remarked under Reg. 17 above, electronic databases should be dated – either by displayable 'date-stamping' of each record, or by indicating to a user upon access a projected end-date for the whole.

Reg. 18 Qualification for database right

Qualification through EEA membership was to be expected, but bodies (incorporated or unincorporated) are included, as well as nationals of EEA member states, provided their administrations are appropriately located and/or linked with the economy of an EEA state.

Comments

The only reference to 'originality' is in new s3A(2), so it is certainly *not a qualification for database right.* Has this been thought through? What happens when a record extracted as an insubstantial part from database X is re-extracted by Y and then by Z?

In new s29(1A) and Reg. 20, the source must be indicated for fair dealing – what is the source after the X-Y-Z progress noted?

Reg. 24 Licensing

The jurisdiction of the Copyright Tribunal (CT) and provisions regarding licensing bodies and schemes closely parallel those in CDPA88 and are stated in Schedule 2 to Part IV of the SI. Possibly the most significant is the equivalent of CDPA88s144 as amended, dealing with *Powers exercisable in consequence of competition report,* namely the powers of the Monopolies and Mergers Commission. MMC would regard the following as operating against the public interest:

'(a) conditions in licences granted by the owner of database right ... restricting the use of the database by the licensee or the right of the owner ... to grant other licences; or

(b) a refusal of an owner of database right to grant licences on reasonable terms.'

The MMC is able to remedy or prevent adverse effects, including the cancellation or modification of licensing conditions and, instead or in addition, to provide that licences in respect of the database right shall be available as of right. Then, in default of agreement, the CT will settle the terms on application by a person requiring a licence.

A3/5.4 Permissions/exceptions re database right

Reg. 12(2) Lending

Making available a copy of a database through an establishment which is accessible to the public, otherwise than for economic or commercial advantage, does not constitute 'extraction or re-utilisation' of contents. The permission is inapplicable to reference access on the spot, which tallies with the rental/lending right provisions already in force.

Comments

From the last sentence above, there seems to be an implication that infringement could occur in the course of reference use in the database right context, with consequent conclusions regarding responsibility – but this should not involve supervision, for which staff time cannot be spared! A generally-applicable phrase to the effect that infringement is an individual responsibility might help.

Schedule 1 to Part IV Public administration

These permissions are listed in Schedule 1 to Part IV of the SI and closely parallel those in CDPA88 ss45-50 in respect of copyright, but none of existing CDPA88 permissions ss28,30-44 and 51-76 is reflected under database right.

Reg. 20 Education and research

Reg. 20 permits 'fair dealing' with a substantial part of the contents of a database by a lawful user for illustration for teaching or research purposes, but excludes commercial purpose. There are three points here:

Comments

(1) This appears to be the only use of the phrase 'fair dealing' outside CDPA88s29. However, if the intention is to balance otherwise unduly restrictive parts of the Directive, it should be appreciated by users, at least for what it is – which is absolutely minimal in view of the restriction to 'illustration'. Illustration for research is the more minimal of the two activities so generously permitted – of what use is it if information cannot be copied and passed around a team or onward to a colleague elsewhere?
But its vagueness could leave users who wish to make maximum use of it open to claims of 'unfairness', with the usual 'sword of Damocles' effect enjoyed (knowingly or not) by publishers when a prospective licensee cannot afford to raise objections because of the cost of using the Copyright Tribunal or making other defence.

(2) As it stands, Reg. 20 effectively overrides by exclusion the educational permissions in CDPA88 in respect of databases. So the new law will prevent an educational establishment from taking advantage of certain permissions in respect of a database of any kind (including image or music) unless only insubstantial parts are involved.

(3) At present, we are working to the definition of 'educational establishment' laid down by SI 1989/1068, as clarified at the time by the DES as embracing any instructional institution and any means of funding. It looks as though teaching by a private institution will now be seen as 'commercial purpose'. If so, a lot of bodies would be affected, starting with the Open University and going on through into private hospital information services.

(4) Whilst taking the implication that a commercially based lawful user would need *additionally* to be licensed for teaching or research uses, it is believed that 'commercial purpose' should not be left undefined

in this or other contexts in the SI. Please see separate comments in A3/5.6(5) below.

A3/5.5 Other Regulations

Reg. 21 Presumptions re maker of a database

Where a name purporting to be that of the maker appeared on copies of the database as published, or on the database when it was made, the person whose name appeared shall be presumed:

until the contrary is proved –
(a) to be the maker of the database, and
(b) to have made it in circumstances not falling within Regulations 14(2) to (4) (employee; Crown officer or servant; joint makers).

This is intended for application in proceedings and is therefore primarily for the use of one publisher or maker against another, infringing one – but this could include a user organisation as producer of another database of some kind.

The use of the past tense 'appeared' is interesting and appears to suggest that the drafter is no more certain of maker identification than most users, who incidentally cannot 'wait around' 'until the contrary is proved'.

Reg. 22 Application of copyright provisions to database right

This makes ss90-93 of CDPA88 (dealings), ss96-98 (rights and remedies) and ss101-102 (exclusive licensee rights and remedies) apply to database right as they do to copyright.

Schedule 1 on exceptions for public administration could have been simply included here, but instead repeats each of ss45-50 of CDPA88 with small changes in wording.

Regs. 23 and 24 Licensing, and Copyright Tribunal jurisdiction

A Schedule 2 on licensing of database right is referred to, and reflects existing copyright provisions on licensing schemes and bodies. CT authority is extended to the latter by Reg. 24.

Regs. 25 to 29 Savings and transitional provisions

Reg. 25 makes CDPA88 Part I definitions applicable to database right where the same expressions are used. Reg. 27 makes nothing in the Regulations affect any agreement made before 1 January 1998; nor any act done before commencement, or after commencement under an agreement made before commencement. Otherwise, under Reg. 26, the Regulations apply to databases made before or after commencement, except for copyright in existing databases covered by Reg. 28 and noted under duration of copyright above.

A3/5.6 Comments on the SI in general and on its application

There would seem nothing at all wrong with treating print and electronic formats alike, indeed much to commend this policy, at last clarified after some doubt since 1988. The following may however require discussion.

(1) Existing CDPA88 permissions

It seems most regrettable that the 'traditional' permissions of CDPA88 ss28, 30-44 and 51-76 are not reflected under database right. A delay in application in respect of printed matter might have helped users to adjust, preferably a moratorium for three years, but this appears to be out of the question.

As matters stand, chaos could theoretically follow, since all bodies concerned with those permissions, and particularly information services, depend on both statute and associated rights-owner guidelines to influence their behaviour. For example, is the extent to which a nonprofit-based library could copy from printed matter to be left unspecified except by 'lawful user' permissions or rights-owner guidelines? The latter may decline without statutory support, and in any event may take some time to produce and proclaim. In practice, however, it would seem that the only sensible course for the average user is to proceed with present permissions in respect of printed databases unless or until notified by rights owners, but check library notices when copying.

The user community will need to pay special attention to consequent problems in readiness for revision pleas at the projected three-year review of the Directive's operation. In particular, data should be sought on the actual use made of traditional permissions in the past, and their continued use for works other than databases, because the remainder of CDPA88 *as a whole* may be under revision from about 2001.

(2) Suggested compulsory sale of electronic records containing noncopyright data

Printed abstracts, by virtue of CDPA88 s60, in effect only carry enforceable copyright in typographical layout at present. Bibliographical data, being factual, is noncopyright already. It is suggested that:

(i) firstly, this situation should be confirmed in respect of the extraction of abstracts and bibliographical data by re-keying from any source;

(ii) secondly, electronic records of noncopyright data which have already been made available to the public should be compulsorily available for sale and downloading, at standard rates to be arbitrated by the Copyright Tribunal (CT) at the outset, *provided* this does not result in a database which competes with any individual source from which data has been extracted.

In (ii), it would not be appropriate to effect the arrangement similarly to other contexts, namely by providing that such data can be extracted unless there is a certified licensing scheme available. This is because no user could believe it reasonable for a database maker to be able to obtain a royalty for every occasion of display or extraction of a noncopyright record for a potentially perpetual period, thus having a monopoly in noncopyright data subject to standard payment rates to be arbitrated by the CT. A maker is nevertheless entitled to recompense for the labour of adding such records to a database, and repetitive sale of records should provide compensation.

During the final run-up to passage of the EU Directive, there were almost frantic efforts by publishers to remove all trace of compulsory or 'non-voluntary' licensing from the draft. This arose mainly, it is suggested, after its coverage had spread to copyright materials and to paper as well as electronic formats. In that atmosphere, the fact that noncopyright data and particularly bibliographic details still required special treatment was overlooked. Rights owners should in any event benefit from greater awareness of their products, but the decision whether or not to license *cannot surely* be left to publishers or producers if they lack understanding of user needs.

To expand on the foregoing, it has been suggested that non-voluntary licensing could be applied in the form of compulsory sale of non-copyright records to any eclectic database covering more sources than each base which is being asked to sell records, provided the resultant eclectic database is not competitive per se with any single large database. This pre-supposes that the outright sale of records to different services requiring to use subsets, whether an in-house system or an extra-murally available service, would more than adequately recompense a database producer for their work in keying-in and indexing, etc a non-copyright item into a compilation. If this be true, there might be some support for claiming that Berne Art. (2) should not be applied in such a way as to prevent greater use of an item when that use should bring more benefit to the copyright owner. All this is arguable, should it prove possible to have this matter discussed when the Directive comes under review. However, an administratively much cheaper solution for all concerned would seem to be a clear statutory permission for non-competitive use of bibliographic data and abstracts without payment, subject of course to rights owners arriving at a consensus on this matter. The Magill case (8.22) should establish a means of enforcing compulsory licensing for publishers but, as this can only apply to specific instances, it is no solution to the above problems for users – nor would operational time-frames and litigation costs permit this approach.

Information services need *reliably* to be able to extract relevant bibiographical data from *any source,* and compulsory licensing seems the only solution. In academe, they also need to be able to recover costs in order to remain reliably viable. Sale of records might be the only way for academe to produce much-needed interdisciplinary databases under specialist local control, tapping other databases selectively and removing the problems of not seeing 'wood-for-trees' and spending costly staff time searching separate databases for *every* occasion of need. Such endeavours are at present seriously inhibited or totally blocked by the inability to get producers to license for this purpose, since they still hold on to the erroneous belief that they can control everything by 'custom' services. Not only should information services and university researchers benefit but publishers also, from advertisement of their wares in a bibliographic database, since sources should be quoted.

(3) Suggested compulsory sale in respect of copyright records also

Provided extracted items were not re-utilised in competition with an individual source database, there appears to be a case for encouraging makers to make them available for sale in electronic format. However, this should be confined to records of which the rights are vested in the publisher/producer. This could help commercial database makers to increase the range of reliable new products, as well as information services needing to build internal files of mixed media whether copyright or not.

This could be effected (unlike noncopyright records, above) similarly to certain existing CDPA88 provisions which allow users to treat uses as licensed unless a suitable scheme is available. It is believed that some such provision would help commercial database making, as well as information services. Also, perhaps much litigation between commercial makers and uncertainty among users could be avoided, all of which represents a waste of costly resources.

(4) Lawful user

Regs. 9 (new s50D), 12, 16 and 19 have to be taken together in order to approximate to the Directive's Art.8(1)-(3). In Reg. 16, as might be expected, the definition of 'infringement' makes it possible by *implication* for anyone (not only a lawful user) to extract or re-utilise insubstantial parts for any purpose whatsoever.

Reg.19 indicates that, if a user has a licence to use a database, that licence shall not prevent him or her from actions which do not infringe database right. In supplementation of an earlier reference, it is assumed that this might be intended to prevent an individual service contract from prohibiting actions under a collective licence, but confirmation is needed.

Additional definitions of 'lawful user' could mitigate and clarify the situation for the user community:

(i) 'lawful user' includes *any* purchaser of materials or services. Such a purchaser can use the purchases *at least* for any of the purposes for which they have been published or produced, without further licence. (This would include an information service of any kind.)
(ii) a nonprofit-based organisation which is a lawful user as in (ii); and which offers an extra-mural service including database usage for which a charge is made; shall only be considered to be acting for a 'commercial purpose' when receipts exceed cost-recovery relating to purchased items/services and to staff etc costs. (cf Reg. 12(2), plus end of 10.4 above.)
(iii) anyone who visits and uses a nonprofit-based service which is a lawful user, whether or not he or his organisation is also a lawful user as subscriber or licensee etc., is himself a lawful user at least for reference and fair dealing purposes.
(iv) a person as in (iii) requiring a staffed copying service in a nonprofit-based library or archive must complete a declaration based on SI 1989/1212 which includes a warranty that the copy is not for a commercial purpose.

(5) Definition of commercial purpose

This is the worst problem of definition. Some difficulties were indicated in a briefing to Parliament during 1987-1988 when the removal of discrimination against commercial purposes from fair dealing was sought, with happy results for users but extreme discontent among publishers, who have since taken their offensive into WIPO and the CEC, obviously with success.

Periodicals

Single copies of single articles per issue of a periodical are the most common kind of copying in industry, commerce and the professions. Since a periodical is usually the result of original intellectual effort in selection and arrangement of contents, and therefore a 'database', the SI could in theory have most serious consequences. It should be recalled that the Government refused to discriminate against 'commercial research' in fair dealing during passage of the CDPA88, because of the projected enormous cost to industry, based on surveys.

Unless a single article per periodical issue can be acknowledged by rights owners as less than a substantial part, publishers may regard an issue as a database and press for licensing coverage of the massive number of single articles copied in a commercial environment. Then the Government's deliberate avoidance of discrimination against 'commercial research' in 1987/88 would come to naught, not only because of definition problems but also forecasts of economic damage to industry, now again looming on the horizon.

Discrimination against 'commercial' purposes in fair dealing, whose removal in the autumn of 1987 from the Copyright Bill was so hard won, will now return. Moreover, the discrimination can be expected to apply to all copying, other than 'public administration' purposes. However, all the reasons given in Parliamentary briefing documents against such discrimination still apply, as detailed by this author more recently than past lobbying (e.g. 'Copyright and text: commercial research and fair dealing', *Managing Information*, **1***(8)*, September 1994, p25-27). It is no clearer now than it was in 1987 just how 'commercial purposes' can be defined, unless all scientific research be treated as potentially commercial. (And then, what about defining 'scientific' and how about statistics?) Can it be guaranteed that no-one will claim a piece of academic research which happens to have commercial as well as non-commercial potential should be regarded as 'commercial purpose'?

Publishers are believed already to obtain full recompense through subscription levels – even for piracy overseas (for which law-abiding subscribers pay – as remarked in App. 2/1.2). The subscription levels are adjusted to meet profit targets, hence the profits are governed by market forces anyway. Is it fair that publishers should expect to be paid twice for reasonable uses of their products? Also, is licensing fair to authors, in that most copying is from periodicals and the sampling basis normally carries no authors' names, hence the net proceeds are liable to go to the Publishers Licensing Society for distribution to periodical publishers?

It is submitted that one article from a printed issue is fair expectation to a journal subscriber, and is absolutely essential for flexibility of working and exchange of ideas. As noted earlier, one article from an issue seems unlikely to be judged a substantial part of the issue in a test case, if anyone can afford one. If the BCC and others should prove inclined to continue claiming that an article is a whole work in itself, this argument should only be given credence when the item is part of a full-text electronic journal. Licensing should therefore not be enforced to cover single articles copied from printed matter (subject to CDPA88 s29(3) and s40, of course.)

Royalties for commercial purpose: printed matter

All information/library services or individuals in profit-based organisations can copy printed matter under fair dealing for any research at present. It is most regrettable that the SI ***might*** prevent this flexibility from continuing, though some mitigation might be possible via two suggestions as follows:

(i) Insert a Regulation containing a proviso to the effect that –

> In respect of a printed database, royalties are only payable for fair dealing for commercial purpose if charging is automatic through an electronic system which records author and other bibliographic details, or if a percentage mark-up has been applied to a subscription for a commercial address, or via a collective licence if available.

This would also cover any printing out from an electronic database. Royalties for CLARCS permissions are already covered automatically. Royalties for electronic applications to BLDSC and other document supply agencies are also charged automatically; and this could also cover all electronic delivery, of course. (This might also help progress towards an Electronic Copyright Management System.)

(ii) Provide that the fees charged in any licensing, whether individual or collective, shall be subject to arbitration by the Copyright Tribunal. However, this would be largely futile unless appeal to the CT were made easier and cheaper. Otherwise, those users who perceive a threat of litigation may fail to question adequately the terms of an offered licence, being unable to afford the costs and time of defence in court. The very inclusion of such a provision could possibly protect such users from rights owners who may make unreasonable demands, perhaps based on unusual or biased interpretations of the law.

(6) Comments on cost/benefit and policy

In distributing copies of the consultative document and draft SI, the Patent Office expressed particular interest in receiving views on exceptions, including cost/benefit elements of making exceptions or removing them. Regrettably, the user community had insufficient time to gather evidence, for which survey finance would be needed in any event. A great deal of information work has 'depth-charge' and other more subtle effects which are quite unquantifiable. Also, it is strongly believed that some of the worst effects of losing some exceptions or permissions would be incalculable and unquantifiable until it were too late. It is hoped therefore that a value judgement may be of interest:

> Sale of electronic records as in A3/4.6(3) above would lead to the creation of a much wider range of databases: interlinking, overlapping, etc but meeting special subset purposes. Also removed would be the 'wood-for-trees' problem and the time plus impossible expense problems of searching separately a range of very large databases individually for each occasion of need.

All information services know that the most useful services are those under local control which can extract essential items from a range of sources.

A3/5.7 General

The changeover to new procedures, development of new licensing methods, new financial provisions, and resultant confusion both to individual users and information services, will be very difficult indeed. Publishers and producers may also require a changeover period. A range of 'damage limitation' proposals was made to the Patent Office on behalf of users. These included some of the points above. To summarise, the main needs are:

(a) better definition of 'lawful user' of a database; 'commercial purpose'; and 'compilation when not a database';
(b) compulsory sale of at least noncopyright electronic records for noncompetitive purposes, to make possible a range of reliably comprehensive specialist information services under local control – these would tap large databases which would require too much time and money to consult for every occasion of need;

(c) fair dealing for education and research for commercial purposes in respect of non-copyright material and/or printed matter databases as a whole;
(d) provide library copying permissions as for copyright, at least for printed matter databases (e.g. dictionaries, directories, encyclopedias, handbooks, serials, and so on);
(e) other permissions also as for copyright in respect of printed matter databases – these include some intended for the disadvantaged.

If these needs do not receive attention, the way is left clear for those publishers/producers who feel so inclined to dictate their own licensing terms, under threat of litigation. The fear of litigation costs, including those of the Copyright Tribunal, is strong among user organisations, especially information/library services. The CT should be subsidised for user organisations. A concise overview appears in Managing Information, **5***(2)*, March 1998 (Aslib), with a footnote exemplifying the confusion concerning 'commercial purpose' which appears to arise in the UK's interpretation in the SI.

The various comments in the above could be regarded as a 'worst-case' scenario. A better one might develop:

- if rights-owner representatives recognise user needs for clarity and guidance, and urgently revise/confirm their various sets of guidelines on permissible actions on a reasonable basis, possibly reflecting traditional permissions as reasonable;
- if information services can afford to be licensed for just about every kind of action, perhaps irrespective of number of actions involved;
- if information professionals 'keep their cool' and proceed with current copying norms and procedures until they themselves discover, or are told by someone, that they may be infringing, then review the situation with expert guidance;
- if publishers can balance their understandable urge towards maximum profits with recognition of the needs of users; that is, the principal users, namely authors, present and future, who are also rights owners but know the need for flexibility and ready access to the works of others.

But the interim before confusion faded could not only be traumatic but might permanently damage any remaining respect among users for the views of militant rights owners in general and, more seriously in the long term, for intellectual property law, leading to clandestine infringement on a large scale.

However, this is not the end of the story, for draft Directives on 'reproduction right' and 'communication to the public right' are now imminent. Although some of their anticipated 'harmonisations' are already in UK law, others may well further reduce user permissions when SIs become passed in compliance in due course, namely the year 2000 at the earliest but probably later. When the harmonisation programme began, its aim was to produce a 'level playing field' for the information industries of the EC member states. This author thinks it would have been much better for the rest to be 'levelled up' to the UK's laws. As it is, although transgressors are quite properly losing any remaining foxholes and hillocks within or behind which to dodge rights owners, the users are losing their little havens against publisher militancy and suffering a reduction in the flexibility of working on which so much creativity depends.

All professionals in whatever sector may be, or could become, authors. Publishers who dig too diligently for a 'crock of gold at the end of the rainbow' should realise that they undermine their own foundations. As creators of intellectual content, authors are among the more important users of copyright materials of others. Their professional associations will need to become involved more deeply and actively involved in copyright concerns. Information service organisations such as Aslib should hold firmly to their tenets which, whilst requiring proper recompense for creators, involve maximum flexibility for users as the keystone of scientific and technical progress.

APPENDIX 4 – FROM CONFLICT TO COLLABORATION?

After years of controversy, sometimes quite bitter, between publishers and user representatives – mostly information service and library professionals – the pressures on both sides are exerting influence at last towards collaboration on solutions to the various problems of the Information Society. Nevertheless the underlying attitudes seem to have changed little so far, and users should still be wary of losing past privileges.

A4/1 Publisher/producer attitudes

Until recent collaborative efforts reported in Appendix 5, it has seemed that a few militant publishers have dominated group attitudes, in a similar manner to that seen at the beginning of the photocopy licensing movement. In those days, it was as though the monies gathered by collecting bodies acting for the film and record industries as were taken to exemplify the scale of benefits that any rights owner should expect of copyright licensing. Few should not know by now that the communication and information world is not fed by torrents of cash like the world of entertainment.

Nevertheless, one view prevails, for apparently there are hardliners who believe that they should be in complete control of all possible markets. And yet, desk-top or Internet publishing is growing apace, as also is university involvement in publishing. Some database producers envisage custom current awareness or abstracting services along with any copying back-up. It has appeared difficult to point out the need for small, highly relevant current awareness services in information services and libraries, including interdisciplinary services to counter the 'wood-for-trees' problem and avoid the impossible expense of regular consultation of a range of large databases for every need.

Strong publisher representations within the EU and WIPO, right up to a December 1996 meeting in Geneva, seemed all too easily to overwhelm user needs and views, and to seek to carry through publisher/producer control to the maximum extent. However, the December 1996 conference did leave users with some promise of more flexibility, but whether that will actually be provided is yet unknown.

A4/2 User attitudes

The attitude of most users continues to be impatience at restrictions which cause delay, but a readiness to pay a fair price for nonfair copying or other actions not subject to statutory permissions. Collective licensing is seen as still falling too far short of its original 'blanket' aim. However, the principle is gaining acceptance as a 'necessary evil' even if some users think point-of-sale licensing would be fairer to rights owners and users alike. The CDPA88 exceptions and permissions, and now the database right permissions, are highly valued for their flexibility. They will be defended in spite of some limitations, which users will seek to overturn where possible. The ECUP material in A4/3 below summarises needs in the electronic context.

Some think that the ruling out of 'commercial purpose' from fair dealing in the new 'database right' may be the thin end of the wedge to remove all permissions and exceptions which currently assist research and education. Others believe this may not happen, since rights-owner profits from subscriptions or purchase could suffer, and that needs will be covered by forms of 'lawful user' service contract with 'common core' terms. Certainly, without the present flexibility in respect of printed matter, self-service copying could be seriously affected, whether in libraries, industry, commerce or professional practices. And, because of staffing difficulties, self-service has become the main way of copying. In this context, the UK's specific statutory nonprofit-based library permissions (6) have particular value which the USA does not have (except via its publisher-challengeable 'fair use' concept and certain guidelines). Non-discriminatory fair dealing was a similar gain compared with the USA.

The rest of this Appendix contains extracts from selected documents of current interest, presented without comment for comparison of rights-owner and user views.

Reproduction of the various quotations is effected with the kind permission of the authorities concerned. Despite space problems in this volume, A4/7 and A4/8 are included as fully as possible. The author believes them to be important but unlikely to have been sufficiently available and studied by information service professionals.

A4/3 European Copyright User Platform (ECUP)

The following statement of user needs, expressed as 'user rights', has arisen from collaboration between 37 library associations which are full members of the European Bureau of Library, Information and Documentation Associations (EBLIDA). The UK is involved via the LA/JCC Working Party on Copyright (12.39). Entitled *Position on user rights in electronic publications* and issued in September 1996, the document first outlines the need for balance between publishing and user interests. Whilst recognising that the new technologies pose uncertainties for economic returns for rights owners –

> The uncontrollability of electronic information is a fear which libraries share with the copyright owners.... The nightmare future for libraries is one in which nothing can be looked at, read, used or copied without permission or payments. In an evolving electronic environment this could mean that information resources are purchased and accessible only to those libraries and members of the public who are able to pay. The public information systems that libraries have developed would be replaced by commercial information vendors and a diminished scope of public rights would lead to an increasingly polarised society of information have's and have-not's.

The balance evolved for printed matter, it is stated, should remain in the digital environment. The user's legitimate rights to use copyrighted material must be protected, and benefits of new technologies should be available to all – the public, libraries and copyright owners. Six principles are listed, the first being the 'guiding principle':

> The user has a right to have access to copyrighted material and to make a copy for private use and research or educational purposes. It is the duty of the library to provide access to copyright material and the library should have the possibility to do so without infringing the principle of the 'normal exploitation of a work' (Berne, Art. 9(2)).

Other detailed principle are set out, such as:

> that copyright control systems (should be) able to differentiate between legitimate and illegitimate usage. The last assures rights owners that libraries will strive to ensure the implementation of .... safeguards ...(and that) their users are informed about the copyright restrictions.

It is concluded that no major revision of law is required at this time. However, libraries and publishers should use pilot projects, within the controllable environment of the library, to experiment with new products and technologies in 'the uncertain times ahead'.

Charts of activities which should be considered lawful are appended to the six pages of text. On the charts:

- 'internal library activities' means those necessary to preserve and organise information and publications in printed or electronic format efficiently;
- 'open user group' is a group of unidentifiable individuals: the general public;
- 'closed user group' is a clearly defined group of individuals who have a formal relationship with the organisation;

- 'registered users' are library members or password holders;
- 'unregistered users' are individuals not known to the library;
- 'on-site access' relates to an activity within the premises where an information service is provided or within a controllable environment, and
- 'off-site access' is the opposite;
- 'allowed' relates to an activity not seen as an infringement – that is, can be done without permission;
- 'licensed' means use of the material obtained in electronic format from the publisher; and
- 'viewing' includes accessing, browsing, searching, retrieving.
- 'free' and 'pay' relate to library intentions for service to users.

In the tables opposite and overleaf, please note:

EDD means the Electronic Document Delivery service of a library

Extensive quotation from ECUP material is permitted by courtesy of Emanuella Giavarra.

	National Library	University Library	Public Library	Other Libraries
internal library activities	**allowed**: digitisation, permanent electronic storage, indexing, one archival copy	**allowed**: digitisation, permanent electronic storage, indexing, one archival copy.	**allowed**: digitisation, permanent electronic storage, indexing, one archival copy.	**allowed**: digitisation, permanent electronic storage, indexing, one archival copy.
open user group registered on-site	**allowed**: viewing full text, copying a limited number of pages - electronically or on paper.	**allowed**: viewing full text, copying a limited number of pages - electronically or on paper	**allowed**: viewing full text, copying a limited number of pages - electronically or on paper	
open user group unregistered on-site			**allowed**: viewing full text, copying a limited number of pages on paper	
open user group registered off-site	**allowed**: viewing full text, copying a limited number of pages - electronically or on paper pay-per-use: EDD	**allowed**: viewing full text, copying a limited number of pages - electronically or on paper pay-per-use: EDD	**allowed**: viewing full text, copying a limited number of pages - electronically or on paper	**allowed**: viewing full text, copying a limited number of pages - electronically or on paper pay-per-use: EDD
open user group unregistered off-site	***no access at all***	***no access at all***	***no access at all***	***no access at all***
closed user group on-site off-site		**allowed**: viewing full text, copying electronically or on paper, EDD		**allowed**: viewing full text, copying electronically or on paper, EDD

ECUP position on user rights in publications digitised by the library

	National Library	University Library	Public Library	Other Libraries
internal library activities	**free**: permanent electronic storage and indexing.	**free**: permanent electronic storage and indexing	**free**: permanent electronic storage and indexing	**free**: permanent electronic storage and indexing
open user group registered on-site	**free**: viewing full text documents, copying a limited number of pages - electronically or on paper.	**free**: viewing full text documents, copying a limited number of pages - electronically or on paper.	**free**: viewing full text documents, copying a limited number of pages - electronically or on paper.	
open user group unregistered on-site			**free**: viewing full text documents, copying a limited number of pages - electronically or on paper.	
open user group registered off-site	**free**: viewing of an abstract or one page. pay: viewing full article, copying electronically or on on paper, EDD	**free**: viewing of an abstract or one page. pay: viewing full article, copying electronically or on on paper, EDD	**free**: viewing of an abstract or one page. pay: viewing full article, copying electronically or on on paper, EDD	**free**: viewing of an abstract or one page. pay: viewing full article, copying electronically or on on paper, EDD
open user group unregistered off-site	***no access at all***	***no access at all***	***no access at all***	***no access at all***
closed user group on-site off-site		**free**: viewing, copying electronically or on paper, EDD		**free**: viewing, copying electronically or on paper, EDD

ECUP position on user rights in electronic publications provided by the publisher
(N.B. The author assumes 'free' in this context to mean 'unrestricted to a lawful user'; compared with 'pay per use'.)

A4/4 ECUP 'Heads of agreement'

This proposal for common heads for site licences for the use of electronic publications was also issued in September 1996. The key heads of the nine proposed are III and IV:

III Permitted activities – by Licensor to Licensee –

- use on site, or within any Local Area Network (LAN);
- electronic transmission to users in open groups registered on or off-site;
- offsite open group users allowed viewing of full text and copying electronically or on paper;
- EDD (Electronic Document Delivery) services to be provided on a pay-per-use basis and royalties to be forwarded to rights owners.

IV Prohibited activities – warranties by Licensee –

- not to permit use on a LAN which is connected to a Wide Area Network;
- not to provide access by users in unregistered open groups off-site;
- no exploitation or activity other than as permitted in III without written consent of the Licensor; and
- no activity which may impede marketing of the product by the Licensor.

A4/5 JISC/PA collaboration

The Joint Information Services Committee (JISC) and the Publishers Association (PA) have been in collaboration for several years. The JISC was set up in April 1993 as part of HEFC, the Higher Education Funding Council, which works together with the several funding councils for Scotland, Wales and Northern Ireland. Membership is not confined to academics and includes commercial representatives, notably of the PA.

Five joint working parties were set up by JISC/PA following a meeting in July 1996, in order to seek solutions to problems between the university and publishing communities in respect of materials in electronic and/or networked forms:

1. Standard licensing agreements;
2. Clearance mechanisms;
3. Fair dealing in the electronic context;
4. Provision of and access to networks;
5. Retention of electronic materials.

Each member of a working party was to put forward personal rather than representative views. This was to be a problem-solving exercise rather than a negotiation procedure, with commissioning of research where necessary.

The JISC is located at HEFC in Bristol (12.39). Dr. Malcolm Read has kindly given permission for quotation from several documents represented here. In the spring of 1997 there appeared: *JISC/PA Working Parties: an analysis of progress to April 1997, a report for the JISC prepared by Mark Bide, Mark Bide and Associates*, from which it is clear that important progress towards problem-solving and/or mutual understanding has been made in all five of the work areas. Some issues are discussed.

From (1), a *JISC/PA Draft model licence for digitisation/electronic use* was issued for comment in June 1997.

Each of the five work areas is necessarily establishing definitions. In the draft licence of (1) a definition, which would be logically applicable in the academic context where CLA coverage is general and 'lawful user' licences will doubtless exist, reads:

> 'Commercial Use' – [external] use for the purposes of monetary reward (whether by or for the Licensee or an Authorized User) by means of sale, resale, loan, transfer, hire or other form of exploitation of the Electronic Material. For the avoidance of doubt Commercial Use does not cover use by the Licensee or by an Authorized User of the Electronic Material in the course of research funded by a commercial organization.

From (3) came an April 1997 *draft* report which contains *Guidelines for electronic fair dealing* covering both do's and don'ts of viewing; printing on to paper; copying of a part on to disk; copying of a whole publication on to disk; transmission to enable printing re whole or part; transmission for permanent storage of whole or part; and posting on a network. As in the last paragraph, this is intended for consideration in the academic context and should not be considered generally applicable at present.

A4/6 Library and Information Commission

LISC issued a report in mid-1997: *New library; the people's network*, said to be:

> a milestone in the development of the public library service, linking it into the National Grid for Learning and the development of an information community that is genuinely global and local in its membership.

Section 6 on *Copyright and licensing issues* (10 pages):

(a) the introduction mentions the need for digitisation, subject to negotiation with rights owners; the need for a standard licence or a set of standard licences; and points to special privileges of UK public libraries:

> Although these cannot easily be transposed into the electronic domain, they should not be neglected in the search for an equitable balance between the UK Public Library Network and copyright owners.

(The only brief mention of fair dealing is in this context and no suggestions are later made, although nonprofit-based library copying is summarised in (d).)

(b) summarises the law for protection of rights on the proposed network;
(c) discusses whether rights owners can be offered an attractive return;
(d) describes the special position of UK libraries arising from ss37-44 of the CDPA88;
(e) suggests which bodies might be approached as rights-owner representatives;
(f) proposes an agency for negotiating licences, separate from a proposed Public Library Networking Agency which will hold the licences;
(g) suggests licence terms (which might be compared with the 'heads' proposed by ECUP) and indicates the need for licences to be:

> as standard as possible ...Specific model licences could be developed for use with public access/educational-type licences ...These licences might contain reciprocal provisions benefiting the copyright owners – for example, by granting hyperlink access to their content on the national network from local library networks, university intranets, and museum or gallery Web sites.

(h) end-user terms, postulates warranties perhaps through screen appearance before a user indicates acceptance of service; and
(i) briefly remarks on several 'other rights', such as in screen explanations and layouts, and in compilations for the network databases. Lastly mentioned are the possible rights of local libraries or library networks in material and databases which they have created, 'which should merit special treatment as falling into the public access/educational category.'

The report has been issued for general comment, as well as comment by information service/library professionals. Written comments should go to Matthew Evans at LIC (12.39). It should be noted that this report and issues/developments arising from it may well be under discussion for several years. (See App. 1/8.2 for citation and a web address, at which a discussion list is available.)

A4/7 Ad Hoc Alliance for a Digital Future

Some 16 computer and telecommunications firms which, whilst doubtless in line for extensive windfalls or 'fallout' from the Information Society, are seeking a proper balance of copyright user and rights-owner aims. The following document was received in April 1997 from the 'ad hoc alliance' named above. This author believes it surveys joint interests of producers and users in a fair manner. Permission for reproduction in full has kindly been arranged by Thomas Vigne of Morrison and Foerster, Brussels.

AD HOC ALLIANCE FOR A DIGITAL FUTURE

Principles for Copyright Directives

Copyright Law Must Strike a Balance

The Information Society promises to make more information available to more people than ever imagined, furthering the advancement of culture, learning entertainment, and democratic participation. To fulfil this promise, as recognised by the WIPO Copyright and Performance and Phonograms Treaties, a balance must be achieved between the interests of copyright holders, performers and producers of phonograms, and the larger public interest. The European Commission has also quite rightly stated in its Follow-up to the Green Paper on Copyright and Related Rights in the Information Society that any EC copyright directive should respect this need for balance.

Those who *provide, deliver and consume* content in the Information Society are each economically dependent on one another. Content providers must have adequate protection and resulting revenue or they will lack the incentive to produce and to place works into a digital environment. Infrastructure providers, which like the postal services simply deliver the messages of others, must have predictability about, and appropriate limitations upon, their ability for copyright infringement. Absent a proper legal framework, infrastructure providers inevitably will be inhibited from introducing open services to deliver information, including copyrighted works, and the building of the Information Infrastructure will be threatened. Consumers must have adequate access to copyright works at reasonable cost or there will be no market for Information Society products.

An unbalanced copyright regime would restrict access to the Information Society and lead to the concentration of copyright ownership and the distribution of copyright works, thus undermining the ability of smaller actors to play a meaningful role in the Information Society.

A balanced copyright regime, which takes into account the legitimate interests of all players, will result in a competitive market and thereby optimise trade in copyright works.

Any Expansion of the Rights of Reproduction and Communication to the Public Must Reflect This Need for Balance

The digital age requires a harmonised copyright regime to eradicate existing market distortions and prevent the emergence of new distortions. However, changes in copyright law can have dramatic economic and social consequences and any such changes should be undertaken only after careful and complete analysis of the consequences they may have on copyright owners, consumers, industrial users, consumer electronics, computer companies and telecos.

In defining how copyright is to be applied in the digital context, the proper boundaries of and between the rights of reproduction and communication to the public should be carefully considered in light of the impact of the digital environment on how copyrighted works are exploited, distributed, accessed and processed through dynamic digital technology.

Copyright law must reflect the economic and technical realities of the Information Society. Specifically, it must take account of the nature of digital networks and technology, and in particular the fact that creating temporary (ephemeral) copies is essential and technically necessary for transmitting information over networks and for using consumer electronic and computer equipment.

The existence of appropriate limitations upon and exceptions to copyright, including those permitting normal acts of reproduction by consumers, is fundamental to maintaining balance in the law. Existing exceptions and limitations to rights should be reduced only after very careful consideration and justification. Moreover, as the Agreed Statements to the WIPO Copyright and Performances and Phonograms Treaties indicate, it may be appropriate 'to devise new exceptions and limitations that are appropriate in the digital network environment'.

Among other things, exceptions must be crafted ensuring that the normal functionality of equipment is not undermined, and that it is permissible to make copies during normal operations of electronic devices, audio, video or multi-media equipment for private use, and in the context of broadcasting and transmission where such copies are temporary or incidental to the primary use of the work.

Any legislation expanding the right of communication to the public must make it clear, as provided in the Agreed Statements to the WIPO Copyright Treaty, that 'the mere provision of physical facilities for enabling or making a communication does not in itself amount to communication'.

Any copyright directive should harmonise Member State law on the scope of copyright protection by implementing Article 2 of the WIPO Copyright Treaty, which provides that 'copyright protection extends to expressions and not to ideas, procedures, methods of operation or mathematical concepts as such'.

Copyright Liability Must Be Appropriately Limited

The issue of liability is closely linked with the question of the scope of rights of copyright holders. Inconsistent rules on liability for copyright infringement are at least as great a threat to the Single Market and to the development of the Information Society as are unharmonised rights. It would be inappropriate to delay consideration of liability issues arising from the updating of rights for the digital environment until after the adoption of harmonised rights.

Clear and fair rules on liability for infringement of any harmonised rights of reproduction and communication to the public, including appropriate limitations of liability for on-line service providers or the providers of similar technology, must be included within any copyright directive. These rules must reflect the fact that infrastructure and other providers are not technically able to review message content and hence cannot monitor nor control the vast quantity of public and private content transmitted over networks.

Infrastructure and technology investment will be severely prejudiced unless infrastructure and technology builders and providers can predict and control when they will be liable for copyright infringement.

Copyright law should not force service providers or network operators to act as censors of the materials delivered on their networks in order to control their potential liability. To do so would introduce an unacceptable and inappropriate restriction of freedom of speech, the free flow of information, and privacy.

Liability for copyright infringement must be limited to situations where the service provider, network operator or equipment manufacturer/retailer has taken responsibility for content. In particular, service providers and equipment manufacturers must be sure that they will not be held liable as a result of users placing material on their networks or using standard consumer electronic and computer products, unless the service provider or equipment manufacturer/retailer has taken responsibility for the content.

Actual knowledge of an infringement must be a prerequisite of liability for copyright infringement in the digital network context, where a multitude of works may be reproduced and distributed instantly without the active intervention of a service provider, network operator or equipment manufacturer.

Any Provision on Technical Protection Systems Must Respect the Existing Copyright Balance

As do Articles 11 of the WIPO Copyright Treaty and 18 of the Performances and Phonograms Treaty, any copyright directive should focus on the *act* of circumvention rather than on the manufacture or sale of devices that facilitate circumvention.

Any person who knowingly circumvents a technical protection system for the purpose of making infringing copies should incur civil liability, and criminal penalties should be available against those who do so for commercial gain. Similar rules and effective sanctions should apply to anyone who interferes or tampers with rights management information.

If any copyright directive is to focus on copy restriction devices, any provision should adhere to the following principles:

- It should avoid effectively mandating the implementation in consumer electronic devices or computer or telecommunications equipment of any unilaterally introduced technical protection system or standard;

- It should not extend to any product or system that has been designed without the object of circumventing technical protection systems to facilitate infringement;
- It should not extend to any consumer electronic device or computer or telecommunications equipment that has a substantial non-infringing use;
- It should not undermine existing copyright privileges; and
- It should permit producers, including in particular manufacturers of consumer electronics devices and computer and telecommunications equipment, to foresee the risk of violating the provision at the time they design their products.

Certain *access protection systems,* such as encryption systems preventing access to television signals, should be regulated in separate legislation, such as the upcoming encrypted services directive, rather than in any copyright directive. Provided they are carefully defined, such access protection systems can properly be subjected to stricter regulation than *copy restriction devices* (which restrict the copying of works already in the process of the copier).

April 1997

Ad Hoc Alliance for a Digital Future

Amdahl Corporation
British Telecommunications plc
Computer and Communications Industry Association
European Association of Consumer Electronics Manufacturers
European Committee for Interoperable Systems
European Public Telecommunications Network
Operators' Association*
France Telecom
MCI Communications Corporation
Nokia Corporation
Philips International b.V.
Storage Technology Corporation
Sun Microsystems
Tele Denmark
Telecom Finland Ltd
Telenor
Telia Infomedia Content Center AB

* *ENTO represents 36 telecommunications operators from 31 European countries.*

A4/8 Publishers' statement

It has been obvious for some years that views differ among publishers on the needs of users. For example, members of the Association of Learned and Professional Society Publishers have long shown greater consideration of and identification with user requirements than many large and more commercially-based publishers. Moreover, this has been apparent in spite of the way in which almost every small UK organisation, once producing documents either gratis or at low cost, was forced by post-Second World War economics to seek income from publishing in order to finance other projects.

This is considered to be one end of the scale. The November 1996 statement below emanates from strongly commercial publishers, and perhaps represents the other end of the scale, where profit is essential not only to the firms involved but also to the national economy. Three points to bear in mind are:

(a) Much is made of Berne Article 9(2), but no account is taken of the strong possibility of benefit to authors (with whom Berne was originally concerned anyway) – and indeed publishers – from compulsory licensing in some circumstances (see App.3/5).

(b) In the second paragraph under the heading 'The future role of libraries', it is noted that the document is concerned solely with use of digitised works. The same paragraph indicates that legitimate library use of 'printed copyright works' and other exceptions need not be affected. Fair dealing is not among the examples, but the reason may be the international nature of the document.

(c) This autumn 1996 statement might be regarded as the 'global word', but the 'European deed' is the removal of most UK permissions on printed databases as a result of compliance with the Directive passed in March of the same year. (Whether some might be restored under a forthcoming new Directive on reproduction right is not at all clear, but that would take several years to come into force anyway.)

It is suggested that readers may wish to study the whole statement in conjunction with the foregoing items in this Appendix. The publisher case appears to this author to be well-argued and persuasively presented in respect of electronic formats. Nevertheless, if the balance achieved for printed matter is going to be permitted to continue to survive to any degree in the Information Society, individual users should be prepared to take a closer interest in issues. Authors in particular, not only as the prime creators but also as the principal users, should work towards compromise solutions which aim to be fair to publishers and producers as well as the user community as a whole. The solutions should reflect the essentials of the present hard-won flexibility of day to day use of printed matter, as well as allow freedom to users to manipulate and communicate information. Such is the essence of the cross-fertilisation of ideas and further creativity. By courtesy of Clive Bradley, Chief Executive of The Publishers Association, the statement is reproduced in full below.

THE USE OF DIGITISED COPYRIGHT WORKS IN LIBRARIES

> A statement on behalf of electronic, book and journal publishers by the International Publishers Association (IPA) and International Association of Scientific, Technical and Medical Publishers (STM), represented by the International Publishers Copyright Council (IPCC) [1]

The development of the information society enables information and ideas of all kinds to be made readily available to users through digital networks, superhighways and other electronic platforms, often in radically new forms which take full advantage of multi-media digital technologies. These dramatic developments are bringing about major changes in the roles of all the parties in the chains through which information is made available to the public, including to the roles of publishers as developers and producers of information materials, and of libraries as resources through which the public can access published information. This statement, made on behalf of the publishers of works commonly used in libraries, sets out how the publishing industry sees the role of libraries developing in the future, in particular in respect of the operation of the copyright systems necessary for the continuance of viable and high quality information services.

Copyright essential to investment in new services

The growth of the information society as a major economic and social resource has been shown in a series of carefully considered government reports, most notably the Lehman report in the United States and the Bangemann report in the European Union, to be dependent on substantial private sector investment in the new digitised 'contents' services. The availability of the investment, the reports confirm, inevitably depends on publishers being able to make a fair return on their investment, which in turn is dependent on making the copyright system fully effective in the digitised environment.

Copyright is the vital support for creativity, but it is also the trading system for literary and other creative works, giving authors, producers and publishers the ability to earn from their work, their skill, and their investment, by granting them the exclusive rights to authorise i) the reproduction (the making) of copies, and ii) the first distribution or communication of their work to the public. An effective world-wide copyright system is a vital stimulus to the availability of works in the required variety and quality.

This essential role of copyright in supporting information services and creativity is common ground between the publishing and library sectors. Neither sector sees a requirement for major changes in existing international and national copyright law. The need is to adapt the system to reflect the requirements of the new environment.

Digitisation and networking jeopardise system unless new practices accepted

Digitisation and networking of creative works offer many valuable benefits, enabling users to search and have access, at their own desks or in libraries, to vast masses of information, published in forms offering considerable added value, from which they can select the precise 'bits' that they need, interact with them, and download them to meet their own requirements. These services may be available on-line or through physically distributed products. Information made available in this way can be readily reproduced and networked so that there is no longer dependence on access to a limited number of physical copies available only in a limited number of places. While this wide availability of digitised services may lead to reduced distribution costs, it nevertheless requires large investments in the initiation and creation, updating, marketing and promotion of high quality materials. The return on such investments, and the quality of the services, is dependent on the ability to earn rewards based on the uses made of the materials and their value.

At the same time, because users may readily download, reproduce, make changes to, and store copies on servers for use throughout networks, or make their own digital copies of printed works, in private and outside the control and knowledge of the copyright holders, the new digitised services put the established copyright system into jeopardy. This process of private copying replicates the very purpose of publishing the works in digitised form in the first place. When this is done outside the agreement or licence of the copyright holder, setting out the terms on which the work is made available for reproduction and dissemination, in return for the payment made for the use of the work, in accordance with copyright law, it inevitably infringes the copyright in the work, and inhibits investment in it.

Publishers, and other copyright holders, are therefore developing new copyright management systems to enable these uses to take place in the new digitised environment on a viable basis.

Traditional and new library services

The established role of libraries - national, public, educational and research – is to make printed copyright works, principally books and periodicals, available to users for consultation and lending. Under many systems of law, non-profit libraries are also permitted, in strictly controlled circumstances which must comply with the Berne International Copyright Convention, to make single copies of limited proportions of printed copyright works for their users, principally for 'private' use, as an exception to the general rules.

Libraries also seek to share their physical resources through inter-library loans of printed works, and in some countries non-profit libraries may be able to provide 'document supply services', providing single copies of parts or the whole of printed works for researchers for use away from the library.

National libraries and their equivalents may also be entitled to statutory deposit copies of printed works for archival purposes, though may be subject to limitations on the uses made of these free copies (for example, they may not usually be used for photocopying or document delivery).

Libraries now wish to be able to offer similar services, including through networks, to their users in respect of digitised copies of copyright works, either by making available digital or printed-out copies of part or all of published digitised works, or by making their own digitised copies of printed works for such use, and argue that they should be entitled to do so at no charge under the terms of the statutory exceptions permitted for printed works.

The publishing industry, however, insists that the publication of copyright works in digitised form, and their availability and reproduction in libraries under sale and licensing of use arrangements which reflect the value of each work and the uses made of it, in themselves provide users with the benefits provided under statutory exceptions. So to extend the statutory exceptions to permit free private copying of digitised works in libraries, with their large number of users, would duplicate and undermine the whole purpose of the licences governing sale and use. Indeed, such licences would become largely redundant, seriously restricting the ability to earn proper rewards for the use of copyright works in libraries, which in many cases may be the principal market for the works, and in other parts of the market. Publishers insist that, indeed, in the digitised environment, such exceptions are excluded under the provisions of the Berne International Copyright Convention.[2]

In the same way, the use of digitised works, outside the terms of licensing arrangements, for inter-library loan or for document delivery, or using deposit copies as material for making such copies[3], precisely replicates the benefits available from publishing works in digitised form.

Similarly, making a digitised copy of a printed work, as a means of overcoming the limited availability of printed copies, in effect permits republishing for wide use to take place contrary to the exclusive rights of the copyright holder, and inhibits the copyright holder from itself publishing in digitised form, for a potential market which can be of high value.

The future role of libraries: a new partnership

The publishing industry does not want to prevent libraries operating effectively in the new digitised environment. Indeed, it sees libraries as vital partners in the information chain. The availability of digitised information requires new legal and organisational systems of licensing, payment and control, and more effective and rapid enforcement procedures, operated with the co-operation of the library community, to mutual benefit. The industry urges, as a matter of vital importance to the future of information services, that traditional forms of making works available through libraries, and of payment for copyright works, need to be changed to comply with new licensing arrangements if investment in many important information resources is not to dry up, to public detriment.

These new arrangements need not affect the continuing legitimate use of printed copyright works by libraries, nor affect other exceptions to copyright permitting, for example, quotation for purposes of criticism, analysis, or news reporting. This statement is concerned solely with 'private' copying and use of digitised works in libraries and similar institutions such as educational and research organisations.

Many different forms of licences and supporting copyright management schemes for use of works in libraries and elsewhere are being developed. In many cases, the objective is to replace outright payments for products which may be constantly developing and changing, and which, because of their extensive content and other added values, can be of very high cost, with payments based on the uses made of the different elements, and their values. This enables a library either to recover the costs of each use (or of a series of uses) from the user, or to decide to meet such charges itself, though many different forms of arrangement may be used by both publisher and library to recover their respective costs. Invariably, licences will limit how far copies may be made and disseminated from the original digitised copy available to the library. The crucial need is to ensure that libraries, and their users downstream, respect the relevant terms. Individual publishers, and their representative bodies, are always ready to discuss how such copyright management arrangements may be made to work more effectively in practice.[4]

In particular, the publishing industry is anxious to avoid systems which are unduly bureaucratic or which are otherwise impractical. There are however some essential requirements for management and control which the industry believes are acceptable given the benefits available to libraries from their ability to provide their users with digitised services.[5]

Vital new role for libraries as service to users

While a limitation on existing library practices to accommodate the changes required by the rapidly growing availability of digitised information may seem to some to threaten the value of libraries as repositories and access points to information, the growth of new electronic information services, far from making the role of libraries redundant, increases the need for professional librarians and library services able to make expensive resources available to the public. Libraries and librarians will become ever-closer partners of other professionals in the information chain by continuing to acquire published information services from publishers to make them available to the public, by guiding users in accessing networks and their electronic resources, and by helping users in the process of search and selection on the most cost-effective and efficient terms. In undertaking this function, libraries will continue to have to pay for the services they acquire at prices reflecting the appropriate values and terms of use, but they will increasingly be able to recover these costs, and their own costs in providing an efficient service, from their users, through the co-operative operation of licensing arrangements.

Inadequacy of public funding as information provider for future

Indeed, it is highly unlikely that, without such a structure, bodies such as university, school, college, public, specialist, and even national libraries, will be provided in the future with the public funding needed to provide expensive digitised services. Funding systems based on the concepts set out in this statement comply with the requirements of modern public sector management systems designed to ensure the most effective use of scarce resources.

Further, access by libraries to electronic information services on the basis of exceptional copyright treatment would manifestly create deeply unfair competition for other information providers who provide equivalent commercial information services on the economic terms needed to secure a proper return on investment.

Information rich and information poor

It is sometimes argued that some library users, including students, less well-off members of the public, and residents of less developed countries, are financially underprivileged, so that requiring libraries to operate within economically viable systems would have the effect of creating discrimination between the 'information rich', able to afford economic charges, and the 'information poor', so increasing existing social divisions.

While it is certainly true, especially in the case of public libraries, that such divisions exist between different users, this is not a logical justification for avoiding the need to establish a working and viable system for supporting investment in electronic services and securing a fair return from the investment. The gap between the information rich and the information poor is a problem for general management of the economy, not a justification for creating a non-viable system of information management or for preventing sensible returns on vital investment.

It is recognised that the digitised environment presents libraries with a major cultural change, equivalent to that being faced by others in the information sector. Instead of libraries providing 'free' services (actually, services provided largely at public expense supplemented by limited privileges designed to overcome physical limitations on the availability of printed products), they will need, like other sectors of the economy, to recover their own costs and overheads, and the costs of their supplies, from their own clients, according to the value of their services, and in competition with other providers on the networks offering similar services.

Only through the development of the type of copyright arrangements described in this statement can an effective international system of creating and disseminating knowledge be maintained and further developed in the digitised information society of the future. The solutions described in this statement offer a fair and well-balanced role for all members of the information chain, enable fair returns to be made on investments in valuable new services, and guarantee the protection of creative work.

29 November 1996

Footnotes

1 This Statement has been prepared in co-operation with the Federation of European Publishers, and is issued by FEP simultaneously.

2 The permitted exceptions enjoyed by libraries for works in printed form are governed by Article 9(2) of the Berne International Copyright Convention. This provides that national laws may only permit exceptions to the exclusive right to authorise the making of copies subject to a three step test: i) the exception must be in respect of a 'special case'; ii) the exception must not conflict with the normal exploitation of the work by rights owner; and iii) the exception must not prejudice the legitimate interests of the rights owner.

It is self-evident that, when a work is published in digitised form, giving it wide availability without limitation on the number of physical copies, copying that work outside the terms of copyright holder's licence is not a 'special case', and inevitably conflicts with the normal exploitation of the work, and with the legitimate interests of the rights owner. The extension of existing 'private use' exceptions, which may be appropriate to printed copies, with their limited physical availability, to the new digitised environment would be in total contradiction of the long-established provisions of the Berne Convention.

The acceptability of the statutory 'private copy' exceptions has in any case been eroded by the relatively recent ability to make photocopies on sophisticated copying machines, which remains a matter of considerable controversy between librarians, researchers and teachers and copyright holders. But while that controversy is far from being resolved, it has proved possible to keep it reasonably in bounds by various forms of agreed voluntary licensing systems, serving as an analogy for future developments in the digitised environment.

3 Since there may be no licence setting out terms of use for a statutory deposit copy, rights holders are likely to accept that the deposit library may give access to the deposit copy in the deposit library itself at a stand-alone work station. Use beyond this, e.g. networking, should only be permissible with the licence of the rights holder.

4 Rights holders are engaged in developing new systems of management of copyrights available to users. Such systems may permit different levels of use, and require different forms of consideration, or payment, for the uses made of a work, dependent on the responsive to the conditions of the particular market. Thus:

- A work may be given away without any restriction. Press releases fall into this category: the originator desires to make the work widely available, and requires no payment - though he or she may want to prevent the work from being altered, for example.

- A work may be sold outright, so that a user (purchaser) faces no further financial obligation, but will nevertheless be prohibited from making duplicate copies available to others, or to be permitted to do so on appropriate conditions.
- The user may be required to pay a subscription, in return for which, for example, updates may be available, with similar restrictions on providing duplicate copies to third parties.
- The user may be required to pay only a small initial sum (or nothing), but then make payments to the copyright holder for each use made of a work.
- The user may be required to make an annual (or other periodical) payment in return for which he may be permitted to use a work within a particular locality or site, or within a particular group of people, probably with some measurement of use to help determine future fair payments.

5 Thus, rights holders are seeking to develop standard licences for different types of use, so reducing the variety of terms and conditions, and to develop 'one stop shop' clearance systems, site licences permitting a variety of uses of a variety of works for agreed payments, sampling systems for measurement of actual uses, and many similar devices to assist libraries in operating within systems compatible with securing a return on investment in new information services. They are also prepared to enter into collective or blanket licensing schemes, or collective administration arrangements, or to form consortia of publishers working together (within the law) to facilitate access to their repertories.

APPENDIX 5 – THE FUTURE FOR COPYRIGHT

Copyright law has long been regarded as a quagmire; or a maelstrom; or a labyrinthine concoction of restrictions which depends very largely on personal honesty, is almost impossible to police at present, can often be extremely irritating and restrictive to the creators of copyright works even though it was initiated to protect their rights; but is nevertheless of principal benefit to publishers and consequently important to national industries. EU harmonisation, aimed at a 'level playing field' in the market for publications, etc, has so far brought even more complexity to the detail and the observance of UK law. Moreover, the field is useless without clear rules and game plans. The Information Society should not be allowed to become a 'litigious society'.

Every new piece of law, from major revision to nuance of meaning, creates further difficulty for a would-be law-abiding user community even if it does help one publisher to sue another. However, publishers have to cope with copyright complexities to a much greater extent than users. 'Something has got to give' as the saying goes, if copyright and database right are to be simplified sufficiently, if all concerned may be able to observe the law. (That is, to observe it as properly as possible, despite its liability to revision not only by new copyright SIs but also by legislation on other subjects such as broadcasting, almost *en passant*.)

Is it worth considering bold, indeed Draconian, changes to improve the situation? In theory, a new law could require the registration of desire to benefit from copyright ownership, this necessarily being registration of copyright also, of course. This need not damage the Berne conception of 'automatic' entitlement to copyright *per se*, but obviously an unregistered work would be in relatively greater danger of copyright theft. However, it should aim to destroy any concept of automatic entitlement to economic benefits when the tracing of ownership details, etc. could hardly be more difficult if there had been deliberate obscuration.

A5/1 Copyright registration

Before the rapid growth of computer systems in the last twenty years, the very idea of registering copyright was considered out of the question on at least three counts:

(1) considered to be against Berne's 'automatic' no-registration provision (12.34), though this need not be relevant if copyright remained automatic but registration became necessary to claim benefits;

(2) too expensive by far as a manual system;

(3) pointless when only first owner would be shown – no longer relevant in the context of an ECMS (3.55) with tracing capability which should require re-registration of ownership when that changes.

Is the concept of an automated registration centre such a mammoth task? Difficult, certainly, but surely justifiable in terms of enormous cost savings in the future? At present, the Public Lending Right system is alone in requiring registration, and PLR administration depends on computers. Why should not at least the 'copying' portion of the copyright regime be administered by computer? Running costs could be met by rights owner charges, since they will need such a system as the basis for an ECMS in any event. An ECMS should be able to employ provenance, duration and current ownership data for its operation. Of course, it would take a long time for a comprehensive 'live' database to be constructed, but the sooner rights owners could start inputting the better! If a desire to benefit were *not* registered, there should be no economic benefit, whether for an author or for a publisher or any other producer of a physical format after a transitional period. What better incentive to set up a central computer-based system which would then be a basis for an ECMS?

A5/2 National centre?

Suggested functions for a national centre have grown since the first proposal by this author in 1981, and take into account CLA's response to the need for rapid clearance, a project previously rejected by the British Library:

(a) expand the CLARCS concept as a basis for further development;
(b) standardisation of contracts;
(c) broker contracts with individual users and/or user groups;
(d) set up a collaborative committee between users and publishers/producers to study continuously the needs of users and the administration of rights;
(e) if new law requires registration of ownership of rights to qualify for benefits, set up and administer a central database to accept author/producer input of new rights and changes in ownership;
(f) coordinate and authorise encryption policies for the Superhighway;
(g) develop concepts towards full electronic copyright management, and then administer a national, then regional (and later contribute to a global) ECMS.

However, as reported in Appendix 4, progress is now being made with (b), following the recent establishment of (d). Central vetting of (e) would be required, including reported changes in ownership and the specific rights concerned, and rights owners should not have direct access for revision of data.

Irrespective of whether the above proposal is thought feasible, all seems now to be set fair for progress in collaboration with publishers to an extent hitherto unknown. Some features which might be worth considering along the way – that is, in addition to some suggestions made elsewhere, such as in Appendix 3 – are offered below for discussion.

A5/3 Central coordination of licensing?

An alternative to comprehensive *blanket* licensing in the electronic context might be the central co-ordination of individual licensing. This would differ from collective licensing in allowing fee variation per producer, which most producers may well prefer. What if a significant number of publishers were to abstain from forthcoming agreed collective licences? Centrally coordinated individual licences would be needed to fill gaps in the user range of interest, not only for full-text services and bibliographic databases but also for scanning published material into databases in academe, research establishments and industry.

A5/4 Collecting societies

Unless or until such time as recurrent clearance tasks may be handed over to computers, the following criteria are suggested for collecting societies:

(a) as few societies as possible should be involved;
(b) each with a high degree of moral and ethical accountability; whether or not there may have been a past tendency simply to 'collect', each should become able readily and speedily to advise confused user organisations, bearing in mind that many may not protest because of litigation costs;
(c) each should aim to simplify their own working procedures and keep administrative costs to the minimum, and reducing the numbers as in (a) above could be the main way to achieve that;
(d) each should help to standardise contractual terms, for example for database service contracts.

A5/5 Copyright currency: an accommodation?

Since the duration of copyright usually involves an author's lifetime, determination of currency can be extremely difficult or even impossible, and take up inordinate amounts of expensive staff time. Simplification could be achieved by replacing author's lifetime with a fixed period, Unless or until fixed terms might be adopted, might an approximate method of judging copyright period apply only to photocopying or electrocopying of published text for *non-publishing* purposes? This would require an agreed approximation of term to be applied to non-publishing user needs, such as 50 years beyond publication to cover *all* rights in a periodical article, and perhaps 100 years for books. Fixed copyright periods have been suggested for this purpose in the past by this author. Periods began with the publication date and ignored certain legal complexities on a swings and roundabouts basis. Such fixed periods could incidentally affect sampling systems in photocopy licensing, hence might this question be worth discussion in the licensing context?

A5/6 Duration

Apart from any consideration of approximate aproaches, is an author's life plus a fixed term *post mortem auctoris* an appropriate formula? Or would a fixed term beyond creation be more suitable and fair?

The EU has worsened the situation by providing protection for life plus 70 years, and made the determination of copyright currency even more difficult by means of extended or revived copyright (2.2). At the time of Rupert Brooke, the protection period was 50 years pma, and his works have been out of copyright worldwide for 32 years. Is not this monstrously unfair, compared with a formula which might help rights owners and users alike? A long-lived author can now have a copyright period of up to a century and a half or more. A fixed period of 100 years from creation should surely be ample for the majority of non-publishing requirements in respect of original works, and users could determine from the creation date whether an item were still copyright or not – items undated, or found to be falsely dated, could immediately go into the public domain. The law required might be regarded as too severe by legislators still concerned about interpretation of Berne's 'automatic' copyright, but it could provide a strong incentive to date original work and that would be the key to protection. (This would tie in with a need for the displayable 'date-stamping' of electronic records, noted elsewhere in this volume.) Published works would be required to bear the creation year as well as publication year. It would be quite clear when copyright were due to end, saving a great deal of uncertainty and time-consuming, therefore expensive, enquiries. It is suggested that it is time to modify the Berne concept now that national computer-based systems of registration are feasible and ultimately essential for proper ECMS control.

A5/7 A copyright Nirvana? – *circa* 2020

Any media or multimedia selections from those created during at least the last 50 years to be available by this date via the Superhighway. Whether reading print on paper, receiving broadcasts, or using a terminal, if there is a need to copy, the portion concerned and key in your requirements. If material is still copyright, the system supplies either clearance to copy at a stated cost, or arranges electronic or hard copy supply from an agency, or permits downloading; with cost agreed before action. The cost would pay for the key to any specific encryption which might have been applied. Other needs than simple copying without publication would automatically be passed on to the current rights owners for direct reply to the enquirer. (This compares with a brief forecast by Hoeren, noted in 12.29 from his report, listed in App. 1/8.1)

The future will require an unhindered electronic flow of information between the desk-tops of specialists. Whilst inhibiting those publishers who have been said to aim at 'total control of the flow of information', precautionary measures should be applied regarding authority in respect of newly created work. Some means are already being developed for peer-reviewing in electronic files, but it is suggested that this cannot be seen as an adequate replacement for publisher authority, marketing skills, and work-specific administration of rights. It is believed that publishers should always have a major role.

A5/8 'Navigation' among rights?

Nevertheless, the urge to profit is naturally great and sometimes may obscure other considerations. Users will need to be encouraged to stand up for their 'rights' – inverted commas because they have long had no rights as such, only permissions to act contrary to an author's exclusive rights. There must be few publishers left who do not realise by now that overzealous drives for profit can undermine their own foundations by obstructing future authors. Those users who form the majority – that is, current and future authors, indeed – should take a closer and stronger interest in the administration of copyright. Rationality in copyright may evolve but slowly unless a national centre is established with appropriate powers, as mooted above. For publishers and users alike, the problems will require increasing collaboration and mutual understanding. It has become extremely difficult for all to steer a sensible course among user needs, cost constraints, profit aims, legal complexity and media variety. The urgency of ECMS grows day by day. As soon as possible, surely we should hand over basic navigation to the computers?

GLOSSARY

This is a glossary of selected terms used in this book or elsewhere in the literature on copyright. It is complementary to the main index to the text, which excludes glossary contents.

acknowledgement, a note of source details associated with a copied extract, necessary not only for courtesy reasons but also to allow tracing of sources by readers, librarians or archivists. 'Sufficient acknowledgement' is specified in law for some circumstances, for example, when copying for criticism or review, and is stated as meaning an acknowledgement identifying the work in question by its title or other description, and identifying the author where possible. In practice, all copying should have annotation which identifies a source with as much detail as would be needed to locate and obtain a copy of the whole work.

acts, permitted/restricted, see **permitted acts; restricted acts.**

adaptation, a translation or modification of a work, including – in the case of a computer program –conversion from one language or code into another.

archivist, a person involved in the collection, organisation, preservation and retrieval of documents, maps and other materials which have historical or other significance in research, history, culture, business, academe, government, or economic and social affairs.

article, periodical, in respect of library copying permissions, an item of any description in an issue of a periodical.

artistic work, any of:

(1) graphic work, photograph, sculpture or collage, regardless of artistic quality;
(2) architectural work – a building or model of a building;
(3) a work of artistic craftsmanship.

author, see **work, copyright**, – in respect of category (a) 'author' means the person who creates the work. In respect of categories (b) and (c), the author, to make a generalisation, is the person responsible for its production or issue to the public; thus a publisher is author of a **typographical arrangement** of a **published edition.** A work bearing the name of a corporate body as author, without indication of personal authors, is treated as anonymous.

back-up copy of a computer program, any copy made by a lawful user which is necessary for the purposes of the agreed use.

breach of confidence, in the context of using, passing on or publishing information acquired in confidence, is a basis for litigation. (See **common law copyright**.)

broadcast, a transmission by wireless telegraphy of sounds, visual images or other information which is capable of lawful reception by members of the public; or is transmitted for presentation to members of the public.

building, any fixed structure or part thereof.

cable programme, means any item included in a **cable programme service**.

cable programme service, a service consisting, wholly or mainly, of sending visual images or sounds or other information by means of a telecommunications system, otherwise than by wireless telegraphy, for reception:

(a) at two or more places; or
(b) for presentation to members of the public, subject to exclusions.

Main exclusions:

(i) services which allow communication between service provider and recipient, other than signals for the operation or control of the service;
(ii) services for individual or business use which are not connected to any other telecommunication system.

cascade copying, a term used by publishers who are concerned about the possibility of one permitted copy being used as a master for multiple copying and, theoretically, any of the multiples being further used for copying. In practice, the law guards against this in many circumstances, and licences cover the eventuality in other circumstances. Some confusion has arisen because of publisher (and some user) belief that copying a photocopy is illegal in any circumstances, which is not always the case – for example, a copy made for library stock with unlimited permission may be used like any other whole work in the stock.

collective licensing, see **licensing scheme.**

commercial publication, see **publication, commercial.**

commercial purpose, a restriction applied at present only to database right, where it is excluded from fair dealing for research, or for illustration for the purposes of teaching or research. No official definition as yet, but it has been mooted that it should apply to seeking profit through dealings in, or other exploitation of, the electronic material itself, rather than use by a lawful user in the course of research financed by a commercial organisation. Case law may further define it, but in any event it is recommended that firms should become licensed against the contingency of unwitting infringement by some member of staff, as recommended elsewhere in this book in respect of photocopying.

common law copyright applied before 1 July 1912 (commencement of Copyright Act 1911) to unpublished works for an indefinite period. Its place has been taken firstly by modern legislation and, secondly perhaps to some extent by 'breach of confidence' in communicating unpublished information, which could still be a basis for litigation today.

computer-generated relates to the generation of a work by computer in circumstances such that there is no human author, and copyright in the work expires 50 years beyond the end of the year of creation.

computer program, a set of instructions for a computer to follow, whatever the code or programming language or other means of communication with the machine. A computer program is a **literary work** regardless of its physical form.

copyright, a bundle of exclusive property rights in respect of recorded or fixed products of the mind. These rights are defined in law by specifying **restricted acts** which only rights owners may control. See also **work, copyright**.

copyright, any, when used in UK copyright law in respect of permissions, this phrase normally includes publishing rights in **typographical arrangements** or printed pages, along with any other form of copyright. Exceptions are the sections on **fair dealing** and **library/archive copying**, where coverage of the printed page is specifically stated where allowable (research or private study) and omitted where questionable (see **criticism** or **review; news reporting**).

copyright in (original works), when used in UK law, this phrase cannot be taken to include **typographical arrangements** unless additionally stated, as in **fair dealing** for research or private study.

copyright work, see **work, copyright**.

criticism or review, the broadest of three permitted purposes of **fair dealing**, ostensibly applicable to any work and any copyright in it, provided there is **sufficient acknowledgement**. Intended to cover quotation of extracts, though no limits are specified.

current events, see **news reporting**.

database, has been traditionally a hard-copy or electronic collection – whether of facts and therefore copyright only as a whole as a compilation, or of copyright items – which is organised to facilitate retrieval of information. Under the new database right from 1 January 1998, database now refers only to a collection of independent works, data or other materials (such as multimedia) which are arranged in a systematic or methodical way and are individually accessible by electronic or any other means. Such a database may also be copyright at compilation level, but only if the selection or arrangement of contents constitutes the author's own intellectual creation. (Reason: originality is necessary to qualify for copyright, but a database need not be original.) This is taken as ruling out a 'sweat of brow' compilation from qualification as a database, but note that such a compilation may still qualify for copyright, whereas a non-original database only gets protection as such. Contents may or may not be copyright in themselves.

database right, is first owned by the **maker of a database** and subsists in any database (as newly defined) if there has been substantial investment in obtaining, verifying or presenting the contents of the database. It is the right to control extraction or re-utilisation of a substantial part or the whole of the contents. (See also **fair dealing**.)

declaration, the copyright declaration form specified as one of the legal conditions governing a manned copyright service in a library or archive, which a requester must sign to warrant his or her purpose, for example, as research or private study, and his or her intention to abide by the details of the declaration.

decompilation, conversion of a computer program expressed in a low level language into a version expressed in a higher level language.

design copyright, a term often used loosely. Designs arising from **artistic works** have copyright as **artistic works**. Design documents and drawings have copyright in themselves only, and not in the making of designs to their specification. (Terms concerning unregistered design right, and registered designs, are excluded from this Glossary.)

digitisation, converting an existing print (or other) work into electronic format.

dramatic work, includes dance or mime.

duration of copyright and/or database right, means the period of monopoly control enjoyed by a rights owner in respect of the **restricted acts**.

edition, published, see **published edition.**

educational establishment, any institution established for the purposes of education or instruction, however funded.

EEA Agreement means the Agreement on the European Economic Area, 2 May 1992, as adjusted by protocol of 17 March 1993. **EEA state** means a contracting party to the **EEA Agreement**. The EEA includes all European Union countries, Iceland and Norway.

e-mail, email, electronic mail, messages passed via a telecommunications system, especially the Internet.

employed, employee, employer, and employment are used in the context of copyright works made during employment under a contract of service or of apprenticeship, whereby the employer is entitled to first ownership of any copyright unless agreed otherwise.

equitable remuneration, means the entitlement of an author or performer under **rental and lending rights** in the event of transferral of rental right to a publisher or producer.

exclusive rights (copyright), see **restricted acts**.

existing, as used at various points in CDPA88 and supplementary legislation, means created or performed before commencement of the law in question.

extraction or re-utilisation, as applied to contents of a database: **extraction** means the permanent or temporary transfer of contents to another medium by any means or in any form (therefore applicable to photocopying or electrocopying); **re-utilisation** means the making available to the public of those contents by any means. Infringement of database right may occur if a substantial part or the whole is involved, whether or not the items of content are copyright in themselves.

facsimile, an exact copy, such as a photocopy or photograph, including an exact copy which is reduced or enlarged in scale, such as **microform**.

fair dealing, a concept of which the definition depends on particular circumstances and is therefore left to the courts. **Fair dealing** is taken to mean actions which should not unduly damage the market for copyright works. In effect, it is a statutory permission, limited to certain purposes (**research or pri-**

vate study, **criticism or review**, and **news reporting**), to plead fair dealing as a defence in an infringement case. **Fair dealing** overrides considerations of **substantial part** and specifies no limits of copying extent, but prohibits more than one copy being made by an individual (including a librarian) when copying for another. In practice, recommended copying limits are applied, based on rights-owner **guidelines** to what may be seen as reasonable. Applicable to an electronic format as well as to a written or printed format. However, although a database may be copied under fair dealing, it may only be copied for research if not for a **commercial purpose**. (See also **library/archive copying**.)

film, a recording on any medium from which a moving image may be produced by whatever means – therefore a video recording is included. (See also **stills**.)

freeze-frame, i.e. video image, see **stills**.

graphic work includes:

(a) any painting, drawing, diagram, map, chart or plan;
(b) any engraving, etching, lithograph, woodcut or similar work.

guidelines, a term often used to describe notes, whether or not actually called 'guidelines', which indicate behaviour in respect of copyright, which is desired by the party issuing the guidelines without necessarily being mandatory. Most guidelines are issued by rights-owner groups or major individual publishers (such as HMSO), but are also prepared by some user groups.

hire, see **rental right**.

ideas, constructs of the mind which are not copyright in themselves, though a complex or sequence of them is to be considered copyright when recorded in an original work.

illustrations, specifically in the context of this book, pictorial or diagrammatic illustrations mentioned in nonprofit-based library permissions. Generally, taken to include any form of two-dimensional representation in any form of record, whether published (including electronic publication) or unpublished, and however produced.

indemnity, see **licensing scheme**.

infringement, copyright, means doing any of the **restricted acts** without permission in respect of the whole or any substantial part of a copyright work.

infringing copy, includes: a copy made without authorisation of a restricted act, whether that authorisation is by licence of or on behalf of a rights owner, or by statute as a **permitted act**; or a copy made with due authorisation for one purpose which is applied for another, unauthorised purpose.

insubstantial parts, of a database, judged both qualitatively and quantitatively; but repetitive extraction or re-utilisation of insubstantial parts can build up into a **substantial part**.

investment, in the context of database right, includes any investment, whether of financial, human or technical resources. Substantial investment means substantial in terms of quantity or quality or a combination of both.

issue to the public, means putting copies of a work into circulation for the first time, within the UK or elsewhere. This includes rental to the public of sound recordings, films and **computer programs**.

item, any component of given material, such as a periodical article, a book chapter, abstract, contents page or statistical table.

lawful user, in relation to a **computer program**, is a person who has a right to use the program, whether under a licence or otherwise (new CDPA88 ss50A-50C apply), and the right may not be overridden by contract (i.e. other than a licence to use). Similarly a lawful user of a database is currently defined as such a person who has a right to use the database, and this right also may not be overridden by contract, but further definition is being sought (e.g. for library clients or other party users).

lending right, this applies to making a copy of a copyright work available for use by the public, on terms that it will or maybe returned, *otherwise* than for direct or indirect economic or commercial advantage [i.e. when any payments do not exceed operating costs] through an establishment which is accessible to the public. **Lending and rental right** apply under the EEA agreement to EEA states. Books covered by **Public Lending Right** are exempt for public libraries but they need licences to lend other materials as would any other organisation wishing to lend to the public. Education establishments are exempt in respect of lending any kind of work. However, if lending becomes 'rental', any organisation needs licensing for the purpose (see also **rental and lending right**).

librarian, a person involved in the collection and organisation of information sources, including – as may be required – the indexing, abstracting and/or cataloguing of sources to facilitate their retrieval and the design of retrieval systems; or a person managing a library.

library/archive copying, nonprofit-based services are permitted to provide single copies within certain limits and subject to **prescribed** conditions, to members of the public. Limited to research or **private study**, or making archival copies for stock in certain circumstances. Research or private study purposes have so far been taken as applying only to written or printed matter as far as libraries are concerned, but under database right it is apparent that no distinction need be made between print and electronic formats, unless a service contract imposes restrictions. The permission overrides any consideration of **fair dealing** or of **substantial part**. Where the law allows discretion (see **reasonable proportion**), it is usual to base decisions on rights-owner guidelines. Any librarian or archivist, like any other person, may also copy under **fair dealing** on someone's behalf, subject to considerations of fairness.

licence, in this context, an agreement whereby some or all of the acts may be carried out, usually subject to payment to rights owners or their representatives.

licence, blanket, a form of **licensing scheme**. As originally conceived, would cover all the needs of a given user group. This aim has not so far been achieved although CLA efforts continues. Rights owners have applied various limits to discourage carte blanche, and a number of owners have still not joined a scheme relevant to their concerns.

licensing body, a society or other organisation whose major object is the negotiation or granting, whether as copyright owner or on their behalf, of licences covering the works of more than one author – that is, of licensing schemes.

licensing scheme, an arrangement by a **licensing body** whereby restricted acts are licensed in respect of the works of more than author – hence, collective licensing – which must by law provide an indemnity against defence costs for licensees who might be accused of infringement despite having followed the terms of the licence.

literary work, any original work, other than a dramatic or musical work, which is written, spoken or sung, including:

(a) a table or compilation other than a database;
(b) a computer program;
(c) preparatory design material for a computer program, and
(d) a database.

maker of a database means the person who takes the initiative in the making of a database *and* assumes the risk of investing in its making. 'Maker' may apply to joint makers. Making by an employee in the course of employment means first ownership by the employer unless agreed otherwise.

microform, microfilm, microfiche, or microcard facsimile representations of works which may or may not be copyright in themselves.

monopoly (copyright), see **duration of copyright**; **restricted acts**.

moral rights, the main moral rights under UK law are the right to be identified as author or creator of a work and to object to derogatory treatment of a work.

multiple copying, expressly excluded from permitted **library/archive copying**, and in some circumstances from **fair dealing**. **Multiple** or **systematic copying** is effectively defined in law as meaning the making, by one individual or members of a group or class, or by a library copying service, of more than one copy of the same item at substantially the same time and for substantially the same or a related purpose.

musical work, means music, excluding any words or actions associated with the music.

neighbouring rights, or **related rights**, defined by some experts as those rights which they see as distinct from copyright per se: such as broadcasting right, performing right, **recording right**, or film distribution right. They protect the medium by which a message is delivered rather than the message itself.

news reporting, excluding photographs, this is one of three permitted **fair dealing** purposes, subject to **sufficient acknowledgement**, though that is required when reporting current events by audiovisual means, including broadcasts or cable programmes. Covers quotation – including re-publication – of extracts, though no limits are specified by statute, but coverage of the printed page should be subject to seeking rights-owner permission.

nonprofit-based, see **prescribed; profit-based library/archive**.

off-air recording, permitted recording of radio or television or cable programmes for educational purposes unless a licensing scheme is available. Also, **timeshift recording** for listening or viewing at a more convenient time for **private and domestic use**.

original, left undefined in UK law, though a work must be original to qualify for copyright (but a database need not be original to qualify for database right). Taken to refer to

(a) a work which is not a copy, in whole or part, of a work by someone else, at least in the form of expression used and the corpus of ideas involved;
(b) a master for replication or production in some other form, such as a film of a book. However, also used loosely to refer to a copy of a publication in the form issued by the publisher.

passing off means the false representation of one thing as another which is made in the course of trade thus creating circumstances which mislead the public and in which damage could occur.

performance of a copyright work, includes: (a) delivery of lectures, addresses, speeches, and the like; (b) any mode of audio or visual presentation, including sound recordings, films, broadcasts, cable programmes.

permitted acts or 'permissions', actions, authorised by statute or associated regulation, which are otherwise **restricted acts** – for example, **fair dealing** or **library/archive copying**.

photocopies, see **cascade copying; facsimile; multiple copying; research or private study**.

photograph means a recording of light or other radiation on any medium on which an image is produced, or any medium from which an image may by any means be produced, when the recording is not part of a film. (See also **stills**.)

pma (post mortem auctoris), after the author's death: phrase used when referring to copyright duration. After creation of a work by a known individual, protection lasts for the rest of the variable period of an author's lifetime, plus a fixed period of 70 years beyond the end of the author's year of death. Rather than the customary '70 years pma', '70 years beyond author's death year' is clearer.

prescribed, this term is used when permitted actions are subject to conditions relating to purpose or similar factors, whether those conditions are in statute or associated regulations or both. Although the phrase 'prescribed libraries' (or archives) is used in law, this must be taken in conjunction with associated regulations, for all libraries are 'prescribed' for certain purposes. In this book the terms 'nonprofit- based' and 'profit-based' have been adopted instead.

printed matter can be copyright both as an original work (e.g. for 70 years beyond an author's death year) and as a **typographical layout** for 25 years beyond publication year. The protection period can become longer through renewal when **database right** is involved.

private and domestic use, the purpose applicable to certain permissions, for example timeshift recording of broadcasts or cable programmes. The 'and' is important.

private study, see **research** or **private study**.

profit-based library/archive, a service which is established or conducted for profit, or which forms part of, or is administered by, a body established or conducted for profit. The term 'profit' in this context is taken to mean that the organisation concerned has the objective of attaining an excess of income over expenditure after all factors are taken into account, and this would exclude mere cost-recovery by an otherwise nonprofit-based body.

public domain, out of copyright, whether at the end of a monopoly period or never protected by copyright law.

Public Lending Right (PLR), is a central system set up under an Act of that name of 1979. PLR uses samples of public library loan records as the basis for annual payments to book authors for loans of their works to the public, provided authors have registered their work with the PLR registry for this purpose. Payments are made through the treasury and not by local authorities. PLR for books now continues alongside broader **'rental and lending right'** provisions.

publication means the issue of copies to the public. In the case of a literary, dramatic, musical or artistic work, the term includes making the work available to the public by means of an electronic retrieval system.

publication, commercial means issuing copies of a work to the public at a time when copies made in advance of orders are generally available; or making the work available to the public by means of an electronic retrieval system.

published edition, defined by the Act only in the context of copyright in a typographical arrangement, means a published edition of the whole or any part of one or more literary, dramatic or musical (but not artistic) works. However, an 'electronic retrieval system' (in practice, a **database**) is a **publication** and could now also be regarded as a published edition even of artistic material.

pupil, in UK copyright law and in the context of an educational establishment, any person who receives instruction.

reasonable proportion, the term used to describe the proportion of non-periodical material of which copying is permitted for **research or private study** purposes by a nonprofit-based library or archive. Being undefined, the term requires discretion and judgement according to circumstances, aided by any applicable rights-owner guidelines.

recording right, a term used in UK law in relation to an exclusive recording contract between a performer and a person or body who is to record.

related copying, see **multiple copying**; **systematic copying**.

related rights, this term can be found applied to rights which, whilst not directly concerned with copyright, are linked to copyright duration – such as public rental or public loan, **moral rights**, and **neighbouring rights**.

release, the issue to the public of **sound recordings** or **films** (including videos).

rental and lending right, is the right of an author to authorise or prohibit rental or lending of copies of his or her copyright work to the public, including those works represented in sound recordings and films; or of a performer to authorise or prohibit rental or lending to the public of copies of sound recordings or films. Rental means making a copy of a work available for use, on terms that it will or may be returned, for direct or indirect economic or commerical advantage. When rental right is transferred by an author or performer to a publisher or producer **equitable remuneration** must be paid by the transferee to the author or performer. The right to equitable remuneration can not be assigned except to a collecting society, hence effectively influences a contract by an author or performer, conceivably to his or her benefit. It follows that anyone wishing to rent works to the public must seek a licence (see also **lending**).

reprographic copy, a copy produced by a reprographic process, which means a process

(a) for making facsimile copies; or
(b) involving the use of an appliance for making multiple copies including, in respect of a work held in electronic form, any copying by electronic means – excluding the making of a film or sound recording.

research or private study, the major permitted purpose, or purposes, of **fair dealing**. The 'or' is important. The order of the words in the phrase is also important, since corruptions can mis-state it, or cause it to be misunderstood, as 'private research' and 'private study' and the like. **Research** is not limited and is taken to mean any kind of research, from personal to corporate needs, including research which may at some time have commercial ends. However, a database may not be copied for research for a **commercial purpose**. **Private study** has been accepted by academe as excluding group study – hence the development of collective licensing to cover **multiple copying** or **systematic copying** for class purposes. Users of a manned copying service in a library for a research or private study copy are required to sign a **declaration** and are only allowed a copy from written or printed matter. When copying under fair dealing, whether as self-service or by any library on a person's behalf, a librarian can copy artistic works, which are otherwise excluded from library copying service.

restricted acts, based on an author's monopoly control, or exclusive rights, to:

- (a) copy the work;
- (b) issue copies to the public;
- (c) perform, show or play the work in public;
- (d) broadcast the work or include it in a cable programme service;
- (e) rent or lend the work to the public;
- (f) make an adaptation of the work or do any of (a) to (e) in respect of an adaptation.

re-utilisation, see **extraction or re-utilisation.**

revived or extended copyright: Revived copyright subsists in a work of UK origin when the formerly applicable pma 50-year period expired on or after 1 July 1995 whilst the applicable period elsewhere in the EEA was still running, thus requiring UK right to be revived for a period of up to another 20 years beyond 1 January 1996. **Extended** copyright subsists in a work, still in UK copyright on 31 December 1995, which became affected by the new 70-year period and is thus extended for 20 years beyond the date which would formerly have ended copyright.

royalty, a sum due to rights owners, usually governed by contract, for each copy made, or each performance, or loan, or rental, of a copyright work.

sculpture, includes a cast or model made for the purpose.

slide/transparency, in common with other still images, defined as a photograph, though designed for repetitive display by means of transmitted light.

sound recording, includes:

(a) a recording of sounds, from which they may be reproduced; or
(b) a recording of the whole or any part of a literary, dramatic or musical work, from which sounds reproducing the work may be reproduced regardless of recording medium or sound production (or reproduction) method.

stills, i.e. film stills or video freeze-frame images, being excluded from the definition of a photograph, are parts of a film (i.e. any moving image).

study pack, a collection of **items** of relevance to a particular class or course of study.

subsistence of copyright, since copyright cannot exist without a work, it is said to 'subsist' in the work. (See **work, copyright**.)

substantial part, that part of a copyright work of which, like the whole, unauthorised copying could be judged to infringe. Being undefined in terms of extent, interpretation requires discretion. Case law has established that 'substantial' can apply to significance of content, and not just to extent. Under database right, required to be defined qualitatively as well as quantitatively. See also **work, whole**.

sufficient acknowledgement, see **acknowledgement**.

systematic copying, a term used by publishers to describe a series of copies taken from the same original by members of the same group, such as a class under instruction on the subject, regarding such copying as constructive **multiple copying**. Although the latter is possibly arguable in law, academic institutions have accepted such 'related' copying as requiring coverage by licence.

teacher, in UK copyright law and in the context of an educational establishment, any person who gives instruction.

telecommunication system, a system for conveying text, visual images, sound or other information by electronic means, from one location to another such as the telephone network.

timeshift recording, see **off-air recording**; **private and domestic use**.

transitional provisions, those legal provisions which apply during a specified transitional period beyond the commencement date of new legislation. Many copyright materials in existence under previous legislation are affected for 50 years to come, hence these provisions can be very important.

transparency, see **slide/transparency**.

typographical arrangement, the layout, of which a publisher is author, of the print on pages of a published edition. Does not have to be text but can be graphic, especially when accompanying **illustrations.** However, electronic records of text (at least) may become regarded as typographical arrangements, irrespective of whether generated by scanning or keying-in plus programmed formatting for display/printout. (See also **published edition.**)

unauthorised (action), a restricted act done without rights-owner permission in some form or other, such as statutory permission or a licence.

video recordings, included in the definition of **film**.

whole work, see **work, whole**.

wireless telegraphy, the sending of electromagnetic energy over non-material paths, excluding the transmission of microwave energy between terrestrial fixed points.

work, copyright, the term covers:

(a) an original literary, dramatic, musical or artistic work;
(b) a sound recording, film (including videos), broadcast or cable programme;
(c) the typographical arrangement of a published edition.

work, whole, any kind of copyright work which is complete in itself, and which may not be found to be covered by a copying permission. Not only applicable to a book, pamphlet, report, etc. but also to complete works embedded in others, such as an individual poem or essay in an anthology, or an art print inside a volume. A periodical article is considered to be a whole work by some publishers, but specific permissions in law – and some licensing – provide for many user needs.

writing, includes any form of notation or code, whether by hand or otherwise (including electronic writing), regardless of method or recording medium.

INDEX

Note

The Bibliography in Appendix 1 and the Glossary have been excluded from this index, and the Quick Reference section has only been indexed at main heading level. The other Appendices (2 to 5) are indexed at main and subheading level and selectively otherwise.

Examples of abbreviations

15.11	*subsection 11 of chapter 15*
5...	*whole of chapter 5*
A3/2	*section 2 of Appendix 3*
def	*definition, shown after a subsection number, e.g. 3.13(def)*
pref	*preface*